Time and Memory in Indigenous Amazonia

UNIVERSITY PRESS OF FLORIDA

Florida A&M University, Tallahassee
Florida Atlantic University, Boca Raton
Florida Gulf Coast University, Ft. Myers
Florida International University, Miami
Florida State University, Tallahassee
New College of Florida, Sarasota
University of Central Florida, Orlando
University of Florida, Gainesville
University of North Florida, Jacksonville
University of South Florida, Tampa
University of West Florida, Pensacola

Time and Memory in Indigenous Amazonia

Anthropological Perspectives

Edited by Carlos Fausto and Michael Heckenberger

University Press of Florida

Gainesville Tallahassee Tampa Boca Raton Pensacola
Orlando Miami Jacksonville Ft. Myers Sarasota

12 11 10 09 08 07   6 5 4 3 2 1

Library of Congress Cataloging-in-Publication Data
Time and memory in indigenous Amazonia : anthropological perspectives /
edited by Carlos Fausto and Michael Heckenberger.
p. cm.
Includes bibliographical references and index.
ISBN 978-0-8130-3060-9 (alk. paper)
1. Indian philosophy—Amazon River Region—History. 2. Indians of South America—
Amazon River Region—Psychology. 3. Indians of South America—Amazon River Region—
Social life and customs. 4. Time—Social aspects—Amazon River Region. 5. Memory—
Social aspects—Amazon River Region. 6. Social change—Amazon River Region.
I. Fausto, Carlos. II. Heckenberger, Michael.
F2230.1.P53T55 2007
981'.01—dc22   2007001324

The University Press of Florida is the scholarly publishing agency for the State University
System of Florida, comprising Florida A&M University, Florida Atlantic University, Florida
Gulf Coast University, Florida International University, Florida State University, New College
of Florida, University of Central Florida, University of Florida, University of North Florida,
University of South Florida, and University of West Florida.

University Press of Florida
15 Northwest 15th Street
Gainesville, FL 32611-2079
http://www.upf.com

To Jim Petersen, in memoriam

Contents

Figures

Foreword

Whose history and history for whom?

Manuela Carneiro da Cunha

This is a book about Lowland South American Indians and their sense of history. What is it not? Well, for one thing, it is not directly about history and it does not use a historical critical apparatus. Hence it is not a history that will back territorial claims in a western Court of Law, a Western official history. Nor, for that matter, is it a history that will back a sense of ethnic identity, an indigenous official history. Those are by now relatively easy waters to navigate, for they have been competently chartered.

Instead, this book is negotiating relatively unchartered waters. The names that navigators carry with them have unstable places to which they might apply. What counts as time? What counts as change, as continuity, as agency? What counts as identity? Or are all these terms utterly inadequate? Are they resting on ontological premises so different from the worlds other people inhabit that words fail us and direct comparison is doomed from the start? Can one elicit what Terence Turner (1988) named ethno-ethnohistory? Is there anything one could call indigenous historicities? And if so, how can one reach them? Infinite regression looms in the dark.

An excellent book, only available in Portuguese, edited by Bruce Albert and Alcida Ramos and published in 2000, *Pacificando o Branco* ("Pacifying Whitemen"), could serve as a prolegomenon to this one. The authors endeavored to look into the modalities by which different Amazonian indigenous groups captured the invasion that befell them. Our historiography renders the events as their defeat: their narrative renders the same events as their labor of domesticating, of pacifying us together with our germs and our commodities.

The present book looks further into the mechanisms that allow such a reversal of what we take to be commonsensical history. How can such ambiguity about what "really" happened persist? Aren't there clear-cut vanquished and victors, even as the vanquished are credited with having their own version of history? Have we assimilated them or have they assimilated us? Can both versions coexist and can they be simultaneously true?

A set of answers rest on what Levi-Strauss first coined as Amerindian "openness to the Other," which translates into the regimentation of alterity for the production of identity, assimilating one's enemy as a mode of reproduction. While the logic of the West lies in the primacy of distinctions, Amazonian logic lies on the primacy of appropriation, of encompassment, cannibalism being one of its manifestations. Predation, as Eduardo Viveiros de Castro (1992) has eloquently shown, is the basic, given, relational mode. Given such assumptions, conversion to catholicism can be conversely seen by neophytes as predation on other people's God(s) (Fausto, Santos-Granero in this volume); what the French called civilizing the native, can be reciprocally seen as the appropriation of foreign practices (Vilaça). Acculturation can thus be understood as a mode of social reproduction, as a kind of endogenous transformation (Gow).

For several decades, a number of Amazonianists have looked into the originality of Amazonian societies and have called into question the universality of familiar categories. While a large sector of North American anthropology was busy with issues of representation, that is, unearthing our own covert assumptions in order to destabilize anthropological narratives, these other anthropologists were asking themselves about other peoples' covert assumptions in order to enlarge our understanding of the different ways people go about living. In contrast, postmodern representation angst eventually led, in its most extreme form, to intellectual isolationism, an apt reaction to (or flip side of) political expansionism.

Emboldened by similar endeavors on New Guinea, anthropologists mostly of neo-structuralist persuasion started to develop some of the consequences of the unfamiliar categories they had found in Amazonian societies. In the late seventies and early eighties, the centrality of the body and the divide between the living and the dead had been foregrounded by a number of us (Seeger, da Matta, and Viveiros de Castro 1979; Carneiro da Cunha 1978; Albert 1985; see also Clastres and Sebag 1963). The issue of the body stands unscathed, while the idea of a generalized severance of kinship links with the dead is being disputed (e.g., by Chaumeil and Heckenberger) but also supported (by Erikson and by Taylor) in this book. A number of other insights followed these early ones looking, in Schneiderian terms, for what is given and what is constructed in Amazonian societies: hence the claim that enmity is given while consanguinity is constructed, and that affinity is a compromise, a lower limit of enmity. Hence also the different claims by Descola (1994, 2005) and by Viveiros de Castro (1998) that Amazonians have specific views on what we would call nature.

The essays in this book largely build on this tradition, and yet they go beyond it. They open up ever more subtle understandings. What, for instance, should we envisage as our unit of analysis in what has been called interethnic situation? Rather than simply contrasting whites and Indians, Anne-Christine Taylor elicits a ternary system: there are 'white' colonists, for sure, but then on the indigenous side, the 'tame,' 'acculturated' Runa and the 'wild' Jivaro are necessarily co-present. Wild Jivaro are not ascribed to one single selfhood, rather they can move into Runa tame identity and yield to otherness, but they can also move back out and appropriate it. Runa and Jivaro each have their own regime of historicity and memory and yet each regime relies on the existence of the other. Runa, in turn, have entangled their five centuries of colonial and neocolonial experience with their ecological practices and perceptions. Kohn (this volume) points to a variety of parallel historical flows that left their prints in Runa animal masters cosmology.

While it may be presumptuous to think one can put one's finger on the different indigenous historicities, on the meaning and connotations such things as time, memory, change might have for indigenous societies, this book throws light on the deceit of taking such notions as unproblematic. It might not give us a key to a full understanding, but it definitely helps us avoid misunderstanding them.

References

Albert, Bruce. 1985. *Temps du Sang, Temps des Cendres: Représentation de la Maladie, Système Rituel et Espace Politique chez les Yanomami du Sud-Est (Amazonie Brésilienne).* Thèse de 3ème Cycle, Université de Paris-X.

———, and Alcida Rita Ramos. 2000. *Pacificando o Branco: Cosmologias do Contato no Norte-Amazônico.* São Paulo: Editora Unesp.

Carneiro da Cunha, Manuela. 1978. *Os Mortos e os Outros: uma Análise do Sistema Funerário e da Noção de Pessoa entre os Indios Krahó.* São Paulo: Hucitec.

Clastres, Pierre, and Lucien Sebag. 1963. "Cannibalisme et Mort chez les Guayakis." *Revista do Museu Paulista* XIV:174–181.

Descola, Philippe. 1994. *In the Society of Nature: A Native Ecology in Amazonia.* Cambridge: Cambridge University Press.

———. 2005. *Par-delà Nature et Culture.* Paris: Gallimard.

Seeger, Anthony, Roberto Da Matta, and Eduardo Viveiros de Castro. 1979. "A Construção da Pessoa nas Sociedades Indígenas Brasileiras." *Boletim do Museu Nacional*, Antropologia 32:2–19.

Turner, Terence. 1988. "Commentary: Ethno-ethnohistory: Myth and History in Native South American Representations of Contact with Western Society," in *Rethinking History and Myth: Indigenous South American Perspectives on the Past*. Edited by J. D. Hill, pp. 235–81. Urbana, Ill.: Urbana University Press.

Viveiros de Castro, Eduardo. 1992. *From the Enemy's Point of View: Humanity and Divinity in an Amazonian society*. Chicago: The University of Chicago Press.

Viveiros de Castro, Eduardo. 1998. "Cosmological Deixis and Amerindian Perspectivism." *Journal of The Royal Anthropological Institute* 4:469–88.

Introduction

Indigenous History and the History of the "Indians"

Carlos Fausto and Michael Heckenberger

This book is about time and change. *Change* is a deceptively simple word (Bynum 2001:19). It implies temporality and decomposes homogeneous time into a past and a present. Whatever is eternal and immutable is out of time; without change neither time nor temporality can be conceived. Indigenous peoples of lowland South America have often been depicted as being out of time—frozen in history, or unable or unwilling to conceptualize change as history. The most popular image of Amazonian indigenous peoples is still as "contemporary ancestors," representatives of a distant past and a mode of living once common in human history. From this viewpoint, Amazonian indigenous peoples have had the privilege (or misfortune) of changing little or not at all, reproducing themselves identically over time until their recent and abrupt plunge into modernity.

This primitivist image is no longer sustainable, given the recent advances in ethnographic, historical, and archaeological research in Amazonia. A "temporal revolution" is under way, a new mode of looking at the continent that not only pushes the human occupation of the Americas further back in time but also accelerates its pace of diversification and complexification (Adovasio and Page 2002; Dillehay 2000; W. Neves, forthcoming; Roosevelt et al. 1996). Today it is clear that the indigenous societies of Amazonia changed, and changed a lot, since the start of the Christian era. Most recent archaeological findings reveal a much more dynamic image of the millennium preceding the European Conquest. Evidence of population growth, increasingly dense social networks, and political complexification are found in various regions of the tropical rainforest. Complex societies extended along the entire length of the Amazon (Guapindaia 2001; Heckenberger et al. 1999; Neves et al. 2003; Neves and Petersen, 2006; Petersen et al. 2001; Roosevelt 1991, 1993; Schaan 2001, 2004), from the Orinoco basin in the north (Gassón 2000; Roosevelt 1980; Rostain 1994) to the southern Amazon periphery

(Heckenberger 2005; Heckenberger et al. 2003) and the forests and savannas of the Llanos de Mojos (Denevan 2001; Erickson 1995). The continent and Amazonia on the eve of conquest might best be pictured as an effervescent cultural pot.

The claim that Amazonian societies underwent significant changes before the arrival of Europeans may seem obvious today. However, it runs against the Stewardian consensus that dominated regional ethnology from the first publication of the *Handbook of South American Indians* (1946) until quite recently. Julian Steward proposed what became the most influential model for comprehending the native societies of the South American continent, classifying them hierarchically into four main types according to their degree of complexity (Steward 1946–50; Steward and Faron 1959). However, his classification of Andean and Caribbean societies was based on information dating back to the sixteenth century, while Amazonian peoples were classified in line with ethnographic data from the first half of the twentieth century, some four hundred years of colonial history later (Fausto 2000a). Amazonian peoples therefore seemed frozen in a natural history, stuck in a time frame matching the evolutionary history of the species.

While Amazonia has undoubtedly seen many changes since the start of the Christian era, it changed even more rapidly after 1492. Indigenous peoples experienced a brutal acceleration of change and rapid transformation of their world—the outcome of the catastrophic processes of demographic loss, mass migrations, and cultural decimation alternating with processes of ethnic reconstitution, transculturation, "cultural cannibalism," and the emergence of new social forms. Many of these histories are definitively lost from humanity's records and can never be recovered; others will be retrieved, but without the experiential detail that would be desirable. Even so, the large number of historical and ethnohistorical works published over the last two decades shows that, although documentation is scarce, it is still possible to produce local and regional histories of indigenous Amazonia. Thanks to these works, large regions of the tropical rainforest have ceased to be *terra ignota* from a historical point of view.[1]

Important historically oriented collections, from broad-ranging works such as *História dos índios no Brasil* (Cunha 1992) and South American volume of *The Cambridge History of the Native Peoples of the Americas* (Salomon and Schwartz 1999) to those focusing on a region or linguistic group (*Ethnohistory* 47(3–4); Franchetto and Heckenberger 2001; Hill and Santos-Granero 2002; Whitehead 2003; Wright 2005), are proof of the vitality of contemporary research into the history of indigenous Amazonian peoples and the possibility of conducting comparative syntheses. At a more localized level, ethnographic monographs increasingly incorporate focus on diachronic perspectives beyond the traditional chapter on the history of the people under study, producing dense local microhistories awaiting new regional syntheses (e.g., Fausto 2001; Heckenberger 2005; Rival 2002; Verswijver 1992; Vilaça, 2006).

Processes of change have also become a key issue for research into themes as diverse as the cosmopolitics of contact (Albert and Ramos 2000), religious conversions (Wright 1999, 2004), indigenous involvement in the monetary economy (Fisher 2000; Gordon 2006; Howard 2000; Hugh-Jones 1992), movements of cultural emergence and ethnogenesis (Hill 1996; Monteiro, forthcoming; Oliveira Filho 1999a; Schwartz and Salomon 1999; Tassinari 2002), new forms of indigenous sociality in the cities (Andrello 2006; Lasmar 2005), schooling and the introduction of writing (Cavalcanti 1999; Franchetto 1995, forthcoming; Rival 1996, 2002; Weber 2004; see also Gow 1990). One should mention as well the flourishing literature on the political processes involved in negotiating identities and rights at the national and international level (Albert 1997; Brown 1993; Chaumeil 1990; Conklin 2002; Conklin and Graham 1995; Greene 2004; Jackson 1994, 1995; Ramos 1998; Rival 1997; Turner 1995; Veber 1998). In all, then, a new ethnology, a new archaeology, and a new history of the indigenous peoples of Amazonia and nearby areas are revolutionizing the Stewardian model and exposing a previously inconceivable dynamism to the region's societies.

The Spirit of the Times

The temporality inscribed in most contemporary works, however varied their empirical object, scale, and theoretical inclinations, certainly diverges from the view that dominated regional anthropology a few decades ago; likewise the key concepts and the thematic fields under investigation have changed. The new directions taken by research in Amazonia have accompanied a general shift in the social and human sciences, a phenomenon we usually define as a series of "turns" (linguistic turn, cultural turn, historical turn, pragmatic turn, reflexive turn) and by a tone of "post"-uality (poststructuralism, postmodernism, and even some post-posts). These terms are symptomatic of general changes in the social sciences, within the heralded new milieu of knowledge production: living from "turn" to "turn," we often find ourselves out of time, incapable of defining our own dynamic intellectual condition, and resort to the prefix "post" to avoid losing our bearings in the absence of labels.[2]

The temporal acceleration of our reflexive consciousness is also reflected in the timescales found in our models and narratives: the long intervals of structural movements give way to evenemential narrations and to the history of the present, while the impersonal forces of the environment, culture, and economy cede their place to human action, history in the making, and intersubjective negotiations. The topics being researched have also changed, along with our classificatory categories: we no longer study kinship, politics, economy, or religion, but subjectification, embodiment, empowerment, agency, and identity. As Sahlins points out, institutions and structures have been emptied to give way to a new "subjectology" (2004:140).

The contributors to this book embrace many of these transformations in anthropological models, such as the incorporation of diachrony, the focus on processes of subjectification, and a certain reincorporation of human creative action. However, our global position is one of caution and critical distance. We feel uncomfortable with the facility with which anthropology has come to adapt itself to the major ideological trends of the post-welfare state. If it is true that anthropology has focused primarily on the normative and structural aspects of social life during the heydays of the nation-state and the planned economy, it is also not by chance that it has recently glorified flexibility, history, and individual agency along with the neoliberal momentum in the global economy. We do not want to imply here that there is an overdetermination of the real economy (and its imagined realities) over theoretical thinking, but simply to remind that what seems to be the last politically correct mood may prove later to be ultimately reactionary (see Sahlins 2004:149). Indeed, this will inevitably occur if we fail to reflect on the risks of projecting onto native peoples our own most cherished cultural notions, those that positively define our contemporary subjective experience, such as historical consciousness and individual agency.[3]

As a way of avoiding the projection of our own notions of history and agency onto Amerindian peoples (as if *they* need these notions to be considered more than passive subjects of colonial and national processes), the ethnographic studies presented here address basic questions such as: How is change conceptualized? How is temporality inscribed in discourse, space, and ritual practices? What are the different modes of producing transformation and what are the regimes of historicity constituted by these practices? Responding to these questions is an essential step in being able to "imbue historiography with ethnographic insight" (Salomon 1999:19) as well as engage ethnography with temporality. Our aim is to study how social memory is produced and mobilized, how change and its agents are conceived, how narratives of the past serve to construct the present. In brief, we wish to comprehend some of the diverse human modes of inhabiting time and producing transformation.

The authors of the following essays take ethnology as a critical tool that seeks not only to explore "unfolding social reality in terms of change" (Salomon and Schwartz 1999:4) but also to reveal a plane of continuities between the past and the present that is not always easy to detect. We approach the dialectic between transformation and reproduction, or historical change and structural continuity, from a dynamic perspective in which transformation is a constitutive part of the plane of permanence. As Sahlins argues, "the continuity of indigenous cultures consists of the specific ways through which they transform themselves" (1997:126; see also Albert 2000:13; Gow 2001).

Alternating to Alterity

A book about time and change is also a book about identity. As Caroline Bynum suggests, the question of change is "the other side of the question of identity. If change is the replacement of one entity by another or the growth of an entity out of another entity in which it is implicit, we must be able to say how we know we have an entity in the first place" (2001:19). *Identity* is also a deceptively simple word, in that, like change, it conflates diverse things and perspectives. It is at the heart of our contemporary experience, as individuals, as members of collectivities (real and imagined), and as anthropologists who are accustomed to seeking out the identity of others. The social sciences tend to reify the social world by creating boundaries, ascribing names, and localizing identities. Without limits, what is *an* entity? Without an entity, who or what possesses an identity? It is near impossible to conceptualize a relational world made up only of hybrids in a constant state of transformation, one in which, as the Heracliteans put it, we can never step twice into the same river. But while a river may be defined by its continuous flow rather than by its shores, human collectivities cannot. From a human point of view, questions of identity imply a kind of temporality that involves both memory and forgetting. What am I now if I cannot remember what I was a moment before? Am I still myself or something else?

These questions, with deep roots extending back to Greek philosophy and Judeo-Christian theology, frame the way we have come to think about identity, change, and temporality. The uneasiness of cultural anthropology with processes of "acculturation," "métissage," and "syncretism" parallels Western philosophy's uneasiness with personal identity, a theme as central to modern philosophy (Schneewind 1998; C. Taylor 1989) as it was to medieval Christianity (Bynum 1995). The classical solution to preserving identity (as self-sameness) was to postulate the continuity of some inner principle (the soul or essence) in opposition to the body or appearance. But while this was never a simple question in terms of personal identity, the case of collective identity proved to be just as problematic, if not more so: what does *Volksgeist* mean without a distinctive language, myths, rites, and the like?

Today, *Volksgeist* and other essentialisms are out of fashion, especially since the "discovery" that no such thing as a "culture" has ever existed. Instead, every social entity is seen to be both constructed and imagined, an effect of discursive practices (including those of anthropologists) and identity politics. In postmodernity, identity assumes another shape, becoming the mechanism through which the always provisional integration of multifaceted subjects (singular or collective) is produced for oneself and for others. Identity is the form in which these subjects appear to other subjects in a field of power practices: "Identity, here, is decisively a question of empowerment. The people without history in this view are the people who have been prevented from identifying themselves for others" (Friedman 1994:117).

This book does not automatically assume that Amerindians are concerned with personal and collective identity to the same degree as Westerners, nor that they are concerned in the same way. They may or may not share the "intense modern concern for identity" (Calhoun 1995:193) as a result of their immersion in new social contexts. But even where this is the case, we approach indigenous socio-cosmologies from another standpoint, according equal emphasis to difference and sameness, transformation and continuity, and exploring how the instability of these dualities generates a very specific dialectics of identity and alterity.[4] In a sense, Amerindians amount to postmoderns *avant la lettre* by making identity "a reversible or provisional state" destined never to last (Lévi-Strauss 1991:305). The problem is knowing whether the uses of identity, and the anxieties over it, are equivalent.

The postmodern celebration of multiform contexts and multi-identity subjects supposes a project of unification (albeit unattainable) that echoes the former sociological vocabulary of status and role (Calhoun 1995:196). In indigenous Amazonia, the problems of subjectification and identity relate to the constitution of both singular and collective subjects via the often predatory relationship with human and nonhuman alterities (Albert 1985; Castro 1992; Chaumeil 1985; Descola 1993; Erikson 1986, 1996; Fausto 1999, 2001; A. Taylor 1985). What haunts the social is not the (impossible) unification of identities but the complete and irreversible transformation into another "species" of subject, as well as the consequent projection of predation onto the sociality of kinship (see Fausto 2002a).

Still, identity politics is an important part of the contemporary lives of indigenous peoples (see Maybury-Lewis 2002; Warren and Jackson 2002). The hegemony of the West has served to universalize the language of identity and to organize the political practice of many of the world's autochthonous peoples in terms of its logic.[5] This is an important topic for understanding contemporary Amazonian indigenous social practices, but we believe it must be addressed in conjunction with an understanding of native ontologies and social philosophies; without this other dimension we risk falling into the sterile debate about authenticity and inauthenticity, a later avatar of mid-twentieth-century cultural change studies (for critical evaluations of the latter, see Conklin 1997; Jackson 1995; Oakdale 2004; Turner 1991). Sahlins is correct to say that the "self-conscious fabrication of culture in response to imperious outside 'pressures' is a normal process," and that, in this respect, "no culture is sui generis" (2000:489). However, the politics of recognition and anxieties over authenticity and inauthenticity are undoubtedly a specific cultural aspect of our own (post)modern condition.

If anthropology is to grasp the indigenization of global trends—which are never born global, just as they have never been entirely local—it must come to terms with difference and resist a paralysis born of the fear of exoticizing the Other. This anxiety results in part from the critique of the Us/Them dichotomy, or "the West and the Rest," intended to free us from the underlying spell of primitivism (Fabian 1983; Kuper 1988; Said 1978).[6] But it also results from the new position assumed by autochthonous peoples in the postcolonial world, a shift that in turn has led to a new politics of ethnographic representation (Asad 1973; Clifford and Marcus 1986). Although the critique of primitivism and exoticism has a number of positive aspects, taken to an extreme it has succeeded in making any evocation of "strangeness" anathema. As an anthropological operation par excellence, "distancing" enables the anthropological study of subjects that in principle are not strange to us. The risk of taking literally the maxim "Nothing human is strange to me" is to turn *our* common sense into what we share in common with (any) others. The danger here lies in performing a reactionary inversion in which critique becomes moralizing and a potentially liberating anthropology becomes patronizing. The anathema of exoticization converts into a rejection of difference, leaving anthropologists satisfied with the belief that, by projecting the values of the metropolis onto others, they morally upgrade native peoples. While autochthonous peoples were unarguably put in "the savage slot" (Trouillot 1991) in the past, the better to be controlled, are we not now requiring them to possess history, identity, and agency *of a certain kind* to qualify as real people?[7]

As Patrick Menget (1999) points out, such a history supposes the construction of a single totalizing narrative as a succession of events and phases lived by an ethnic group. This construction responds to demands stemming from the sociohistorical context in which South American indigenous populations nowadays find themselves. In Brazil, the production of these narratives by specialists, in particular anthropologists assigned to write technical reports, has become essential to the acquisition of rights over traditional lands and in some cases to the construction of an ethnic identity for oneself and for others (see Cunha 1986;

Oliveira 1999b, 2002). As a result, the applied work of anthropologists in land claims, fundamental to the political and legal gains of indigenous peoples in Brazil, suffers from a paradox typical of all "entangled" (*impliquée*) action (Albert 1995): it becomes an instrument of the logic of the state it ostensibly aims to counter. As Menget suggests, "Putting the legitimate rights of Indians into effect undoubtedly requires ethnologists to provide them with the weapons for resisting. But today we demand that they assert themselves by rewriting their past, as though their survival, after what for them was centuries of turmoil and bloodshed, were not ample proof of their resilience, their resistance, and their will to live" (1999:164).

This book reasserts an anthropological commitment to understanding difference, an ambition that has been drowned in suspicion over the last few decades. However, it is not intended as a return to the modernist knowledge practices of the past. We fully recognize the importance of the postmodernist critique of certain aspects of anthropological theory, but we wish to avoid its intellectual pitfalls and its ethnographic paralysis. This book favors a relationist approach to the problem of "getting to know the Other," one that implies recognizing, as Eduardo Viveiros de Castro puts it, that the relation is both our subject and our method. Approached in these terms, the anthropological problem is "less to determine what the social relationships that constitute its subject are than to ask what its subject constitutes as a social relation, what a social relation is in the subject's terms or, more exactly, in the terms that can be formulated by the relation between the 'anthropologist' and the 'native'" (Castro, forthcoming).

Hot Theories, Warm Historicities

The contributors to this book come from diverse intellectual traditions and address the issues of change, temporality, and memory in different ways. Many of us have been taking part in an intellectual conversation in progress since the 1960s, including authors from different national backgrounds and styles of anthropological practice, and focusing on a number of theoretical and empirical problems specific to Amazonian indigenous peoples. This conversation has two distinctive characteristics. Firstly, it breaks with the normal center-periphery hierarchical structure, since Brazil is as much a center of theoretical production as France, England, or the United States. Secondly, it developed from Lévi-Strauss's Americanist legacy, and despite expanding beyond these origins, it has conserved a structuralist resonance—a background radiation, so to speak. This amounts to a certain "sense of structures" as well as a predisposition to approach the process of transformation in terms of continuity (and continuity in terms of structural transformation). These preferences are not impediments to investigating phenom-enological and pragmatic aspects of social life, nor to incorporating diachrony in our studies. In fact, most of the authors included here have been writing about indigenous history and historicity for more than a decade now.[8]

The book results from the session "History and Historicity in Amazonia: Time Conceptualized, Experienced, and Enacted," held at the 98th Annual Meeting of the American Anthropological Association in 1999.[9] The central issue of the meeting was how concepts of time structure our work as anthropologists and the lives of the peoples we study. Two previous meetings congregating Amazonian specialists focused on related topics: the 1976 symposium "Time and Social Space in Lowland South America," held at the XLII International Congress of Ameri-canists (Overing, see Kaplan 1977), and a 1984 session at the AAA, which resulted in the book *Rethinking History and Myth: Indigenous South American Perspectives on the Past* (Hill 1988a).[10]

The "Time and Social Space symposium addressed the question of how time is conceptualized in Amazonia by exploring indigenous social philosophies of time. Its agenda was born of the need to distinguish Amazonian collective repre-sentations of time from the notion of genealogical time characteristic of British Africanist models. As part of this paradigm shift, emphasis was accorded to the mechanisms of obliterating time and forgetting genealogical ties, both now well-known aspects described in a series of Amazonian ethnographies (but perhaps not quite as universal as was once thought—see Chaumeil, this volume). For Overing Kaplan, indigenous representation of time implied its denial; if not a denial of time's passage per se, at least an attempt to "deny the changes that occur through time" (1977:389). Such a philosophy of time or regime of historicity was closely inspired by Lévi-Strauss's distinction between "cold" and "hot" societies.

The other meeting uniting specialists from Amazonia (and the Andes) resulted in what has proved to be perhaps the most influential ethnographic book on the myth/history debate. *Rethinking History and Myth* is devoted to dismantling what Jonathan Hill calls "the myth of 'cold' societies" (Hill 1988b:3). It looks to read-dress the distinction between myth and history by exploring the ways in which Indian-white contact appears in narratives, rituals, and oratory. In a sense, the book takes precisely the opposite tack to the earlier symposium, seeking to free itself from the formal and synchronic side of structuralism and lend a new em-phasis to politics and performance in social life: "myth in South America," writes Turner in his closing comments, "has not been merely a passive device for clas-sifying historical 'events' but a program for orienting social, political, ritual, and other forms of historical action" (1988:236). This shift from classificatory reason to the logic of politics and practice exemplifies not only Americanist production over recent decades but also poststructuralist anthropology in general, a shift accompanied by a closer attention to history.[11]

However, comparing the various chapters included in the publications from the two symposia (Overing Kaplan 1977; Hill 1988a), we can see that, analytically speaking, they are not quite so opposed as the theoretical discussions would imply. Both collections focus on apprehending the culturally specific forms of relating to temporal sequences, although with different takes on the relation between structure and practice. Part of the problem here resides in a different understanding of the Lévi-Straussian distinction between hot and cold societies.[12] Indeed, it may be argued that many of the cases analyzed in *Rethinking History and Myth* are good examples of what Lévi-Strauss had in mind when he proposed this distinction. By exploring how Indian-white relations are incorporated into and expressed by ritual performances and narratives, the contributors show how certain cultural devices absorb new events and relations. The fact that this necessarily implies change does not contradict Lévi-Strauss's argument, since the latter is predicated not upon stability and fixity but upon the notion of structural transformation—the sort of transformation that structures his *Mythologiques*. As he points out in "The Scope of Anthropology," he adopts, in contrast to history, "a *transformational* rather than a *fluxional* method" ([1960] 1976:18).

We take this transformational model as an important analytical instrument in studying issues of continuity and change, revealing their mutual implication without resorting to romantic motifs such as essence, *Volksgeist*, or cultural core, which suppose self-similarity across time. A productive critique of Lévi-Strauss's ideas must therefore question the *limits* of this model of structural transformation rather than attribute a lack of dynamics to his theory. The lower limit of this model is the issue of human agency, since structural dynamics implies a diachrony without agency. The question then is how much agency we wish to infuse in our descriptions (see Schwartz and Salomon 2003:510). This is a highly complex issue since, at least for anthropologists, it implies a further question: What is agency and what does it mean in specific ethnographic situations? The upper limit of the model has two aspects: how to conceptualize radical transformation, and how to conceptualize the encounter of societies with different structures (see Sahlins 1981, 1985; also Turner 1993:63). We deal with the problem of agency in the next section, and with so-called cultural contact in the penultimate one.

Despite their divergences, both symposia provided an important impulse toward research into indigenous temporality and memory. The inscription of memory in the landscape, the temporality involved in interactions with the environment, and the study of indigenous cartographies have emerged as important themes of investigation, particularly among specialists in Arawakan peoples (Balée

1998; Gow 1995; Heckenberger 2005; Hill 1989; Santos-Granero 1998; Vidal 2000, 2003; Whitehead 1998). The construction of kinship and the meaningful experiences of dwelling have been treated as key elements of indigenous historicities (Gow 1991; Viegas, forthcoming). Ritual has been studied as a primary means of producing and actualizing social memory (Conklin 1995; Cormier 2003; Cunha and Castro 1985; Graham 1995; McCallum 2000; Oakdale 2001, 2005a; A. Taylor 1993), a theme that has acquired a more theoretical formulation in the works of Carlo Severi (1993, 2004). Narratives—whether "mythical," "historical," or "autobiographical"—and other verbal genres have been investigated, revealing singular ways of constructing temporality, as well as the inscription of historical events in discursive forms (Basso 1995; Fausto 2002b; Franchetto 1993; Gallois 1993; Hendricks 1993; Kohn 2002; Oakdale 2005b). Here we can also highlight the themes of cultural cannibalization and mimesis that have emerged as new ways of conceiving processes previously subsumed under the label of "acculturation" (Santos-Granero 2002; Taussig 1993; see also in this volume Santos-Granero's and Fausto's chapters).

In sum, a significant number of contemporary ethnographic works look to comprehend the regimes of historicity developed by Amazonian peoples; their findings, in turn, can be used as a critical tool for the development of historical studies, supplying parameters—always relative, since we cannot suppose a simple identity between the past and the present—that in turn enable us to produce histories that are "at once intelligible in the non-native orbit, and authentic to native categories" (Salomon 1999:51).

The Otherness of Indian History

The recent development of diachronic research on indigenous peoples in Amazonia is not without its internal frictions. As Frank Salomon observes, there is an "underlying tension between respect for the 'otherness' of 'Indian history' (which demands epistemological caution about representing native viewpoints) and recognition of indigenous peoples' 'agency' in the making of early modernity (which demands bold synthetic representations)" (1991:51). Such tension is not confined to anthropology in Amazonia. In his monograph on Tanga Islanders, Foster underlines the difficulty of reconciling two distinct lineages of Melanesian anthropology. On one hand, Foster writes, a New Melanesian Ethnography has flourished, led by Strathern (1988; also see 1999) and Wagner (1967, 1981) and emphasizing the "fundamental differences between Melanesian and Western presuppositions about social reality." On the other hand, we find a New Melanesian History, the outcome of a close symbiosis between history and anthropology in the works of authors such as Thomas (1991) and Carrier (1992), which, on the contrary, stresses the "similarities generated out of shared histories of colonialism and commerce" (Foster 1995:2–3).

The same tension can be detected in Amazonian ethnology, although some works try to accommodate both positions. This is the tone set by *Pacificando o branco* (Albert and Ramos 2000), for example, which aims to "reconcile analyses of cosmological systems with the socio-history of contact situations" (Albert 2000:10). Yet this tension is perhaps irreducible, more a continual byproduct of the dualisms—between myth and history, structure and agency, reproduction and transformation—that we all reject at the outset only to reencounter, or reinvent, in the end. If we cannot escape them, perhaps we can counteract the global nature of these series of binarisms by following Strathern (1981) and taking each of the opposed pairs to be tangential to the rest without ever forming a single set of oppositions. For, as Ingold argues, what is characteristically Western is "a propensity to think in parallel dichotomies" (1994:21), and not binarism per se.

In terms of the topics covered by this book, the tension between a New Amazonian History and a New Amazonian Ethnography is expressed in the way the category of "agency" is claimed by each line of research. Used to define the creative capacity to act in a transformative form on sociocultural reality, agency has been taken either as a universal human quality—one previously ignored by structural anthropology (see Rapport and Overing 2000:8)—or, in contrast, as a culturally defined quality, not necessarily located in the singular or collective individual, whose definition varies in accordance with native ontological premises and their relational practices. The latter understanding of agency can be traced in large part to the contributions of Strathern (1988) and Wagner (1991) on Melanesian notions of personhood, a body of work that today has a sizeable influence on Amazonian ethnology (e.g., Castro 2001; Fausto 2002a; Gow 1991; Heckenberger 2005; Hugh-Jones 2000; McCallum 2001; A. Taylor 2000; Vilaça 2002).

These two ways of deploying the notion of agency have an important bearing on the myth/history debate. Contemporary definitions of historical agency, historical consciousness, and even history presuppose if not the suppression of myth then at least the emergence of a theoretico-practical sphere in which human actions are taken to be effective in themselves. A historical narrative is obtained wherever the capacity for transformative action is attributed to humans in their ordinary condition. This is a definition extending back to ancient Greece, but it also reflects the way in which modern philosophy and history retrospectively narrated their origin myths as the overcoming of *mythos* by *logos* (see Lincoln 1999).[13] Be that as it may, this is the usual definition in South American anthropology. Salomon, for example, defines historical narratives as "narratives about change as a humanly made phenomenon" (1999:59). Turner, for his part, defines historical consciousness as the perception that the social world is the product of "creative social agency as a property of contemporary social actors" (1988:244), while Hill calls it "a reflexive awareness on the part of social actors of their abilities to make situational and more lasting adjustments to social orderings," an idea founded in turn on the perception that "the historical past is . . . inhabited by fully human, cultural beings who, although perhaps living in different conditions from those of the present time, had essentially the same powers for making changes as do people living in the present" (1988b:6–7).

From this viewpoint, history and historical perception are necessarily rooted in human praxis, or, as François Châtelet says, in the "recognition of the sensible-profane nature of human existence" (1962:40). This human "making," which molds society as much as nature and which can be narrated a posteriori, is conceived here as a universal potential that is realized as historical consciousness only when recognized as human action—that is, when perceived as creative human action capable of producing transformations in the social world. At once historical and political, this consciousness supposes the homogeneity of past, present, and future—Lyell's uniformitarianism applied to human things.

The question is whether these definitions, fairly productive when it comes to reconstructing a history on the basis of oral accounts, respect the "otherness" of "Indian history." Recovering the link between human action and narrated fact is certainly an essential step in producing historical narratives of peoples without writing (as we two have, in fact, already done: Fausto 2001, n.d.; Heckenberger 2005). However, nothing guarantees that this history of the Indians is also an indigenous history (Menget 1999; see also Basso 1995). The problem lies in negotiating not only the difference between indigenous and Western regimes of social memory but also their different social theories of action and agency. Historical *agency*, defined as a *human* capacity, presumes an ontological separation between humans and nonhumans that fits awkwardly with Amerindian animist ontologies (Castro 1998; Descola 1992, 2005). It could be argued, therefore, that the indigenous equivalent of what we term *historical* action would be *shamanic* action on the world, with the implication that transformative action is not limited to those cases in which human praxis is recognized as a condition, in and by itself, for social transformation (Fausto 2002b; see also Hill 1999:391–394).

This argument has two further implications. One is that, in this context, the concepts of action and agency are linked to the problem of producing transformations in a world that is *not* seen as a product of social conventions. Agency here supposes the possibility of producing transformations in the order established by myth and not the substitution of one convention for another convention, one contract for another contract. Transformative action is a differentiating act in relation to the postmythical order, which also implies the actualization of mythic time to produce effective transformations.[14] The second implication is that transformative action demands an interaction with beings that may be agents without being human in kind. Creative human activity depends on mobilizing capacities that are not just human and of which humans were (partially) deprived in the postmythical order. The equivalent of our "making history" is, then, a mythopraxis that is narrated as a past and a future in a shamanic key (Fausto 2002b:85).[15]

Our argument echoes that of Salomon on the famous Huarochirí Quechua Manuscript, a compilation of oral accounts made at the start of the seventeenth century in Peru. The history that emerges from the manuscript is one of interaction between humans and divinities (*huacas*). Its chronology seems to have been subjected to every kind of manipulation, yet, as Salomon argues, "even if the [oral] sources had been spared such manipulation, they would not have embodied a view of diachrony much like that of European historians. The tellers were not chiefly interested in compiling a chain of human causes for human events. Rather, their main preoccupations were 'mythohistoric'" (1999:37). The history that unfolds is thus a history of relationships between humans and gods—and between humans through gods. Likewise, in Amazonia it is more accurate to conceive indigenous history (not the history of Indians) as the outcome of sociocosmic interactions between different types of persons, human and nonhuman, expressed in a set of always multiple narratives only partially totalizable through ritual action that reaffirms "the fundamental process of transformation, which provides the ontological basis of culture" (Menget 1999:164). The constitution of historical agents depends not on a reflexive capacity (historical consciousness) but on the fabrication of people's agential capacities through involvement in shamanic and ritual practices.[16]

It is worth noting that this does not imply an absence of indigenous historical accounts, in the sense we usually give to history; neither does it mean that indigenous societies are imprisoned by the "machine of myth." The problem is precisely one of supposing that the structure/agency dualism is part of the same equation involving myth/history. Aligning these dualisms in a single series is our way of producing what we call modernity; in the indigenous case, though, myth and its reactualization are precisely the conditions for producing social agency.[17] As Rappaport notes, when associated with political strategies, oral traditions assume an entirely different character to when they are approached simply as myths. However,

> Notwithstanding the centrality of the practical sphere in Nasa history making, we cannot lose sight of the importance of ritual, symbol and pattern

in insuring the efficacy of these narratives over space and time. While they are practical in that they derive from activities that solve problems on the ground, they accomplish this by articulating powerful symbols that move people to action by forging a moral link to a distant past. Their efficacy lies in their very merging of myth and history, and not in any separation of the two (1998:208).

In seeking to relate our concept of history to other sociocultural contexts, therefore, we must be prepared to explore conceptual equivalences rather than objective identities. This is not a question of asking whether history exists among Amerindians and whether they are aware of it, but of determining what they constitute as history and how we can describe it in terms of the relation between them and us (Castro, forthcoming).

Geometries of Relations

We return to the tension indicated by Salomon and by Foster from the other side of the equation, one that emphasizes the plane of similarities and the mutual entanglement in a shared colonial and national history. The shift from a structural idiom to one of ontology, which characterizes both the Melanesian and the Amazonian New Ethnography, has enabled an exploration of the (onto)logical continuity of the indigenous lived world and, therefore, an emphasis on the dissimilarities between Us and Them, even in contexts of intense social change and growing interaction with the surrounding society.

A recent example of this position is Gow's book, which combines structural, phenomenological, and historical approaches in order to understand what kind of continuity inheres in the ceaseless transformation of the Piro people of Peruvian Amazonia. From this perspective, he rephrases the issue of historical agency: "the present study," he writes,

> would have achieved little if all it said was that what Piro people have done, historically, is react to those features of the ongoing consequences of European colonial expansion that have impinged upon them. Instead, it is necessary to demonstrate that the specific form of successive colonial situations arose from within *the ways Piro people set about constituting them.* This is not because, in the sentimental language of resistance theories, Piro people are not passive victims but active agents. For much of their recent history, Piro people have indeed been victims of exploitation, brutality, and injustice, in situations where they had no say and few means to fight back, and it would be grotesque for me to pretend that things had been otherwise. Instead, the reason why it is necessary to demonstrate that the specific form

of successive colonial situations arose from the ways Piro people set about constituting them is because Piro people are made by other Piro people, and have no choice but to constitute the world around them in ways that are intrinsically meaningful to them (2001:303, our emphasis).

The authors of this book adopt a similar position and look to understand the ways in which the indigenous societies of Amazonia *set about constituting* the specific historical situations in which they find themselves embroiled. However, the exploration of this plane of continuities, even when associated with the notion of structural transformation, involves two parallel risks: on one hand, the danger of emptying the structural content of global and local historical processes (Turner 1993:63); on the other hand, the danger of taking the indigenous world as a universe apart, capable of transforming itself continually, cannibalizing historical situations, in order to remain the same. By adopting this line of thinking, we simply invert the terms of the world system theorists who find structure in global processes alone and pure discontinuity at the local level.

Various authors have searched for alternative solutions to this conundrum. Oliveira (1964, 1972) coined the concept of "interethnic friction," highlighting the conflictual nature of culturally diverse intersocietal zones, as a way of circumventing the dualism of acculturation studies. Sahlins believes it necessary to reconfigure "the usual binary opposition as a triadic historical field, including a complicated intercultural zone where the cultural differences are worked through in political and economic practices" (2000:486), a zone in which new "structures of conjuncture" emerge. Ferguson and Whitehead have proposed the notion of "tribal zone" to characterize the "physical and conceptual spaces that radiate out from the borders of the intrusive state system" (1999:xii), an idea that renders the geometry of contact more complex. This is not a minor question, since spatial metaphors such as margin and periphery designate a center and thereby represent the perspective of the intrusive state system.[18] Geometry serves in locating perspectives and so can also be used to invert points of view, as Waddel, Naidu, and Ha'ufa achieve by designating Oceania "Our sea of islands" (*apud* Sahlins 1997:103–108).

There are, though, some difficulties in appropriating the idea of intercultural or interethnic zones. The first is geometric; the second is perspectival. Such an idea supposes a linear, continuous, and localized geography. This may have been the spatial conformation during some early periods of colonial history, but it does not apply well to the present situation. The contemporary experiences of indigenous peoples in Amazonia differ from those of past centuries in at least three sociospatial and scalar aspects: the present absence of interactional discontinuity;

the multiplication of relations at various scales; and, finally, the paradoxical process of territorialization and delocalization (see Fausto 2000b).

Discontinuity was a crucial feature of the colonial process in Amazonia. Moments of expansion were intermingled with periods of retraction in such a way that interethnic relations were based on cycles of contact and isolation. These reflected to some degree the rhythm of the extractivist economy, which was highly sensitive to world system trends (Hemming 1987; Santos-Granero and Barclay 1998, 2000; Sweet 1974; Weinstein 1983; see Kohn, this volume). This tidal movement had two basic consequences. First, it generated new "discoveries." The nineteenth-century rubber economy drew back into the system peoples who had been subjected to missionary influences more than a century before. Twentieth-century state agents contacted "pristine" peoples already attacked by seventeenth- and eighteenth-century *bandeirantes*. Native groups also enacted the "discovery" of whites and commodities more than once (Fausto 2001:56–58; Howard 1993). The second consequence was that these cycles of contact and isolation created a special dynamic for social and cultural phenomena. Periods of retraction were particularly rich in terms of the reorganization and re-creation of native societies, prompting historical processes whose rationale was only partially—or even marginally—colonial.[19] This fact is commonly obscured by ethnohistory, whose focus tends to be either on processes of regression under external pressure or on the interaction between whites and natives, as though indigenous history becomes history only when *we* enter the equation (see Fausto, this volume).

Nowadays there is no perspective of discontinuity in white-Indian relations, a fact that is reinforced by a new scale of interaction. There is a multiplication of relations, which reverses the insularity promoted by late colonial processes and the former monopoly of mediation held by the state during the twentieth century. In a sense, contemporary indigenous Amazonia is more favorably compared with pre-Columbian Amazonia than with late colonial Amazonia. Network structures, multiplicity of connections, and regional and supraregional fluxes of goods and information were probably common features of certain parts of lowland South America, especially along the main rivers, in the fifteenth century (Boomert 1987; Lathrap 1973). Colonialism promoted insularity by causing the demographic and social disruption of native networks. The cultural isolate studied by functionalists and culturalists in the twentieth century is a real product of this historical process. But here lurks a paradox: now that we consider the cultural isolate to be an essentialization produced by anthropological discourse, it seems that each aggregate we call an "Amazonian people" tends to represent itself as a cultural isolate among other cultural isolates in the world, all of them distinguished from "white society."[20]

This counterinvention of the local is paradoxically accompanied by "delocalization"—though not by "deterritorialization," which characterizes the colonial period. Much to the contrary, there is a definitive territorialization of indigenous people in Amazonia, which results from political conquests in lands and rights (for the Brazilian case, see Oliveira 1998). Delocalization stands for the process of being able to skip local chains and build links outside the local context. In the past, the contiguity of space was inescapable. In the rubber economy, for instance, each node of the system represented a more inclusive perspective (Cunha 1998; Gow 1994), but no one could skip a local node and reach a higher one. This was sometimes physically enforced by the *seringalistas* who controlled strategic spots along downstream routes (Taussig 1986). The same is true for state control, which tended to bar interactions further away from the reservations. The first agency for indigenous affairs of the Brazilian Republican State was born in 1910 as the Service for the Protection of the Indian and for the Localization of National Workers (SPILTN). To be able to confine people within the local amounted to domination.[21]

The production of these local geographic spaces, with their associated control mechanisms, was never monolithic. Even the Jesuit *aldeamentos* were far from being the Foucauldian panoptic. Today, though, the experience of delocalization is not merely an outcome of multiple journeys and social interactions: it also involves the entry of communications media into the villages. Televisions, radios, and the Internet delocalize even those who do not travel. It is now possible to skip local contexts in imaginary and real ways, building connections that elude the intermediary nodes of the system. These processes produce a nonlinear geometry that makes it increasingly difficult to locate intermediary areas of "contact" or cultural "friction."

The second difficulty with the notion of intercultural zone concerns the perspective we choose to describe these relational fields. Addressing this problem, Foster asserts that the solution involves recognizing that "Melanesians understand themselves and act in terms . . . conditioned by the continued encounter between agencies of (post)colonial states, capitalism, and Christianity, on one side, and highly localized practices for making meaning, on the other" (1995:5). Few would be apt to disagree with this assertion. Indigenous peoples are part of this wider social field that includes a myriad of relations (which indeed always extended beyond the borders of any cultural isolate, even before European colonialism). Nonetheless, the problem is perhaps one of perspective, since we may occupy only one position at a time, even in the gray zone, without ever encountering a global viewpoint. For Viveiros de Castro, there is no solution to this conundrum: "The alternative is clear: either we take indigenous peoples to be creatures of the objectifying gaze of the national state, duplicating in theory the political asymmetry between the two poles; or we look to determine the fully creative activity of these peoples in constituting the 'white world' as one of the components of their own lived world, that is, as historical raw material for the 'culturing culture' of indigenous collectivities" (1999:115). For Hill, the way out of state reification is a politics that can "recognize that the indigenous systems of representation, still embodied today in the shamanic practices and the poetic evocations of a mythic and historical past, constitute a parallel and very sophisticated approach to the contradictions between nationalism and indigenous identities" (1999:394).

Parallel or incompossible worlds, then? We continue to believe, just like the Amerindian shamans, that relating incompossible worlds remains possible, and politically necessary. That is to say, the work of anthropology, as often as not, is not about writing or reconstructing history but about relating alternative histories, each with a unique perspective and voice.

The Book

This book, containing nine essays by different authors, favors an intensive examination of various ethnographic cases rather than an extensive survey. Geographically speaking, the book concentrates on the western portion of Amazonia (see map, figure 0.1), focusing on peoples located in Ecuador (the Quechua Runa and Jívaro), Peru (Yanesha and Cocama), the Brazil-Peru border (Matis), and the Brazil-Bolivia border (Wari'). To these peoples are added the Xinguanos in the geographical center of Brazil and, outside Amazonia, the Guarani, dispersed between the south of Brazil, Paraguay, Argentina, and the south of Bolivia. From a linguistic viewpoint, the book has a wider scope, covering peoples representing a very diverse range of language groupings, including the Pano, Tupi-Guarani, Jívaro, Chapakura, and Arawak, as well as a Quechua-speaking people. The essays are sequenced in the form of a fugue—that is, a theme presented by one author is taken up by the authors that follow, "establishing a fabric of out-of-phase similarities" (Wisnik 1990:120)—but without any final chord of resolution.

The book opens with Santos-Granero's essay on the Yanesha, one of the Arawakan peoples that joined together under the leadership of Juan Santos de Atahuallpa to expel the Spanish invaders from Peruvian Amazonia in 1742. In the most successful indigenous uprising seen in the South American lowlands, these peoples succeeded in ridding the whole region of European intruders until the mid-nineteenth century. The Yanesha, however, do not emerge from Santos-Granero's account as a traditionally closed people. On the contrary, they appear to have been extremely permeable to Andean and, later, European influences. Incan

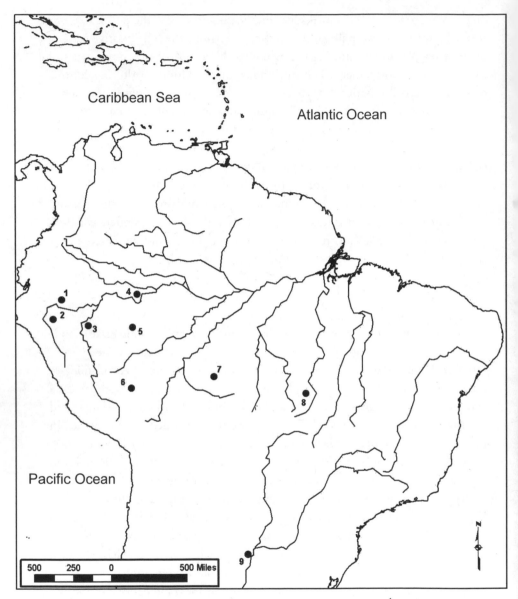

Fig. 0.1. South America, showing location of indigenous peoples, including: (1) Ávila Runa, (2) Shuar,
(3) Yanesha, (4) Cocama, (5) Matis, (6) Piro, (7) Wari', (8) Xinguano, (9) Guarani.

and Catholic figures people their religion and social life, bringing to the fore the theoretical issue of how to conceptualize this mimetic appropriation of alien ideas and practices by Amerindian peoples. Santos-Granero addresses this issue as a temporal process unfolding in the context of asymmetric relations between the Yanesha and other people (the Incas, Europeans, and non-indigenous Peruvians). The key question is how they construct this past of ceaseless transformation. "What do they remember but, above all, what do they choose to forget?" asks Santos-Granero. The author goes on to reveal the way in which the Yanesha make and unmake the past through selective remembering and forgetting, a process as much concerned with the past as it is with the future.

Fausto raises similar issues in his chapter. He critically assesses the dominant view cultivated in Guarani studies of a pure religious core upon which their identity is founded. Fausto explores the issue of transformation both as a process that unfolds in time (a history) and as a topological transformation (a structure). He also points to the need to adapt our models of social change to the specific indigenous conceptions and practices of transformation. He looks at the contemporary Guarani from the standpoint of colonial chronicles, as well as more recent ethnographic accounts of Amazonian Tupi-Guarani peoples. A very different image of Guarani history emerges from his analysis. Much in the same way as the Yanesha, the Guarani appropriated countless features of Catholic origin, yet this did not lead them to think of themselves as others. They erased the very process of appropriation from their memory, forgetting how they appropriated and transformed an alterity that simultaneously transformed them. Fausto, as much as Santos-Granero, tries to define this form of forgetting, the making and unmaking of history, without resorting to some metaphysical necessity of remaining identical through time.

Kohn takes the same lead from the perspective of the Quechua Runa of the Ávila Viejo village in Amazonian Ecuador. Instead of centering his analysis on interethnic relations, Kohn focuses on interspecies relations between humans and nonhumans, exploring the perspectival ontology of the Ávila Runa. The image that emerges is of a cosmology suffused with history, although phenomenologically experienced as timeless and changeless. More specifically, the chapter's theme is the cosmological role of animal masters. These are powerful beings who control the forest and its animals, and whose relationship to humans is predicated upon an ambivalent social contract that enables and at the same time restricts predation on both sides. Kohn shows how the Ávila Runa came to incorporate their historical experience into this cosmology, such that, for them, living "in the society of nature" is based on a translocal and transhistorical image of sociality. The animal masters encompass a number of diverse historical figures: the indigenous lords of the region, the headmen of "wild Indians," and the bosses and priests of colonial and postcolonial times. By examining Ávila Runa relations with the beings of the forest, Kohn ends up uncovering layers of historical experiences with humans of different kinds. In the end, then, the essay is as much about interethnic relations as it is about interspecies relations between humans and nonhumans, underlining the fact that Amerindians seem to pose no ontological divide between relations across species and relations across cultures.

The next chapter, by Taylor, analyzes different regimes of historicity present within the regional system composed of Jivaroan people, their Quechua-speaking neighbors, and nonindigenous colonists in the upper Amazon. Taylor argues that there are two modes of construing the past at the regional level: one that is Jivaroan and built upon the dynamics of internal vengeance, and another, characteristic of their Runa (Quechuan) neighbors, that emphasizes interethnic relations and the processes through which they emerged as hybrid cultures. These two regimes are simultaneously opposed and complementary, meaning that the Jivaroan insulation of their tradition from outside influences depends on others. The continuity of their tradition is thus predicated upon transformation and hybridization among the Quechua-speaking people. Through an analysis of Jivaroan conceptions of illness as a process involving the dissolution of the self, Taylor describes the passage from one identity (Jivaroan) to the other (Runa), furnishing a microsociological depiction of the dynamics of transformation that manifests at the regional and historical level as a macro process of "acculturation" and "ethnogenesis." As a result, her work reveals specific notions of history, agency, and transformation in which no ontological distinction between sociological and cosmological domains is made.

Tackling similar issues in the context of "interethnic contact," Vilaça addresses cultural change from the perspective of Amazonian conceptions of body metamorphosis. Her procedure is similar to Kohn's and Taylor's, applied here to Indian-white relations and more specifically to the issue of changing indigenous identities. She criticizes recent approaches for not paying sufficient attention to indigenous practices and conceptions of body fabrication and transformation, a topic that has been on Amazonian ethnology's agenda since the 1960s. Vilaça bases her case on her research with the Wari', a Chapakuran-speaking people of the state of Rondonia, Brazil. She shows how Wari' shamans inhabit a double self-position—one human, the other animal—and can switch from one to the other, a switch that equals a changing in bodily attributes and, consequently, in perspectives. Selfhood and identity are, in fact, concepts that fail to describe what is at issue here. It is actually inexact to say that shamans have a double, split, or multiple personality, since in our culture these notions describe an undesirable dissolution of a unitary self or its complete absence. Amerindians, however, strive to acquire more than an internally homogeneous self in order to become (pro)creative persons. From cannibal practices to vision quests, from shamanic trances to ritual transformation, from posthomicidal seclusion to funerary practices, we observe the same effort to be more than *one*self. Given that this notion of personhood has guided millions of Amerindians for thousands of years, why should it not also shape the more recent context of Indian-white relations? Most of us consider that there is something special about modern Western societies, and tend to see other contemporary lived worlds as a projection of our own predicaments. Vilaça questions this assumption: Can we interpret the Amerindian appropriation and use of Western goods, especially clothes, using our own categories of identity and selfhood? Can we turn everything into a positive or negative symbol of ethnic identity? We are so convinced about the power of our objects to seduce hearts and minds that we often forget to ask what hearts and minds are for the people being seduced by them.

Gow follows a similar path in dealing with another traditional theme in Amazonian ethnology: personal names. His subject is not the acquisition or transmission of names in a local context, however, but their attribution and social meaning in the context of asymmetric relations within a regional system in Peruvian Amazonia. He focuses on the Cocama and Cocamilla people, Tupi-speaking populations, who were supposedly on the way to vanishing as a distinct ethnic group by the 1960s. Called "ex-Cocama" by Lathrap and "invisible Indians" by Stocks, these populations were assumed to have passed from one set identity to another, namely, from that of "Indian" to that of "rural mixed-blood people." Gow argues that this interpretation is modeled upon the idea of "passing as" another ethnicity—a notion originating in the United States—in which the ex-Cocama phenomenon simply appears to be a case of hiding a "real" identity as "Indian" in order to operate better in a social context where being "Indian" is a social handicap. This is not entirely false, but it is wholly insufficient and trivial. Gow looks to show that this phenomenon can be interpreted as a transformational variant of other indigenous Amazonian kinship systems, and in this sense should be taken not as the eclipsing of an indigenous social logic but as evidence of its ongoing transformation.

A new thematic strand is now introduced into the book: the concept of ancestrality in indigenous Amazonia. Since the symposium organized by Overing Kaplan in 1977 and Cunha's paradigmatic monograph in 1978, Amazonian ethnologists have taken the absence of the concept of ancestrality and the shallowness of genealogical time as general empirical facts with many implications for the understanding of indigenous social reproduction and social memory. This set of features was also instrumental to the development of a more general approach in Amazonian ethnology, which Viveiros Castro (1996) named the "symbolic economy of alterity." If Amerindians conceive of their dead as Others, they fall in the same category as the many other Others in indigenous sociocosmologies, such as brothers-in-law, enemies, animals, and gods.

Erikson's analysis focuses on the masked figures produced by the Panoan-speaking Matis, living in Brazilian Amazonia. These masked figures, called *mariwin*, have previously been depicted as the representation of "ancestral" spirits. The author casts a new light on the matter by exploring the fact the *mariwin* are at once "ancestors" and "non-kin." They amalgamate features of otherness and ancestrality, raising the question: How can a people represent their ancestors through others (or others through their ancestors)? Erikson shows that although the *mariwin* are associated with the dead and the preceding generations, and hence stand for the group's continuity and self-assertion, they appear less as forebears than as virtual affines. The *mariwin* ambivalence is not uncommon in Amazonia. An interesting parallel is found in the different meanings attributed to the concept of *arutam* among the Jivaroans (see Descola 1996). As with the *mariwin*, the *arutam* are neither entirely other nor entirely self—a result that matches well with contemporary discussion on the notion of the person in indigenous Amazonia (see Castro 2001; Fausto 2002a; A. Taylor 2000).

If, as it seems, ancestrality is inflected through alterity in Amazonia, even among social groups where one finds the vertical perpetuation of identities, does it mean that the "cult of the dead" is entirely absent in the South American lowlands (in marked contrast to the Andean highlands)? Chaumeil scrutinizes a vast literature on past and present lowland indigenous peoples to answer this question. The shallowness of genealogical memory in Amazonia, as well as the well-known practices for effacing the memory of the deceased, seem to indicate that little continuity can exist between the living and the dead, and even where it does exist, it is tinged with alterity. Chaumeil argues, though, that there is more diversity to both the treatment and the conceptualization of the dead than is commonly acknowledged. He shows that the image of the deceased-as-enemy, expelled from the memory of the living, is far from being a universal paradigm in Amazonia, whether in the past or today. In response, he sets out to compile and analyze a number of practices that do not fit with this general idea, revealing a much more diverse picture of funerary and postfunerary practices in the lowlands.

Recognition of this diversity has a particular appeal for archaeological studies in Amazonia, since it is not a simple task to reconcile the ethnographic image of the dead as "people to be forgotten" with examples of funerary pottery found in archaeological excavations along the Amazon floodplain—most items of which have already been known for more than a century. The simple fact that the vast majority of the region's indigenous population perished during the first century of colonization means that no easy analogy can be made between the present and the past. Fortunately, there are still a few places in Amazonia where past and present come together in cultural traditions that extend into the distant past, such as the upper Xingu, where one can study more than a thousand years of in situ cultural development. The region is a laboratory for investigating the issue of continuity and discontinuity. Over a millennium, an amazing permanence of very basic cultural schemas can be observed, which are clearly marked out in space and recognizable archaeologically; at the same time we can see an eventful history of migration and mixture of different peoples, leading to the formation of today's multiethnic and multilingual single cultural system. No one can recount the last millennium of Xinguano culture without a firm "sense of structure," nor can one perceive it as less then eventful.

In the final chapter, Heckenberger focuses on several critical elements of Xinguano ethnoarchaeology, which provides an Amerindian perspective on large, settled, regional, and hierarchical peoples. Such peoples, rare today, dominated various areas of Amazonia in pre-Columbian times. Heckenberger's text resonates with the points made by Chaumeil, particularly insofar as it questions the idea of "genealogical amnesia" and an absence of "ancestrality." He explores how history and social hierarchy are objectified in ritual performance and the environment. Building on discussions of village space, houses (Lévi-Strauss [1977] 1984), and the ritual construction of the body, he argues that the upper Xingu regional complex represents the type of historicity that is usually attributed to small- to medium-sized complex societies elsewhere in the world. He also challenges the strict distinction between archaeology, history, and ethnography, adding a fresh spin to the questions of history, memory, and identity that permeate the whole volume. In closing the book, this chapter tries to reach back into an Amazonian past whose distinct features have been obliterated by the massive changes that have transpired in the region since 1500 A.D.

Taken as a whole, all the authors deal, in one form or another, with the same set of problems concerning time and change. Indeed, how could it be otherwise? The problems of cultural form, social identity, history, and memory interate in highly complex ways. There is no easy approach, nor any singular perspective, for describing social entities in a world subject to the dynamics of transformation and the ravages (and benefits) of time. Through the presentation of insightful ways of discussing the matter of time in the context of South American indigenous peoples, we aim at contributing to a renewal of anthropological theory, one that takes a critical and reflexive stance toward our contemporary predicaments and cultural anxieties. The book, then, is also about our times. After all, time matters, it always matters, but it does not matter always in the same way.

Acknowledgments

Our thanks to Fernando Santos-Granero, Peter Gow, Eduardo Kohn, and Luiz Antonio Costa for their comments on this introduction. Portions of the final text were translated and/or revised by David Rodgers. All quotations from non-English texts were translated by the authors.

Notes

1. Such is the case with the upper Amazon (Brown and Fernández 1991; Renard-Casevitz et al. 1986; Santos-Granero 1992a, 1992b; A. Taylor 1992, 1999), the Guianas (Arvelo-Jiménez and Biord 1994; Farage 1989; Whitehead 1988, 1990, 1993a, 1999a, 1999b), to a certain extent Central Amazonia and the Rio Negro (Amoroso 1992; Menéndez 1992; Porro 1994, 1996; Wright 1991, 1992, 2005), and the Atlantic coast and the basin of the Paraná-Paraguay rivers, inhabited by Tupi-Guarani peoples (Ganson 2003; Melià 1986; Monteiro 1992, 1999; Pompa 2003; Wilde 2003).

2. This is also the effect of the current dynamics of academic competition on the construction of anthropological theory. Critical thinking seems to be driven more by academic survival strategies than by intellectual engagement per se. The overall result of this competition is less a constant intellectual renewal than the (false) impression that there is no accumulation in anthropological knowledge, only endless ruptures and "turns": continuous "post"-erization (which amounts to a continuous pasteurization of previous ideas).

3. Agency is a critical cultural category in contemporary Anglo-American social consciousness. It connotes the capacity of individuals qua individuals to consciously guide their lives and act upon the world. This culturally specific concept stems from a particular notion of the person, predicated upon self-identity and self-consciousness, in which free choice is the model of action and property relations characterizes the agents connections to their acts (see Schneewind 1998; Strathern 1996, 2004; Tully 1993). As anthropologists, we cannot take this notion for granted, not just because we have alternative conceptions of agency in our own cultural traditions, but also because other cultures have their own specific conceptions of agency.

4. The concept of "alterity" is quite current in Amazonian anthropology, more than in other regional traditions. It designates a certain quality or "state of being other or different" (OED), describing thus an ontological condition where perfect identity is not only unattainable but also undesirable. The productivity of this concept in Amazonian anthropology derives from Lévi-Strauss's legacy, and, more generally, from modern French philosophy (for an excellent overview, see Descombes 1980).

5. However, we must perfect our gaze, since what sometimes appears purely reactive may

be the outcome of an indigenization of our own obsession with identity. The content of native identity claims may be a particularly convoluted form of the other's incorporation into the self, so well described by Amazonianists in other contexts. *Plus ça change . . .*

6. The binarism of modernity produces difference through projection, taking identification as its ideological horizon. Binary opposition, in this case, contains an internal movement that is processual, temporal, and teleological in kind: the position of the Us/Them distinction indicates a development whose arrival point is the dominant pole of the opposition—explaining the pregnancy of notions such as cultural assimilation, civilizing process, social development, and modernization.

7. The risk here is also one of turning the critique of exoticization into a machine of derealization, capable of converting any form of thought or practice that fails to meet our moral standards and exigencies of rationality into a figment of the Western imagination. The European mythmaking argument (see Obeyesekere 1992, 1998; Sahlins 1995, 2003) is a symptom of this more general state of the discipline. No doubt all empires are given to mythomania, but this is no justification for demanding that colonized peoples cease to believe in their myths or, say, refrain from practicing anthropophagy (unless we wish to behave like missionaries and colonial administrators). An antiexoticist anthropology, with its derealization of other realities, accomplishes conceptually what colonialism sought to achieve politically: to assimilate and identify.

8. We use "historicity" here in the sense of a general relation that a human collectivity maintains with the past and the future, without implying any "historic quality or character" (OED) as opposed to myth or fiction (Lefort 1978). This allows us to talk about regimes of historicity and historicities in the plural

9. Originally, the session included the participation of William Fisher and Stephen Hugh-Jones, who unfortunately were unable to contribute to this volume.

10. Recently, Neil Whitehead edited a book with a similar title to our AAA session, compiling some of the papers presented at the Wenner-Gren conference "The Ethnohistory of the So-Called Peripheries" in 2000 in London, Ontario, organized by Marshall Sahlins and bringing together specialists on Amazonia, Melanesia, and Asia. Although Fausto also took part in this conference, we make no direct reference to it here since it had a much wider geographical scope and a more ethnohistorical focus.

11. A fact observed by Ortner in an earlier critical survey (1984; also see 1996). This shift was the result of a veritable new spirit of the times at the end of the millennium, expressed in the publication (or translation into English) of key works such as *Outline of a Theory of Practice* (Bourdieu 1977), *Ilongot Headhunting* (Rosaldo 1980), *Historical Metaphors and Mythical Realities* (Sahlins 1981), *The Constitution of Society* (Giddens 1984), and *Writing Culture* (Clifford and Marcus 1986).

12. There is a recurrent misunderstanding concerning this distinction. As early as midcentury, Lévi-Strauss ([1952] 1958) was arguing against the idea of peoples without history, attacking the then common view that hunter-gatherers were frozen in an archaic state. The distinction between cold and hot societies appeared for the first time in "The Scope of Anthropology," in which, after stating that the "so-called primitive societies belong in

history," he adds the proviso that "they have specialized in ways different from those we have chosen" ([1960] 1976:28). It is this recognition of different ways of dealing with the passage of time that enables Lévi-Strauss to propose the distinction between hot and cold societies, noting above all that this is a theoretical distinction, since no actual society corresponds entirely to one or the other type. The same argument reappears in *The Savage Mind*, as the author prepares his critique of Sartre's historicist transcendental humanism. Here he writes: "It is tedious as well as useless, in this connection, to amass arguments to prove that all societies are in history and change: that this is so is patent. But in getting embroiled in a superfluous demonstration, there is a risk of overlooking the fact that human societies react to this common condition in very different fashions" (1966:234).

13. As Sahlins points out, the danger of taking historical action as transcultural and agency as a universal human capacity lies in producing a decidedly anticultural history: "in a historiography without anthropology, our accounts are reduced to the indeterminacies of a generic human nature or the implicit common sense of the historian's own tribe" (2004:123–124). Abercrombie highlights a similar problem in the relationship between historians and mythology: "Historians have long thought themselves to be debunkers of myths rather that students of them" (1998:410).

14. We use "differentiating" here—*pace* Wagner (1981:42–45)—as a nonconventional symbolization that brings forth invention but at the same time specifies the conventional world. The postmythical order is reinvented only through the radical transformation of what was given in mythic times.

15. On this question, see in particular the literature on the so-called millenarian or messianic movements among Indians and mestizos that flourished in the South American lowlands (Agüero 1992; Brown 1991; Brown and Fernández 1991; Cunha 1973; Hill and Wright 1988; Santos-Granero 1992c, 1993; Vainfas 1995; Wright 1998). For more recent contributions, see Veber's critical evaluation of this literature (2003) and the comments on her article.

16. This need not require a transcendent historicity, produced only by heroes and extraordinary events, since, as McCallum argues (2000:376), it may comprise a historicity of the processes involved in the everyday production of sociality. In this sense, the indigenous equivalent of our quotidian history—"histories of private life," for example—would be a memory inscribed in the processes of producing persons (also see Gow 1991), though these processes also imply the domain of ritual and shamanism. On history and shamanism, see Albert (1993) and Baines (2000).

17. Note, for example, what Toren has to say about myth and history in Fiji: "for us ritual and tradition denotes fixity. From this point of view, it is difficult to understand ritual or tradition as a historical process. . . . In Fijian terms tradition, ritual and custom cannot be distinguished from one another and they are all allowed to be processual. . . . The notion of fixity is reserved for history" (1999:64).

18. See Boccara's discussion (2001) on the notion of frontier.

19. The best-studied cases of cultural re-creation are those of the Selva Central in Peru

(Renard-Casevitz 1992, 1993; Santos-Granero 1991, 1993), the upper Rio Negro (Hugh-Jones 1994; Wright 1998), and the upper Xingu (Heckenberger 2001a, 2001b, 2005), from the mid-eighteenth to the end of the nineteenth century. By saying that the rationale here was marginally colonial, we mean that these local processes, though linked to the wider colonial process, unfolded during moments of greater autonomy, which enabled the rein-digenization of the "tribal zone."

20. It is a simplification to call this process "ethnification" if one sees it as a mere reaction to systemic forces or as a strategic response to new market conditions (Sahlins 1997). Although it is true that the invention of the global counterinvents the local—that is why contemporary struggles take the form of cultural claims for recognition—it seems absurd to simply move from the position that "people have a culture although they don't know" to the assumption that "they think they have a culture although culture doesn't exist."

21. A consistent project of deterritorialization and localization of indigenous populations had begun much earlier, with the Jesuit *aldeamentos* in Portuguese America (M. Almeida 2003; Castelnau-D'Estoile 2000) and the *reducciones* in Spanish America. The same problem was later confronted at the level of state legislation and practices during the Pombal Directorate (1757–98), when a new plan for civilizing Brazil's Indians was put into operation (see R. Almeida 1997). In practical terms, this was also the problem posed by the spatial structure of the *seringais* during the Amazonian rubber boom (1870–1920). The SPILTN therefore inherited a series of colonial ideas and practical experiences, all of which proved disastrous for the indigenous populations (see Lima 1989).

References

Abercrombie, Thomas A. 1998. *Pathways of Memory and Power: Ethnography and History among an Andean People*. Madison: University of Wisconsin Press.

Adovasio, J. M., with Jake Page. 2002. *The First Americans: In Pursuit of Archaeology's Greatest Mystery*. New York: Random House.

Agüero, Oscar Alfredo. 1992. *The Millenium among the Tupí-Cocama*. Uppsala: Department of Cultural Anthropology, Uppsala University.

Albert, Bruce. 1985. "Temps du sang, temps des cendres: Représentation de la maladie, système rituel et espace politique chez les Yanomami du sud-est (Amazonie brésilienne)." Ph.D. diss., Université de Paris X–Nanterre.

———. 1993. "L'Or cannibale et la chute du ciel: Une Critique chamanique de l'économie politique de la nature (Yanomami, Brésil)." *L'Homme* 33(2–4):349–378.

———. 1995. "Anthropologie appliquée ou 'anthropologie impliquée.'" In *Les Applications de l'anthropologie: Une Essai de réflection collective depuis la France*, edited by Jean-François Baré, 87–118. Paris: Karthala.

———. 1997. "'Ethnographic Situation' and Ethnic Movements: Notes on Post-Malinowskian Fieldwork." *Critique of Anthropology* 17:53–65.

————. 2000. "Introdução: Cosmologias do contato no Norte-Amazônico." In Albert and Ramos, *Pacificando o branco*, 9–24.

Albert, Bruce, and Alcida Rita Ramos, eds. 2000. *Pacificando o branco: Cosmologias do contato no Norte-Amazônico*. São Paulo: Editora UNESP.

Almeida, Maria Regina Celestino de. 2003. *Metamorfoses indígenas: Identidade e cultura nas aldeias coloniais do Rio de Janeiro*. Rio de Janeiro: Arquivo Nacional.

Almeida, Rita Heloísa de. 1997. *O Diretório dos Índios: Um projeto de "civilização" no Brasil do século XVIII*. Brasília: Editora da UNB.

Amoroso, Marta Rosa. 1992. "Corsários no caminho fluvial: Os Mura do rio Madeira." In Cunha, *História dos índios no Brasil*, 297–310.

Andrello, Geraldo. 2006. *Cidade de Índio*. São Paulo: Isa/Unesp/ Nuti.

Arvelo-Jiménez, Nelly, and Horacio Biord. 1994. "The Impact of Conquest on Contemporary Indigenous Peoples of the Guiana Shield: The System of Orinoco Regional Interdependence." In Roosevelt, *Amazonian Indians*, 55–78.

Asad, Talal, ed. 1973. *Anthropology and the Colonial Encounter*. New York: Humanities Press.

Baines, Stephen. 2000. "O xamanismo como história: Censuras e memórias da pacificação Waimiri-Atroari." In Albert and Ramos, *Pacificando o branco*, 311–345.

Balée, William, ed. 1998. *Advances in Historical Ecology*. New York: Columbia University Press.

Basso, Ellen B. 1995. *The Last Cannibals: A South American Oral History*. Austin: University of Texas Press.

Boccara, Guillaume. 2001. "Mundos nuevos en las fronteras del Nuevo Mundo." *Revista Nuevo Mundo–Mundos Nuevos* 1:448–507. http://nuevomundo.revues.org/document426.html.

Boomert, Arie. 1987. "Gifts of the Amazon: 'Green Stone' Pendants and Beads as Items of Ceremonial Exchange in Amazonia and the Caribbean." *Antropológica* 67:33–55.

Bourdieu, Pierre. 1977. *Outline of a Theory of Practice*. Translated by Richard Nice. Cambridge: Cambridge University Press.

Brown, Michael F. 1991. "Beyond Resistance: A Comparative Study of Utopian Renewal in Amazonia." *Ethnohistory* 38:387–413.

————. 1993. "Facing the State, Facing the World: Amazonia's Native Leaders and the New Politics of Identity." *L'Homme* 33 (2–4):307–326.

Brown, Michael F., and Eduardo Fernández. 1991. *War of Shadows: The Struggle for Utopia in the Peruvian Amazon*. Berkeley and Los Angeles: University of California Press.

Bynum, Caroline Walker. 1995. *The Resurrection of the Body in Western Christianity, 200–1336*. New York: Columbia University Press.

————. 2001. *Metamorphosis and Identity*. New York: Zone Books.

Calhoun, Craig. 1995. *Critical Social Theory: Culture, History, and the Challenge of Difference*. Cambridge, Massachusetts: Blackwell.

Cardoso de Oliveira, Roberto. *See* Oliveira, Roberto Cardoso de.

Carneiro da Cunha, Manuela. *See* Cunha, Manuela Carneiro da.

Carrier, James G., ed. 1992. *History and Tradition in Melanesian Anthropology.* Berkeley and Los Angeles: University of California Press.

Castelnau-L'Estoile, Charlotte. 2000. *Les Ouvriers d'une vigne stérile: Les Jésuites et la conversion des Indiens au Brésil, 1580–1620.* Paris: Centre Culturel Calouste Gulbenkian.

Castro, Eduardo Viveiros de. 1992. *From the Enemy's Point of View: Humanity and Divinity in an Amazonian Society.* Translated by Catherine V. Howard. Chicago: University of Chicago Press.

———. 1996. "Images of Nature and Society in Amazonian Ethnology." *Annual Review of Anthropology* 25:179–200.

———. 1998. "Cosmological Deixis and Amerindian Perspectivism." *Journal of the Royal Anthropological Institute* 4:469–488.

———. 1999. "Etnologia brasileira." In *O que ler na ciência social brasileira: 1970–1995,* edited by Sérgio Miceli, 1:109–224. São Paulo: Sumaré.

———. 2001. "GUT Feelings about Amazonia: Potential Affinity and the Construction of Sociality." In *Beyond the Visible and the Material: The Amerindianization of Society in the Work of Peter Rivière,* edited by Laura Rival and Neil Whitehead, 19–44. Oxford: Oxford University Press.

———. Forthcoming. *A desmedida de todas as coisas.* São Paulo: Cosac e Naif.

Castro, Eduardo Viveiros de, and Manuela Carneiro da Cunha, eds. 1993. *Amazônia: Etnologia e história indígena,* São Paulo: NHII (Núcleo de História Indígena e do Indigenismo) USP/FAPESP (Fundação de Amparo à Pesquisa do Estado de São Paulo).

Cavalcanti, Ricardo Antonio da Silva. 1999. "Presente de branco, presente de grego? Escola e escrita em comunidades indígenas do Brasil central." Master's thesis, PPGAS/Museu Nacional, Universidade Federal do Rio de Janeiro.

Châtelet, François. 1962. *La Naissance de l'histoire: La Formation de la pensée historienne en Grèce.* Paris: Minuit.

Chaumeil, Jean-Pierre. 1985. "Échange d'énergie: Guerre, identité, reproduction sociale chez les Yagua de l'Amazonie péruvienne." *Journal de la Société des Américanistes* 71:149–163.

———. 1990. "Les Nouveaux Chefs: Pratiques politiques et organisations indigènes en Amazonie péruvienne." *Problèmes d'Amérique Latine,* 96:93–113.

Clifford, James, and George E. Marcus, eds. 1986. *Writing Culture: The Poetics and Politics of Ethnography.* Berkeley and Los Angeles: University of California Press.

Conklin, Beth A. 1995. "'Thus are our bodies, thus was our custom': Mortuary Cannibalism in an Amazonian Society." *American Ethnologist* 22:75–101.

———. 1997. "Body Paint, Feathers, and VCRs: Aesthetics and Authenticity in Amazonian Activism." *American Ethnologist* 24:711–737.

———. 2002. "Shamans versus Pirates in the Amazonian Treasure Chest." *American Anthropologist* 104(4):1050–1061.

Conklin, Beth A., and Laura R. Graham. 1995. "The Shifting Middle Ground: Amazonian Indians and Eco-Politics." *American Anthropologist* 97(4):695–710.

Cormier, Loretta. 2003. "Decolonizing History: Ritual Transformation of the Past among the Guajá of Eastern Amazonia." In Whitehead, *Histories and Historicities in Amazonia*, 123–140.

Cunha, Manuela Carneiro da. 1973. "Logique du mythe et de l'action: Le Mouvement messianique canela de 1963." *L'Homme* 13(4):5–37.

———. 1978. *Os mortos e os outros: Uma análise do sistema funerário e da noção de pessoa entre os índios Krahó*. São Paulo: Hucitec.

———. 1986. *Antropologia do Brasil: Mito, história, etnicidade*. São Paulo: Brasiliense/ EdUSP.

———, ed. 1992. *História dos índios no Brasil*. São Paulo: FAPESP, Companhia das Letras.

———. 1998. "Pontos de vista sobre a floresta amazônica: Xamanismo e tradução." *Mana: Estudos de Antropologia Social* 4(1):7–22.

Cunha, Manuela Carneiro da, and Eduardo Viveiros de Castro. 1985. "Vingança e temporalidade: Os Tupinambás." *Journal de la Société des Américanistes* 71:191–217.

Denevan, William M. 2001. *Cultivated Landscapes of Native Amazonia and the Andes: Triumph over the Soil*. Oxford: Oxford University Press.

Descola, Philippe. 1992. "Societies of Nature and the Nature of Society." In *Conceptualizing Society*, edited by Adam Kuper, 197–226. London: Routledge.

———. 1993. "Les Affinités sélectives: Alliance, guerre et prédation dans l'ensemble jivaro." *L'Homme* 33 (2–4):171–190.

———. 1996. *The Spears of Twilight: Life and Death in the Amazon Jungle*. Translated by Janet Lloyd. New York: New Press.

———. 2005. *Par-delà nature et culture*. Paris: Gallimard.

Descombes, Vincent. 1980. *Modern French Philosophy*. Translated by L. Scott-Fox and J. M. Harding. Cambridge: Cambridge University Press.

Dillehay, Thomas D. 2000. *The Settlement of the Americas: A New Prehistory*. New York: Basic Books.

Erickson, Clark L. 1995. "Archaeological Perspectives on Ancient Landscapes of the Llanos de Mojos in the Bolivian Amazon." In *Archaeology in the Lowland American Tropics*, edited by Peter W. Stahl, 66–95. Cambridge: Cambridge University Press.

Erikson, Philippe. 1986. "Alterité, tatouage et anthropophagie chez les Pano: La Belliqueuse Quête de soi." *Journal de la Société des Américanistes* 72:185–210.

———. 1996. *La Griffe des aïeux: Marquage du corps et démarquages ethniques chez les Matis d'Amazonie*. Paris: Peeters.

Ethnohistory. 2000. "Venezuelan Anthropology." Special issue, *Ethnohistory* 47(3–4).

Fabian, Johannes. 1983. *Time and the Other: How Anthropology Makes Its Object*. New York: Columbia University Press.

Farage, Nádia. 1991. *As muralhas dos sertões: Os povos indígenas do rio Branco e a colonização*. São Paulo: Paz e Terra.

Fausto, Carlos. 1999. "Of Enemies and Pets: Warfare and Shamanism in Amazonia." *American Ethnologist* 26 (4):933–956.

———. 2000a. *Os índios antes do Brasil*. Rio de Janeiro: Jorge Zahar.

———. 2000b. "Local and Global History in Amazonia." Paper presented at the Wenner-Gren Conference, "The Ethnohistory of the So-Called Peripheries," American Society for Ethnohistory, London, Ont., October 18–22.

———. 2001. *Inimigos fiéis: História, guerra e xamanismo na Amazônia*. São Paulo: EdUSP.

———. 2002a. "Banquete de gente: Comensalidade e canibalismo na Amazônia." *Mana: Estudos de Antropologia Social* 8(2):7–44.

———. 2002b. "Faire le mythe: Histoire, récit et transformation en Amazonie." *Journal de la Société des Américanistes* 88:69–90.

———. n.d. *Forms in History: A Hundred Years in the Life of an Amazonian People (c. 1890–1995)*. Manuscript.

Fausto, Carlos, and John Monteiro, eds. Forthcoming. *Tempos índios: Histórias e narrativas do Novo Mundo*. Lisbon: Assírio e Alvim.

Ferguson, R. Brian, and Neil L. Whitehead. 1999. Preface to *War in the Tribal Zone: Expanding States and Indigenous Warfare*, 2nd printing, xi–xxxv. Sante Fe, New Mexico: School of American Research Press.

Fisher, William H. 2000. *Rain Forest Exchanges: Industry and Community on an Amazonian Frontier*. Washington, D.C.: Smithsonian Institution Press.

Foster, Robert J. 1995. *Social Reproduction and History in Melanesia: Mortuary Ritual, Gift Exchange, and Custom in the Tanga Islands*. Cambridge: Cambridge University Press.

Franchetto, Bruna. 1993. "A celebração da história nos discursos cerimoniais kuikúro (Alto Xingu)." In Castro and Cunha, *Amazônia*, 95–116.

———. 1995. "O papel da educação escolar no processo de domesticação das línguas indígenas pela escrita." *Revista Brasileira de Estudos Pedagógicos* 75:409–421.

———. Forthcoming. "A guerra dos alfabetos: Escrevendo línguas indígenas na Amazônia." In Fausto and Monteiro, *Tempos índios*.

Franchetto, Bruna, and Michael Heckenberger, eds. 2001. *Os povos do Alto Xingu: História e cultura*. Rio de Janeiro: EdUFRJ.

Friedman, Jonathan. 1994. *Cultural Identity and Global Process*. London: Sage.

Gallois, Dominique Tilkin. 1994. *Mairi revisitada: A reintegração da fortaleza de Macapá na tradição oral dos Waiãpi*. São Paulo: NHII-USP/FAPESP.

Ganson, Barbara Anne. 2003. *The Guaraní under Spanish Rule in the Río de la Plata*. Stanford, California: Stanford University Press.

Gassón, Rafael. 2000. "Quirípas and Mostacillas: The Evolution of Shell Beads as a Medium of Exchange in Northern South America." *Ethnohistory* 47(3–4):581–609.

Giddens, Anthony. 1984. *The Constitution of Society: Outline of the Theory of Structuration.* Berkeley and Los Angeles: University of California Press.

Gordon, Cesar. 2003. "Folhas pálidas: A incorporação Xikrin (Mebêngôkre) do dinheiro e das mercadorias." Ph.D. diss., PPGAS/Museu Nacional, Universidade Federal do Rio de Janeiro.

Gow, Peter. 1990. "Could Sangama Read? The Origin of Writing among the Piro of Eastern Peru." *History of Anthropology* 5:87–103.

———. 1991. *Of Mixed Blood: Kinship and History in Peruvian Amazonia.* Oxford: Clarendon Press.

———. 1994. "River People: Shamanism and History in Western Amazonia." In Thomas and Humphrey, *Shamanism, History, and the State,* 90–113.

———. 1995. "Land, People, and Paper in Western Amazonia." In *The Anthropology of Landscape: Perspectives on Place and Space,* edited by Eric Hirsch and Michael O'Hanlon, 43–62. Oxford: Clarendon Press.

———. 2001. *An Amazonian Myth and Its History.* Oxford: Oxford University Press.

Graham, Laura R. 1995. *Performing Dreams: Discourses of Immortality among the Xavante of Central Brazil.* Austin: University of Texas Press.

Greene, Shane. 2004. *Paths to a Visionary Politics: Customizing History and Transforming Indigenous Authority in the Peruvian Selva.* Ann Arbor, Michigan: University Microfilms.

Guapindaia, Vera. 2001. "Encountering the Ancestors: The Maracá Urns." In McEwan, Barreto, and Neves, *Unknown Amazon,* 156–173.

Heckenberger, Michael J. 2001a. "Estrutura, história e transformação: A cultura xinguana na *longue durée,* 1000–2000 d.C." In Franchetto and Heckenberger, *Os povos do Alto Xingu,* 21–62.

———. 2001b. "Epidemias, índios bravos e brancos: Contato cultural e etnogênese no Alto Xingu." In Franchetto and Heckenberger, *Os povos do Alto Xingu,* 77–110.

———. 2005. *The Ecology of Power: Culture, Place, and Personhood in the Southern Amazon, A.D. 1000–2000.* New York: Routledge.

Heckenberger, Michael J., James B. Petersen, and Eduardo G. Neves. 1999. "Village Permanence in Amazonia: Two Archaeological Examples from Brazil." *Latin American Antiquity* 10(4):535–576.

Heckenberger, Michael J., Afukaka Kuikuro, U. Tabata Kuikuro, Morgan Schmidt, Christian Russel, Carlos Fausto, and Bruna Franchetto. 2003. "Amazonia 1492: Pristine Forest or Cultural Parkland?" *Science* 301(5640):1710–1714.

Hemming, John. 1987. *Amazon Frontier: The Defeat of the Brazilian Indians.* London: Macmillan.

Hendricks, Janet Wall. 1993. *To Drink of Death: The Narrative of a Shuar Warrior.* Tucson: University of Arizona Press.

Hill, Jonathan D., ed. 1988a. *Rethinking History and Myth: Indigenous South American Perspectives on the Past.* Urbana: University of Illinois Press.

———. 1988b. Introduction to *Rethinking History and Myth*, 1–17.

———. 1989. "Ritual Production of Environmental History among the Arawakan Wakuénai of Venezuela." *Human Ecology* 17(1):1–25.

———, ed. 1996. *History, Power, and Identity: Ethnogenesis in the Americas, 1492–1992.* Iowa City: University of Iowa Press.

———. 1999. "Nationalisme, chamanisme et histoires indigènes au Venezuela." *Ethnologie Française* 29(3):387–396.

Hill, Jonathan D., and Fernando Santos-Granero, eds. 2002. *Comparative Arawakan Histories: Rethinking Language Family and Culture Area in Amazonia.* Urbana: University of Illinois Press.

Hill, Jonathan D., and Robin M. Wright. 1988. "Time, Narrative, and Ritual: Historical Interpretations from an Amazonian Society." In Hill, *Rethinking History and Myth*, 78–105.

Howard, Catherine V. 1993. "Pawana: A farsa dos visitantes entre os Waiwai da Amazônia setentrional." In Castro and Cunha, *Amazônia*, 229–264.

———. 2000. "A domesticação das mercadorias: Estratégias waiwai." In Albert and Ramos, *Pacificando o branco*, 25–60.

Hugh-Jones, Stephen. 1992. "Yesterday's Luxuries, Tomorrow's Necessities: Business and Barter in Northwest Amazonia." In *Barter, Exchange, and Value: An Anthropological Approach*, edited by Caroline Humphrey and Stephen Hugh-Jones, 42–74. Cambridge: Cambridge University Press.

———. 1994. "Shamans, Prophets, Priests, and Pastors." In Thomas and Humphrey, *Shamanism, History, and the State*, 32–75.

———. 2001. "The Gender of Some Amazonian Gifts: An Experiment with an Experiment." In *Gender in Amazonia and Melanesia: An Exploration of the Comparative Method*, edited by Thomas A. Gregor and Donald Tuzin, 245–278. Berkeley and Los Angeles: University of California Press.

Ingold, Tim. 1994. "Humanity and Animality." In *Companion Encyclopedia of Anthropology*, edited by Tim Ingold, 14–32. London: Routledge.

Jackson, Jean E. 1994. "Becoming Indians: The Politics of Tukanoan Ethnicity." In Roosevelt, *Amazonian Indians*, 383–406.

———. 1995. "Culture, Genuine and Spurious: The Politics of Indianness in the Vaupés, Colombia." *American Ethnologist* 22:3–27.

Kohn, Eduardo O. 2002. "Infidels, Virgins, and the Black-Robed Priest: A Backwoods History of Ecuador's Montaña Region." *Ethnohistory* 49:545–582.

Kuper, Adam. 1988. *The Invention of Primitive Society: Transformations of an Illusion.* London: Routledge.

Lasmar, Cristiane. 2005. *De Volta ao Lago de Leite: gênero e Transformacão no Alto Rio Negro*. São Paulo: Isa/Unesp/Nuti.

Lathrap, Donald W. 1973. "The Antiquity and Importance of Long-Distance Trade Relationships in the Moist Tropics of Pre-Columbian South America." *World Archaeology* 5:170–186.

Lévi-Strauss, Claude. [1952] 1958. "La Notion d'archaïsme en ethnologie." In *Anthropologie structurale* 1:113–132. Paris: Plon.

———. [1960] 1976. "The Scope of Anthropology." In *Structural Anthropology: Volume II*, translated by Monique Layton, 3–32. New York: Basic Books. First published as *Chaire d'Anthropologie sociale: Leçon inaugurale* (Paris: Collège de France, 1960).

———. 1966. *The Savage Mind*. Chicago: University of Chicago Press.

———. [1977] 1984. "La Notion de maison (année 1976–1977)." In *Paroles données*, 189–193. Paris: Plon.

———. 1991. *Histoire de Lynx*. Paris: Plon.

Lefort, Claude. 1978. *Les Formes de l'histoire: Essais d'anthropologie politique*. Paris: Gallimard.

Lima, Antonio Carlos de Souza. 1995. *Um grande cerco de paz: Poder tutelar, indianidade e formação do Estado no Brasil*. Petrópolis: Vozes.

Lincoln, Bruce. 1999. *Theorizing Myth: Narrative, Ideology, and Scholarship*. Chicago: University of Chicago Press.

Maybury-Lewis, David, ed. 2002. *The Politics of Ethnicity: Indigenous Peoples in Latin American States*. Cambridge, Massachusetts: Harvard University Press.

McCallum, Cecilia. 2000. "Incas e Nawas: Produção, transformação e transcendência na história Kaxinawá." In Albert and Ramos, *Pacificando o branco*, 375–401.

———. 2001. *Gender and Sociality in Amazonia: How Real People Are Made*. Oxford: Berg.

McEwan, Colin, Cristiana Barreto, and Eduardo Góes Neves, eds. 2001. *Unknown Amazon: Culture in Nature in Ancient Brazil*. London: British Museum Press.

Melià, Bartomeu. 1986. *El Guarani—conquistado y reducido: Ensayos de etnohistoria*. Asunción: Centro de Estudios Antropológicos, Universidad Católica.

Menéndez, Miguel A. 1992. "A área Madeira-Tapajós: Situação de contato e relações entre colonizador e indígenas." In Cunha, *História dos índios no Brasil*, 281–296.

Menget, Patrick. 1999. "Entre memória e história." In *A outra margem do ocidente*, edited by Adauto Novaes, 153–165. São Paulo: Companhia das Letras.

Monteiro, John Manuel. 1992. "Os Guarani e a história do Brasil meridional: Séculos XVI–XVII." In Cunha, *História dos índios no Brasil*, 475–500.

———. 1999. "The Crises and Transformations of Invaded Societies: Coastal Brazil in the Sixteenth Century." In Salomon and Schwartz, *South America*, 1:973–1023.

———. Forthcoming. "Entre o etnocídio e a etnogênese: Identidades indígenas coloniais." In Fausto and Monteiro, *Tempos índios*.

Neves, Eduardo Góes, and James B. Petersen. 2006. "The Political Economy of Pre-Co-lumbian Amerindians: Landscape Transformations in Central Amazonia." In *Time and Complexity in Historical Ecology: Studies in the Neotropical Lowlands*, edited by William Balée and Clark Erickson, 279–309. New York: Columbia University Press.

Neves, Eduardo Góes, James B. Petersen, R. N. Bartone, and C. A. da Silva. 2003. "His-torical and Socio-cultural Origins of Amazonian Dark Earths." In *Amazonian Dark Earths: Origins, Properties, Management*, edited by Johannes Lehmann, Dirse C. Kern, Bruno Glaser, and William I. Woods, 29–50. Dordrecht, Netherlands: Kluwer.

Neves, Walter A. Forthcoming. "Origem do homem na América: Fósseis versus molécu-las." In *Novas questões sobre o povoamento das Américas: Visões interdisciplinares*, edited by Hilton P. Silva and Claudia Rodrigues-Carvalho. Rio de Janeiro: Viera and Lent.

Oakdale, Suzanne. 2001. "History and Forgetting in an Indigenous Amazonian Com-munity." *Ethnohistory* 48:381–401.

———. 2004. "The Culture-Conscious Brazilian Indian: Representing and Reworking Indianness in Kayabi Political Discourse." *American Ethnologist* 31(1):60–75.

———. 2005a. "Forgetting the Dead, Remembering Enemies." In *Interacting with the Dead: Perspectives on Mortuary Archaeology for the New Millenium*, edited by Gordon F. M. Rakita, Jane E. Buikstra, Lane A. Beck, and Sloan R. Williams, 107–141. Gaines-ville: University Press of Florida.

———. 2005b. *I Foresee My Life: The Ritual Performance of Autobiography in an Amazo-nian Community*. Lincoln: University of Nebraska Press.

Obeyesekere, Gananath. 1992. *The Apotheosis of Captain Cook: European Mythmaking in the Pacific*. Princeton, New Jersey: Princeton University Press.

———. 1998. "Cannibal Feasts in Nineteenth-Century Fiji: Seamen's Yarns and the Ethno-graphic Imagination." In *Cannibalism and the Colonial World*, edited by Francis Barker, Peter Hulme, Margaret Iversen, 63–86. Cambridge: Cambridge University Press.

Oliveira, Roberto Cardoso de. 1964. "Estudo de áreas de fricção interétnica do Brasil." *O índio e o mundo dos brancos*. São Paulo: Difel, 127–132.

———. 1972. "Problemas e hipóteses relativos à fricção interétnica." *A sociologia do Brasil indígena*. Rio de Janeiro: Tempo Brasileiro, 85–129.

Oliveira Filho, João Pacheco de, ed. 1998. *Indigenismo e territorialização: Poderes, rotinas e saberes coloniais no Brasil contemporâneo*. Rio de Janeiro: Contra Capa.

———, ed. 1999a. *A viagem da volta: Etnicidade, política e reelaboração cultural no Nor-deste indígena*. Rio de Janeiro: Contra Capa.

———. 1999b. "Romantismo, negociação política ou aplicação da antropologia: per-spectivas para as perícias sobre terras indígenas." In *Ensaios em Antropologia Histórica*, 164–190. Rio de Janeiro: EdUFRJ.

———. 2002. "O antropólogo como perito: Entre o indianismo e o indigenismo." In *Antropologia, impérios e estados nacionais*, edited by Benoit de L'Estoile, Federico Nei-burg, and Lygia Sigaud, 253–276. Rio de Janeiro: FAPERJ/Relume Dumará.

Ortner, Sherry B. 1984. "Theory in Anthropology Since the Sixties." *Comparative Studies in Society and History* 26:126–166.

———. 1996. "Making Gender: Toward a Feminist, Minority, Postcolonial, Subaltern, etc., Theory of Practice." In *Making Gender: The Politics and Erotics of Culture*, 1–19. Boston: Beacon Press.

Overing Kaplan, Joanna. 1977. "Orientation for Paper Topics" and "Comments." In *Social Time and Social Space in Lowland South American Societies*, edited by J. Overing Kaplan, 2:9–10, 387–394. Paris: Peeters.

Petersen, James B., Eduardo Góes Neves, and Michael J. Heckenberger. 2001. "Gift from the Past: *Terra Preta* and Prehistoric Amerindian Occupation in Amazonia." In McEwan, Barreto, and Neves, *Unknown Amazon*, 86–105.

Pompa, Maria Cristina. 2003. *Religião como tradução: Missionários, Tupi e Tapuia no Brasil meridional*. São Paulo: EDUSC/ANPOCS.

Porro, Antonio. 1994. "Social Organization and Political Power in the Amazon Floodplain: The Ethnohistorical Sources." In Roosevelt, *Amazonian Indians*, 79–94.

———. 1996. *O povo das águas: Ensaios de etno-história amazônica*. Petrópolis, Brazil: Vozes/EdUSP.

Ramos, Alcida Rita. 1998. *Indigenism: Ethnic Politics in Brazil*. Madison: University of Wisconsin Press.

Rappaport, Joanne. 1998. *The Politics of Memory: Native Historical Interpretation in the Colombian Andes*. Durham, North Carolina: Duke University Press.

Rapport, Nigel, and Joanna Overing. 2000. *Social and Cultural Anthropology: The Key Concepts*. London: Routledge.

Renard-Casevitz, France-Marie. 1992. "História kampa, memória ashaninca." In Cunha, *História dos índios no Brasil*, 197–212.

———. 1993. "Guerriers du sel, sauniers de la paix." *L'Homme* 33(126–128):25–44.

Renard-Casevitz, France-Marie, Thierry Saignes, and Anne-Christine Taylor. 1986. *L'Inca, l'Espagnol et les sauvages: Rapports entre les sociétés amazoniennes et andines du XVe au XVIIe siècle*. Paris: Éditions Recherches sur les Civilisations.

Rival, Laura M. 1996. *Hijos del sol, padres del jaguar: Los Huaorani de ayer y hoy*. Quito: Abya-Yala.

———. 1997. "Modernity and the Politics of Identity in an Amazonian Society." *Bulletin of Latin American Research* 12:137–151.

———. 2002. *Trekking through History: The Huaorani of Amazonian Ecuador*. New York: Columbia University Press.

Roosevelt, Anna Curtenius. 1980. *Parmana: Prehistoric Maize and Manioc Subsistence along the Amazon and Orinoco*. New York: Academic Press.

———. 1991. *Moundbuilders of the Amazon: Geophysical Archaeology on Marajo Island, Brazil*. San Diego, California: Academic Press.

———. 1993. "The Rise and Fall of the Amazon Chiefdoms." *L'Homme* 33 (2–4):255–283

———, ed. 1994. *Amazonian Indians from Prehistory to the Present: Anthropological Perspectives*. Tucson: University of Arizona Press.

Roosevelt, A. C., et al. 1996. "Paleoindian Cave Dwellers in the Amazon: The Peopling of the Americas." *Science*, April 19, 1996, 373–384.

Rosaldo, Renato. 1980. *Ilongot Headhunting, 1883–1974: A Study in Society and History*. Stanford, California: Stanford University Press.

Rostain, Stéphen. 1994. L'Occupation amérindienne ancienne du littoral de Guyane. Ph.D. thesis. Paris: Université de Paris I–Panthéon/Sorbonne.

Sahlins, Marshall. 1981. *Historical Metaphors and Mythical Realities: Strucuture in the Early History of the Sandwich Islands Kingdom*. Ann Arbor: University of Michigan Press.

———. 1985. *Islands of History*. Chicago: University of Chicago Press.

———. 1995. *How "Natives" Think: About Captain Cook, for Example*. Chicago: University of Chicago Press.

———. 1997. "O 'Pessimismo Sentimental' e a experiência etnográfica: Por que a cultura não é um 'objeto' em via de extinção." *Mana: Estudos de Antropologia Social* 3(1):41–74; 3(2):103–150.

———. 2000. *Culture in Practice: Selected Essays*. New York: Zone Books.

———. 2003. "Artificially Maintained Controversics: Global Warming and Fijian Cannibalism." *Anthropology Today* 19(3):3–4.

———. 2004. *Apologies to Thucydides: Understanding History as Culture and Vice Versa*. Chicago: University of Chicago Press.

Said, Edward W. 1978. *Orientalism*. New York: Pantheon.

Salomon, Frank. 1999. "Testimonies: The Making and Reading of Native South American Historical Sources." In Salomon and Schwartz, *South America*, 1:19–95.

Salomon, Frank, and Stuart B. Schwartz, eds. 1999. *South America*. Vol. 3 of *The Cambridge History of the Native Peoples of the Americas*. 2 pts. Cambridge: Cambridge University Press.

Santos-Granero, Fernando. 1991. *The Power of Love: The Moral Use of Knowledge amongst the Amuesha of Central Peru*. London: Athlone.

———. [1992?]a. *Etnohistoria de la Alta Amazonia: Siglo XV–XVIII*. Quito: Abya-Yala.

———, ed. 1992b. *Opresión colonial y resistencia indígena en la alta Amazonía*. Quito: Abya-Yala

———. 1992c. "Anticolonialismo, mesianismo y utopia en la sublevación de Juan Santos Atahuallpa, siglo XVIII." In *Opresión colonial y resistencia indígena*, 103–134.

———. 1993. "Templos e ferrarias: Utopia e reinvenção cultural no Oriente peruano." In Castro and Cunha, *Amazônia*, 67–93.

———. 1998. "Writing History into the Landscape: Space, Myth, and Ritual in Contemporary Amazonia." *American Ethnologist* 25(2):128–148.

———. 2002. "Saint Christopher in the Amazon: Child Sorcery, Colonialism, and Violence among the Southern Arawak." *Ethnohistory* 49(3):507–543.

Santos-Granero, Fernando, and Frederica Barclay. 1998. *Selva Central: History, Economy, and Land Use in Peruvian Amazonia.* Translated by Elisabeth King. Washington, D.C.: Smithsonian Institution Press.

———. 2000. *Tamed Frontiers: Economy, Society, and Civil Rights in Upper Amazonia.* Boulder, Colorado: Westview.

Schaan, Denise. 2001. "Into the Labyrinths of Marajoara Pottery: Status and Cultural Identity in an Amazonian Complex Society." In McEwan, Barreto, and Neves, *Unknown Amazon,* 108–133.

———. 2004. *The Camutins Chiefdom: Rise and Development of Social Complexity on Marajó Island, Brazilian Amazon.* Ann Arbor, Michigan: University Microfilms.

Schneewind, J. B. 1998. *The Invention of Autonomy: A History of Modern Moral Philosophy.* Cambridge: Cambridge University Press.

Schwartz, Stuart B., and Frank Salomon. 1999. "New Peoples and New Kinds of People: Adaptation, Readjustment, and Ethnogenesis in South American Indigenous Societies (Colonial Era)." In Salomon and Schwartz, *South America,* 2:443–501.

———. 2003. "'Un Américain (imaginaire) à Paris': Réponse à Carmen Bernand." *Annales,* Mars–Avril, 499–512.

Severi, Carlo. 1993. *La memoria rituale: Follia e immagine del bianco in una tradizione sciamanica amerindiana.* Firenze: Nuova Italia.

———. 2004. *Il Percorso e la voce: Un'antropologia della memoria.* Turin: Einaudi.

Steward, Julian H., ed. 1946–50. *Handbook of South American Indians.* 7 vols. Washington, D.C.: Smithsonian Institution, Bureau of American Ethnology.

Steward, Julian H., and Louis C. Faron. 1959. *Native Peoples of South America.* New York: McGraw-Hill.

Strathern, Marilyn. 1981. "Self-Interest and the Social Good: Some Implications of Hagen Gender Imagery." In *Sexual Meanings: The Cultural Construction of Gender and Sexuality,* edited by Sherry B. Ortner and Harriet Whitehead, 166–191. New York: Cambridge University Press.

———. 1988. *The Gender of the Gift: Problems with Women and Problems with Society in Melanesia.* Berkeley and Los Angeles: University of California Press.

———. 1999. *Property, Substance, and Effect: Anthropological Essays on Persons and Things.* London: Athlone.

———. 2004. "Losing (Out on) Intellectual Resources." In *Law, Anthropology, and the Constitution of the Social,* edited by Alain Pottage and Martha Mundy, 201–233. Cambridge: Cambridge University Press.

Sweet, David Graham. 1974. *A Rich Realm of Nature Destroyed: The Middle Amazon Valley, 1640–1750.* Ann Arbor, Michigan: University Microfilms.

Tassinari, Antonella M. I. 2002. *No bom da festa: O processo de construção cultural das famílias Karipuna do Amapá*. São Paulo: EdUSP.

Taussig, Michael. 1986. *Shamanism, Colonialism, and the Wild Man: A Study in Terror and Healing*. Chicago: University of Chicago Press.

———. 1993. *Mimesis and Alterity: A Particular History of the Senses*. New York: Routledge.

Taylor, Anne-Christine. 1985. "L'Art de la réduction: La Guerre et les mécanismes de la différenciation tribale dans la culture Jivaro." *Journal de la Societé des Américanistes* 71:159–173.

———. 1992. "História pós-colombiana da alta Amazônia." In Cunha, *História dos índios no Brasil*, 213–238.

———. 1993. "Remembering to Forget: Identity, Mourning and Memory among the Jivaro." *Man* 28:653–678.

———. 1999. "The Western Margins of Amazonia from the Early Sixteenth to the Early Nineteenth Century." In Salomon and Schwartz, *South America*, 2:188–256.

———. 2000. "Le Sexe de la proie: Représentations jivaro du lien de parenté." *L'Homme*, nos. 154–155:309–334.

Taylor, Charles. 1989. *Sources of the Self: The Making of the Modern Identity*. Cambridge, Massachusetts: Harvard University Press.

Thomas, Nicholas. 1991. *Entangled Objects: Exchange, Material Culture, and Colonialism in the Pacific*. Cambridge, Massachusetts: Harvard University Press.

Thomas, Nicholas, and Caroline Humphrey, eds. 1994. *Shamanism, History, and the State*. Ann Arbor: University of Michigan Press.

Toren, Christina. 1999. "Making the Present, Revealing the Past: The Mutability and Continuity of Tradition as Process" In *Mind, Materiality and History: Explorations in Fijian Ethnography*, 45–66. London: Routledge.

Trouillot, Michel-Rolph. 1991. "Anthropology and the Savage Slot: The Poetics and Politics of Otherness." In *Recapturing Anthropology: Working in the Present*, edited by Richard G. Fox, 17–44. Santa Fe, New Mexico: School of American Research Press.

Tully, James. 1993. *An Approach to Political Philosophy: Locke in Contexts*. Cambridge: Cambridge University Press.

Turner, Terence. 1988. "Ethno-Ethnohistory: Myth and History in Native South American Representations of Contact with Western Society." In Hill, *Rethinking History and Myth*, 235–281.

———. 1991. "Representing, Resisting, Rethinking: Historical Transformations of Kayapo Culture and Anthropological Consciousness." In *Colonial Situations: Essays on the Contextualization of Ethnographic Knowledge*, edited by George W. Stocking Jr., 285–313. Madison: University of Wisconsin Press.

————. 1993. "Da cosmologia à história: Resistência, adaptação e consciência social entre os Kayapó." In Castro and Cunha, *Amazônia*, 43–66.

————. 1995. "An Indigenous Amazonian People's Struggle for Socially Equitable and Ecologically Sustainable Production: The Kayapo Revolt Against Extractivism." *Journal of Latin American Anthropology* 1:98–121.

Vainfas, Ronaldo. 1995. *A heresia dos índios: Catolicismo e rebeldia no Brasil colonial*. São Paulo: Companhia das Letras.

Veber, Hanna. 1998. "The Salt of the Montaña: Interpreting Indigenous Activism in the Rain Forest." *Cultural Anthropology* 13:382–413.

————. 2003. "Asháninka Messianism: The Production of a 'Black Hole' in Western Amazonian Ethnography." *Current Anthropology* 44(2):183–211.

Verswijver, Gustaaf. 1992. *The Club-Fighters of the Amazon: Warfare among the Kayapo Indians of Central Brazil*. Ghent, Belgium: Rijksuniversiteit te Gent.

Vidal, Silvia M. 2000. "Kuwé Duwákalumi: The Arawak Sacred Routes of Migration, Trade, and Resistance." *Ethnohistory* 47:635–667.

————. 2003. "The Arawak-Speaking Groups of Northwestern Amazonia: Amerindian Cartography as a Way of Preserving and Interpreting the Past." In *Histories and Historicities in Amazonia*, edited by Neil L. Whitehead, 33–58. Lincoln: University of Nebraska Press.

Viegas, Susana M. Forthcoming. "Compatibilidades equívocas: A permuta de terra entre brancos e índios Tupi na costa sul da Bahia." In Fausto and Monteiro, *Tempos índios*.

Vilaça, Aparecida. 2002. "Making Kin out of Others." *Journal of the Royal Anthropological Institute* 8(2):347–365.

————. 2006. *Quem somos nós: Os Wari' encontram os brancos*. Rio de Janeiro: EdUFRJ.

Viveiros de Castro, Eduardo. *See* Castro, Eduardo Viveiros de.

Wagner, Roy. 1967. *The Curse of Souw: Principles of Daribi Clan Definition and Alliance in New Guinea*. Chicago: University of Chicago Press.

————. 1981. *The Invention of Culture*. 2nd ed. Chicago: University of Chicago Press.

————. 1991. "The Fractal Person." In *Big Men and Great Men: Personifications of Power in Melanesia*, edited by Maurice Godelier and Marilyn Strathern, 159–173. Cambridge: Cambridge University Press.

Warren, Kay B., and Jean E. Jackson. 2002. *Indigenous Movements, Self-Representation, and the State in Latin America*. Austin: University of Texas Press.

Weber, Ingrid. 2004. "Escola Kaxi: História, cultura e aprendizado escolar entre os Kaxinawá do rio Humaitá." Master's thesis, PPGAS/Museu Nacional, Universidade Federal do Rio de Janeiro.

Weinstein, Barbara. 1983. *The Amazon Rubber Boom, 1850–1920*. Stanford, California: Stanford University Press.

Wisnik, José Miguel. 1990. *O som e o sentido: Uma outra história da música*. São Paulo: Companhia das Letras.

Whitehead, Neil L. 1988. *Lords of the Tiger Spirit: A History of the Caribs in Colonial Venezuela and Guyana, 1498–1820*. Dordrecht, Netherlands: Foris.

———. 1990. "The Snake Warriors—Sons of the Tiger's Teeth: A Descriptive Analysis of Carib Warfare, ca. 1500–1820." In *The Anthropology of War*, edited by Jonathan Haas, 146–170. Cambridge: Cambridge University Press.

———. 1993a. "Ethnic Transformation and Historical Discontinuity in Native Amazonia and Guayana, 1500–1900." *L'Homme* 33(126–28):285–305.

———. 1993b. "Recent Researches on the Native History of Amazonia and Guayana." *L'Homme* 33(126–28):495–506.

———. 1998. "Indigenous Cartography in Lowland South America and the Caribbean." In *The History of Cartography*, vol. 2, bk. 3, *Cartography in the Traditional African, American, Arctic, Australian, and Pacific Societies*, edited by David Woodward and G. Malcolm Lewis, 301–326. Chicago: University of Chicago Press.

———. 1999a. "The Crises and Transformations of Invaded Societies: The Caribbean (1492–1580)." In Salomon and Schwartz, *South America*, 1:864–903.

———. 1999b. "Native Peoples Confront Colonial Regimes in Northeastern South America (c. 1500–1900)." In Salomon and Schwartz, *South America*, 2:382–442.

———, ed. 2003. *Histories and Historicities in Amazonia*. Lincoln: University of Nebraska Press.

Wilde, Guillermo. 2003. "Antropología historica del liderazgo guarani misionero (1750–1850)." Ph.D. diss., Universidad de Buenos Aires.

Wright, Robin M. 1991. "Indian Slavery in the Northwest Amazon." *Boletim do Museu Paraense Emílio Goeldi* 7:149–179.

———. 1992. "História indígena do noroeste da Amazônia." In Cunha, *História dos índios no Brasil*, 253–266.

———. 1998. *Cosmos, Self, and History in Baniwa Religion: For Those Unborn*. Austin: University of Texas Press.

———, ed. 1999. *Transformando os deuses*. Vol. 1, *Os múltiplos sentidos da conversão entre os povos indígenas no Brasil*. Campinas: FAPESP/Unicamp.

———, ed. 2004. *Transformando os deuses*. Vol. 2, *Igrejas evangélicas, pentecostais e neopentecostais entre os povos indígenas no Brasil*. Campinas: FAPESP/Unicamp.

———. 2005. *História indígena e do indigenismo no alto rio Negro*. Campinas: Mercado das Letras.

I

Appropriating Transformations

Time Is Disease, Suffering, and Oblivion

Yanesha Historicity and the Struggle against Temporality

Fernando Santos-Granero

> "What do you [remember] about this business?" the King said to Alice.
> "Nothing," said Alice.
> "Nothing *whatever*?" persisted the King.
> "Nothing whatever," said Alice.
> "That's very important," the King said, turning to the jury.
>
> —after Lewis Carroll, *Alice's Adventures in Wonderland*

Following Comaroff and Comaroff's invitation "to disinter the endogenous historicity of local worlds" (1992:27), this essay aims at understanding ways of making and unmaking history that differ from our own. It addresses the issue of how the Yanesha people of eastern Peru, as well as other Amazonian indigenous peoples upholding "millenarian ideologies," conceive of time, space, the past, and the future.[1] According to Yanesha thinkers, time is not homogeneous. The present era is a time-riddled period in between a timeless past and an equally timeless future. It began with the loss of immortality and the introduction of differences, two events that inaugurated time and history. It is, thus, an era in which the Yanesha began to experience the miseries of the human condition: suffering, pain, death, and oblivion. But it is also an era ruled by alterity, hierarchy, and inequality.

The Yanesha, I argue, are engaged in a struggle to put an end to the afflictions of time and the agonies of history. In this essay I analyze the means through which they fight time and history. Two aspects are of particular interest to me. First, how do the Yanesha construct their past? What do they remember and, above all, what do they choose to forget? Second, how do they imagine their future and, more particularly, what role do they attribute to their own agency in achieving their imagined future? In brief, this essay is concerned as much with Yanesha historical consciousness (see Hill 1988), or historical vision (see Rappaport 1998), as with their historical imagination (see Comaroff and Comaroff 1992).

The Heterogeneous Nature of Time

Unlike other Amazonian peoples, the Yanesha, an Arawak-speaking people living in the Andean piedmont (see map, figure 1.1), have a highly structured notion of time, conceived of as a linear sequence of events organized in fixed eras. This is expressed in their myths, which generally begin with the expression *ahuat,* "in the past" or "in ancient times," followed by a phrase indicating with more precision the point in time to which it refers, such as "when Yompor Rreŧ, the malign solar divinity, still illuminated this earth" or "before women began to give birth to human beings" or "after Yompor Ror, the present solar divinity, ascended to heaven."

In addition, mythical events are grouped in three distinct eras. The first is the era of primordial creation, when Yato' Yos, Our Grandfather Yos, created the world and all the good beings that inhabit it, and his envious classificatory brother Yosoper perversely mimicked his creation by giving birth to all evil beings.[2] This era ended with the creation of Yompor Rreŧ, the first solar divinity. His ascension to heaven marked the advent of the second era. This was initially a period of fear in which the malignant Rreŧ enjoyed harassing people by throwing stones at them. It was also a time of social and biological chaos in which people were immersed in a Hobbesian "state of Warre" and women gave birth to objects and nonhuman beings. Harmonious sociality was achieved after a woman stole the knowledge of *coshaṁñats* sacred music and the preparation of manioc beer from the land of the murdered ones. Biological order was obtained after the birth of the twins Yompor Ror, Our Father the Sun, and Yachor Arrorr, Our Mother the Moon. These two events inaugurated a brief period of absolute harmony—the Yanesha golden age—in which divinities, humans, animals, plants, and things, all of them immortal and in human guise, shared this earth in peace.

The ascension to heaven of the Sun and the Moon, and the defeat of the previous Sun and his banishment to the sky of a higher earth, put an end to this paradisiacal period, giving rise to the third, present era.[3] This event was preceded by what can be called a second creation. On his way to the hill from which he was going to ascend to heaven, Yompor Ror changed the landscape and the beings he met with his divine transformational powers. After he ascended to Yomporesho, the celestial realm, this earth and its inhabitants acquired their present form. Animals, plants, and things lost their human shape, and the divinities abandoned

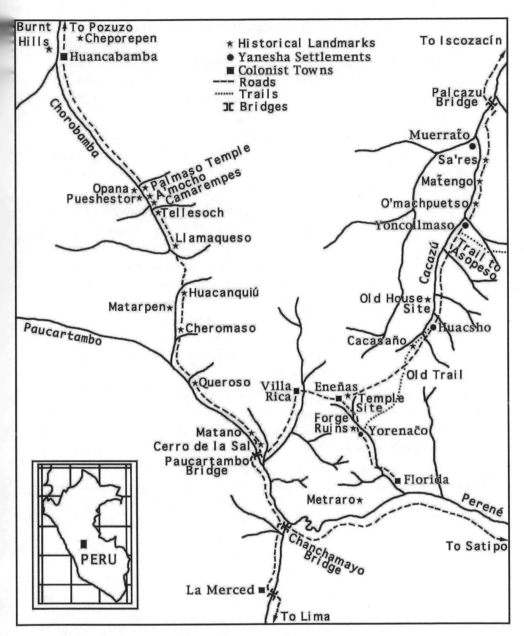

Fig. 1.1. Yanesha territory and important landmarks.

this earth or hid in lakes and mountains, no longer sharing their lives with their human creatures. Worst of all, out of ignorance, laziness, and indifference, humans lost the opportunity of following the divinities and becoming immortal. As a result, they were left behind to experience illness, hard work, suffering, and death. It was thus that Yanesha people became *a'rromñaternesha'*, "mortal beings," and that this earth became *rromue patsro*, "the earth where people die."

It was thus, also, that the Yanesha began to experience the effects of "real" time. Yanesha thinkers and myth tellers conceive of time as a linear sequence of events, but not as a homogeneous continuum. The first two eras, corresponding to the times of creation and re-creation of the cosmos, are thought of as a closed cycle. They are eternal and, therefore, timeless times that are hermetically sealed and closed to the present-day Yanesha (see Wright 1998:104, for a similar view among the Baniwa). Yanesha people conflate these two eras under the expression *ahuaï mella*, or "ancient sacred times." The period when humans and divinities lived together is seen as a *mellapo*, "a timeless period when the earth and its inhabitants were in a sacred state" (Smith 1977:107). Death was unknown in ancient sacred times. Ancient sacred peoples (*mella acheñ*) could fight, could be defeated, transformed, locked up, or deprived of their mystical powers, but they could not be killed and they never died. They continue to live, and will always live, on other earths, in other skies, or hidden in this mortal earth.

In contrast, the present era is a time-riddled era, a period in which the Yanesha are subjected to the afflictions of time: illness, suffering, death, and oblivion. However, according to Yanesha millenarian beliefs, as there was a beginning of time, there will be an end of time. This will happen when, out of compassion for the suffering of their mortal creatures, the divinities send a savior, which will mark the beginning of a second *mellapo*, or sacred timeless period.[4] This divine emissary will make people immortal (*mellañochterr*) and take them to the abode of the higher divinities. The end of time will not be a peaceful event. It will be a cataclysmic occurrence marked by earthquakes, floods, and conflagrations, a veritable end of the world as we know it in which only a few will be saved. This will inaugurate the fourth and last era of human existence, an era of happiness and harmony devoid of the hardships of work, disease, and death, but also characterized by the full satisfaction of the life of the senses, including plenty of food, drink, songs, dances, and sex. Conversion to Adventism (since the 1920s) or Evangelism (since the 1940s) has not eradicated these messianic expectations, but has rather accentuated them.

In brief, the Yanesha conceive of the present, time-riddled era as an interlude between a timeless past and a timeless future. From their viewpoint, time is not homogeneous—a characteristic that Turner (1988:248) has already pointed out as central to Amerindian conceptions of temporality. In Yanesha thought, the present era is the age of time and history. It began with the loss of immortality and will end only with the restoration of immortality. It is, thus, inextricably associated with the miseries of the human condition but also, as we shall see, with the nefarious consequences of alterity. Yanesha people are engaged in a battle against the ravages of temporality, and they fight to transcend the human condition. Their fight against time and history assumes two forms: the struggle against oblivion and the quest for divine salvation. These, however, are not different phenomena but two sides of the same coin. There is no remembrance of the past that is not linked in one way or another to the hope for immortality, and there can be no salvation without remembrance of the past. Yanesha historical awareness is nurtured by these two drives.

Memory of Significant Others

Among the Yanesha, what Danièle Dehouve (1993) calls the struggle against oblivion ("la lutte contre l'oubli") has little to do with the West's obsession with not forgetting. Based on the oft-quoted dictum of Santayana that those who cannot remember their past are condemned to repeat it, Western societies have embarked on a crusade to remember that involves not only the ruling classes but also all kinds of social segments and interest groups. This is manifested in the proliferation of museums, libraries, and archives of all types that have benefited from the development of new electronic means of storing vast amounts of information. The urge to remember is associated with the atrocities committed during the twentieth century in the name of political ideologies of diverse types. Simon Wiesenthal's 1989 appeal not to forget the Shoah, the Nazi massacre of the Jews, and to "build a defense against repetition" through remembrance, finds echo in Carolyn Forché's 1993 anthology of "poetry of witness," entitled precisely *Against Forgetting*. In it she asks us to fight the "diseased complacency" of oblivion and protest against violence, for "The resistance to terror is what makes the world habitable" (32, 46).

I suggest that the Yanesha's struggle against oblivion is more about remembering the past to remind us of who we are than to remind us of the barbarous and unacceptable. In other words, it is more about ethnic awareness and identity than about political conscience and mobilization. Hill (1988:10) has already underscored the fact that "social otherness" is a central concern in indigenous representations of the past. Whitten (1988:301–302) has further argued that these representations often deal with social relationships with "significant others," who are classified in terms of relative cultural similarity and political power. Amerindian historical consciousness would be mostly about alterity and power. This certainly holds true for the Yanesha, among whom this concern is manifested in a series of myths that are set in the present era and that refer to three significant others: the cannibalistic Pano people, the authoritarian Incas, and the rapacious white men (Santos-Granero 1988b:43).

As I have argued elsewhere, Yanesha memory of the past is kept alive not only through myths (*serrparñats*) and songs (*morreñets*) but also through such means as topographic writing, ritual performances, and bodily practices (Santos-Granero 1998). Analysis of the discursive and nondiscursive means by which Yanesha people have kept the memory of these significant others, and a comparison with what we know of their relationships with them from historical documents, can reveal, I suggest, what the Yanesha consider important to remember. It can also reveal the ways in which Yanesha historical imagination proceeds in the construction and reconstruction of the past, for as Aurore Becquelin has argued, forgetting is "the motor of historical creativity" (1993:34).

Memory of the Pano-speaking peoples is preserved in the myth of the Muellepen, a cannibalistic people that each year came upriver along the Palcazu River to attack and eat the Yanesha of the Cacazú valley.[5] Yato' Caresa, also known as Yato' Po'sholl, was a powerful *mellañoteñ* spirit in charge of defending the Yanesha. To prevent Muellepen attacks, he used to post guards upstream from the confluence of the Cacazú and Yoncollmaso rivers, which was the limit of Yanesha territory. He painted his Yanesha warriors with a magical ointment that made them invulnerable, allowing them to kill their enemies. Once, however, while pursuing the Muellepen at night, Yato' Caresa did not have time to paint his warriors, and all of them were killed. Alone, and fearing that if he escaped he would not be able to resurrect his warriors, Caresa surrendered his mystical powers, allowing the Muellepen to kill him and cut his head off. Holding his head in his hands, he returned to the Cacazú valley, where he mystically hid with his followers in a lake known as Cacasaño.

Some of the elements of this narrative are corroborated by archaeological and documentary evidence. There is evidence that the ancestors of Pano-speaking peoples displaced the proto-Yanesha from the Ucayali River, pushing them upriver along the Pachitea and Palcazu rivers to their final location along the Andean piedmont (Lathrap 1970:135). There is also plenty of historical evidence that in colonial times the Pano continued to wage war against Yanesha and other Arawak-speaking peoples. Such was the case of the Pano-speaking Conibo, who lived at the confluence of the Pachitea and Ucayali rivers, and Cashibo, who inhabited the interior lands of the left bank of the Pachitea River. These peoples practiced funerary endocannibalism, which in some cases involved eating the body of deceased kin (Maroni [1738] 1988:180), and in others the cremation of the deceased and the ingestion of his or her ashes mixed with fermented beer (Huerta [1686] 1983:121).

Colonial sources state that the Conibo chopped off the heads of their enemies and ripped their hearts out to display them in their homes as a sign of their courage (Rodríguez Tena [1774] 1977:60). It is also said that they drank their enemies' blood mixed with fermented beer. None of these sources, however, asserts that the Pano ate war prisoners. Hostilities between the Yanesha and their Pano neighbors were so intense that well into the nineteenth century the Palcazu River continued to be a poorly inhabited area, a no-man's-land that acted as a buffer zone (see, for instance, Ordinaire 1892).

Interestingly enough, the myth about the Muellepen omits what was the most important feature of Panoan raids against Yanesha and other Arawak-speaking peoples: the capture and removal of women and children to be taken as wives, adopted, or kept as slaves (Amich 1975:298). Neither this nor other Yanesha myths referring to confrontations with ancient cannibalistic peoples make any reference to the abduction of women and children. Instead they stress the military, male aspects of the relationship, extolling the bravery and battle feats of Caresa and his warriors. In fact, an associated myth narrates how the Yanesha organized a war party to punish the Muellepen for the death of Caresa. They attacked them on the Sungaroyacu, a tributary of the Pachitea River where the present-day Cashibo live, and killed everybody except for a chief and two children, a girl and a boy. This, the myth teller asserted, explains why today there are so few Cashibo left. The myth also omits the importance that Panoan polychrome pottery had in the trading networks centering on the salt mines of the Cerro de la Sal. Although this kind of pottery reached the Yanesha through the mediation of the Asháninka along the Ucayali-Tambo-Perené fluvial axis, they must have known that it was manufactured by the same people who raided them along the Ucayali-Pachitea-Palcazu fluvial axis.

Selective memory, or rather selective forgetting, also plays an important role in the myth of Enc, a semidivine figure that represents the Inca people (Santos-Granero 1991:73–74, 247–249).[6] Enc was born of a Yanesha virgin impregnated by an envoy of Yato' Yos, the creator god, who wanted to provide his mortal creatures with a loving and compassionate leader. When Enc became a man, he decided to find his divine father. To stop Enc from ascending to heaven, Yato' Yos sent his daughter Yachor Palla to marry him. Enc was a tyrant. He demanded from the Yanesha's priestly leaders a constant supply of feather tunics. If they failed to bring them, or if the feather tunics were not well woven, he beheaded the leaders and replaced them with their eldest sons. Enc gave Yanesha men stone axes and forced them to clear gardens for him. He did not feed his workers, but if one of them was found stealing food from his gardens, Enc ordered his decapitation. He paid his workers in gold and silver, which they rejected, as they had no use for it. Finally, he obliged his followers to impose a fidelity test on their wives. Those who were found guilty of adultery were also beheaded. According to the myth, the creator god grew tired of Enc's crimes and punished him by depriving him of his mystical powers.

It is impossible to know the exact character of the relationship between the Yanesha people and the Inca Empire.[7] However, archaeological and early colonial documentary evidence corroborates many elements of this narrative, suggesting that the ancient Yanesha experienced some form of Inca domination. We know, for instance, that to reinforce their domination, Inca rulers used to take as secondary wives high-ranking women from the peoples they conquered. Like Enc's mythical Yanesha wife, these concubines had the title of *palla*. We also know that the Incas obtained prized tropical forest products through a diversity of means, including colonization of the lowlands, subjection of Amazonian peoples, and establishment of trading relationships (Saignes 1985). Chief among these products were coca leaves, hardwoods, and feathers; of the three, feathers seem to have been the most important. For instance, we are told that the Chupaychu, Andean neighbors of the Yanesha, had to provide the Inca annually with 120 persons to gather feathers as tribute, whereas they provided only 60 for the cultivation of coca leaves (Ortiz de Zúñiga [1562] 1967:306). The most skillful Chupaychu feather specialists were sent to Cuzco, where they were exclusively devoted to making feather tunics and feather-ornamented weapons.

The Yanesha remember mostly the authoritarian, coercive aspects of their relationship with the Inca Empire—a relationship marked, according to myth, by despotism, economic exploitation, sexual policing, and an outrageous curtailment of personal autonomy. Omitted are a series of elements that we know made a great impression on the imagination of other Amazonian peoples that had close contact with the Incas. There is no mention in the myth of Enc, or in other related oral narratives, of such normally awe-inspiring Inca technologies as stonework, architecture, hydraulics, and metallurgy. And there are no references to objects obtained from the Incas in exchange for Yanesha labor or Yanesha products, except for a contemptuous reference to Inca gold and silver. No mention is made of copper and bronze axes, which are so prominent in the mythologies of other Amazonian peoples (Renard-Casevitz et al. 1986), and which we know were important objects in the long-distance trading networks linking the Andes with the Amazonian lowlands (Lathrap 1973; Myers 1981). At most, the Incas are credited with giving the Yanesha stone axes. In brief, there is no memory of the numerous exchanges made with Andean peoples, exchanges that we know persisted long after the Spanish conquest (Tibesar 1950). The only thing that Yanesha people "remember" is a "nonexchange" or "antiexchange," namely, receiving useless stuff (gold and silver) for valuable work.

References to the white men (*ocanesha*) appear in various myths.[8] The Yanesha attribute their origin to Enc's folly. On his way to heaven to retrieve his wife, who had abandoned him, Enc opened the magical gates that kept the white men locked in. He was in such a rush that he did not bother to close them. He told his four sons to lock the gates, but they did not obey him. The white men came out in great numbers. They killed Enc's sons Enca Capa and Huascar and took all his silver.[9] It was thus that the Yanesha people were forced to share their lands with the white men.

However, if it is true that the appearance of the white men was linked to Enc's fallibility, their success was, according to myth, the direct consequence of the fallibility and lack of devotion of the Yanesha themselves. It is said that Yompor Yompuer, one of the brothers of the present-day solar divinity, whose body was half stone, told the Yanesha to take care of him because otherwise the white men would take him with them. When the white men came to see Yompuer singing and dancing, the Yanesha panicked and abandoned the divinity, who could not walk. The white men took Yompuer to their land, where they still venerate him. For this reason, Yanesha myth tellers claim, the white men multiply while the Yanesha grow fewer each day.

In another myth it is said that when Yompor A'penerr, Our Father Milky Way, was about to ascend to the heavens, he asked the Yanesha people to follow him. As they would not, he asked them to allow at least one of their children to follow him, so that he could become as powerful as the divinities and could one day come back to this earth to make the Yanesha immortal. But the Yanesha did not allow even this. In contrast, some white men followed Yompor A'penerr. They are now visible as bright stars in the summer night sky. This explains, according to myth tellers, why nowadays the white men have extraordinary creative powers and can invent marvelous things, such as cars and other machines, whereas the Yanesha have no money and are as poor as orphans.

The Yanesha contend that, thanks to the powers acquired from their divinities, the white men multiplied so much that they soon occupied most of the Yanesha territory. By then most Yanesha had become like the whites, losing their native language, their sacred songs, and their traditional dress. Worse still, they no longer worshipped the old divinities. Worried that his mortal creatures would disappear, the creator god sent his son Yompor Santo to make them immortal (Santos-Granero 1991:80–83). However, in his eagerness to help the Yanesha people, Yompor

Santo came to this earth before finishing his period of acquisition of divine powers. When he arrived on this earth, he revealed himself to the only pious Yanesha man that was left. After the devoted man recognized Yompor Santo as a divine emissary, the Yanesha people started multiplying rapidly. Yompor Santo gathered all the Yanesha in Metraro, where he taught them how to live a correct and moral life. Yanesha built a large house for Yompor Santo and provided him with beautiful cotton tunics, feather crowns, and other ornaments. Unfortunately, Shellmeñ, Yompor Santo's classificatory brother and the first Yanesha sorcerer, betrayed his confidence. He ordered the decapitation of many of his followers and eventually killed Yompor Santo himself. As Yompor Santo lacked full divine powers, he failed to make the Yanesha immortal. Moreover, after dying he was not able to return to life as promised. Eventually the white men took his bones to the Andean town of Tarma; with them they made an image of him that they still worship.

Yanesha representations of white men in these and other oral narratives and songs are full of references to historical "events," but they also contain some significant omissions. The Yanesha version of the origin of the white men retains the fact that their arrival coincided with the demise of the Inca Empire. Attributing the origin of the white men to the fallibility of the Inca adds to the negative views that Yanesha people have about this personage. We find a similar anchorage in historical events in the myth of Yompor Santo, which is inspired by the historical figure of Juan Santos Atahuallpa, a highland Indian who in 1742 led the Yanesha and their neighbors in a successful revolt against the Spanish (Varese 1973; Castro Arenas 1973; Zarzar 1989; Santos-Granero 1992b; Torre López 2004). Juan Santos claimed that he descended from the Inca, the Sun, and the Holy Spirit, and that he had been sent to eliminate Spanish oppression, recover his kingdom, and guide his people (San Antonio 1750).

He established his headquarters in Metraro, which became a sort of "Land without Evil" or "new Jerusalem" for his large following, consisting mostly of Arawak-speaking peoples—the Yanesha, Asháninka, Ashéninka, Piro, and Nomatsiguenga. In Metraro Juan Santos led an ascetic and spiritual life, surrounded by his personal guard and an elaborate protocol (San Antonio 1750). The rebel dressed like an Amazonian Indian. His followers constantly supplied him with fine cotton tunics and other ornaments. Juan Santos died sometime in the 1760s. His tomb became an object of annual pilgrimages linked to the hope of his resurrection until 1891, when his remains were removed from the tomb and taken to Tarma by order of the local governor, presumably to suppress his memory and crush indigenous resistance (Castro Arenas 1973:148–149).

Together with these historical references, however, there are some important historical omissions that raise interesting questions about Yanesha historical awareness. According to myth, Yompor Santo appeared in a time when the white men had occupied Yanesha territory, and most Yanesha had become like them. This is partly validated by historical documentation. By the time Juan Santos initiated his revolt, the Spanish had been in the region for thirty-three years, founding numerous mission posts, a few military garrisons, and some big ranches, and reducing thousands of Arawak-speaking Indians to Christian life. But the myth makes no reference either to the Franciscan missionaries, who were the main colonial agents in the region, or to mission life, which we know Yanesha people disliked intensely. Likewise the myth does not allude to the economic exploitation to which the Yanesha and their neighbors were subjected by missionaries, colonial authorities, and large landowners, and which constituted an important element in Juan Santos's anticolonial discourse (Santos-Granero 1992b). Even more puzzling is the fact that there is no mention of the fatal epidemics that decimated the Yanesha during this period and that generated much unrest and many rebellions (Santos-Granero 1987). But most striking of all is the omission of the revolt itself.

There is no mention whatsoever in the myth of Yompor Santo of a military confrontation with the whites. This is all the more surprising given that Juan Santos's was one of the largest and most successful Amazonian insurrections against Spanish colonial rule. So much so, it kept Spaniards and Peruvians away from the region for more than a century. Rather than historical "facts," what Yanesha people remember, I argue, are the emotions, feelings, and moods resulting from their relationship with significant others. It is a "history of the senses" (Taussig 1993), rather than a history of events. These sentiments are linked with particular characterizations of others, which, as is generally the case, are sketchy and stereotyped.

Thus, in Yanesha imagination, Pano peoples are bloodthirsty, deceitful cannibals for whom Yanesha can feel only abhorrence and spite. They are the quintessential savages, the inferior "others like us," who deserve only extermination—a feat that, in myth at least, the Yanesha almost achieved. Inca rulers, personified in the semidivine figure of Enc, are mean, cruel, but powerful "others like us." They have no respect for personal autonomy and do not comply with the most basic norm of civilized life, that of reciprocal exchange. They represent the antithesis of legitimate authority, which in Yanesha political philosophy is always about love, compassion, generosity, and service—in other words, about giving life rather than taking it (Santos-Granero 1991). Finally, the white men are the "real others." They are an accident of history, the unforeseen result of the folly of a mean and irresponsible semidivinity. White men are opportunistic and powerful people who have consistently taken advantage of the Yanesha's fallibility and lack of devotion to deprive them of the divine powers that should have been theirs. But their main defect derives from their main virtue. According to Yanesha thinkers, the white men are more devoted and pious than the Yanesha; this allowed them to acquire the powers of fertility and creativity of Yanesha divinities. This is why Yanesha feelings toward the white men are so ambivalent.

Although Yanesha historical memory is selective, favoring remembrance of emotions rather than of events, it does not operate at random. The analysis of what is remembered and what is forgotten in myths and in other, less structured oral narratives and songs shows that, while the Yanesha remember what makes the others other, they seem to omit any suggestion that the others are superior. In other words, they underscore cultural differences but obliterate power differences that place them in a subordinate position. This they do by denying any intrinsic superiority to others and attributing the others' temporary positions of power to forces from within their own culture. Thus, from a Yanesha point of view, the Incas are powerful not because of their technology, administrative acumen, and military might but because they are semidivine children of the creator god. In turn, the white men are powerful because they obtained Yompor A'penerr's fertility powers by following him to heaven; they captured and took with them Yompor Yompuer and his powers of creation; and they stole the remains of the divine emissary Yompor Santo. As we shall see below, negation of the power of others is also found in processes of mimetic appropriation.

Mimesis or the Art of Forgetting

Michael Taussig argues that through the magic of mimesis—what was once called "sympathetic magic"—the copy is granted "the character and power of the original, the representation the power of the represented" (1993:xviii). In other words, through the magical replication of beings, objects, rituals, or bodily practices believed to be powerful, those who replicate hope to obtain power over that which is replicated. Mimetic processes are best seen at work in colonial and neocolonial settings—that is, in contexts of extreme power inequalities, whether social, political, or economic. However, Taussig asserts that mimesis is not only a mechanism of magically appropriating the power of the other but, above all, a means to "explore difference, yield into and become the Other" (xiii). In this he follows Walter Benjamin, who defined the mimetic faculty as a "compulsion to become the Other" (Taussig 1993:xviii). This is true, I would suggest, if and only if we analyze processes of mimetic replication from a synchronic point of view. The minute we introduce time into the equation, mimesis can be characterized, I argue, as a means to appropriate the power of the other while at the same time erasing the memory of such appropriation. This is also a way of negating the power of the other.

There are numerous instances of mimetic replication among Yanesha people, particularly in relation to the Incas and the European missionaries, the most powerful others of Yanesha recent history. This phenomenon is consistent with what Eduardo Viveiros de Castro (1993:369) has called "la voracité idéologique des Indiens" (the ideological voracity of Indians), that is, the Amerindian openness to hearing and assimilating new religious messages. But it is also of a piece with what Stephen Hugh-Jones (1992:43) has called the "consumerism" of lowland South American Indians, that is, their fascination with foreign manufactured goods.

The most outstanding example of mimetic appropriation of Inca elements by the Yanesha is the *wakas*, the sacred sites or objects of Andean tradition. This is particularly true of a specific type of *wakas*: those of ancient beings and divinities transformed into stone, a theme that is common throughout the Andes (Zuidema 1989:457). Yanesha mythology is full of references to ancient peoples and deities turned into stone as a result of the transformative powers of the higher divinities. Their stone figures are scattered throughout the Yanesha landscape, forming part of what I have elsewhere called their topographic history (Santos-Granero 1998). Pueshestor and Arrarpeñ, two powerful *mellañoteñ* spirits, were transformed by the solar divinity as punishment for attempting to keep for themselves the fish he had created for the Yanesha. Today their stone bodies can be seen along the Chorobamba River together with the stone sieves they used to capture the fish. Yompor Caresa transformed the bodies of his followers who were killed by the cannibalistic Muellepen to spare them from being decapitated. They can still be seen as elongated stone slabs submerged in a shallow strand of the Cacazú River (see figure 1.2).

Yanesha people consider the stone figures of Pueshestor, Arrarpeñ, and Caresa's warriors to be numinous, but they do not worship them. In contrast, the figures of the divinities Yompor Yompere, his wife Yachor Mamas, and his classificatory son Yemo'nasheñ Senyac, who were transformed into stone by the angry solar divinity before he ascended to the heavens, were the object of elaborate rituals (Navarro 1924; Smith 1977; Santos-Granero 1998). Until the 1920s their stone bodies were sheltered in a large temple at Palmaso, a site along the Chorobamba River, where they were visited and venerated not only by the Yanesha but also by the Perené Asháninka and the Gran Pajonal Ashéninka (see figure 1.3). As in the Andes, pilgrims attending the ceremonies held at the temple made offerings of coca leaves, limestone powder, tobacco, and manioc beer to the stone divinities. They also prayed to them, asking for health, fecundity, and abundance, and above all for aid in achieving immortality. According to Richard Chase Smith

Fig. 1.2. "Petrified body" of one of Yompor Caresa's warriors, Cacazú River.

(1977), Yanesha people also made pilgrimages to visit the stone body of Yompor Efetar, another brother of Yompor Ror, whom the solar divinity transformed in Huancabamba before going to his sky abode. Yanesha people do not make any association between these sacred stone figures and the Incas. In fact, according to Yanesha historical chronology, these transformations took place before the appearance of Enc. With the passage of time, what began as a copy meant to extract the power of the original was appropriated as one's own. The filiation of the original was forgotten; the copy became a new original.

Christian elements mimed by Yanesha people in colonial and postcolonial times underwent a similar process. This was the case of "St. John's fires." Both written and oral sources assert that the Yanesha worshipped fires in their ceremonial centers (Navarro 1924; Santos-Granero 1991:285). These fires had a divine origin. Priests claimed that they had found them during spiritual retreats into the forest. Known generically by the term *cantell*, a word derived from the Spanish *candela* or "fire," sacred fires were kept constantly alight. People venerated them by making offerings, praying to them, and singing and dancing in their honor. Sacred fires were conceived of as manifestations of the strength and power of Yompor Ror, the present-day solar divinity, and were thus referred to as Yompor Poyoročhen, Our Father's Portent. However, they were also attributed to other divinities of the *yompor*, or "our father," category. Among them oral sources mention Yompor Parehuanch, a divinity whose name derives from Padre Juan or

Fig. 1.3. Stone figures of divinity Yompor Yompuer and his wife and son at Palmaso.

Father John. We know that in seventeenth- and eighteenth-century Europe the feast of St. John was as prominent in the Catholic calendar as Christmas, to the extent that the liturgies established by the Church for the two festivals were very similar (Catholic Encyclopedia 2005). The central feature of the popular celebration of St. John's Day was the lighting of bonfires immediately after sunset. People burned old things in these fires in the belief that this act would purify and renew their lives. Yanesha people mimicked the bonfires the Franciscan missionaries lit on St John's Day in the hope of appropriating their purifying powers. Copied in the context of eighteenth-century missionary domination, these fires continued to be worshipped in Yanesha ceremonial centers until the 1950s. In the process, however, their Christian origin was obliterated from Yanesha memory.

I suggest that, together with selective memory, the mimetic faculty conspires to obliterate and/or revert power differences with significant others in contexts of extreme inequality. In the short term, it constitutes a means of magically appropriating what are considered to be the mystical powers of others; in the long term, however, it becomes a means of turning the power of the other into one's own. Thus, if it is true, as Taussig (1993) asserts, that mimesis constitutes a means to become the other, seen from a diachronic perspective, it does so only to turn the other into oneself. In brief, whereas selective memory makes use of forgetting in order to attribute the power of the other to the forces of one's own culture, mimesis elevates forgetting to a state-of-the-art activity by appropriating the power of the other as if it had always been one's own. It is thus that the Yanesha obliterate from historical memory—or perhaps it would be better to say that they redress in historical memory—the crude realities of power and alterity. By forgetting, the Yanesha disempower the others, to empower themselves. This is why not remembering—as the King told the jury—is so important.

Raising Up the Memory of the Future

The Yanesha people's fight against time and history is as much about hastening the occurrence of the *mellapo*, the end of time, as it is about selective remembering and forgetting. Until recently, this was achieved through the spiritual routines of the *cornesha'*, the Yanesha priestly leaders, and the ceremonial activities carried out by their followers under their direction.[10] Yanesha religiosity, past and present, is very much founded on a messianic hope for salvation. Both the Yanesha divinities of old and the new Christian god left this earth promising that they would come back to rescue their children and grant them immortality. Central to the discourse of both past *cornesha'* and present-day Adventist and Evangelical ministers is the imminence of the god's return and, thus, of the end of time. In the following paragraphs I shall concentrate on the mnemonic practices involved in the more "traditional" quest of the *cornesha'* for salvation. However, the reader should bear in mind that such a quest is not a thing of the past; adapted to Christian discourse and ritual practice, it survives today.

Coshamñats sacred music is central to the Yanesha quest for salvation, as Smith (1977) has demonstrated in his insightful doctoral dissertation.[11] Yanesha people stole the knowledge of *coshamñats* music from the land of the murdered ones—the land where the souls of murdered Yanesha live, located in the uppermost of the five planes of the Yanesha cosmos. The *coshamñats* celebration, in which household heads take turns inviting their kin, friends, and neighbors to sing, dance, and drink manioc beer in honor of the divinities, encapsulates the Yanesha ideals of mutual love and reciprocal generosity. However, only the divinities have the power to invent *coshamñats* music and songs. Because they are divine creations, these songs have powers of their own—the power to cure, the power to induce animals to multiply and plants to bear in abundance—extraordinary life-giving powers. But the powers of *coshamñats* songs are not confined to utilitarian, economic purposes.

More important, it is through *coshamñats* songs that the higher divinities remind Yanesha people of their promise of salvation and convey important messages related to the imminence of the end of time. For this reason the quest for divine revelation in the form of sacred songs and music was one of the most significant spiritual activities of the Yanesha priestly leaders of old. Through fasting, sexual abstinence, prolonged vigil, and the consumption of coca leaves, concentrated tobacco juice, and in some cases hallucinogenic plants, priests—but also other devout men and women—sought to excite the love and compassion of the divinities in order to obtain the revelation of a song.

The aim of these ritual practices, as Smith (1977:177) asserts, is "to accrue sufficient power to momentarily cancel the distinction between mortal and immortal, to suspend the truth of human existence long enough to enter the world of immortality and pure power, and to return with a song, a concrete symbol of that power, as well as an object imbued with the power to create order from chaos and to free one from the inevitability of death." Because each song is the result of an individual quest, the memory of a *coshamñats* song is always associated with that of the song seeker to whom it was revealed. It is also associated with the chain of persons through whom it was passed from generation to generation. Smith (1977:181) refers to these persons as "song custodians." Although some persons are credited with knowing a large number of *coshamñats* songs, there are no specialized song keepers as in other Amazonian societies (see, for instance, Hill 1993). Until recently, every Yanesha man and woman knew one or more *coshamñats* songs. In a given settlement, however, only one person was recognized as the custodian of a particular song and, as such, had exclusive rights to perform it on public occasions. At the broader ethnic level there could be several custodians of the same song, learned from independent sources. Thus, chains of custodianship of particular songs involved all adult Yanesha, crisscrossed Yanesha social space, and united the living with the dead.

Songs are generally learned from same-sex parents, or from older same-sex members of one's extended kindred (Smith 1977:188). This, however, is not a rule, and the issue of who teaches whom is largely a matter of interpersonal sympathies and negotiations. Whatever the arrangement, the transmission and learning of songs establishes a link between past, present, and future custodians. According to Smith (1977:195), by performing a song its custodian "preserves the immortality of previous custodians and ultimately of the divinity whose song it is," and by transmitting it the custodian protects the song from oblivion and "fosters his own immortality by keeping the memory of himself alive." Before beginning to sing a particular song, its custodian tells the audience which divinity revealed the song to whom, and through which singers the song was passed down.

The act of recalling a song and the memory of its previous custodians is described by the term *tantateñets*, which literally means "to lift" or "to raise up" something, but which can be glossed as "to bring to life" or "to resurrect." Thus, according to Smith (1977:196), "A song is 'raised up' in the sense that it is brought to life again with each new performance," whereas "a former owner is 'raised up' from oblivion when his song is performed." *Coshamñats* songs embody the spirit of their former custodians in the form of memories that are resurrected whenever the song is performed. In that way, Yanesha song keepers guarantee the immortality of previous custodians, but also that of the song's original divine owner (Smith 1977:198). They also keep alive the hope for immortality, which was promised to them by their divinities before leaving this earth, and which the divinities have renewed with each new song they have revealed to the Yanesha. In doing so, they raise up, as it were, the memory of the future.

Despite pressures from foreign and local Christian ministers to abandon *coshamñats* music, Yanesha people continue to perform it not only in private but in public settings, such as regular and extraordinary meetings of their ethnic political organization, the Federación de Comunidades Nativas Yanesha (FEC-ONAYA). For many Christian Yanesha, however, *coshamñats* songs have lost their original meaning and are preserved more as powerful signs of Yanesha identity than as key elements of their religiousness. This in no way means that they have renounced the hope of salvation. The hymns that the Christian Yanesha have learned from Adventist and fundamentalist Evangelical missionaries—or in some cases have created themselves—continue to transmit this messianic hope, as is shown in the following fragments:

> The return of our King is near.
> Let's rejoice, for He comes to take us with Him.
> That day the crying, the suffering, the pain and the sorrow
> Will come to an end.
>
> The end of the world is near.
> The Gospel will come to an end,
> And the signs are coming true,
> They are coming true as it was written.
>
> Jesus is coming on clouds
> To raise up His church.
> If you do not get ready, here you will remain.
> I won't stay here, I won't stay here,
> Flying with my Christ I shall ascend to heaven.[12]

The three central elements of Yanesha "traditional" messianic hopes, before their mass conversion to Christianity, persist in these verses: the hope for the arrival of a divine savior, the hope for the end of suffering, and the hope for an immortal life in a celestial sphere. I suggest that by singing *coshaññats* sacred songs or Christian hymns, Yanesha people resurrect the memory of their divinities—past and present—and remind them of their promise of salvation. In so doing they strive to put an end to time and history, to the miseries of the human condition, but also, it should be stressed, to the vexations of alterity and hierarchical relations.

Conclusions

What are we to conclude from the Yanesha people's struggle against time and history? It would be tempting to see this as another example of a Lévi-Straussian "cold society," firm in its negation of history and minimizing change for the sake of social equilibrium and continuity. But even if we subscribe to Lévi-Strauss's original notion—which has often been distorted, as Teixeira-Pinto (1997:199–200) and others have pointed out[13]—the Yanesha do not qualify as a cold society. Firstly, they neither feel "obstinate fidelity to a past conceived as a timeless model" nor legitimize every present practice on the basis that "the ancestors taught it to us," and secondly, they do not assume that "nothing has been going on since the appearance of the ancestors except events whose recurrence periodically effaces their particularity" (Lévi-Strauss 1966:236).

The Yanesha not only accept that things change, they preserve the memory of change in the present historical era in terms of "before" and "after" specific events, with special emphasis on those events linked to the appearance of new social actors. What they seem not to accept are the consequences that these events have on the interethnic balance of power. Thus, one of the main features of Yanesha representations of the past is the constant elimination of any reference that might imply that significant others are in some essential way superior—culturally, technologically, or politically—to themselves. This does not mean that they negate the existence of situations in which they occupy a subordinate position. On the contrary, as we have seen, Yanesha people are always ready to accept and even exaggerate their material poverty vis-à-vis powerful others. Such acknowledgment, however, is mainly a rhetorical device meant to underscore the unfairness and absurdity of history and, thus, reinforce the desirability of the *mellapo*, the end of time.

One might also be tempted to assert, following Terence Turner, that the Yanesha consider that "social agency in the full sense," meaning the "power to create or change the forms and contents of social existence" (1988:244), is not available to them—in other words, that they do not consider their society and culture to be "historical products of a collective social activity," but rather "fetichized products of super-human beings," as is the case among the Kayapó (1993:58). The fact that they tend to suppress the memory of their political agency, even with respect to their participation in the insurrection of Juan Santos Atahuallpa, and that they tend to attribute major historical events to the agency of their divinities, would seem to support this view. However, I would argue that it is not that Yanesha people deny their own agency, but rather that their notion of historical agency differs from that of the West insofar as it privileges spiritual over political agency.

Ever since the Enlightenment and Voltaire's call for "positive action" to improve the human condition and redress society's evils, social agency in Western thought has been associated with political action, which in its extreme manifestation assumes the form of revolutionary struggles. As they have demonstrated throughout colonial and postcolonial history, the Yanesha do not shun political strife, even if this takes the form of armed confrontation. It seems clear, however, that they do not consider this type of agency a significant means of empowerment, at least not significant enough to preserve its memory in their narratives.

In contrast, they ascribe the highest importance to spiritual agency. They believe that their behavior, both individual and collective, vis-à-vis their divinities determines the divinities' course of action. From a Yanesha point of view, political agency is always subordinated to spiritual agency. The best way to put an end to situations of inequality, exploitation, and oppression is to embark on a life of devotion aimed at exciting the divinities' compassion, so that they will grant immortality to their human creatures. This feature is, precisely, what most attracted Yanesha people to Juan Santos Atahuallpa. The myth of Yompor Santo indicates that the divine emissary was sent to renew Yanesha devotion to their divinities, and to announce the end of time. Interestingly enough, the myth says that he was recognized and welcomed by a *cornesha'*, or Yanesha priestly leader. In fact, the historical Juan Santos Atahuallpa behaved in many ways as *cornesha'* are said to have behaved, always searching for a divine indication of the coming of the *mellapo*. Historical documents confirm this particular aspect of the myth. Contemporary witnesses assert that Juan Santos led an austere life, avoided the company of women, chewed coca leaves, practiced fasts, and was counseled by an old "sorcerer" (Santo and García [1742] 1942:58; Loayza 1942:33–34). All these practices coincide with the asceticism attributed to *cornesha'* embarked on a quest for a divine acoustic revelation (Smith 1977). In this sense, it could be said that there was a mutual influence between Yanesha priestly leaders and Juan Santos Atahuallpa in which each served as model for the shaping of the other (Santos-Granero 2004:207).

Yanesha spiritual agency does not preclude political action, but as I have argued elsewhere (Santos-Granero 1991), Yanesha politics is always subordinated to religious principles of action. If Yanesha people took up arms against the Spanish, it was not so much because they were enticed by the possibility of putting an end to Spanish exploitation, but rather because they were attracted by Juan Santos Atahuallpa's promise of salvation. Their final aim was not the attainment of political freedom or equality but the elimination of oppression and hierarchy through spiritual salvation and the achievement of immortality. That they achieved the former but not the latter cannot be construed as indicating that the aims of Yanesha insurgents were political rather than spiritual. What motivated—and still motivates—Yanesha people to confront their oppressors is not a desire for temporal redress of social inequalities "in history" but the desire to obliterate alterity, hierarchy, and power by extricating themselves "out of history." In other words, the point is not to make history but, rather, to bring history to an end. Such messianic expectations are still in force, and have been triggered even by modern leaders who have not adopted a millenarian discourse.[14]

In sum, what Yanesha people remember is that time has not always existed; that they did not always suffer and die; that time and history came to be because of human fallibility; and that the only way to put an end to them is through spiritual action. This is the crux of the millenarian ideology and historicity of peoples such as the Yanesha. They do not negate time, but fight against the ravages of time. They do not negate history, but contest the hierarchy and inequalities inherent in history. They do not negate their own historical agency, but endorse the idea that agency is meaningful (and memorable) not in order to make history but, rather, to unmake it.

Acknowledgments

I wish to thank Carlos Fausto for his insightful comments on an earlier draft of this chapter. I would also like to thank Olga F. Linares, who, as always, has helped me to polish my English.

Notes

1. In a 2003 article in *Current Anthropology*, Hanne Veber called into question the much proclaimed "messianism" of the Asháninka—Arawak-speaking neighbors of the Yanesha people—on the grounds that it seems to be more a projection of the theoretical biases of authors who have studied their society and history than a well-substantiated social phenomenon. In my comments on her article (Santos-Granero 2003:204), I argued

that whereas there might be doubts about the depth of the messianic beliefs and millenarian expectations of some of the regional groups that compose the Asháninka cluster, there can be no doubt that these beliefs are central to the Perené and Pichis Asháninka, as well as to the Yanesha people—an assertion with which Veber (2003:208) agreed in her reply. The data presented in this article confirm the centrality of millenarian beliefs both in Yanesha conceptions of time and in Yanesha historical agency.

2. Smith (1977:85) suggests that the names of the creator god and his evil classificatory brother may derive from the Spanish names for God and the Devil: Dios = Yos, and Lucifer = Yosoper. This Christian influence in Yanesha theology has been adapted, however, to native Amazonian structures of thought, so that in the Yanesha myth of creation God and the Devil appear as rival classificatory brothers, and creation itself as the result of their interpersonal competition of wills.

3. The Yanesha people conceive of the cosmos as composed of five terrestrial planes, each with its own sky. This earth, the "earth where people die," occupies the second position from bottom to top.

4. Smith (1977:107) asserts that the root *mell-*, found in the terms *mella* and *mellapo*, "looks suspiciously like the Spanish *mil* (one thousand), the root of *milenio* (millennium), a period of one thousand years which, according to Christian thought, Christ will reign when he returns to earth." He asserts, however, and I agree with his view, that even if the Yanesha borrowed the root from colonial missionaries, "the underlying concept of millennium is, I am convinced, indigenous." The root *mell-* is used in many different contexts, always related to notions of eternity, immortality, and sacredness (cf. Smith 1977:107–108). It is found in the noun *mellañoteñ*, the invisible powerful spirits that inhabit this earth; these beings are immortals, they have existed and will exist forever. It is also found in the verb *mellañochterr*, which means to turn something or someone into a *mellañoteñ* spirit, and by extension refers to the capacity "to immortalize" or "to sanctify," a power exclusive to the higher divinities. In more secular contexts, it is also present in the adjective *mellasheñ*, which means "very ancient, old and worn out."

5. I was first told this myth in 1977, while on a trek along the forest trail linking Huacsho to Muerraťo. This is the area where Yanesha people used to fight against the invading Muellepen, and where I took the picture that appears in figure 1.2. In addition, I took notes on three versions of this myth in 1982–83 and recorded a complete version in 1983 from a myth teller of Muerraťo, renowned for his knowledge of Yanesha historical tradition. These different versions are very much alike in structure and content.

6. I heard—and noted down—three versions of the myth of Enc in 1977, 1978, and 1979. The first two versions were told by young people and were fragmentary; the last was a very complete version told by the son of a renowned shaman. In addition, in 1983 I recorded two complete versions from well-known myth tellers living in different settlements. All versions agree as to the main events of the story, and present the same omissions.

7. Elsewhere I have argued that Amazonian peoples' representations about the Incas

vary according to geographical distance, with those closest to the Andean range and having a more direct experience of Inca domination having more negative views than those living farther to the east (Santos-Granero 1992a:279–295).

8. Information on the origin and past deeds of white people appears in a variety of myths. Here I focus on four: Enc, Yompor Yompuer, A'penerr, and Yompor Santo. On the myth of Enc, see note 5 above. In 1983 I took notes on two abridged versions of the myth of Yompor Yompuer, and recorded one complete version narrated by one of the oldest myth tellers of Muerrafo. I noted down two versions of the myth of A'penerr in 1977, and in 1983 recorded a complete version told to me by the same man from Muerrafo. I wrote down one fragmentary version of the myth of Yompor Santo recounted to me in 1979, and three more complete versions during the 1982–83 period. In 1983 I recorded a full version told to me by the son of the last priestly leader of the Palmaso ceremonial center. With greater or lesser detail, the diverse versions of each of these myths narrate the same events.

9. Enca Capa and Huascar are the names of Inca rulers. Huayna Capac was, according to Inca mythical history, the twelfth Inca ruler. Huascar and Atahuallpa were his sons. At Huayna Capac's death, Huascar and Atahuallpa fought for control of the Inca Empire. Atahuallpa defeated Huascar, but later he was captured and executed by Francisco Pizarro and his troops.

10. The distinction between Yanesha priestly leaders (*cornesha*) and tobacco shamans (*pa'llerr*) began before contact times. In the early eighteenth century, only seven years after the establishment of Franciscan missions in Yanesha territory, Spanish chroniclers already reported the existence of sorcerers/enchanters (*brujos/encantadores*) who worshipped and offered sacrifices to the Sun (San Joseph [1716] 1750:14v). Worship of the solar divinity Yompor Ror was central to the activities of the historical *cornesha'* mentioned in Yanesha oral tradition, as well as in colonial and postcolonial documents (e.g., Navarro 1924). Indeed, this is one of the most important traits differentiating them from tobacco shamans, whose main mystical relationships are with animal familiars and jaguar spirits. In addition, historical sources say that these "enchanters" were central in instigating Yanesha people to oppose the missionary presence (San Joseph [1716] 1750:15v), suggesting that they already played an important role as supralocal political leaders. There is evidence, however, that the role of priestly leaders acquired its "modern" traits—e.g., adoption of some elements of Catholic theology, appropriation of the knowledge of iron forging techniques, and building of large ceremonial temples—in colonial times and, especially, after the revolt of Juan Santos Atahuallpa in 1742 (Santos-Granero 2004:206–207; 1988a). Like most Yanesha social and cultural practices, the *cornesha'* priest/temple complex was a work in progress, the product of multiple internal developments and external influences. This is probably true of most native Amazonian peoples, the difference being that we know much less about their histories than what we know about Yanesha history.

11. Much of the following discussion on the mnemonic aspects of custodianship and performance of *coshamñats* sacred music and songs is based on the disquisition on the topic by Smith (1977:Chapters 5–6).

12. These verses, published in Spanish but probably translated from English, were copied from a small mimeographed hymnbook used extensively by Yanesha members of the Peruvian Evangelical Church (Iglesia Evangélica Peruana).

13. Lévi-Strauss does not contend that cold societies are "peoples without history"; he actually asserts that the fact that "all societies are in history and change . . . is patent" (1966:233–234). Instead he is concerned with how different societies react to the realities of the "common condition" of history—a legitimate concern from my point of view, and one that I share.

14. In the late 1960s, Moisés Gamarra, a Peruvian mestizo who had adopted native attire, language, and customs, began to exert great influence over both Yanesha and Asháninka leaders. He spent most of his time visiting their communities and denouncing the injustices experienced by native people. Gamarra insisted that the only way to eradicate these injustices was through political action. He opposed the government and advocated "a small war against Peru." He admired the historical figure of Juan Santos Atahuallpa and asserted that native people "should follow his example." Although, as far as I know, Gamarra never adopted millenarian ideas or images, his profile fitted Yanesha and Asháninka paradigms of messianic leaders: unknown origins, claims to indigeneity, adherence to traditional customs in the face of rampant acculturation, great knowledge of sacred music, command of the ways of the white men, introduction of new social practices (in this case emphasis on formal education and techniques of personal defense), and, last but not least, subversive discourse. As a result, some Yanesha started regarding Gamarra as a possible divine emissary. His sudden disappearance in the late 1970s—some say he married a Swedish woman and now lives in Sweden—reinforced these suspicions.

References

Amich, José. 1975. *Historia de las misiones del convento de Santa Rosa de Ocopa*. Lima: Milla Batres.

Becquelin, Aurore. 1993. "Temps du récit, temps de l'oubli." In Becquelin and Molinié, *Mémoire de la tradition*, 21–50.

Becquelin, Aurore, and Antoinette Molinié, eds. 1993. *Mémoire de la tradition*. Nanterre: Société d'Ethnologie.

Carroll, Lewis. 1865. *Alice's Adventures in Wonderland*. London: Macmillan.

Castro, Eduardo Viveiros de. 1993. "Le Marbre et le myrte: De l'inconstance de l'âme sauvage." In Becquelin and Molinié, *Mémoire de la tradition*, 365–431.

Castro Arenas, Mario. 1973. *La rebelión de Juan Santos*. Lima: Milla Batres.

Catholic Encyclopedia. 2005. "St. John the Baptist." http://www.newadvent.org/cathen/08486b.htm.

Comaroff, John, and Jean Comaroff. 1992. *Ethnography and the Historical Imagination*. Boulder, Colorado: Westview.

Dehouve, Danièle. 1993. "À la recherche du sens perdu: La Lutte contre l'oubli chez les Nahuas du Mexique." In Becquelin and Molinié, *Mémoire de la Tradition*, 51–70.

Forché, Carolyn, ed. 1993. *Against Forgetting: Twentieth-Century Poetry of Witness*. New York: W. W. Norton.

Hill, Jonathan D., ed. 1988. *Rethinking History and Myth: Indigenous South American Perspectives on the Past*. Urbana: University of Illinois Press.

———. 1993. *Keepers of the Sacred Chants: The Poetics of Ritual Power in an Amazonian Society*. Tucson: University of Arizona Press.

Huerta, Francisco de la, ed. [1686] 1983. "Relación . . . de la entrada y sucesos a las santas conversiones de San Francisco Solano en los gentiles Conibos hecha por el padre . . ." *Amazonía Peruana* 4(8):113–124.

Hugh-Jones, Stephen. 1992. "Yesterday's Luxuries, Tomorrow's Necessities: Business and Barter in Northwest Amazonia." In *Barter, Exchange, and Value: An Anthropological Approach*, edited by Caroline Humphrey and Stephen Hugh-Jones, 42–74. Cambridge: Cambridge University Press.

Lathrap, Donald W. 1970. *The Upper Amazon*. New York: Praeger.

———. 1973. "The Antiquity and Importance of Long-Distance Trade Relationships in the Moist Tropics of Pre-Columbian South America." *World Archaeology* 5(2):170–186.

Lévi-Strauss, Claude. 1970. *The Savage Mind*. Chicago: University of Chicago Press.

Loayza, Francisco A., ed. 1942. *Juan Santos, el Invencible: Manuscritos del año de 1742 al año de 1755*. Lima: D. Miranda.

Maroni, Pablo. [1738] 1988. *Noticias auténticas del famoso río Marañón*. Edited by Jean-Pierre Chaumeil. Monumenta Amazónica B4. Iquitos, Peru: IIAP/CETA.

Myers, Thomas. 1981. "Aboriginal Trade Networks in Amazonia." In *Networks of the Past: Regional Interaction in Archaeology*, Proceedings of the Twelfth Annual Conference, Archaeological Association of the University of Calgary, edited by Peter D. Francis, F. J. Kense, and P. G. Duke, 19–30. Calgary: Archaeological Association.

Navarro, Manuel. 1924. *La tribu Amuesha*. Lima: Escuela Tipográfica Salesiana.

Ordinaire, Olivier. 1892. *Du Pacifique à l'Atlantique par les Andes péruviennes et l'Amazone*. Paris: Plon. Translated in *Del Pacífico al Atlántico y otros escritos*, Monumenta Amazónica D1 (Iquitos, Peru: IFEA/CETA, 1988).

Ortiz de Zúñiga, Iñigo. [1562] 1967. *Visita de la provincia de León de Huánuco en 1562*. Vol. 1, *Visita de las cuatro Waranqa de los Chupachu*. Huánuco: Universidad Hermilio Valdizán.

Rappaport, Joanne. 1998. *The Politics of Memory: Native Historical Interpretation in the Colombian Andes*. Durham, North Carolina: Duke University Press.

Renard-Casevitz, France-Marie, Thierry Saignes, and Anne-Christine Taylor. 1986. *L'Inca, l'Espagnol et les sauvages: Rapports entre les sociétés amazoniennes et andines du XVe au XVIIe siècle*. Paris: Éditions Recherches sur les Civilisations.

Rodríguez Tena, Fernando. [1774] 1977. "Sigue la Mission de Panatahuas." *Amazonía Peruana* 1(2):157–168.

Saignes, Thierry. 1985. *Los Andes orientales: Historia de un olvido*. Lima: Instituto Francés de Estudios Andinos; Cochabamba, Bolivia: Centro de Estudios de la Realidad Económica y Social.

San Antonio, Joseph de, ed. 1750. *Colección de informes sobre las misiones del Colegio de Santa Rosa de Ocopa*. Madrid.

San Joseph, Francisco de. [1716] 1750. "Copia de un informe hecho por el V. Padre Fr. Francisco de San Joseph, comissario de missiones del Cerro de la Sal, y prefecto de la Sagrada Congregación de Propaganda Fide, en el reyno del Perú, y provincia de los doce Apóstoles de Lima: al Rmo. Padre Fr. Joseph Sanz, comissario general de Indias." In San Antonio, *Colección de informes*, 13v–16v.

Santo, Fr. Manuel del, and Fr. Domingo García. [1742] 1942. "Copia de carta, escrita por los padres . . . missioneros apostólicos del Colegio de Santa Rosa de Ocopa, y missiones de infieles del Cerro de la Sal, al R. P. Fr. Joseph Gil Muñoz, comisario de dichas missiones." In Loayza, *Juan Santos*, 1–8.

Santos-Granero, Fernando. 1987. "Epidemias y sublevaciones en el desarrollo demográfico de las misiones Amuesha del Cerro de la Sal, siglo XVIII." *Histórica* 11(1):25–53.

———. 1988a. "Templos y herrerías: Utopía y re-creación cultural en la Amazonía peruana, siglo XVIII." *Bulletin de l'Institut Français d'Études Andines* (Lima) 17(3–4):1–22.

———. 1988b. "The Ideological and Political Implications of doing Anthropology 'At Home.'" *Revindi* 2:39–50.

———. 1991. *The Power of Love: The Moral Use of Knowledge amongst the Amuesha of Central Peru*. London: Athlone.

———. 1992a. *Etnohistoria de la Alta Amazonía: Siglos XV–XVIII*. Quito: Abya-Yala.

———. 1992b. "Anticolonialismo, mesianismo y utopía en la sublevación de Juan Santos Atahuallpa, siglo XVIII." In *Opresión colonial y resistencia indígena en la Alta Amazonía*, edited by Fernando Santos-Granero, 103–134. Quito: CEDIME/FLACSO-Ecuador.

———. 1998. "Writing History into the Landscape: Space, Myth, and Ritual in Contemporary Amazonia." *American Ethnologist* 25(2):128–148.

———. 2003. "Comments to Hanne Veber's article 'Asháninka Messianism: The Production of a 'Black Hole' in Western Amazonian Ethnography.'" *Current Anthropology* 44(2):204.

———. 2004. "Los Yanesha." In *Guía etnográfica de la Alta Amazonía*, vol. 4, *Matsigenka, Yánesha*, edited by Fernando Santos-Granero and Frederica Barclay, 159–359. Lima: Smithsonian Tropical Research Institute/Instituto Francés de Estudios Andinos.

Smith, Richard Chase. 1977. *Deliverance from Chaos for a Song: A Social and Religious Interpretation of the Ritual Performance of Amuesha Music*. Ann Arbor, Michigan: University Microfilms.

Taussig, Michael. 1993. *Mimesis and Alterity: A Particular History of the Senses*. New York: Routledge.

Teixeira-Pinto, Márnio. 1997. *Ieipari: Sacrifício e vida social entre os indios Arara (Caribe)*. São Paulo: Hucitec/ANPOCS.

Torre López, Arturo E. de la. 2004. *Juan Santos Atahualpa*. Lima: Pontificia Universidad Católica del Perú.

Tibesar, Antonine S. 1950. "The Salt Trade among the Montaña Indians of the Tarma Area of Eastern Peru." *Primitive Man* 23:103–109.

Turner, Terence. 1988. "Ethno-Ethnohistory: Myth and History in Native South American Representations of Contact with Western Society." In Hill, *Rethinking History and Myth*, 235–281.

———. 1993. "Da cosmologia à história: Resistência, adaptação e consciência social entre os Kayapó." In *Amazônia: Etnologia e história indígena*, edited by Eduardo Viveiros de Castro and Manuela Carneiro da Cunha, 43–66. São Paulo: NHII-USP/FAPESP.

Varese, Stefano. 1973. *La sal de los cerros: Una aproximación al mundo Campa*. Lima: Retablo de Papel.

Veber, Hanne. 2003. "Asháninka Messianism: The Production of a 'Black Hole' in Western Amazonian Ethnography." *Current Anthropology* 44(2):183–211.

Whitten, Norman E., Jr. 1988. "Historical and Mythic Evocations of Chthonic Power in South America." In Hill, *Rethinking History and Myth*, 282–306.

Wiesenthal, Simon. 1989. Interview. *Baltimore Jewish Times*, February 24. Quoted in www.wiesenthal.com/site/pp asp?c=fwLYKnNOLzII&b=242924.

Wright, Robin M. 1998. *Cosmos, Self, and History in Baniwa Religion: For Those Unborn*. Austin: University of Texas Press.

Zarzar, Alonso. 1989. *"Apo Capac Huayna, Jesús sacramentado": Mito, utopía y milenarismo en el pensamiento de Juan Santos Atahualpa*. Lima: Centro Amazónico de Antropología y Aplicación Práctica.

Zuidema, R. Tom. 1989. *Reyes y guerreros: Ensayos de cultura andina*. Lima: FOMCIEN-CIAS.

2

If God Were a Jaguar

Cannibalism and Christianity among the Guarani (16th–20th Centuries)

Carlos Fausto

> Every coming-to-be is a passing-away of something else and every passing-away some other thing's coming-to-be.
>
> —Aristotle, *On Generation and Corruption* I.3

> To perish is to cease to be what one was; to be changed is to exist otherwise.
>
> —Tertullian, *The Resurrection of the Flesh* LV

"Ore kurusu ñe'ëngatu ra'y, kurusu ñe'ëngatu rajy, ore ára jeguaka ra'y" (We are sons and daughters of the cross of the good word, we are sons of the crown of time). This self-description comes from the Kaiová, a Guarani subgroup from Brazil and Paraguay.[1] Kaiová is a corruption of *kaaguá*, meaning "forest dwellers," a generic term applied to Guarani populations that evaded absorption by the colonial system. *Kurusu*, in turn, is an indigenization of the Spanish and Portuguese word *cruz*, or "cross," and functions as an extremely productive concept in present-day Kaiowá cosmology. The term refers to the support of the earth, set to collapse in the final cataclysm. But it can also mean a person, since someone who has died is referred to as an ex-cross (*kurusu kuê*), and it refers also to an instrument used by shamans, who carry a cross in one hand while shaking a maraca in the other (Chamorro 1995:61–62).

What do the Kaiowá mean when they claim they are the children of the "cross of the good word," those who emerged from the "foamy base of the cross" (Chamorro 1995:60)? What status should we ascribe to this self-definition and how should it be interpreted? Is it an imitation of misunderstood Christianity or a mere veneer concealing an authentic indigenous religion beneath? These are just some of the questions that haunted twentieth-century Guarani ethnology, and that had earlier tormented missionaries as far back as the first centuries of colonization, men for whom deconversion and cryptopaganism were problems on a par with teaching the mysteries of the Faith.

However, this is not the usual image of the Guarani living in the Jesuit missions of Paraguay. Here they are more often depicted as passive recipients of catechism, thanks to the virtue of the priests or to a sort of cultural preadaptation to Christianity. As early as the sixteenth century, chroniclers mentioned the greater propensity of the Guarani toward conversion (when compared to the Tupi)—an idea later reinforced by seventeenth- and eighteenth-century mission historiography, which boasted of the missionaries' apparent success in religious conversion.[2] Modern anthropology has tended to concur with this image: "on the face of the earth," wrote Schaden in the 1950s, "there is undoubtedly no people or tribe to whom the Evangelical Word is better suited than the Guarani: my kingdom is not of this world. The entire mental life of the Guarani converges toward the Beyond" (1954a:248).

But rather than assuming that this inclination "toward the beyond" reflects a disposition to conversion, anthropology has interpreted it as the source for resistance, tradition, and memory. Although far from monolithic, the image of the Guarani produced by twentieth-century anthropology implies such a high degree of religious continuity that contemporary indigenous cosmologies come across almost as protohistorical relics that somehow survived the colonial process unscathed. We are faced by a dilemma, then: How can we reconcile the image of miraculous conversion with the tenacious resistance of a creed that apparently underpins an identity impervious to change and alterity?

I propose that examining the zone of ambiguity between these two poles—pure discontinuity and pure continuity—is much more productive. Over recent decades, new approaches to the history and anthropology of religious missions in native South America have enabled us to reconstruct the complexity of the phenomenon (Wright 1999; 2004) and to question the myth of the Jesuit reductions (Castelnau-L'Estoile 2000; Pompa 2003; Wilde 2003a). However, the same critique has yet to be applied to the ethnography of the Guarani. Even historical studies continue to repeat entrenched mistakes and questionable interpretations as though they comprised raw empirical data.[3] Here I attempt to make a start on this critical work by exploring—rather than repudiating—the idea of transformation, taken here as a process that unfolds in time (a history), as the production of a topological space (a structure), and as a native category. My aim is to dissolve some of the traditional views found in the literature and thereby make room for new interpretations. The limits of the text are determined by this objective, meaning that I shall restrict myself to what Melià (2004:176) has called "El Guarani de papel; esto es en papel" (the paper Guarani—that is, the Guarani on paper).[4]

In previous works I have examined some of the classical dichotomies of anthropology—structure and action, myth and history, form and process—and proposed fresh analyses which, though making use of these binary opposites, do so by altering the relationship between them. When employing the notion of "mythical agency," I have maintained the distinction between myth and history while rejecting a widely accepted contrast framed in terms of passivity and activity (Fausto 2002a). Likewise, by emphasizing the pragmatic conditions through which certain beliefs are actualized in particular historical situations, I have insisted on their persistence over the long term (Fausto 2002b). I now wish to tackle these issues within a wider time frame, focusing on Guarani "religion," information on which extends back as far as the sixteenth century. My purpose is to show how this religion was transformed and to examine the directions taken in the process of becoming modern Guarani "religion." My working hypothesis is that contact with mission-based Christianity and the experiences of colonialism led to a growing denial of cannibalism as a source of shamanic power and social reproduction—a process I call "dejaguarization." I also suggest that the eclipsing of cannibalism created space for the emergence of a new concept, love, that acquired a central place in Guarani cosmology.

To pursue this hypothesis, I begin with a synopsis of the colonial situation experienced by the Guarani in Paraguay. I then discuss and criticize the composite image produced by Guarani ethnography via two procedures: firstly, a revision of the history of the missions and, secondly, a structural analysis of the transformations found in latter-day Guarani and Amazonian cosmologies. I conclude with a number of comparative observations concerning other processes of "dejaguarization" in Amazonia.

The Guarani during the Early Colonial History

The huge indigenous population inhabiting the Atlantic coast of South America and the Rio de la Plata estuary in the sixteenth century came to be known as Tupi-Guarani. The term combines the names of its two constituent blocks: the Tupi, who lived north of present-day São Paulo, and the Guarani, who extended south as far as the Lagoa dos Patos and along the Paraná, Paraguay, and Uruguay rivers. Ascertaining precisely when this distinction became consolidated in the literature is difficult, but it was already starting to take shape in colonial times (see Edelweiss 1947, 1969). Nonetheless, local designations tended to predominate during the sixteenth and seventeenth centuries: names such as Tamoio, Tupinambá, Tupiniquim, Tabajara for the Tupi and Carijó, Itatin, Tapé, Guarambarense for the Guarani. Derived from the native word for "war" (Montoya 1876), it was the latter term, Guarani, that became the generic designation for the southern block.

The first contacts of the Guarani with Europeans date from the beginning of the sixteenth century. The oldest information is the report produced by the Norman captain Paulmier de Gonneville, who landed on the coast of Santa Catarina in 1503 and remained there for six months. Until the mid-sixteenth century, the Guarani lands and the Rio de la Plata basin served merely as an eastern route to the Andean mountains and their abundant mineral wealth. In 1524 the Portuguese explorer Aleixo Garcia, escorted by the Guarani, succeeded in reaching the Incan Empire from the Brazilian coast. News of his expedition stimulated the Spaniards to explore the Rio de la Plata, founding Buenos Aires in 1536 and Asunción the following year.

Colonization of the region gained impetus, though, only when it became clear that the Andean mines had been monopolized by the conquistadors of Peru. In 1556 the *encomienda* system was established in Paraguay, designed to control the use of indigenous labor in the region surrounding Asunción.[5] This system entailed a rupture with the previously more volatile relations, regulated by alliance and kinship, between the Guarani and the vastly outnumbered Spaniards (Necker 1979:31–32). Implantation of the *encomiendas* may well account for the escalation in indigenous rebellions, already violently repressed since at least the beginning of the 1540s.[6]

From the 1570s onward, these rebellions began to be expressed in a shamanic and/or messianic idiom. The earliest records of these movements coincide with the start of missionary activity in Paraguay, an enterprise carried out by the Franciscans with the support of the governor Hernando Arias de Saavedra, who saw in the system of *reducciones* a solution to two problems: limiting the power of the *encomenderos* and pacifying the Guarani.[7] The combination of military action and Franciscan catechism—in a context of brutal demographic decline caused by epidemics and warfare—paved the way for the installation of the Jesuit missions. These flourished in the first decade of the seventeenth century and soon achieved hegemonic control over missionary work in Paraguay, although they were severely hit by slave hunters from São Paulo between 1628 and 1641. Several centers of Jesuit activity were destroyed or abandoned during this period.

The 1640s witnessed the economic, spatial, and military reorganization of Paraguay, which led to a stabilization in the reduction system (Monteiro 1992:493). This stabilization did not mean the isolation of the missions, though. They remained linked, albeit in somewhat tense fashion, to both the colonial politico-economic system and to the Amerindians who resisted reduction—the so-called *monteses* or *cá'águara* (forest dwellers). In fact, these appellations encompassed a wide variety of people. The *monteses* included refugees from uprisings, fugitives from the *encomienda* system, and former neophytes from the missions, alongside people and groups who had no experience of living with non-Amerindians. Despite the constraints imposed by the *encomienda* system and the reduction regime, the colonial situation was much more flexible than commonly imagined, including in terms of the circulation of people and things. Indeed, the history of the missions was always marked by large demographic fluctuations, whether these comprised the silent and constant movements of indigenous individuals and families or the intense migrations and epidemic crises that occurred at various moments from the very outset of missionization.[8]

The demographic crisis and the concentration of the Guarani population in the provincial and missionary villages had created uninhabited zones that afforded relative isolation to the *monteses*. However, the expansion in yerba mate harvesting led to new incursions into these areas in search of fresh fields, leading to contacts with supposedly isolated Guarani populations. The diversity in the historical experiences of these *monteses* can be glimpsed in missionary reports. For example, already in the eighteenth century, Jesuit priests established contact with the Tarumaés "who had learned about the *cruciferos* ('cross bearers,' i.e., the missionaries) through 'hearsay' and had adopted the '*kurusú poty*' [the flower of the cross]" (Susnik 1980:188). This indicates a prior history of relations with the colonial religious universe. During the same period, the Jesuits made contact with another Guarani people, the Mbaeverá, who supposedly showed no signs of Christian influence, living as their ancestors had done and following their shamans who, in the words of Father Dobrizhoffer, "arrogate to themselves full power of warding and inflicting disease and death, of predicting future events, of raising floods and tempests, [and] of transforming themselves into tigers" ([1784] 1970:63).

Cutting a long story short, around this time we start to observe a growing cultural distinction between the *monteses* and other Guarani populations, combined with a progressive merging of the Guarani inhabiting the provincial towns and local missions, as well as a blending of these latter populations with the poor mestizo population. This process was strengthened by the expulsion of the Jesuits in the second half of the eighteenth century, which helped weaken the system of reductions and accelerate the absorption of the native population into the surrounding economy and society.[9] The end result was, on one hand, the forming of a rural population that eventually became part of independent nation-states in the nineteenth century (Argentina, Bolivia, Paraguay, and Brazil) and, on the other, an indigenous population recognized as Guarani, the subjects of anthropological study in the twentieth century.

The Guarani and Their Ethnography

The first ethnography on the Guarani was published in Germany in 1914 by Curt Nimuendajú. His work focused on Guarani groups living in the state of São Paulo, although they had originally come from Mato Grosso do Sul. This population began migrating eastward at the start of the nineteenth century, stirred by the messianic hope of reaching *ywy maráey*, an expression that Nimuendajú translated as the "Land-without-Evil," a translation that achieved common acceptance in the subsequent literature.[10] The migrations were led by shamans who announced the imminent end of the world and called on people to follow them, amid chanting and dancing, to a land of plenty with no disease or death, which was often believed to lie overseas.[11]

At the start of the twentieth century, the Apapocuva—People of the Long Bow, the self-designation used by the principal group studied by Nimuendajú—were in permanent contact with national society. They had adopted a series of nonindigenous traits, such as clothing and the use of crosses and Christian names, but, according to the author, maintained a typically indigenous mythoreligious conception of the universe, founded on the idea of an eventual (and recurrent) cataclysm. As far as Nimuendajú was concerned, "Christian tendencies" were entirely absent from the Apapocuva worldview since the key motifs of their religion were "archi-indigenous." Its specificity lay in the theoretical elaboration and practical productivity of these motifs, an outcome of the suffering inflicted on the people over the preceding centuries (Nimuendajú 1987:131). This prompted Nimuendajú's comparison with crypto-Judaism: just as Heine became a Christian in order to be left in peace as a Jew, so the Apapocuva adopted the outward signs of Christianity as a way of remaining inwardly Guarani (1987:27).

Nimuendajú's book set out the main issues for Guarani ethnography over the following decades, especially questions concerning the authenticity of their contemporary religion. The latter topic reemerged during the 1950s in the work of Egon Schaden, likewise an ethnologist of German extraction and an adherent of acculturation studies. Concerned with tracing the nontraditional aspects of indigenous life, Schaden argued that Guarani religion had suffered profound Christian influence but, rather than obliterating native culture, the assimilation of new elements had accentuated "to an extreme certain key values of primitive tribal doctrine, reinterpreting Christian teaching in light of these" (1969:105).

This vague idea of historico-structural transformation remained unexplored in Guarani ethnography over the 1960s and 1970s. Instead, discussion focused on cultural preservation and identity.[12] The key work from this period is *Ayvu rapyta: Textos míticos de los Mbyá-Guaraní del Guairá*, published by León Cadogan in 1959. The book presents the Mbyá of the Guairá as an isolated population that had conserved, as Schaden writes in the preface, "their traditions in their original purity: that is, with no modification caused by Christian influence, whether at the time of the Jesuit missions, or in more recent times" (1959:5). Among the narratives collected and translated by Cadogan, it was the first set, entitled "Ñe'ẽ Porã Tenonde" (The first beautiful words), that attracted the attention of most later scholars.

Presented as a secret and esoteric tradition to which the author succeeded in gaining access only after years of working with the Mbyá, "Ñe'ẽ Porã Tenonde" describes the origin of the supreme divinity, the foundations of love and human language, the creation of the first earth, and its subsequent destruction by the universal flood. For Cadogan (1959:68–70), the flood closed the first part of the "religious annals of the Mbyá," their "most sacred chapters," and what follows, he argues, are no more than legends similar to those of other Amerindian peoples.

This passage from mystical religion to primitive mythology leads Cadogan to ask whether this contrast indicates grafting or syncretism: "the profound religious concepts," he writes, and "the elevated language . . . of the chapters which make up the first part . . . could well have been extracted from the annals of a race much more cultured than the Mbyá" (1959:70). But he rejects this hypothesis, proclaiming the uncorrupted authenticity of the "Ñe'ẽ Porã Tenonde" on the basis that these First Beautiful Words were unknown to the whites and supposedly preserved from missionary influence. We thus move from Nimuendajú's cryptopaganism, seen as a defense mechanism against national society, to a secret religion transmitted over the centuries in the depths of the forest.

This is the move that Pierre Clastres would ultimately achieve when he published many of Cadogan's texts in 1974, along with others collected by himself. In his introduction, Clastres characteristically collapses opposite poles of Western thought into one single formulation as a way of undermining its structure. Images of purity succeed each other, but not of primitiveness. For the author, the Beautiful Words of Guarani religion, which still today "resonate within the most secret part of the forest . . . preserved from all corruption" (1974:7–8), harbor a profound metaphysics, comparable to the great traditions of reflexive thought. They express a desire for superhumanity and immortality, contemplating the world and its misfortunes, and providing the apex to a religious universe that is "the substance of Guarani society," "its very source and the goal of the Guarani will to live" (8).

This profound adhesion of the Guarani to their religion was, the author argues, primarily a political fact—both a sign of resistance to the ethnocidal process of conquest, and the result of an autochthonous political crisis that predated European colonization. Clastres postulates a growth in the power of Tupi-Guarani chiefs and the emergence of chiefdoms around the end of the fifteenth century, in turn provoking a wave of opposing religious movements stirred by the prophetic discourse of the great shamans. Urging the people to abandon everything and depart in search of the Land-without-Evil, these shamans, Clastres suggests, catalyzed the desire of a society keen to retain its self-identity and prevent the emergence of any irreversible political division.[13] European arrival in the Americas, however, had an immediate impact on this process. Colonial violence and the takeover of indigenous territories made large-scale migrations unviable. Hence, "closed from praxis, the Guarani desire for eternity found its outlet in the elaboration of the Word; it flowed to the side of *logos*" (1974:10).

Clastres' hypothesis replied to the question that first puzzled Cadogan: What was the origin of these Beautiful Words explaining the origin of our First and Last Father (Ñande Ru Pa-pa Tenonde), of Him who gave birth to Himself in the primordial darkness and who, through His wisdom, engendered human language and love, even before creating the first earth, which He created only to destroy, commanding another divinity to build it anew, but now suffused with sorrow? Its origin, said Clastres, was Guarani religion folding in on itself, provoking the replacement of mythology by metaphysics.

Thus the problem of conversion that haunted the seventeenth-century Jesuits was transformed into a twentieth-century anthropological problem of contamination and identity. While ethnographic studies have correctly shown how contemporary Guarani religion lacks a series of dichotomies typical of Christian soteriology, it has tended to exclude any transformation whatsoever in favor of a pure and impermeable nucleus of Guarani religiosity.[14] This essentialism—already expounded by Nimuendajú—was reinforced by the "discovery" of the Mbyá of the Guairá, immediately depicted as the last representatives of an untouched "Guarani-ness."

Histories of Un-conversion

The conception of culture and tradition underlying the ideas of purity and authenticity in Guarani "religion" is difficult to sustain in light of contemporary Amazonian ethnology. It is particularly difficult to match this conception with structuralist-inspired ethnographies, whose emphasis on alterity and affinity provide a non-identity-centered formulation of indigenous societies and cosmologies. How are we to reconcile this perspective—which has proved highly productive in ethnographic terms—with the portrayal of the Guarani as a people closed in on themselves, resistant and impermeable to the otherness of the whites?[15]

This impermeability appears in stark contrast to what we read in sixteenth- and seventeenth-century chronicles. Here we find numerous passages exemplifying the complex appropriation and reworking of Christian symbols by Guarani chiefs and shamans. As early as 1594, Father Alonzo Baranza mentions rebel movements led by Indians claiming to be the pope or Jesus Christ (*apud* Melià 1986:39). The same themes surface in Barco de Centenera's poem (1602) that recounts the revolt in 1579 of Guarambaré, commanded by Oberá, a messianic leader who claimed to be the son of God, born of a virgin. The poem tells of a baptized Amerindian who, having lived in a village subjected to the *encomenderos,* left it to preach throughout the land, promising liberty to the natives and ordering them to sing and dance. The most common of these chants was "Obera, obera, obera, pay tupa, yandabe, hiye, hiye, hiye," which can be translated as "Splendor, splendor, splendor of the priest, God for us too, let us pray, let us pray, let us pray" (Melià 1986:36, 113).[16]

The Jesuit reductions provided the setting for various conflicts between priests and Guarani, confrontations in which each side made use of the other's weapons.[17] In the case of priests, this was usually a ploy to curb a "magician" or "sorcerer." But in general the two sides converged, albeit equivocally, in terms of their imagery of the supernatural and the intervention of extrahuman powers in the human lived world. Chiefs and shamans, for their part, were avid consumers of Catholic rituals and liturgical objects, prompting accusations by the Jesuits of their "pretending to be priests." Father Antônio Ruiz de Montoya narrates how the cacique Miguel Artiguaye, "donning a small cape made of beautiful feathers and other adornments, simulated mass. He placed some towels upon a table and on them a manioc pie and a vase, elaborately painted and filled with maize wine, and, talking through his teeth, held many ceremonies" ([1639] 1985:57).

Although these religious conflicts were often dissipated through threats and derision, occasionally they escalated into actual violence. In 1628, for example, after initially permitting missionaries to enter his lands, Neçu, a Guarani cacique and shaman, ordered them all to be killed. After their deaths, Neçu, "to show he was a priest, albeit a false one, donned the liturgical paraphernalia of the priest and, thus attired, presented himself to the people. He summoned the children before him and proceeded to eradicate, through barbaric ceremonies, the indelible character which baptism had impressed upon their souls" (Montoya [1639] 1985:201–202). This "debaptism" seems to have been just as important an act to the Guarani as baptism was to the priests. They scraped the tongues of children who "had tasted the salt of the sapient spirit," as well as their backs and necks to "smudge the holy ointments," and inverted the ritual, washing the children from their feet up to their heads.

This use and abuse of Jesuit imagery indicates that, from the native point of view, what was at stake was not a conflict between two "religions" in the sense of two mutually exclusive orthodoxies or creeds (see Greer 2003).[18] As Viveiros de Castro (1993) has shown, the Tupi-guarani style of religiosity was opposed to any kind of orthodoxy. Unlike the Catholic missionaries' belief in God and the Scriptures, their faith in their shamans was entirely provisional, a credence based on trial and error. Moreover, the reduction system did not consist of two watertight worlds divided by an impermeable frontier; it formed a social network involving not only the circulation of goods but also a constant flow of reinterpreted signs. The missionaries had no control over the meanings produced in their interactions with natives: once placed in circulation, their ideas acquired autonomy (Griffiths 1999:9). In fact, this process was already under way in the adaptation of native categories required in translating the catechism into indigenous languages—a task that relied on the aid of bilingual informants and continued from one ritual event to the next.

The main problem for the Guarani was not how to return to a lost identity but how to appropriate the powers that the Europeans, especially the priests, seemed to possess.[19] And here the reworking of rituals and the use of sacerdotal clothing and liturgical objects played an equally crucial role. Such practices were not simply disrespectful parodies of Christianity or artifices of the devil, as the Jesuits thought. Nor were they mere subterfuges to conceal a pure "Guarani-ness," as Nimuendajú would conjecture centuries later. These objects and habits were like the masks used in indigenous rituals to make a spirit present, or the jaguar skins worn by shamans to metamorphose into the feline (Fausto 2003, 2004). At issue was not representation in the dramatic sense but transformation. The intention was to appropriate the special capacities that priests seemed to possess—an idea that the missionaries reinforced by likewise attributing mystical powers to the habit that went beyond its institutional function.[20] Here we can take literally the saying that the habit makes the monk.

Native appropriation of the imagery and power associated with the missionaries rarely took the form of actual devouring, which was otherwise one of the classic Tupi-Guarani methods for capturing external identities and subjectivities. The Jesuits were not a favored target for anthropophagy. Much the opposite: eating them seems to have been avoided, this fate being reserved for native neophytes (see Montoya [1639] 1985:83, 165–166, 235). At the start of the seventeenth century, the martyrs of the Company of Jesus killed by the Guarani had their bodies dismembered and burned, insinuating it was necessary to reduce them to nothingness in order to avoid shamanic vengeance and deny them the posthumous immortality they had proclaimed in life. There is a notable similarity between the way in which the priests were killed and the way in which, in indigenous myths, a demiurge is put to an end[21]—the difference being that, in the latter narratives, the bodies of primordial shamans are indestructible, a sign of their power and their immortality.[22]

Montoya's account of the dialogue between priests and their killers prior to their execution suggests that immortality was one of the disputed issues, although native and European conceptions of it diverged ([1639] 1985:202–203, 234–235). Faced with his imminent death, the missionary would affirm that his captors could kill his body but not his soul, for this was immortal. Concerned as much with the soul as with the body (or maybe because they did not postulate this dichotomy), the Guarani proceeded to tear the victims apart before burning them. They separated their members, cut open the torso, and removed the heart. This was the fate of Father Cristóvão de Mendoza, whose heart, "which burned with love for them," was shot by "obstinate archers" who pronounced: "Let us see if your soul dies now" (Montoya [1639] 1985:234–235).

If God Were a Jaguar

We do not know if the priests' souls were immortal or not. But did their words and deeds leave their trace in the religious discourse of the Guarani? As we have seen, most ethnographers have answered this question with a simple denial, or have appealed instead to the dichotomy between essence and appearance by asserting that Guarani religion (culture) remained self-identical over time. Conceived as a set of firmly interiorized and zealously protected beliefs, this religious essence was identified as the core of Guarani existence and identity: an inner nucleus preventing them from dissolving into an amorphous state of syncretic indifference. But here we must pause to ask whether transformation has to be denied in order to affirm the identity of a culture and hence its distinctiveness. Is it really necessary to conflate the problem of individuation with the problem of the Same and the Identical? And finally, "what does it mean to remain the same through time?" (Ricoeur 2000:98). From a structural point of view, duration over space and time implies transformation, and the problem becomes one of recognizing the limit beyond which a structure ceases to be itself. From a phenomenological point of view, the question is, how can one become an other and still think of oneself as the same? Let us leave this last question pending and turn first to the problem of transformation at the structural level.

This question brings us to what I have dubbed "dejaguarization": the negation of cannibalism as the general condition of the cosmos and as a mechanism for social reproduction. Contemporary Guarani cosmology is characterized by an antithesis between people and substances that are otherwise closely associated among other Tupi-Guarani peoples, including the diametrical blood/tobacco and warrior/shaman oppositions. This disjunction is manifested in various areas of Guarani thought, beginning with their concept of the person, where we encounter a dichotomy between two animating principles that can be roughly identified as a "divine" soul and an "animal" soul.[23] The first is normally called *ayvu* or *ñe'ē* and glossed as "word-soul." Its origin is divine and it falls to the shaman to determine its exact source during the naming ceremony. This he undertakes through chants, quizzing the various divinities about the origin of the soul and its name (Nimuendajú 1987:30).

This preformed heavenly soul is followed by another, generally called *acyguá*, a word that, Nimuendajú tells us (1987:33), derives from *acy*, meaning "pain" and "lively, violent, vigorous." *Acyguá* is both what causes pain and something that is vigorous. The literature betrays a fair degree of ambiguity in characterizing this soul. Sometimes it appears as a regressive animal-soul responsible for sexual urges, violent impulses, and the desire to eat meat. At other times it is identified as the soul of a specific animal whose qualities determine the character of the person, such that the *acyguá* of a butterfly will not pose the same threat as that of a jaguar. Nonetheless, the jaguar seems to correspond to the ideal-type dominating the symbolism of the *acyguá*, and to become a jaguar is the fate of every human being who fails to behave in a properly religious and generous fashion.

This dichotomy between distinct animating principles is expressed in two extreme configurations of the Guarani male person: on the one hand, the man who allows himself to be dominated by the animal soul and the desire to eat raw meat, and whose fate is to become a jaguar; on the other, the ascetic who dedicates his life to achieving a state of maturity-perfection (*aguyje*) and whose fate is to become immortal. As Hélène Clastres has shown (1975:113–134), this dichotomy possesses both ethical and alimentary implications: the first is the selfish hunter, who eats his prey in the forest so as to avoid sharing its meat; the second is the generous hunter who hands over all of the game to his kin and abstains from eating meat.[24] Vegetarianism is an essential condition—along with dancing and chanting, accompanied by manioc beer drinking—for joining the gods. "Because of this way of life," the Apapocuva say of the great shamans, "their bodies became light: the *acyguá* . . . has been subjugated, while the *ayvucué* returned whence they came: during shamanic dances their souls left the earth and returned to *Ñandecy* [Our Mother], *Ñanderyquey* [Our Older Brother] or *Tupã*. At times, one found their dead bodies, at other times they ascended in their living body" (Nimuendajú 1987:62).

Tameness, generosity, avoidance of meat, participation in rituals—all these should guide the conduct of a Guarani man so that his word-soul controls his animal-soul. Finally, at death, these two components of the person are definitively sundered. The ex-word-soul (*ayvu-kwe*) returns to the sky after a journey littered with obstacles, while the *acyguá* becomes a dreaded specter, the *anguéry*. This kind of posthumous duality is also found in various Tupi-Guarani groups in Amazonia, but the Guarani case reveals a crucial permutation: the eclipsing of cannibalism as a central operator associated with death and shamanism.

For the sake of comparison, we can take the Araweté case as an example. Here we also find a verticalized cosmology and an emphasis on shamanic relations with divine beings. The Araweté postulate the existence of a single soul called *i*, naming both the vital principle and a person's shadow. At death, this soul splits into two components: a posthumous projection of the shadow (a specter known as *ta'owe*) and a spirit (also referred to as *i*), which ascends to the sky. This spirit is then devoured and made immortal by the gods, whose epithet is "eaters of the raw"—that is, jaguars. Araweté shamanism occupies precisely the mediatory space between humans and these jaguar-gods (Castro 1992:90, 201–214).

Similar ideas are found among the Asurini of the Tocantins with, however, an interesting twist. They postulate the existence of a single soul during life known as *iunga*, which is deposited in women by the divinity Mahira. As death approaches, it splits into a celestial aspect and a terrestrial one: the first joins Mahira in Tupana, while the second becomes a specter known as *asonga*, a cognate of the Tupinambá *anhanga*, a cannibal spirit associated with the dead. The spirit that ascends to *Tupana* ceases to be of any importance to the living, while the specter remains earthbound and becomes an auxiliary spirit for dreamers, playing a key role in the encounters between shamans and the celestial jaguar, the ultimate source of all shamanic power (Andrade 1992:217–249).

In both cases—and despite these permutations—the jaguar-operator is positively associated with shamanism. Indeed, this is the case among most Amazonian groups, where the most powerful shamans are those who have fearsome predators as their spirit familiars, eaters of blood and raw meat (see Fausto 2002c). But this articulation has been severed in the case of the contemporary Guarani: the shaman is an anticannibal and the spirits who supply him with chants are either the divine souls inhabiting the "country of the dead" or themselves divinities lacking predatory traits. While initiating the anthropologist Miguel Alberto Bartolomé, the Chripá shaman Avá Ñembiara asked him to remember the animal he had last killed. He then described the vegetarian diet the anthropologist was to follow thereafter and advised Bartolomé to allow himself to be guided by love alone (Bartolomé 1977:103). Cannibalism as a model for a person's relation with the Other seems to have been substituted by another relational form whose central category is love (*mborayhu*).[25]

The disjunction between shamanism and predation—as well as the exclusive association of the first with an immortal, divine soul—opened up the way for a transformation in the Guarani notion of the person and the emergence of the concept of the *acyguá*: the jaguar-part of the person, representing the Other of the gods and the human desire for immortality. Thus *acyguá* is what traps us in this existence of misfortunes (*teko achy*) and prevents us from reaching the Land-without-Evil (H. Clastres 1975:114). As constitutive alterity, the animal-soul must be denied and controlled through a vegetarian diet, a particular aesthetic (witness the productivity of the concepts of beauty and adornment), and through what various authors, perhaps under the influence of Ignatius Loyola, have termed *spiritual exercises*. The male ideal is not the warrior who captures an alien subjectivity by killing his victim, thereby acquiring knowledge and creativity. Rather it is the shaman who strips himself of his alterity in order to become divine in the image of a god who is not a jaguar.

Maize Religion

Let us return to corporeal immortality, a condition that elides the experience of death. As we have seen, this destiny is reserved for the great ascetics who achieve maturity-perfection (*aguyje*) rather than for the killer. A Chiripá shaman explains that "our ancestor left the living world without dying. . . . As a result, we must not eat meat when we dance; we can only eat the food that Ñanderu [Our Father] sent us" (Bartolomé 1977:87). But what is this food that Our Father left for us?

In the case of the Chiripá studied by Bartolomé, part of the answer can be located in a mythical episode inserted into the saga of the twins—a variation of a myth found throughout South America, but one that, to my knowledge, has no counterpart among the Amazonian Tupi-Guarani peoples. The Chiripá myth tells us that every time Kuarahy—the sun, son of Ñanderú Guazú (Our Great Father) and the older of the twins—created/raised an animal, the Tupi-Guarani demon Añang invented a way of hunting it. Here predation emerges not as an *a priori* given, nor as a condition set down by the demiurge, but as an artifice employed by his cannibalistic rival. The myth stresses the absolute disjunction between divinity and predation. The shamans establish relations with nonpredatory divine beings, whose pacificity contrasts with many of the spirit familiars of Amazonian shamans.

While meat should be avoided, other foods must be consumed. These include white maize, the core element of one of the main contemporary rituals: *avati-kyry*, frequently glossed as "baptism of the white maize" but literally meaning fermented maize drink. This is a beer festival, but one very different from those practiced by the sixteenth-century Tupi-Guarani in the run-up to their cannibal feasts, or those held by the Parakanã as a means of acquiring the speed and agility to track game. Rather than transform drinkers into agile and voracious predators, Guarani maize beer makes them light enough to approach the divinities.

The Guarani feast is held to baptize the new crop of maize and resembles various Amazonian rituals that aim to desubjectify animal prey to make them edible. Maria Kaiowá, a Guarani woman, explains: "we need to love [the maize], because it is a child, we need to sing for it to ripen . . . so that when we eat it . . . it doesn't make our bellies swell or make us angry. We have to pray so as to prevent it from killing us" (quoted in Chamorro 1995:91; see also Schaden 1954b:57).[26] Maize is for the Guarani—as game is for Amazonian peoples—a person, and it needs to be shamanized to become safe for daily consumption. Eating it without praying first, failing to treat it with due love, would be tantamount to a form of cannibalism.

Although use is made of crosses, altars (*mba'e marangatu*), kneeling and even mention in the songs of biblical figures like Noah, the crucial idea is that the ritual represents the baptism of Jakaira, the divinity who created the second earth after the flood—a function that other Guarani groups attribute to Kétxu Kíritu (Schaden 1969:109, 110, 125). The ritual's central theme is the renewal of the maize and takes place at the end of its period of ripening: this corresponds to the divinity's departure. The body of the maize remains behind to be eaten, while its "master" (*avati jára*) leaves for the heavens, from where he returns with each new crop.

If we imagine this cycle to contain an echo of Christ's saga and the maize to be his body, it is perhaps safe to assume blood corresponds to the "indigenous wine" or maize beer. Indeed this appears to be the function of the fermented beverage, which causes drunkenness but makes the drinker well-behaved and tame: precisely the opposite of Tupinambá beer and other substances—frequently associated with the blood of victims and menstrual blood—which in Amazonian rituals inspire a violent and creative energy in people (see Fausto 1999). For the Kaiowá, maize contains a vital force called *jasuka*, which guarantees its continual renewal. Paulito Kaiowá explains this concept: the beer "is the first juice of *Jasuka*. . . . *Jasuka* is for us what the motor is for whites, with the difference that *Jasuka* is natural rather than artificial. . . . it serves to give us life and renew us. Some people are so renewed by *Jasuka* that they no longer die, they remain new like a child who has just had his lip pierced" (Chamorro 1995:99).

The fermented drink also appears in another Kaiowá ritual, the boy's lip-piercing rite, also known as *mitā ka'u*, "the child's drunkenness." The purpose of the ritual is to "cook" the boys to prevent them from becoming violent and angry (Chamorro 1995:115). Those who fail to have their lips pierced stay raw and tend to become either predators or prey, since they "smell more pleasant to the jaguar" (Schaden 1954b:111). Prohibited to women, the ritual aims to induce a pacific disposition rather than instill a predatory potency in the young—the goal of Tupi-Guarani rites in the past, and of the initiation of boys among the Barasana (see C. Hugh-Jones 1979) or the *arutam* quest among the Jívaro. By donning ritual clothes and adornments, which likewise enter seclusion, the boys are said to "become true son[s] of Tupã," children "without evil" (*marane'y*) (Chamorro 1995:111, 118).

The "boy's drunkenness" ritual involves cooking and cooling the novices. The feast "makes them cold" (*emboro'y*) and prepares them to live according to the nonviolent, "cold way of being" (*teko ro'y*), a theme developed in the prayer chants:

My father cools our mutual body, bringing joy to the earth;
My father cools our mutual word, bringing joy to the earth;
My father cools anger, bringing joy to the earth.

(Chamorro 1995:115–116).[27]

Perhaps this idea of "cooling" was already present in the universe of the seventeenth-century reductions, when Montoya compiled his *Vocabulario y tesoro de la lengua guarani*, illustrating the entry for the word *roi*, "cold," with the expressions "Roiçã hápe ahaihú Tũpã" (I coolly love God) and "Cheracubo cũe Tũpã raihûbari iroi imã" (I cool myself in God's love).

The Work of Forgetting

Let us now turn to my second question, concerning the problem of transformation and temporality, which I expressed in phenomenological terms as follows: How can one be different and yet continue to think of oneself as the same? Or, to adapt this question to our present topic: How did the Guarani make theirs a religious discourse that bears the marks of an alien discourse? How can they truly be the "sons of the Cross of the Good Word"?

The religious universe of the Guarani is filled with symbols, ritual routines, and figures derived from Catholicism. Various authors, Schaden in particular, have dedicated themselves to identifying these elements. The cosmic sequence of divinities commences with a supreme deity called Our Father (Ñanderu) or

Our Master (Ñandejara) who gives birth to himself in the primordial darkness, adorned with a crown of flowers from which emerges the primogenital bird, the hummingbird, who later reappears as the messenger of the gods (Cadogan 1959:14; P. Clastres 1974:18; Bartolomé 1977:105). In the Apapocuva version, Ñanderuvuçu emerges amid the darkness and finds himself alone save for his antithesis, the Eternal Bats, cannibal beings who fight endlessly among themselves. In his chest he carries the sun (Nimuendajú 1987:143), the resplendent heart that permeates Guarani religious imagery and can probably be traced back to the cult of the Sacred Heart.[28] The Chiripá say that when someone reaches the state of perfection (*aguyjê*), when he is dry and incorruptible (*kandire*), "flames [emerge] from his chest as evidence that his heart is illuminated by divine wisdom" (Bartolomé 1977:84–85). This is the same wisdom that enabled Ñamandu Ru Eté to produce the light of the flame out of himself and create the foundations of both human language (*ayvu rapyta*) and love (*mborayú rapyta*) (Cadogan 1959:19–20).

Turning to the saga of the twins that, according to Cadogan, inaugurates the second part of the "religious annals" of the Mbyá of the Guairá, we find that the main protagonist is Kuarahy, the Sun, the older brother of the Moon. Among the Mbyá of other regions, Kuarahy is conflated with Kétxu Kíritu and with Ketxuíta, personae frequently identified with each other.[29] The Mbyá of Chapecó say that after the first earth was destroyed by the flood, Kétxu Kíritu re-created the world (Schaden 1964:109, 123)—a world once again about to end since the cross holding it up will soon give way. The gods will then come with "*ponchito, chiripá* and *tembetá* of destroying fire . . . [and] all the earth will burn" (Chamorro 1995:63). There will be a new flood. Then the gods will change their fiery clothes for cold clothes (*ro'y*) and prepare a new earth, perfect and eternal, "that nothing petty could ever change" (P. Clastres 1974:140).

The version of the twins saga found among the Guairá Mbyá reveals an important transformation. This Pan-American myth recounts the adventures of two brothers—sons of the same mother but different fathers. Among the Tupi-Guarani, the elder brother is the son of the demiurge Maíra and represents shamanism and immortality, while the younger is the son of Opossum, symbol of death and decay. In the First Beautiful Words, however, the Sun creates the Moon from himself after the jaguars kill his mother. He makes a companion, whom he calls brother, but denies they are twins since they did not share the same uterus.[30] Perhaps we can extract a more general observation here, bearing in mind that, according to Lévi-Strauss, the myth of the twins deals with the impossibility of a perfect identity and expresses the "opening toward the Other" (1991:16) typical of Amerindian cosmologies. Perhaps the Guarani have been drifting toward this identity-based temptation, this "self-folding" (*pli sur soi-même*) mentioned by

Pierre Clastres. If so, wasn't he right, except for the fact that the Beautiful Words were not "sheltered from all stain"?

Despite all the marks of an alien discourse and these multiple signs of trans-formation, the Guarani were not led to think of themselves as others, for they made this alterity entirely their own. This meant forgetting the process through which they appropriated and transformed an alterity that simultaneously trans-formed them. But how do we define this other form of forgetting? Is it simply a failure to remember typical of a society without history and without writing—an unfortunate pathos that blocks any conscious recognition of the fact that human activity is a making that unfolds over time? Or are we faced with an active-pas-sive phenomenon that implies a specific mechanism for producing a sociocultural world and a collective memory?

Analyzing a similar process among the Yanesha, Santos-Granero in this volume suggests that such a mechanism results from a combination of mimesis and for-getting, which works to revert or neutralize relational asymmetries by appropriat-ing the power of the other as if this had always been one's own. Extending this idea, perhaps we can see in this process, as Severi (2000) suggests, a paradoxical mode of social memory, one capable of simultaneously obliterating and record-ing a traumatic history in an imagetic and ritual form. This may explain the sadness that the Guarani say pervades maize baptism, an emotional tone difficult to understand within the more general context of Amazonian rituals, frequently translated by Amerindians themselves as fiestas.[31]

Appropriation and forgetting haunted the sixteenth-century Jesuits. For them, the difficulty in converting the Tupi-Guarani lay in the fact that their memory and will were incapable of retaining God's word. They avidly consumed the Good News, only to forget everything soon afterward. As Viveiros de Castro suggests, "the problem is thus one of determining the meaning of this blend of open-ness and stubbornness, docility and inconstancy, enthusiasm and indifference with which the Tupinambá received the Good News—one of understanding the meaning of this "weak memory" and "defective will" of the Indians, comprehend-ing this modality of believing without faith, fathoming the object of this obscure desire of being the Other, but in their own terms" (1993:371).

While this blend was a structural feature of the relationship between Tupi-Guarani peoples and whites, the historical situation also favored such mixture. Epidemics, forced migrations, the collapse of social networks, *mestizaje*, and new interethnic contexts in which people of different origins were brought together—all of these factors disrupted the traditional networks of cultural transmission, while simultaneously expanding the possibility of cultural reinventions. The very discontinuity of the colonial process—which alternately advanced into indigenous territories and withdrew from them, either attracting or repulsing indigenous populations, in response to economic cycles and political variations—strengthened the work of forgetting.[32] This dynamic flow and counterflow allowed native societies a degree of autonomy in reelaborating and re-creating contents produced and circulated during periods or within regions of denser interethnic interaction (see S. Hugh-Jones 1996:52–53, for example). Rarely documented, these facts have tended to remain overlooked. Ethnohistory has focused its attention on those moments when the world system expanded and on those areas were there was a continuous interaction between whites and Amerindians. This creates the false impression that indigenous history is history *only within this relationship* and that only two ways of conceiving this history therefore exist: either a gradual and inexorable imposition of an external dominant model (in which case indigenous history is simply the history produced by others), or the repetition of the Same against the alterity of history (in which case indigenous history is merely an affirmation of the identical, irrespective of the passage of time).

Conclusion

In order to found a new ethic of love (*mborayhu*)—which was probably built on native concepts of generosity and reciprocity, and nurtured by the "love thy neighbor" ethic of the Christian message—the Guarani concealed the footprints of the jaguar. They either turned the jaguar into pure negativity or shrouded it in silence. Although the shaman-ascetic's zoomorphic stool (*apyka*) frequently represents the feline, the head is nonetheless absent, for "one should neither see nor recognize the jaguar, nor even say its name" (H. Clastres 1975:133).

Indigenous people living in the missions were taught to imitate the pathos of Christ (and the priests) while simultaneously refraining from any attempt to appropriate the agency of the jaguar. As Guillermo Wilde notes, the Jesuits' annual reports (*cartas anuas*) reveal a recurrent association between "forest tigers," sorcerers, and the devil. For the Jesuits, this was all the same battle. God-made-as-man subverted the predatory logic of indigenous ontologies (Castro 1993; Fausto 2001): the divine pole became the pole of passive prey, a role played out in each act of communion.[33] Moving from the enemy eaten publicly in the central plaza to the divinity devoured in the mass involved a profound shift, unleashing a series of transformations. This explains the notable absence of blood in Guarani rituals and cosmologies, a symbol as central to indigenous cultures as it is to Christianity. The blood of Jesus—token of a sacrifice that the missionaries yearned to emulate through martyrdom—could not be appropriated. The ethic of tameness and ascetic shamanism implied a new combination of three basic substances: blood, beer, and tobacco. The Guarani assimilated the last two and negated the first. It is no accident that Jakaira, the owner of the maize used to make beer, is also the creator of tobacco, a substance meant to protect humans from misfortune.

This process of transformation was neither random nor amorphous, as might be imagined. Although unfolding in a context of sociodemographic crisis, these appropriations and reappropriations, interpretations and reinterpretations, did not just evolve into an array of disparate cosmologies. Much the opposite: today we can speak of a contemporary Guarani cosmology and recognize versions of one and the same structure through its variations. We can also identify various Christian motifs that have been particularly productive, like the concept of love. As Montoya would say, the missionaries conquered the Amerindians, "with love and gifts" ([1639] 1985:208)—accompanied, of course, by the armed interference of the Spaniards and converted Amerindians.[34] But we should not overlook the love of the devoted missionary who, as he is executed, asks of his killers: "sons, why do you kill me?" (200). The imperative of love had a longer-lasting impact on Guarani thought than the threat of punishment and hell, a response similarly found among the Yanesha described by Santos-Granero (1991 and this volume).

This does not imply the disappearance of all figures of devoration, but most likely the channeling of cannibalism into magical forms of aggression and sorcery. A "religion of love" may be accompanied by extreme levels of violence, as we can see in the Yanesha complex of child sorcery accusations and executions (Santos-Granero 2002), or in the eruption of factional conflicts among the Kaiowá-Ñandeva at the beginning of the twentieth century, which led to the dissolution of political unities and the death of many people accused of witchcraft (Mura, 2006).

Be that as it may, I would argue that, in the Guarani case at least, we observe a replacement of familiarizing predation as the hegemonic scheme of relating with others by love as the basis of power and religion. And here we can see a real shift in point of view: persons and collectivities are no longer perceived to be constituted through an identification with the predator position but, on the contrary, with the position of familiarized prey. Such perspectival inversion may serve as a form of resistance in contexts of great asymmetry of power, as Rival (1998, 2002) and Bonilla (2005) have similarly argued.[35]

But what breach allowed the Christian message of universal love, peace, and brotherhood among human beings to penetrate into the indigenous lived world? It appears to have resonated precisely where predation is projected onto social relations among kin—where an ethic of reciprocity and generosity is continually assailed by cannibalism as an essential mechanism for social reproduction. The question is: How can predation of the outside be prevented from becoming the measure for relationships on the inside? How can one be a jaguar without eating one's own kin? Wherever this paradox was acutely posed, we can observe a series of transformations in the notion of the person, in the diet, and in ritual practices. These did not always result from Christian influence or even from the presence of Europeans—at least not directly. In the case of the upper Xingu, for example, this appears to be the product of an Arawak cultural base and a historical neces- sity to absorb peoples with distinct linguistic and ethnic origins in the wake of the territorial pressure caused by the European Conquest (see Heckenberger 2001, 2005; Franchetto and Heckenberger 2001; Fausto et al., forthcoming). In the case of the upper Rio Negro, on the other hand, the diminution in the space of predation involves a long history of contact with colonial agents followed by periods of isolation, likewise in a context of accommodation between different ethnic groups (S. Hugh-Jones 1994, 1996:145; Wright 1998).

Although I shall have to develop these points another time, I wish to conclude with an observation concerning what Stephen Hugh-Jones (1994) has called "dual shamanism"—that is, the distinction between two types of religious specialists, who occupy complementary poles of Amazonian shamanism. The disjunction I discussed in relation to the Guarani has been emerging as a constitutive element of the shamanism of upper Rio Negro peoples from at least the nineteenth cen- tury, actualized in the figures of the *payé* (the jaguar-shaman: morally ambigu- ous, concerned with relations with the outside, and associated with hunting and warfare) and the *~kubu* (the divinity-shaman: pacific and generous, concerned with relations with the ancestors, and associated with collective rites of passage and the baptism of first fruits).

In contrast to the Guarani case, this dichotomy implies the complementarity of shamanic functions rather than the negation of one of the poles. Nonetheless, we can observe the progressive decline of the jaguar-shaman in the upper Rio Negro, after a flourishing during the messianic movements that spread through- out the region from 1857 onward. According to Hugh-Jones, the leaders of these movements, the *"pajés* of the cross," were people who had some contact with national society and who blended jaguar-shamanism with Christian elements. Following the decline in prophetism and the effective installation of new Catholic missions in the region by the beginning of the twentieth century, we witness a growing rejection of jaguar-shamans, whose position was associated with both warfare and hunting (1996:145).

The sixteenth- and seventeenth-century Guarani shamans who led large or small revolts against the colonial system were, evidence suggests, warriors and jag- uars too: they sang and danced, drank beer, prophesied, favored hunting and war- fare, and may well have continued to eat human flesh. Perhaps like the Santidades of the sixteenth century, they also continued to wish that the invading Europeans could be converted into game so they could eat them (Monteiro 1999:1012). All of them were ultimately defeated through violent repression, missionary activity, epidemics, internal rivalry, or growing disbelief. The contemporary shamans, perhaps "closed off from *this* praxis," founded their action and authority upon another source, love (*mborayhu*), and another practice, asceticism. As a result, today they are able to reprimand whites for not possessing what the shamans were once told they lacked: "if this world is going badly and heading toward destruction," said *ñanderu* Fernando Taper to the anthropologist Egon Schaden (1969:118), "it is because civilized people are not very religious."

Acknowledgments

This article was written during my stay at the Laboratoire d'Anthropologie Sociale (CNRS/Collège de France). I would like to thank Philippe Descola for the invitation and the Coordenação de Aperfeiçoamento de Pessoal de Ensino Superior for making my stay in Paris possible. Versions of the paper were presented at the École Pratique des Hautes Études, the Maison des Sciences de l'Homme, the Laboratoire d'Anthropologie Sociale, the Centre André-Georges Haudricourt, the Instituto de Filosofia e Ciências Sociais (UFRJ), and the University of Chicago. A final version was first published in 2005 in *Mana: Estudos de Antropologia Social* 11(2), in Portuguese. I have deeply benefited from the questions and criticisms of many people on these occasions, and cannot do justice to them all. Allow me to acknowledge, in the name of all the others, Patrick Menget, Guillaume Boccara, Anne-Christine Taylor, Carlo Severi, and Manuela Carneiro da Cunha. I would also like to thank John Manuel Monteiro and Guillermo Wilde for commenting on the manuscript, as well as Fábio Mura and Olivier Allard for helping me with ideas and books. Luiz Costa translated the first version of this article into English, and David Rodgers revised/translated this final version.

Notes

1. Today the Guarani number approximately 125,000 people. They are divided into four major blocks: the Kaiowá or Paï-Taviterã, with about 30,000 individuals living in Brazil and Paraguay; the Mbyá, with about 20,000 distributed along the Brazilian coast, in Paraguay, and in Argentina; the Chiripá or Ñandeva, whose 15,000 people live in Brazil and Paraguay; and finally the Chiriguano, most of whose population of 60,000 live in Bolivia (Assis and Garlet 2004). I do not deal with the Chiriguano case in this essay, and hardly take into consideration the internal differences among the Guarani peoples. I

hope to overcome these shortcomings in a future work. The opening quote is taken from Chamorro 1995:35; I changed the translation of *ara* from "universe" to "time."

2. The idea that the Guarani were more susceptible to catechism than the Tupi began to circulate among the Jesuits in Brazil around the 1550s, especially in São Paulo where the border zone between these two large Tupi-Guarani blocks was located (Monteiro 1992:487). As Eduardo Viveiros de Castro suggests (1993:419), there was a large degree of idealization in this judgment.

3. A common mistake is to take the ethnological literature relating to the Guarani as a description of the Guarani pre-Conquest and, therefore, as a ground zero providing the basis for measuring post-Conquest transformations. This ethnographic projection onto the historical past creates a vicious circle in which later facts end up explaining earlier facts; see, for example, Bailey's characterization of pre-mission Guarani (1999:148–150) as well as Ganson's portrayal of Guarani culture (2003:12–24). Another common error is to collapse the spatial and temporal, as when a Tupi migration begun on the coast of Pernambuco in the mid-sixteenth century is used as evidence of the originary nature of the search for the Land-without-Evil by the Guarani, which was observed only from the nineteenth century onward.

4. Hence, I fail to distinguish with due care the different ethnographical and historical situations involving the distinct Guarani groups. Furthermore, I limit myself to the hegemonic view of shamans and religion, though I suspect that there is much more to be said about contemporary shamanism in relation to accusations of sorcery and magical violence; see, for instance, Mura, 2006, on the Kaiowá and Lowrey 2003 on the Guarani-speaking Izoceño of Bolivia.

5. The system assigned the entire Guarani population living within a 250-kilometer radius of Asunción to some three hundred Spaniards, called *encomenderos*, who had the right to demand services from them (Necker 1979:31).

6. On Guarani resistance, see, among others, Susnik 1965:215–228; 1980:164–172; Necker 1979; Melià 1986:31–41; Rípodas Ardanaz 1987; Roulet 1993.

7. *Reducción* (henceforth "reduction") was the term applied to designate the mission's physical location and its function, since the missionaries were said to "reduce" the Indians to "civil and political life" (Montoya [1639] 1985:34). At the start of the seventeenth century, new legislation regulating the relations between natives and non-natives helped strengthen the power of the religious orders and restrict the activity of the *encomenderos*. Of particular importance are the Ordinances of Alfaro, published in 1611, which ended up codifying these relations for much of the colonial period (see Necker 1979:118 et passim).

8. In the eighteenth century, large oscillations occurred between 1715 and 1720, and between 1735 and 1740, as well as after the Madrid Treaty (1750) and the so-called Guarani war (1754–56) (Ganson 2003:108–112).

9. Thirty years after their expulsion, the population of the thirty Jesuit missions in the Paraná-Paraguay basin, which amounted to almost 90,000 people in 1768, had collapsed

to half that number. This depopulation resulted from the combined effect of epidemics and migrations. Many Guarani headed to the towns, while some found work in the countryside. They temporarily or definitively entered the local economy as unskilled workers, cowboys, artisans, bakers, and the like (Ganson 2003:125–136). Others—about whom we know very little—returned to the forest, becoming *monteses* once more. For a description of the social transformations in the wake of the expulsion of the Jesuits, see Wilde 2003a, chap. 5.

10. This is how Nimuendajú explains his translation: ". . . Land Without Evil, *Yvy marãey*. *Mará* is a word no longer used in the Apapocúva dialect; in ancient Guarani it means 'disease,' 'evil,' 'slander,' 'mourning-sadness,' etc. *Yvy* means 'land,' and *ey* is the negation 'without'" (1987:38). Meliá (1986:106) suggests that the meaning of *yvy maraney* in the seventeenth century was the one given by Montoya (1876), "intact land," and that it acquired a religious connotation only in the nineteenth century when the migrations studied by Nimuendajú took place (Meliá 1990:45; see also Noelli 1999 and Pompa 2000). It is also important to note that the term *maraney* was an extremely productive concept in the missions, designating the virginity of Ñandesy (Our Mother), the chastity of priests, purity, and the absence of sin. In Parakaná we find the cognate -*marony'ym*, which appears in warfare narratives and means "not injured," "untouched."

11. Some Mbyá groups identified this place as the Land of the Ketxuíta, or Ketxu Kíritu (Schaden 1969:125). Schaden relates the tragicomic episode involving the Mbyá of the coast of São Paulo who, in the 1940s, met with Brazil's president of the republic "in the hope of obtaining tickets to travel by sea to Portugal, which they believed to be closer to paradise" (1951b:178). In vain. Instead they were transferred to the village of Pancas, which, ironically enough, lay in the state of Espírito Santo (Holy Spirit).

12. This is due to various factors, some of them internal to anthropology, others external. In the 1940s and 1950s, we can observe—at least in Brazil—higher value being attributed to the notions of tradition and cultural preservation, which led to important changes in the indigenist policies of the Brazilian state.

13. An analysis of Pierre Clastres' hypotheses, which was based on scarce historical and archaeological evidence, lies beyond my present scope.

14. It would be interesting to analyze how this ideal of resistance, identity, and spirituality approximated the views of the new Christian missionary tradition (post–Vatican II) to the ethnology of Guarani peoples. This tradition took the Guarani to be a privileged expression of *human* religiosity (if we take seriously the Christian theory of the divine soul, religiosity is necessarily internal to every human being and anterior to the Gospel). The contradiction inherent in this tolerant posture is that it cannot deny the unique and true character of the Christian Revelation without also denying the institution itself. Another kind of "tolerant" posture has recently appeared in evangelical missionary work. The Fale network of evangelical organizations nowadays campaigns in favor of the "religious freedom of indigenous peoples" as part of the "right to free choice" (see www.fale.org.br). In one of its pamphlets we can read, alongside phrases by indigenous pastors, a declaration by

Marcolino da Silva, identified as a "Guarani shaman": "I replied [to a pastor who appeared in my village]: No, I'm sorry. You can take your Bible and your car and leave. . . . I have my own religion . . . and I cannot swap my religion for another one." *Plus ça change, plus c'est la même chose*: the Guarani continue to be the only Indians in the South American lowlands to whom Christian churches (and some ethnologists) like to attribute a true religion.

15. See, however, Anne-Christine Taylor's analysis in this volume of the two different regimes of relating to the outside found among the Jivaro.

16. It is important to note the presence of mestizos among the followers of Oberá. Mestizos and Amerindians with experience in the reductions had a noteworthy participation in various "messianic" movements, suggesting that they occupied an important mediatory position in the circulation and digestion of new ideas (see Hugh-Jones 1996:53). Examples include the figure of Juan Santos Atahuallpa, who commanded the uprising of the pre-Andean Arawakan groups in the eighteenth century (Santos-Granero 1993), and Venancio Cristo and his successors who made themselves into prophets among the Baniwa in the nineteenth century (Wright and Hill 1986). See also Vainfa's analysis (1995) of the Santidade do Jaguaripe, which emerged in the Recôncavo of Bahia in the 1580s, and whose imagery appears to have been gestated in the Jesuit missions.

17. This is a phenomenon observable throughout the New World, since the convergence between the functions of missionaries and of shamans inevitably led to rivalry. As Gruzinski (1974) has pointed out, whenever a priest sought to show his superiority over the shaman as a religious specialist, he admitted to confronting him in his own field and, therefore, facilitated his incorporation into the native cosmology. The Jesuits, in particular, knew how to make use of this convergence, in both South America (Haubert 1966; Fausto 1992; Castro 1993) and North America (Griffiths 1999:15–18; Steckley 1992).

18. The Amerindians did not show themselves to be resistant to matters of faith, but rather to matters of custom. In the seventeenth century the greatest impediment to conversion, at least in the eyes of Montoya, was no longer anthropophagy but polygamy, particularly that of "chiefs." The Spanish Crown recognized the chiefs' special status, giving them titles and the staff of office, exempting them from obligatory services to the Crown and the *encomenderos*, and entrusting them with the organization of the *encomienda* system at the local level (see Ganson 2003:57–68 on the *cabildo* system). In the reductions, frequently excluded from the network of *encomiendas*, the priests conquered local leaders by means of "gifts of little value" (Montoya [1639] 1985:197), but demanded that they take only one woman in legitimate matrimony. It was not rare for the chiefs to rebel and mobilize not only troops but also shamans (actually, many caciques were also shamans).

19. As Wilde points out, this appropriation had a paradoxical effect in the eighteenth-century missionary context, when it served as a "potent means of symbolic absorption into the dominant society" in conditions of subordination (2003b:218). Here Wilde is referring to the staffs and other insignia of office conferred on the indigenous *cabildantes* by the Jesuit priests. It is difficult to ascertain whether symbols of power existed among the Gua-

rani before the European Conquest. We know for sure, though, that the "staffs of power" had a considerable impact on Guarani religion, appearing for example at the beginning of the Beautiful Words, where Ñanderu is said to carry the "insignia rods" (*ywyra'i*) in his hands (Cadógan 1959:14). The *chiru* (crosses and insignia rods) of the contemporary Kaiowá can be traced back to the same context. The assistants of current Kaiowá shamans, who must protect the *chiru*, are called *ywyra'ija*, the "rod owners," just like those who occupied the position of bailiff in the missions (Mura 2004; Wilde 2003b:220).

20. In his *Crónica Franciscana de las Provincias de Perú*, Diego de Córdova Salinas tells of a Spaniard who, on seeing his expedition surrounded by fire on the pampas, made use of Father Bolaños's robe to calm the flames, leading the fire to recognize "la virtud que Dios había puesto en él y, prestando a su poder obediencia, se apagó todo, dejando a los circunstantes tan maravillados como tiernos, de ver el respeto que el fuego tuvo al manto" ([1651] *apud* Necker 1979:49).

21. In a Guarani version of the saga of the twins, for example, the grandmother-jaguar tries in vain to roast them but is incapable of destroying their bodies, and ends up raising them as pets (Cadogan 1959:73–74). Likewise, in the Gê myth of Auké, the protagonist becomes white after being incinerated by his maternal uncle, who had already tried to kill him many times because of his constant metamorphoses (Nimuendajú 1946:245–246).

22. Montoya appears to believe that something similar occurred to the bodies of the martyrs of the Church (even though they died): when the Guarani killed Fathers Afonso and Roque, "so as to eliminate all traces of the martyrs, they made a great fire, in which they threw the two bodies and the heart of Father Roque. This, however, remained whole, the fire of charity winning over the flames which burned from the material log, the purity of that heart remaining as gold purified in the fire, that heart which is today kept in Rome with the same arrow that pierced it" (Montoya [1639] 1985:203). Father Roque's bones were kept at the Concepción Mission. On the eve of the Guarani War, which followed the Treaty of Madrid (1750), a group of seventy armed Indians headed there in order to ask for his protection (Ganson 2003:95). On the importance of Father Roque as a Guarani symbol of the alliance between Jesuits and the Indians in the reductions, see Wilde 2003b:98–99.

23. Important variations exist among the various Guarani subgroups. Here I use the Mbyá data, recorded by Nimuendajú at the start of the twentieth century.

24. With the exception of the meat of the white-lipped peccary, an animal designated as "the fine pet" of the divinities (see H. Clastres 1975:127; Ladeira 1992; Larricq 1993).

25. I lack the data to carry out an in-depth analysis of this category among the contemporary Guarani. I am unaware of any dense phenomenological description of this affect in the literature. Montoya used the term in the seventeenth century to translate the Christian notion of the loving God and God's love into Guarani. Cadogan translates it in the Beautiful Words as "love (those near to you)." Pierre Clastres corrects him, suggesting that the original meaning of *mborayhu* was "tribal solidarity" (1974:27). Hélène Clastres prefers "reciprocity" (1975:116). It would be interesting to look for evidence of the appro-

priation/transformation of the concept of love in the historical records, focusing not only on the repressive and pedagogical practices of missionaries but also on the ambivalences and anxieties lived by indigenous peoples. Such experiences may be inscribed in bas-relief in the less edifying chronicles and the description of particular cases.

26. The prayer is a dance-chant performed under the auspices of a shaman, a *ñanderu*. It describes the cyclical process of maize renewal, which ripens but never dies, adorns itself with "liturgical" clothes and feathers, and makes itself into seed again (Chamorro 1995:79–81).

27. "Che ru ojoeté emboro'y embohory ywy / Che ru oñoñe'ë emboro'y emborohy ywy / Che ru piraguái emboro'y embohory ywy." I have altered the translation slightly. On cooling and warming in the context of producing the rod-insignias (*chiru*), see Mura 2004.

28. The cult of the Sacred Heart—whose iconography typically involves depiction of the organ on the chest or in the hands of Jesus, from where it emits rays of light in all directions—dates from the end of the seventeenth century, following Jesus's appearances to Saint Maria Margarita Alacoque. The Sacred Heart is strongly associated with the Catholic notion of love. In his appearances, Jesus told the future saint: "This is the Heart which so loved man; which spared nothing of itself in showing them its love until it was finally expended and consumed. And in recognition I receive from most of them nothing but ingratitude through the contempt, irreverence, sacrilege, and coldness that they have for me in this Sacrament of love" (*Catolicismo*, July 2004. www.catolicismo.com.br). We know that the iconography of the Sacred Heart was adopted by Jesuits in the eighteenth century; the Chapel of the Sacred Heart in the church of Saint Ignatius in Rome dates from this period. We also know that nine hundred engravings of Jesus's heart were sent to Argentina and Paraguay in 1744 in a single ship (Bailey 1999:164).

29. Other versions suggest that the Ketxuíta was not a god, but a Guarani from Paraguay who had reached a state of maturity-perfection (Schaden 1969:109).

30. One of Cadogan's informants explained this absence of twinness in the myth by saying that the birth of twins is a divine punishment on the couple: "the young Indian who revealed the belief told me that it would be a great inconsistency for the Mbyá to worship twin gods, if they themselves believed twins to be an incarnation of the devil and did away with them at birth" (Cadogan 1959:70–71).

31. A Guarani man said to Chamorro, "Those who are not Kaiowá think that the *jerosy* is all feasting and happiness, but the *jerosy* is pure sadness!" (1995:94).

32. A two-sided forgetting, by the way, since it also enabled whites (including anthropologists) to "rediscover" populations who very often had already been under missionary influence, traded with the colonizers or resisted them centuries earlier. The rubber boom that swept Amazonia after the 1860s was one of these key moments of "rediscoveries," and left us with many of the ethnic designations that today make up the ethnographic map of the region.

33. I thank Wilde for personal communication about the *cartas anuas*. On the use of

images of Christ and martyrs in the South American Jesuit missions as a way of "inciting *pathos,*" see Bailey 1999:147; 167–169. On the active-passive makeup of relations and persons in Amerindian ontologies, see Fausto 2002c.

34. Epidemics also played an important role here. Missionaries exploited the idea of divine punishment, associating it with the diseases (Montoya [1639] 1985:208). Since those born and raised in the reductions were probably less susceptible to Western diseases than the unreduced population, it is possible that epidemics claimed more victims among resistant souls: "The other delinquents, the pestilence exiled from this life. . . . It was very visible that the pestilence claimed victims only among them, for it forgot the remaining populations, who kept their health and life" (191).

35. Bonilla shows how the Paumari of Western Amazonia tried to control nonindigenous predation by identifying themselves as "familiarized prey," that is, as clients adopted by "good patrons."

References

Andrade, Lucia M. M. de 1992. "O corpo e os cosmos: Relações de gênero e o sobrenatural entre os Asurini do Tocantins." Master's thesis, Universidade de São Paulo.

Assis, Valéria de, and Ivori J. Garlet. 2004. "Análise sobre as populações guarani contemporâneas: Demografia, espacialidade e questões fundiárias." *Revista das Índias* 64(230):35–54.

Bailey, Gauvin Alexander. 1999. *Art on the Jesuit missions in Asia and Latin America, 1542–1773.* Toronto: University of Toronto Press.

Bartolomé, Miguel Alberto. 1977. *Orekuera royhendu (lo que escuchamos en sueños): Shamanismo y religión entre los Ava-Katú-Eté del Paraguay.* Mexico: Instituto Indigenista Interamericano.

Bonilla, Oiara. 2005. "O bom patrão e o inimigo voraz: Predação e comércio na cosmologia paumari." *Mana: Estudos de Antropologia Social* 11(1):41–66.

Cadogan, León. 1959. *Ayvu rapyta: Textos míticos de los Mbyá-Guarani del Guairá.* São Paulo: Universidade de São Paulo.

Castro, Eduardo Viveiros de. 1992. *From the Enemy's Point of View: Humanity and Divinity in an Amazonian Society.* Translated by Catherine V. Howard. Chicago: University of Chicago Press.

———. 1993. "Le Marbre et le myrte: De l'inconstance de l'âme sauvage." In *Mémoire de la Tradition,* edited by Aurore Becquelin et Antoinette Molinié, 365–431. Nanterre: Société d'Ethnologie.

Chamorro, Graciela. 1995. *Kurusu ñe'ēngatu: Palabras que la historia no podría olvidar.* Asunción: Centro de Estudios Antropológicos, Universidad Católica; São Leopoldo: IEPG/COMIN.

Clastres, Hélène. 1975. *La Terre sans mal: Le Prophétisme Tupi-Guarani.* Paris: Seuil.

Clastres, Pierre. 1974. *Le Grand Parler: Mythes et chants sacrés des Indiens Guarani.* Paris: Seuil.

Cunha, Manuela Carneiro da, ed. 1992. *História dos índios no Brasil.* São Paulo: FAPESP, Companhia das Letras.

Dobrizhoffer, Martin. [1784] 1970. *An Account of the Abipones, an Equestrian People of Paraguay.* Reprint of 1822 translation from the Latin. 3 vols. in 1. New York: Johnson Reprint.

Edelweiss, Frederico G. 1947. *Tupís e Guaranís: Estudo de etnonímia e linguística.* Bahia: Museu da Bahia.

————. 1969. *Estudos tupi e tupi-guaranis: Confrontos e revisões.* Rio de Janeiro: Livraria Brasiliana.

Fausto, Carlos. 1992. "Fragmentos de história e cultura tupinambá: Da etnologia como instrumento crítico de conhecimento etno-histórico." In Cunha, *História dos índios no Brasil,* 381–396.

————. 1999. "Of Enemies and Pets: Warfare and Shamanism in Amazonia." *American Ethnologist* 26(4):933–956.

————. 2001. *Inimigos fiéis: História, guerra e xamanismo na Amazônia.* São Paulo: EdUSP.

————. 2002a. "Faire le mythe: Histoire, récit et transformation en Amazonie." *Journal de la Société des Américanistes* 88:69–90.

————. 2002b. "The Bones Affair: Knowledge Practices in Contact Situations Seen from an Amazonian Case." *Journal of the Royal Anthropological Institute* 8(4):669–690.

————. 2002c. "Banquete de gente: Comensalidade e canibalismo na Amazônia." *Mana: Estudos de Antropologia Social* 8(2):7–44.

————. 2003. "Masks, Trophies, and Spirits: Making Invisible Relations Visible." Paper presented at the 51st International Congress of Americanists, Santiago de Chile.

————. 2004. "A Blend of Blood and Tobacco: Shamans and Jaguars among the Parakanã of Eastern Amazonia." In *In Darkness and Secrecy: The Anthropology of Assault Sorcery and Witchcraft in Amazonia,* edited by Neil L. Whitehead and Robin Wright, 157–178. Durham, North Carolina: Duke University Press.

Fausto, Carlos, Bruna Franchetto, and Michael J. Heckenberger. Forthcoming. "Ritual Language and Historical Reconstruction: Towards a Linguistic, Ethnographical, and Archaeological Account of Upper Xingu Society." In *A World of Many Voices: Lessons from Documented Endangered Languages,* edited by Adrienne Dwyer, David Harrison, and David Rood. Amsterdam: John Benjamins.

Franchetto, Bruna, and Michael Heckenberger, eds. 2001. *Os povos do Alto Xingu: História e cultura.* Rio de Janeiro: EdUFRJ.

Greer, Allan. 2003. "Conversion and Identity: Iroquois Christianity in Seventeenth-Century New France." In *Conversion: Old Worlds and New,* edited by Kenneth

Mills and Anthony Grafton, 175–198. Rochester, New York: University of Rochester Press.

Griffiths, Nicholas. 1999. Introduction to *Spiritual Encounters: Interactions Between Christianity and Native Religions in Colonial America*, edited by Nicholas Griffiths and Fernando Cervantes, 1–42. Lincoln: University of Nebraska Press.

Gruzinski, Serge. 1974. "Délires et visions chez les Indiens de Méxique." *Temps Modernes* 86:445–480.

Haubert, Maxime. 1966. "L'Oeuvre missionaire des Jésuites au Paraguay, 1585–1768: Genèse d'un 'paradis.'" Third-cycle thesis, Ecole Pratique des Hautes Etudes, Paris.

Heckenberger, Michael J. 2001. "Estrutura, história e transformação: A cultura xinguana na *longue durée*, 1000–2000 d.C." In Franchetto and Heckenberger, *Os povos do Alto Xingu*, 21–62.

———. 2005. *The Ecology of Power: Culture, Place, and Personhood in the Southern Amazon, A.D. 1000–2000*. New York: Routledge.

Hugh-Jones, Christine. 1979. *From the Milk River: Spatial and Temporal Processes in Northwest Amazonia*. Cambridge: Cambridge University Press.

Hugh-Jones, Stephen. 1994. "Shamans, Prophets, Priests and Pastors." In *Shamanism, History, and the State*, edited by Nicholas Thomas and Caroline Humphrey, 32–75. Ann Arbor: University of Michigan Press.

———. 1996. "Bonnes raisons ou mauvaise conscience? De l'ambivalence de certains amazoniens envers la consommation de viande." *Terrains* 26:123–148.

Ladeira, Maria Inês. 1992. *"O caminhu sob a luz": O território Mbyá à beira do oceano*. Master's thesis, Pontifícia Universidade Católica, São Paulo.

Larricq, Marcelo. 1993. *Ipytuma, construcción de la persona entre los Mbya-Guaraní*. Misiones: Editorial Universitaria, Universidad Nacional de Misiones.

Lévi-Strauss, Claude. 1991. *Histoire de Lynx*. Paris: Plon.

Lowrey, Kathleen Bolling. 2003. *Enchanted Ecology: Magic, Science, and Nature in the Bolivian Chaco*. Ann Arbor, Michigan: University Microfilms.

Melià, Bartomeu. 1986. *El Guarani—conquistado y reducido: Ensayos de etnohistoria*. Asunción: Centro de Estudios Antropológicos, Universidad Católica.

———. 1990. "A Terra sem Mal dos Guarani." *Revista de Antropologia* 33:33–46.

———. 2004. "La novedad Guarani (viejas cuestiones y nuevas preguntas): Revisita bibliográfica, 1987–2002." *Revista das Índias* 64(230):175–226.

Monteiro, John Manuel. 1992. "Os Guarani e a história do Brasil meridional: Séculos XVI–XVII." In Cunha, *História dos índios no Brasil*, 475–500.

———. 1999. "The Crises and Transformations of Invaded Societies: Coastal Brazil in the Sixteenth Century." In *The Cambridge History of the Native Peoples of the Americas*, vol. 3, *South America*, edited by Frank Salomon and Stuart B. Schwartz, 1:973–1023. Cambridge: Cambridge University Press.

Montoya, Antônio Ruiz de. [1639] 1985. *Conquista espiritual feita pelos religiosos da Companhia de Jesus nas províncias do Paraguai, Paraná, Uruguai e Tape.* Porto Alegre: Martins.

————. 1876. *Vocabulario y tesoro de la lengua guarani, ó mas bien tupi.* Vienna: Faesy & Frick; Paris: Maisonneuve.

Mura, Fábio. 2004. "A trajetória histórica dos Chiru na construção da tradição de conhecimento kaiowá." Paper presented at the 24th meeting of the Associação Brasileira de Antropologia, Recife.

————. 2006. "A Procura do 'bom viver': Território, tradição de conhecimento e ecologia doméstica entre os Kaiowá." Ph.D. diss., PPGAS, Museu Nacional, Universidade Federal do Rio de Janeiro.

Necker, Louis. 1979. *Indiens guarani et chamanes franciscains: Les Premières Réductions du Paraguay (1580–1800).* Paris: Anthropos.

Nimuendajú, Curt. 1946. *The Eastern Timbira.* Translated by Robert H. Lowie. Berkeley and Los Angeles: University of California Press.

————. 1987. *As lendas da criação e destruição do mundo como fundamentos da religião dos Apapocúva-Guarani.* Translated by Charlotte Emmerich and Eduardo B. Viveiros de Castro. São Paulo: Hucitec.

Noelli, Francisco. 1999. "Curt Nimuendajú e Alfred Métraux: A invenção da busca da 'terra sem mal.'" *Suplemento Antropológico* (Asunción) 34 (2):123–166.

Pompa, Maria Cristina. 2000. "Per ripensare il 'profetismo' indigeno: I Tupinambá." *Studi e Materiali di Storia delle Religioni* (Roma), n.s., 24(1):145–200.

————. 2003. *Religião como tradução: Missionários, Tupi e Tapuia no Brasil meridional.* São Paulo: EDUSC/ANPOCS.

Ricoeur, Paul. 2000. *La Mémoire, l'histoire, l'oubli.* Paris: Seuil.

Rípodas Ardanaz, Daisy. 1987. "Movimientos shamánicos de liberación entre los Guaraníes (1545–1660)." *Apartado de Teología* (Buenos Aires) 24(50):245–275.

Rival, Laura M. 1998. "Preys at the Center: Resistence and Marginality in Amazonia." In *Lilies of the Field: Marginal People Who Live for the Moment,* edited by Sophie Day, Evthymios Papataxiarchis, and Michael Stewart, 61–79. Boulder, Colorado: Westview.

————. 2002. *Trekking through History: The Huaorani of Amazonian Ecuador.* New York: Columbia University Press.

Roulet, Florencia. 1993. *La resistencia de los Guaraní del Paraguay a la conquista española (1537–1556).* Posadas, Argentina: Editorial Universitaria, Universidad Nacional de Misiones.

Santos-Granero, Fernando. 1991. *The Power of Love: The Moral Use of Knowledge amongst the Amuesha of Central Peru.* London: Athlone.

————. 1993. "Templos e ferrarias: Utopia e reinvenção cultural no Oriente peruano." In *Amazônia: Etnologia e história indígena,* edited by Eduardo Viveiros de Castro and Manuela Carneiro da Cunha, 67–94. São Paulo: NHII/FAPESP.

————. 2002. "Saint Christopher in the Amazon: Child Sorcery, Colonialism, and Violence among the Southern Arawak." *Ethnohistory* 49(3):507–543.

Schaden, Egon. 1954a. "O estudo do índio brasileiro ontem e hoje." *América Indígena* 14(3):233–252.

————. 1954b. *Aspectos fundamentais da cultura guaraní.* São Paulo: Universidade de São Paulo.

————. 1969. *Aculturação indígena: Ensaio sobre fatores e tendências da mudança cultural de tribos índias em contato com o mundo dos brancos.* São Paulo: Pioneira.

Steckley, John L. 1992. "The Warrior and the Lineage: Jesuit Use of Iroquoian Images to Communicate Christianity." *Ethnohistory* 39(4):478–509.

Susnik, Branislava. 1965. *El indio colonial del Paraguay.* Vol. 1, *El Guarani colonial.* Asunción: Museo Etnográfico Andrés Barbero.

————. 1980. *Los aborígenes del Paraguay.* Vol. 2, *Etnohistoria de los Guaraníes (epoca colonial).* Asunción: Museo Etnográfico Andrés Barbero.

Vainfas, Ronaldo. 1995. *A heresia dos índios: Catolicismo e rebeldia no Brasil colonial.* São Paulo: Companhia das Letras.

Viveiros de Castro. *See* Castro, Eduardo Viveiros de.

Wilde, Guillermo. 2003a. "Antropología historica del liderazgo guarani misionero (1750–1850)." Ph.D. diss., Universidad de Buenos Aires.

————. 2003b. "Poderes del ritual y rituales del poder: Un análisis de las celebraciones en los pueblos jesuíticos de Guaraníes." *Revista Española de Antropología Americana* 33:203–229.

Wright, Robin M. 1998. *Cosmos, Self, and History in Baniwa Religion: For Those Unborn.* Austin: University of Texas Press.

————, ed. 1999. *Transformando os deuses.* Vol. 1, *Os múltiplos sentidos da conversão entre os povos indígenas no Brasil.* Campinas: FAPESP/Unicamp.

————, ed. 2004. *Transformando os deuses.* Vol 2, *Igrejas evangélicas, pentecostais e neopentecostais entre os povos indígenas no Brasil.* Campinas: FAPESP/Unicamp.

Wright, Robin M., and Jonathan D. Hill. 1986. "History, Ritual, and Myth: Nineteenth Century Millenarian Movements in the Northwest Amazon." *Ethnohistory* 33(1):31–54.

3

Animal Masters and the Ecological Embedding of History among the Ávila Runa of Ecuador

Eduardo O. Kohn

The Runa, Quichua (Quechua)-speakers from the village of Ávila in Ecuador's upper Amazon, interact with nonhuman realms in a variety of ways. Through a creative use of language that accentuates particular semiotic modalities, they capture sensations and qualities of the biotic world, thereby creating vivid simulations of forest experience in such a way that signs become thoroughly entangled with materiality (Kohn 2005). In other contexts their concern is the challenges that ensue when treating forest animals as "persons," who possess their own intentions, motivations, and subjective perspectives (Kohn, n.d., chap. 2). But in such matters as success in the hunt, danger in distant forests, and the realm of the afterlife, the Runa's interest turns especially to *who* controls the animals, processes, and events of the forest. This question is a decidedly sociological one, and its answer requires understanding Runa interactions with forest beings within a social context that extends spatially beyond the local community and temporally beyond the present to include the regionwide legacy of a long colonial history. This chapter, then, focuses on those beings that exert control over the forest as a way to understand how interaction with them reflects the impact of history, Runa notions of historicity, and the diverse ways in which multiple temporalities come to be embedded in ecological practice. Describing these intersections is an important aspect of a historical ecology (see Crumley 1994) in that it recognizes how history both is visible in landscape and structures the possibilities for interaction with that landscape.

Whereas the Runa live "above" (*jahuata*), these beings who control the forests and the animals that inhabit it live "inside" (*ucuta*). The Runa call these the forest lords (*sacha curaga*), game animal lords (*aicha curaga*), or, more commonly, simply the forest beings (*sachaguna*), the lords (*curagaguna*), or the bosses (*amuguna*). Here I call them animal masters. These masters are extremely important to the

Runa because they control game animals (as well as many other forest creatures) and it is only by establishing relations with them that one can successfully hunt. Furthermore, they control the weather, especially in distant forests, and they can thus cause harm to hunters. Finally, theirs is one of the domains where Runa souls go after death.

The different ways in which the Runa and animal masters perceive the forest are aligned by means of metaphoric correspondences that assume a perspectival logic (see Castro 1998; Kohn 2002a). What the Runa see as wild, the animal masters see as domestic. For example, what the Runa see as jaguars are the hunting and guard dogs of the animal masters. Peccaries are the domestic pigs of the masters. What the Runa see as gray-winged trumpeters, guans, curassows, and chachalacas—all prized game birds that are primarily terrestrial—are chickens of the animal masters. Where the Runa see lethargic leaf-eating sloths clinging to tree branches, the animal masters see furry urticating caterpillars that inch their way along the rafters of their houses. Armadillos, with their bony armor plates, near-blindness, and curious lack of incisors and canines, are seen by the animal masters as squashes—hard-rinded and innocuously sessile. Similarly, the forests that the Runa walk are the fallows of the masters. Just as the Runa return to their long-abandoned gardens to harvest fruit from their planted stands of trees such as peach palm, guava, and *patas*,[1] and to hunt the wild animals that are attracted to these, the animal masters draw on the resources of their "fallows" to feed their own "pets." And when the Runa find peccaries eating fallen *huapa*, or virola fruits,[2] this is because the animal masters have released these "pigs" from their pens into their fallows to forage.

Animal masters are a central part of the forest landscape, even if they are not always readily visible. At times, however, their presence becomes acutely manifest. Being captured by them is something that, on occasion, happens to people; I have heard several firsthand accounts in Ávila of such experiences (see Kohn 2002a). Besides the gifts of game provided by these beings, small hints of their domain are visible in everyday life. Sometimes when walking by waterfalls the Runa will catch the scent of food being cooked by the forest lords "inside," and the early morning sound of distant water can signal that the animal masters are bathing. Shamans can readily converse with these beings, and sometimes they appear in people's dreams as well.

Among the Runa, there is one set of social norms that governs all relations among beings; animals, masters, and people all interact among themselves and with each other according to the same logic of sociability. Philippe Descola (1996a), on the basis of his extensive research among the Achuar, calls this particular mode of interacting with the nonhuman "animism." The origins of these social norms, however, are not just human (see Ingold 2000:107–108). They also have roots in nonhuman forms of sociability such as the jaguar's solitary predatory nature and the dominance hierarchies visible among dogs (Kohn n.d.). Furthermore, in the Runa case at least, those roots that are grounded in the human reach well beyond the domain of local sociability. The Achuar have maintained relative autonomy from the outside world and, accordingly, the forms of sociability this group extends to the beings of the forest correspond to images of society that are primarily local and indigenous. The Runa, by contrast, have had sustained contact with colonial and national society since the sixteenth century (see Oberem 1980; Muratorio 1987; Hudelson 1987; Kohn 2002a), and this has had a great impact on Runa "animism." Despite the importance of cash markets, colonists, and state presence in Ávila, virtually all food is gardened, gathered, fished, or hunted, and hence an intimate relationship continues to exist with the forest and its beings. However, this relative economic autonomy does not mean that the forest is imagined as some separate domain of traditional indigenous lifeways divorced from greater political economic frameworks. The social template that the Runa extend to the forest realm is one that encompasses not only local relations of sociability—those related to local kin relations, the household, the house and garden—but also the way in which that intimate sphere of domesticity is inserted into a regional and even national web of social, economic, and political relations.

What form does animism take when the social world is not limited to the local and, moreover, when that greater social world constrains, in many ways, the conditions under which local modes of social interaction are possible? Whereas the Achuar social template is the autonomous household and it is this "domestic" image of society that these people project onto nature (Descola 1994), the Runa one posits local sociability as part of a much larger regional system that stretches well beyond the indigenous. In keeping with this more expansive image of the social, the Runa describe animal masters as wealthy white priests and estate owners who drive pickup trucks and fly airplanes and live in cities deep inside the forest. It is with these powerful beings that the Runa must establish appropriate relations in order to access the forest and its goods.

In examining historically laden images and the ways in which they have come to inhabit parts of the ecological landscape, this chapter is part of a larger concern with the ways in which ecological activity is undertaken within the context of colonial legacies; nature and history are intimately "entangled" in this part of the world (Raffles 2002). Elsewhere I explore how historically contingent conceptions of personhood have been adopted and are extended to animals (Kohn, n.d., chaps. 4, 6), how certain elements of ecological cosmology emerged through interaction with foreigners and the constraints of landscape that locals and foreigners share (Kohn 2002a:316–335; Kohn, n.d., chap. 5), and how dialogue with the animal masters of the forest is part of a broader set of strategies for negotiating with powerful outsiders (Kohn 2002a:336–390). Here I wish to examine the contours of the world of animal masters and its relation to history and local notions of historicity. In the first part of the chapter, I examine how the animal master realm exhibits qualities captured from a variety of historical periods—evidence of the way in which it changes with changing historical circumstances. In the second part, I demonstrate that although such relations clearly reflect historical change, Ávila animal master cosmologies appear to the Runa, in some contexts, as stable. I also argue that this particular modality of engagement with the animal master realm interweaves with other modalities. Some of these appear in dream images that are quite sensitive to current social realities. Others are preserved in biological nomenclature and have a deeper time-depth. Each has its own susceptibility to different moments of sociopolitical and economic configuration. What emerges in this process is a variety of parallel temporal flows that interweave in ecological practice.

The Animal Masters and Their Realms

The most prominent inhabitants of the domain of the animal masters are those described as *curaga*. These exhibit attributes of a variety of figures: the pre-Hispanic and early colonial indigenous leaders of the Quijos chiefdom that included under its jurisdiction the region that is now Ávila; a traditional *auca* (non-Christian indigenous) "big man"; and, perhaps most important, a white priest or estate owner.

Curaga (or *curaca*) means "lord" in Quechua (see González Holguín [1608] 1952:55). During the early colonial period, the Spaniards used the Arawakan synonym *cacique* to refer to the leaders they found in the Quijos region.[3] Caciques were hereditary leaders associated with specific geographical regions (Ordóñez de Cevallos [1614] 1989:431). Their position of authority became important primarily in times of crisis. They were also hierarchically nested; groups of lesser caciques would unite loosely under the temporary command of paramount ones (ibid.:429; Oberem 1980:225). At the time of contact, the Quijos region was united into approximately five such higher chiefdoms. One of these, called either Ávila or Sumaco, was composed of thirty or so caciques that inhabited the northern and western slopes and adjacent areas of the Sumaco Volcano, including the region where present-day Ávila is located. During the important uprisings against the Spaniards of the late 1570s, these were united under a *cacique principal* or chief lord named Jumande (Martin [1563] 1989:119).[4] The Spaniards dismantled this system of chiefdoms or *cacicazgos* toward the end of the sixteenth century and supplanted them with indigenous officials they appointed, known as *varayu* (Oberem 1980:226–227).

The animal master lords, as they are imagined today in Ávila, share a number of features with the sixteenth-century *curaga*. They are organized in a nested hierarchy and the apical *curaga* is associated with Sumaco Volcano. Indeed, the early colonial administrative unit known as the *provincia de Sumaco* corresponds roughly to the modern-day territory of the animal master lord. These similarities can be seen from the following myth that explains the scarcity of game in Ávila:

> There used to be a lot of game in the Ávila region. Then a *curaga* from Terere (a mountain island on the Napo River, downriver from Ávila) came. He tricked the Sumaco *curaga* by getting him drunk. He made him sleep and then stole his horn. Then he went back downriver and sounded the horn to call all the animals. At that time there were no large animals, such as the white-lipped peccary, downriver. There were only small animals. Attracted by the call, all the game went down to Terere while the Sumaco *curaga* was still sleeping. That's why there's a lot of game down there. Even the woolly monkeys abandoned this area. When the Sumaco *curaga* awoke, he called the game with another horn, but only some of the small game, such as agoutis, collared peccaries, and curassows, came back. Very few of the large animals, such as the white-lipped peccaries and woolly monkeys, came back.

This Sumaco lord is thought of as paramount in relation to the lesser animal masters from whom the Ávila Runa attempt to procure meat. The Ávila Runa explicitly recognize this relation, and it is also implied in the myth; the loss of the Sumaco lord's herds affects the abundance of game in the entire region.

Because animal and human societies share the same social attributes, the Runa also recognize lords in animal "societies." In troops of coati (*mashu*), dominant males are called lords of the coatis (*mashu curaga*). And a large species of stinkbug (*pacu*) is referred to as the *curaga* of smaller stinkbug species. Other animals labeled *curaga* have qualities that specifically match those related to the political caciques of the sixteenth century. For example, the cinereous antshrike (*cuchiquiri*) is considered a "lord of the small birds" (*pishcu curaga*) because of its propensity to lead mixed flocks of antwrens and flycatchers as they flit about in the low levels of the forest canopy in search of insects (see Hilty and Brown 1986:389). This antshrike is known in Ávila for warning the flocks of approaching raptors. Since "it leads around lots of small birds," as one person explained to me, the *cuchiquiri* shares some qualities with the sixteenth-century *curaga*. In a mixed flock, with different species that all forage for their own food and that have no readily apparent hierarchy, this bird, by alerting the flock when predators threaten, emerges as a leader and protector—much as the sixteenth-century lords of the Ávila region led loose confederations, sometimes including people who spoke different languages, that united in moments of crisis.

The animal master *curaga* also shares attributes with the "big man," the leader or household head still potent, at least until recently, both as a political figure of the various *auca* (non-Christian indigenous) groups and as a model for a powerful Runa shaman. For example, in Ávila the animal masters are thought to sit on benches or thrones consisting of caymans and turtles.[5] Lucas Siquihua, a powerful Ávila shaman who died many decades ago, recounted to Juanicu, a man now in his sixties, how he had once gone to live in the world of the animal masters for two weeks. Upon first entering the house of the animal masters, he was afraid to sit down because, instead of the usual improvised bench of stacked *huama* sleeping planks,[6] he saw a large cayman and, instead of the carved wooden benches, he saw a terrestrial turtle. The Runa of Archidona by my own observation, as well as those from the Canelos region according to Norman Whitten (1976:149), see such animal benches as sources of shamanic power. Household heads of the Canelos Runa receive visitors while sitting on such benches (1976:67), as do the Achuar (Descola 1996b:34).

In Ávila the animal masters not only embody the characteristics of powerful indigenous leaders, they are also "white."[7] What does it mean to say that a *curaga* is white? It would be inaccurate, I think, to see the world of the animal masters as a rigid caste society with Indians in one role and whites in another. True, it is believed that the animal masters employ Runa workers who live in this realm as field hands. And the masters are also thought to control modern technology usually associated with whites, such as airplanes and pickup trucks. In other contexts, however, the animal masters are portrayed as if they were Runa without focusing particularly on their "white" attributes. The wives of animal masters tend chickens in the same way that Runa women do, and animal masters drink manioc beer, a beverage that many outsiders do not drink. They also have hearths, live in thatch-covered houses, eat game meat, and hold weddings similar to those of the Runa. It must be remembered that attributes of whiteness are just some of several possible indices of power in a perspectival system in which shamanic metamorphosis can allow the Runa to capture some of the bodily attributes, and hence power, of different kinds of beings, including Europeans (see Vilaça, this volume). Animal masters, then, are not "white" in a racial sense; they are powerful and they occupy a certain place in a hierarchical organization, and this status, in part, has come to be associated with the authority that white attributes confer (see Kohn 2002a:265–315).

The abodes of the animal masters are found deep in the forest, and their entry portals are often striking features of the natural landscape, especially the waterfalls found at the headwaters of rivers and streams. Although deep in the forest, these spaces are decidedly urban (see also Mercier 1979:139; Wavrin 1927:325; Muratorio 1987:236). In Ávila, people say that the paramount *curaga* lives in a large city. The Runa refer to this as Quito and generally locate it inside the Sumaco Volcano. Lesser animal masters live in cities and villages akin to the smaller towns and cities that make up the parish and provincial seats of Ecuador's Amazonian provinces. These correspond to other features of the landscape such as smaller mountains and hills.

Underground roads connect these metropolises, and the animal masters travel back and forth by car, motorcycle, bicycle, even by airplane. One man, Hilario, in his mid-fifties, was able to observe evidence for these links between animal master abodes as they are inscribed in the landscape. In his youth, he was one of several Ávila men recruited to serve as guides and porters for members of the Ecuadorian military who were intent on building a heliport and erecting a set of relay antennas near the volcano summit. This volcano, in whose foothills Ávila is nestled, forms a near-perfect cone. Although it is readily visible from Ávila, it took the expedition ten days to get to the top. From the barren conical peak, many of the major rivers of the region originate. At the top, however, these headwaters are nothing more than empty streambeds carved into stone that fan out radially like spokes from an axle. Describing these, Hilario matter-of-factly remarked that these canals are the *carreteras* (roads) of the *amuguna* (lords). His sister Luisa added that these are where the lords drive their cars.

The "Quito within the jungle" is a place that people, on occasion, are thought to visit. The mother of one man with whom I worked in Ávila became lost in the forest. After she miraculously emerged five weeks later, emaciated and infection-ridden but alive, she told how a boy who resembled one of her teenage grandsons led her "halfway" to the underground city she called Quito. She later commented to her relatives that this city was beautiful and opulent like "the real Quito."

The possibility of a Quito in the forest, and the opportunities for exchange that it might afford, has a long history in the Ávila region. In the early colonial period there was a concerted effort on the part of residents of the Quijos region, including the ancestors of the Ávila Runa, to persuade Spaniards to build a "Quito" in the Amazon: in 1559, as part of peace negotiations with Spaniards, leaders from this region met in Atunquyxo with the governor of Quito, Gil Ramírez Dávalos, and supplicated him to "make another city like Quito" (Ramírez Dávalos [1559]

1989:50, see also 39). Their reasoning, it seems, was economic. They were "so impressed by the gifts that the governor gave them that they asked him to found in their territory a Christian settlement like Quito, where they would gladly serve, given that through it, commerce would improve tremendously" (Oberem 1980:74–75).

Of course, this "other" Quito was never founded in the lowlands and, to the continuing chagrin of local inhabitants, the region remained an economic backwater largely isolated from broader networks of trade. To this day, the descendants of the Quijos lords who met with Ramírez Dávalos lament this "failed Quito" in the Amazon. In Oyacachi, a cloud forest village that once formed part of one of the Quijos chiefdoms (Oberem 1980:226), people recount that if their ancestors had not caused a miraculous image of the Virgin Mary to abandon them—it was moved to El Quinche in the highlands by the bishopric of Quito in 1604—Oyacachi would have become an important city like Quito and there would have been no mountains separating Oyacachi from the prosperous populations of the highlands (Kohn 2002b). One man in Oyacachi explained to me, "If a Quito had been built here, Oyacachi would have become a real city."[8] People in Ávila today recount a myth that plays on similar themes:

> A king passed through the Ávila region coming, possibly, from downriver. He crossed the Suno River and continued upriver to a place called Balsiti near the Sumaco Volcano. There he began to establish a city by first throwing stones in every direction using a *huaraca* (sling).[9] The Sumaco lord became angered and stopped him from making the city, so the king left for the highlands. On his way, however, he made Huamani Mountain (the high Andean peak by which Amazonian travelers to Quito must pass before reaching the temperate inter-Andean valleys) and also made it very rainy there. Then he went to Quito and built his city there because the *curaga* of the Pichincha Volcano wanted it so. Again he threw the stones with the sling in all directions, and there was enough space for a large city (see also Wavrin 1927:330).

Some people can discern the remnants of this failed "Quito in the jungle" in the landscape. On a plain to the north of the Suno River headwaters, several people say, there are remnants of "cement" steps and a stone road. Ventura, a man in his mid-forties who saw these as a teenager, feels that these are all that remain of the city that the king failed to build. Ventura concluded that if Quito had been built there, Ávila, because of its proximity, would have also become a big city, and by now its inhabitants would have become hispanicized like the highlanders (*jahuallacta*).[10]

These examples illustrate how people of the Quijos region, past and present, explain their economic and geographical isolation from a wealthy metropolis in terms of a failure to reproduce that metropolis locally. In all these cases, local decisions and acts—the inability to properly care for the Virgin in Oyacachi, or the Sumaco lord's rejection of the king and his city—explain why Quito does not exist in the lowlands. Such personal investments in bringing a Quito "home" have made this city a potentially tangible presence today in the forest.

Quito seems to have been imagined by the Runa as a kind of worldly paradise of opulence and freedom to which whites, such as priests, had privileged access. Emilio Gianotti, a Josephine missionary, wrote in 1924 of encountering a Runa peon on one of the oppressive rubber estates of the Napo River, which was ironically named La Libertad. The peon wanted to escape with the priests, thinking that he would thus be able to live in this idealized Quito:

> Arriving on a dark and rainy night at Belleza . . . we found a poor Indian (*indiecito*) soaked and shivering with cold and hunger. "Who are you? Where do you come from? Where are you going?" we asked.
>
> With great effort he managed to answer that he wanted to go with us to Quito.
>
> "But, do you know were Quito is? We live in Tena and not in Quito. Where did you escape from?"
>
> "From Libertad."
>
> "Your master doesn't love you?"
>
> "No."
>
> "And why do you want to come with us?"
>
> "Because the *padres* love me."
>
> Then I remembered that in Florencia, after having gotten some forty kids to sing and pray, I taught them to dance the tarantella. Poor fellow, he thought that with us he would go to sing, pray, and dance forever.[11]
> (Gianotti 1997:60–61)

In response to the priest's "do you know where Quito is?" the Runa peon would respond, I think, with an emphatic "yes." Quito is a place of tremendous wealth and power located in regions that are difficult for the uninitiated to access—places like the cities in the deepest reaches of the forest, or those in the high Andes.

From the mid-nineteenth century until well into the twentieth, the inhabitants of Ávila, along with those from the nearby Runa villages Loreto and Concepción, made occasional treks to Quito to trade products such as pita fiber,[12] and to meet with government officials (Villavicencio [1858] 1984:389). Marcos, the father of

Hilario and Luisa, was one such man. Born at the turn of the twentieth century, as an adult he was appointed *capitán* by the government and would make regular trips to Quito to settle disputes and sell pita fiber. Hilario and Luisa accompanied him once, making the eight-day trip barefoot to marvel at the wonders of this city. These trips were another way by which Quito became a tangible presence in people's lives.

The status of Quito as a utopia coexists uneasily with an image of this city as a source of suffering. It is said that an epidemic illness known as *murhui*, which killed many Runa, originated in Quito and that it is still there, locked away in a suitcase somewhere. People in Ávila say that this illness killed half the population at some time before the rubber boom. Indeed, an anonymous document written by a rubber boss in 1913 refers to a smallpox epidemic that swept through the Runa communities of the Upper Napo in 1896 as *muruy* (possibly from *morir* cf. murrain) and says it killed "65 percent of the population" (in Porras 1979:28).

The abundant references that the Runa make to fallows and pens, to farm animals and *patrones* in speaking of the animal master world indicate that another important influence on the architecture of this realm is the Amazonian hacienda. As Blanca Muratorio (1987:186) has shown, the hacienda of the upper Napo, especially in its heyday between approximately 1915 and 1950,[13] when the *patrones* were the undisputed political authorities in the region, is a unique institution, adapted to specific local culture and economic features of the upper Amazon. The Amazonian hacienda was much more like the colonial *encomienda* (Taylor 1999:215) than the Andean hacienda in that the status and wealth of the *patrón* depended more on the coercive control of people than it did on the control of land as property.

Ecological, economic, and sociological factors dictated that these estates be extractive. Their wealth was not a product of converting the Amazonian jungle into arable land. Such a feat would require extensive amounts of labor. More important, the region's isolation made it impossible for perishable products to be transported to the markets of the highlands. Rather, these estates focused primarily on creating debt obligations among the natives through the forced distribution at inflated prices of commercial goods such as clothing, beads, and steel tools in exchange for extractive products. These products included rubber, gold, and pita fiber. Although the agropastoral aspect of the estate itself, for which native labor was also used, was symbolically important, it was primarily for the subsistence of the hacienda (Muratorio 1987:186).

The haciendas of the upper Amazon were nodes in a vast network. These were sources of wealth and power from which manufactured goods originated and spread throughout the region through the networks of Indian debtors that were drawn in. At these nodes, rubber from widely dispersed trees was collected, as was gold panned in the tentaclelike network of streams and creeks. Pita fiber was produced in the distant secondary residences to which Runa families often retreated (Villavicencio [1858] 1984), and it too was brought to these collection points.

Some of the unique properties of this economic institution are reflected today in descriptions of the animal master world. The animal masters' wealth is concentrated in enclosed areas; their animals are kept on their estates in pens. Yet, like the *hacendados*, their presence can be felt throughout the forest. Furthermore, their relationship to the forest is not one of extensive transformation through labor but one of usufruct. In this sense it is fitting that the Runa refer to the forest not as the pastures of the animal master—for these would require extensive upkeep—but as fallows. Like Runa fallows, the forest for the animal master and *hacendado* is a source of wealth that requires labor only in collection and extraction and not in maintenance. In the same way that manufactured goods are stockpiled by *patrones* in the hacienda even though only a small portion is ever allowed to reach Runa hands, the animals of the animal masters are overly abundant in the pens even though they can only occasional be spotted and hunted in the forest after they have been let out of the pens by their masters. This is how Juanicu, frustrated when the animal masters gave us no game on our hunting trip, explained to his son-in-law the discrepancy between the wealth of the masters and the scarcity of game in the forest:

> for no good reason [the masters keep them] shut up, in their overfull [pens]: white-lipped peccary, collared peccary, woolly monkey, curassow. What else? Trumpeter. What else? Tinamou. And a whole bunch of other things. Until they're completely overfilled. Keeping them only for themselves, they don't send them out. They're just stingy for no good reason.[14]

Although the Ávila Runa have been economically self-sufficient in many respects, their attraction to the estates of rubber merchants and other *patrones* stemmed in large part from their desire for certain manufactured goods. In Ávila, some people refer to the period lasting until approximately the early 1970s as *nativu uras*, native times. What distinguished that period from the present was that the Runa used minimal amounts of purchased goods. A few men had crude muzzle-loading shotguns. The rest used blowguns. Cloth and some clothing was purchased, but these were colored using local plant dyes.[15] Cookware and storage vessels were made locally from clay. Many of the goods that are purchased today—rubber boots, nylon fiber and rope, cookware and tableware, firearms and ammunition, flashlights and batteries—were not part of everyday life in *nativu uras*. Nevertheless, items such as clothing, steel tools, blowgun poison, salt, and glass trade beads, were central to Runa lifeways, and these were mostly acquired via relationships with the *patrones*.

The dependency that the Runa had on the hacienda for manufactured goods mirrors their dependency on the forest for meat. In terms of food, Runa households are for the most part self-sufficient. Gardens produce plantains and manioc year-round, and orchards provide a variety of other products on a more seasonal basis. Yet the Runa must complement these by venturing into the forest to acquire other resources, especially meat.

The haciendas never occupied vast areas of land, and they rarely displaced the Runa permanently. Unlike the peons of the highland hacienda, the Runa generally retained access to their own land-based resources. They were rarely forced to live on the hacienda and therefore did not become dependent on it for access to land, as the highland system required (Muratorio 1987:187). In this sense, the *patrón* was like the historical lords of the early colonial period and, by extension, like the animal master lords that populate the forest today. The relationship with a particular *patrón* was dependent on residential kin group (*muntun*) affiliation. About fifty families were usually within the sphere of influence of a single *patrón* (186). This is similar in many ways to the relationship of commoner to *curaga* as recorded in early colonial times. A local *curaga* had one hundred or two hundred people under him (Oberem 1980:224). As a demographic ratio, this number corresponds to the extent of a *patrón*'s influence over the Runa at the height of the estate system.

The Runa were often quite dependent on alliances with *patrones*. In the 1920s, especially in the region of Tena, Archidona, and Puerto Napo, practically all the Runa were affiliated with a *patrón* (Oberem 1980:117).[16] In this sense too, these *patrones* are like powerful lords. The entire local population is aligned with one or another, and the *patrones* are able to allocate these people as they see fit. A *patrón* could pursue the Runa aggressively and mercilessly unless the Runa managed to ally themselves with another master (Gianotti 1997:132). Similarly, animal masters that do not "know" the Runa that are passing through their domains can be extremely aggressive. They can cause dangerous wind and lightning storms, for example.

The animal master realm is a space of marked hierarchy, and this is rooted in *patrón*-Runa relations as well as earlier ones between government officials (colonial and, later, republican) and the Runa. In the 1840s, for example, Gaetano Osculati observed in the Puerto Napo region that the possessions with which the Runa were buried included the wooden troughs (*batea*) with which gold is panned ([1850] 1990:114). At the time that Osculati wrote, the Runa of Puerto Napo panned gold in order to fulfill tribute requirements to the government.

Tribute, it seems, also had to be paid in the afterlife. This is why the dead were buried with the tools they needed to procure payment. Similarly, in Ávila, Runa souls, particularly those of older men and women, are thought to inhabit the bodies of jaguars after death. Although the jaguar is the most awesome Amazonian predator, it is simultaneously seen as the obedient dog of the animal master; Runa werejaguars, then, become servants of white masters in the afterlife. That the Runa werejaguars are both top predators and servants captures something important about Runa life: people can be simultaneously autonomous in their households and subservient to more powerful masters in other contexts (see Kohn, n.d.).

Just like Quito, which is imagined both as a paradise and also as a source of suffering, the hacienda-inflected imagination of the animal master space is seen to reflect not only the hierarchy inherent to *patrón-peón* relations but also its utopian qualities. The Runa who go to live there are free of earthly torment. People in Ávila often remark that "the dead are free" (*huañugunaca luhuar*). By this they mean specifically that in the world of the animal masters, the dead can escape Judgment Day (*juiciu punja*). The term *luhuar* is derived from the Spanish word *lugar*. Its primary meaning in that language is "place." It also is used in the phrase *tener lugar*, to have the time or opportunity to do something. This phrase is infrequently used today in Ecuadorian Spanish. However, the meaning of *luhuar* is related to *tener lugar*. *Luhuar* often refers to having a period of respite from labor or work obligations (*trabaju*). In Ávila, work can often be seen as a source of suffering. In this context the term *turmintu*, from the Spanish *tormento*, meaning anguish, oppression, suffering, is used. The afterlife, above all, is seen as a time and place where one can be free of suffering, free of torment. The world of the animal masters has spatial and temporal qualities that differentiate it from the world of everyday life. It is both a distant place and outside temporality (people never age there; for example, old women who go there after death revert permanently to a nubile state). These qualities are brilliantly captured by *luhuar*, a Spanish loan that, in its original meaning, alludes to a place outside time.

The idea of escaping worldly *turmintu* by going to the afterlife is illustrated by the following legend:

> A *patrón* came to Ávila to exchange clothing and cloth for pita fiber. He advanced a large amount of these items to one Runa family, saying, "Become indebted to me" (*debiachihuai*). The family accepted and incurred a debt much larger than they would ever be able to pay in fiber. Meanwhile, in order to improve his fishing abilities, the Runa man had been cultivating a relationship with the river lords (*yacu curaga*) by ingesting a variety of riverbank herbs. These masters live underwater and look just like people. They have abundant food and drink and live in Runa villages. At night, however,

they take off their clothing and turn into anacondas. They also keep pet jaguars. Because of his debt, this man, however, ingested the herbs a fourth time—one more time than is usually prescribed for proficiency at fishing. He additionally gave it to his entire family with the exception of two boys who were out bird hunting. When the trader returned to collect his debt, loud thunder was heard and the entire house site turned into a lake. Only the coals of the fire, now floating, remained. The trader was unable to find the family, so he dove underwater to search for them. There the anaconda ate him. All that remained of him were his lungs, which floated up to the water's surface. The two boys that had been hunting went to another lake, each imploring, "Father, take me with you." They then also went to live with their family underwater. Nobody dies in that realm.

Although the animal master world is seen as a paradise free of suffering, most people are not willing to give up their worldly lives to move there permanently. There are, however, some exceptions. On a visit to San José de Payamino in 1997, I was told that a woman from the community had disappeared in the forest about three years before to escape her abusive husband. Her departure was sparked by this incident: One day she found a giant land snail, a *sacha churu*.[17] When she presented him with the snail for dinner,[18] her husband angrily asked, "Is that all you give me to eat?" The woman was so enraged by this remark that she abandoned her husband and went instead to live with the animal masters. Since then she has appeared twice in her husband's dreams, still upset about his remark. In these dreams she repeats to him that "we, the animal masters, will no longer give you meat."

The Runa of Ávila, along with the Runa of Loreto and Concepción, were heavily impacted by the rubber boom. Colombians and Peruvians came up to these villages to capture slave laborers (Muratorio 1987:107). Udo Oberem, who visited Loreto in the 1950s, recounts how, in the generation of the parents of his informants, more than a thousand people were sold to rubber bosses in Peru as well as Brazil and Bolivia, most of them taken by force. Of these, he was told, only forty returned (Oberem 1980:117).[19] Paradoxically, however, the hacienda of the rubber-boom era is imagined in Ávila today as an idyllic space. This may be due in part to the fact that those that suffered most under the rubber bosses never returned. They either perished or settled permanently in the region of their relocation, primarily downriver in Peru. Another factor accounting for this idealization seems to be that the *patrones* consciously cultivated the idea that these estates were utopian. The names of their estates were taken from affluent or distant and exotic-sounding countries such as Bélgica or Armenia, or from utopian terms connected to progress or religious themes—Oasis, Libertad, Providencia (Gianotti

1997). For example, the Hacienda Arcadia, on the Napo somewhat upriver from the Aguarico confluence, was reputed to be the most productive hacienda of the region and was clearly depicted by Gianotti in utopian, self-sufficient terms:

> It has one hundred eighty Indian families and five white ones, in addition to the [owner's] large family. Arcadia is an important center for work and progress, where the Indians are like our workers [in Italy], well dressed, educated, and fluent in the Spanish language. The Indians are paid here in excess, given that they have everything: clothing, sewing machines, soap, pots, salt, meat, shoes, hats, caps, etc. 53)

These utopian images were aimed primarily at the society of colonists, and their establishment was a step toward fulfilling their own ideals of wealth, home, and stability. Some *hacendados* also tried overtly to incorporate the Runa into their vision of utopia. The *teniente político* of Coca, who had a hacienda known as Coronel Montúfar on the Napo, told Gianotti of his plans to

> build and settle, on the other side of the river, a town of free Indian servants with a church, plaza, and bell tower; he already gathered the Indians from the hacienda that belonged to Pérez who were left without a *patrón* after the death of the aforementioned Mr. Pérez, and now he wants to resettle there the Indians from Loreto, Ávila, and San José de Payamino. (43–44)

In sum, Runa ecological cosmology is not unchanging. Rather, it is a product of specific historical circumstances. At least formally, however, Runa ecological cosmology is very similar to the more traditional Achuar system in that in both the same social norms govern conduct in human as well as forest realms. Descola has argued that this "animistic" way of understanding nature tends to lead to a stable, unchanging way of life because the Achuar representation of nature, as well as their relation to it, is modeled after a specific form of social organization. Any change in this organization would necessitate a major realignment of the conceptual model and a concomitant change in the ways in which the Achuar actually manipulate and adapt to nature. This is why, Descola argues, production systems like that of the Achuar "continue unchanged over long periods of time" (1994:329). In light of Descola's comments, the Runa case is very interesting, for these people have experienced tremendous socioeconomic and political change, and this is reflected in the ways in which they describe the domain of the animal masters. Yet, in formal terms, the animistic quality of this domain has changed very little. A tension exists in Ávila between an ideology of fixity and a world in flux (see also Hugh-Jones 1989). And it is to tracing the multiple temporalities made evident by this tension that I turn in the next section.

The Forest and its Histories

Even though the realm of the animal masters clearly reflects changing political economic institutions, it is also portrayed as unchanging. Elsewhere (Kohn, n.d., chap. 5) I try to explain why this might be. Here I simply want to describe some of the discrepancies between these different ways of understanding temporality. That the master realm can be understood as static is possible because the images of society the Runa extend to the forest do not exactly correspond to contemporary sociopolitical realities. Rather, these are often drawn from the past. There is a historical time lag between such images and present reality. For example, although demons in Ávila are described as wearing priestly habits, modern missionaries in the region no longer wear these. In addition, the opulent haciendas on the Napo, which serve so prominently as models for the animal master realm, were in a state of ruin by the mid-1920s (Gianotti 1997:119). Powerful landowners still exist, but the majority of outsiders in the region are now poor colonists who do not figure prominently in the animal master realm. Clearly, Ávila ecological cosmology would be seen as having changed tremendously if it could be compared to its precontact equivalent. Yet these systemic transformations also reveal a continuity of structure (Gow 2001), and the maintenance of a kind of stability seems to be important to this.

Such stability is evident in plant nomenclature. To my queries about the etymology of a particular plant name, people would usually respond with something to the effect that "that's what the old-timers would call it." Many people state that all plants were originally named by God our Father (*Yaya Dyus*). Naming is ahistorical; people do not name plants, and these designations do not change. Etymology, then, is not a locally relevant concern. The fact that many plants are unnamed does not prompt people to come up with names for them. Although younger people may admit ignorance of the names of some taxa, older people will feel that they know all plants that are named. Confronted with a tree for which they do not have a name, they might say, as Juanicu did, "It's just a plain-old tree." People consider names to be attached permanently to taxa, and this relationship is unchanging.

Yet other elements of plant naming seem to suggest a much more malleable system. For example, people will often taste leaves or bark slash of an unknown plant. If they deem these bitter (*jaya*), it is supposed that the plant in question "might be suitable as a remedy"; bitterness, according to local understanding, is equated with medical potency. On a plant-collecting trip in premontane forest with Ascencio, a man in his early sixties, I came across a small midcanopy tree of the genus *Coussarea* (Rubiaceae). Ascencio at first said he did not know the name.

Then he smelled the bark and commented, "[It's good] for making medicine." Ascencio felt it could be used to make vapor baths to treat aches and pains and began calling it *juya yura*, the vapor bath tree.

Even though they are not thought of as such, the names of many organisms are tied to historical moments, events, and eras. For example, the praying mantids are often called *huangana caya*, callers of the white-lipped peccary, because the direction in which they point their raised forelegs is thought to indicate the location of white-lipped peccary. This name persists despite the fact that herds of white-lipped peccary have not passed through the region for at least twenty years.

The *aya martillu* (hammer of the dead) is a kind of nocturnal cricket that occasionally finds its way into houses, where it rubs its forewings to produce a series of chirps that the Runa imitate as "*tin tin tin*." The presence of this cricket is an omen that a relative will die, for its call resembles the sharp metallic ring of a hammer striking a nail firmly planted in the hardwood lid of a coffin. This cricket, with its name and attributes, is thought to be an unchanging part of a stable biotic universe. Yet its name and meaning are derived from a specific historical moment. The use of hammers and nails has been adopted only in the last generation or so. Before this time, the dead were buried in a sheet of bamboo-like *huama* slats that was rolled up around the body.

Other names can be linked to specific historical events, as with several organisms that are named after Catholic feasts. For example, of the folk genus *cara caspi* (*Guatteria*, Annonaceae), whose fruits are primarily eaten by large game birds, one species, *navidad cara caspi*, is distinguished from its congenerics because it fruits around Christmas (*Navidad*). Similarly, *navidad pacai* is a species of *Inga* (Fabaceae-Mimosoideaeae) that fruits in December. Another *Inga* species fruits during Easter (*Pascua*) and is therefore referred to as *pascua pacai*. The fruits of *Gustavia macarenensis* (Lecythidaceae), coveted for their edible oily flesh, ripen around Easter (*Pascua*). This tree is therefore known as *pasu* (Quechua for *Pascua*). Because the white-necked thrush lays eggs during Easter, its name *pasu pishcu* also refers to this feast. Of the folk genus of understory trees known as *anduchi caspi* (primarily *Miconia* spp., Melastomataceae), whose berries are eaten by a variety of birds, *sajuan anduchi caspi* is known as such because it flowers and fruits around the *día de San Juan*, St. John's Day, June 24.

I have been unable to document from written historical sources the process by which taxa acquired Catholic feast-related names. It is, however, likely that missionaries renamed these plants in an attempt to align local yearly calendars—based on the fruiting of important resources, fish migrations, and the mating flights of edible leaf-cutter ants—with the festival cycle of the Catholic calendar they wished to impose. Through linking of local phenology with important Catholic festivals, Catholicism becomes naturalized and, more practically, the Runa are reminded—in the absence of a resident priest—when they should reconvene at the community center for the festivals.

Although the plants mentioned above retain their association with Christian holidays, some with similarly derived names have lost these links, owing to a shift in Catholicism over recent decades away from processional celebration and feast days to focus on individual worship. Whereas Catholic ritual in Ávila was oriented around the fiestas as late as the 1970s (see Hudelson 1987), this system has now disappeared completely. For example, *curpus* is an understory shrub of the genus *Palicourea* (Rubiaceae) whose very showy inflorescences generally bloom in May and June. It is replaced ecologically, according to local thinking, by similar flowery shrubs in different regions: *urai curpus* (lowland *curpus*, *Ruellia colorata*, Acanthaceae) at lower elevations east of Ávila and *urcu curpus* (mountain *curpus*, *Coussarea* sp., Rubiaceae) in the premontane forests to the west. The names of these are derived from Corpus Christi, a movable Catholic feast held in May or June. Many know this plant but do not remember that its name once referred to a Catholic feast that is no longer celebrated in Ávila.

Other taxa refer to specific, datable events. In Ávila I collected a specimen of *Tetrathylacium macrophyllum* (Flacourtiaceae). This is a tree with a cascading panicle of translucent dark red fruits whose Quechua name, *hualca muyu*, means, appropriately, bead necklace. Rather than resembling the opaque glass necklace beads of Bohemian origin that have been a mainstay of Amazonian trade for the past century, these fruits bear an uncanny resemblance to an earlier Venetian trade bead, dark red and translucent, that circulated in Ecuador around the time of the presidency of Ignacio Veintemilla (1878–82) and was therefore called *veintemilla*. The passage of a trade item through a local economy can be marked by a plant name even after people have long forgotten it.

One kind of grasshopper—probably *Eumastax* sp. (see Hogue 1993:163 and plate 1c)—has a body that is streaked with iridescent stripes of green, blue, and yellow. It is referred to as *soldadu jiji*, the soldier grasshopper.[20] The long hind wings, when tucked back, and the bright colors resemble the tails and epaulettes, respectively, of the uniform of nineteenth-century soldiers. Although the members of Ecuador's armed forces seen today in the Amazon all wear camouflage fatigues, the guards that stand at attention in front of the presidential palace in Quito continue to wear the traditional uniform. Forty years ago, when the Ávila Runa still traveled to Quito and the city was small enough that life was organized around the Plaza Grande and its presidential palace, these soldiers and their uniforms would have made quite an impression.

Local attitudes to plant names reveal an attempt to deny change, even though their names can exhibit accretions of history. Animal master cosmologies, by contrast, do not exactly deny history, but they do reflect social reality with a certain time lag. The Runa tendency to understand the forest in terms of categories that extend beyond local relations of sociability is also evident in the hunting omens of dreams. These, however, are different from the images of the animal master realm I have discussed in that they reflect a sense of the Runa's place in the larger society, which is much more sensitive to current social vicissitudes. For example, early one morning when I was staying at Juanicu's, his son Adelmo suddenly bolted out of bed, announcing loudly for all to hear, "*Nuspani*" (I've dreamt), before grabbing his shotgun and rushing out of the house. Later that morning he returned with a collared peccary. When I asked him what dream had prompted him to rush out into the forest and kill a peccary, he responded that he had dreamt of buying new leather shoes. The shoe stores in Loreto, the nearby colonist town, filled with shelves of leather shoes and rubber boots of all sizes, colors, and models, provide an apt image for the profusion of tracks left by a herd of peccaries at a mud wallow or salt lick. Peccaries, with their threatening canines, musky odor, fondness for mud baths, gregarious propensity to travel in herds, and omnivorous habits, often represent outsiders or enemies for Amazonians. Like "real" people, they are very social. Yet they also seem to ignore the kinds of taboos that distinguish such "real" people from their enemies (see, for instance, Rival 1993; Fausto, n.d.). In Ávila, dream images of peccaries are now, fittingly, represented via the hypersocial image of the town, and its goods and inhabitants.

Similarly, during a visit to his parents' hunting camp in the foothills of the Sumaco Volcano, a young man commented to me that he had dreamt of a well-stocked general store filled with things like rice and cans of sardines and tended by a young priest. He explained that this augured killing woolly monkeys. These travel in troops deep in the mountains, far away from Runa settlements. When found, they provide a veritable cornucopia. They are relatively easy, once spotted, to hunt—usually several can be taken—and they are coveted for their thick layers of fat. Like the forests that these monkeys frequent, the well-stocked general stores are at some distance from Runa settlements. And, like the troops of monkeys, these stores offer a bonanza of food. Both the store and the monkey troops are controlled by powerful whites, and the Runa, by establishing appropriate relations with them, can gain access to some of the wealth of both.

Conclusion

I have traced elements of Runa ecological cosmology especially as these pertain to the world of the animal masters. Although this cosmology is very traditional in logic, it is outward-looking in content. In "traditional" Amazonian societies, people socialize nature by extending local ideas of the social order to the realm of nature. The Runa view of society, by contrast, includes the greater nation-state in which Ávila is inserted, and this greater society is what is projected on the forest realm. A study of Runa ecological cosmology is thus also a way of studying history.

An exploration of the animal master realm indicates how environment and history become aligned. It is not that an environment is historically constructed, but that certain meaningful historical relations have come to be mapped onto features of the environment. Yet this is more than a process of mapping social relations onto an inert nature. The nonhuman world has its own properties, and modes of sociality, and these also constrain what kinds of relationships are possible. Both estate owners and the Runa have had to make a living from the same environment in much the same way; amassing gold and rubber is similar to hunting and fishing in that these are all extractive activities. As such, they all require similar relations to the environment. It is not enough, then, to say that the animal masters are reflections of a larger political and economic order, for such orders have had to respond to the same environment that hunters encounter. And these orders are impacted by environmental factors. That the animal masters see forests as fallows, and not as pastures or gardens, says something about the nature of an extractive economy that must engage with a landscape that imposes its own constraints on social possibilities.

History is visible everywhere in the landscape, but the forest does not provide some objective mirror of political economic circumstances. Although the landscape exudes history, it is not always interpreted as such—indeed, the Runa often portray it as unchanging. My aim here has been to point to how this tension between fixity and fluidity, visible in the world of the animal masters, plant names, and hunting dreams, reflects upper Amazonian attempts to engage with a changing world and to harness its powers, and how this changing world is brought into alignment, via a series of ecologically embedded histories, with the myriad social relationships that gave rise to it.

Notes

1. The cacao relative *Theobroma bicolor* (Sterculiaceae).

2. *Virola* spp. (Myristicaceae).

3. The term *curaga* (as *curaca* or *curacka*) seems to have been adopted later in Amazonia to refer to indigenous leaders (see Magnin, in Maroni 1988:477). In the mid-nineteenth century, the *varayu* indigenous leaders appointed by government authorities to mediate

between Runa communities and the state were also referred to by this term (Osculati [1850] 1990:113).

4. Jumande was also known as Jumandy or Jumandi.

5. The authority of sixteenth-century caciques of the Quijos region, such as Senacato, was based in part on their right to sit atop wooden thrones (Oberem 1980:225).

6. While not true bamboo, *huama—Guadua* sp. (Poaceae)—is functionally and taxonomically closely related.

7. This has important antecedents in the upper Amazon. For example, by the eighteenth century the Tupian Cocama of the Huallaga River region already had a vision of an afterlife peopled by powerful whites (Maroni [1738] 1988:193).

8. *"Oyacachipi Quituta ruashpa . . . propio llacta canman carca."*

9. The meaning of the term *huaraca* is all but forgotten in Ávila. Ventura, one of the people who recounted this myth, knew the term only from the myth until he remembered that as a child, playing, he would use a net bag to hurl stones and that this was called a *huaraca*. The Tupian Omagua of the sixteenth century were described as using slings as weapons. They are also from "downriver." (Oberem 1967–68:153). The Omagua, then, may be an additional source from which the image of the mythical king is drawn.

10. This plain is the location of the early colonial chiefdom known as Mote, which survived as a village by the name of San José de Mote at least until the late nineteenth century. The present village of San José de Payamino is populated in part by people of this region.

11. This man had his wish fulfilled; he went to live with priests. Unfortunately, however, instead of traveling to Quito, he ended up as a servant of the Josephines in one of their lowland missions: "now he is one of our charges (*criadito*)," wrote Gianotti, "and very useful" (1997:61).

12. *Aechmea* sp. (Bromeliaceae).

13. In Tena, the hold of the *patrones* ended in the 1950s with the completion of the road connecting this region to the highlands. At this time itinerant Sierran merchants settled and established a merchant middle class (Muratorio 1987:217). Although the hold of the estate owners seems to have always been more tenuous in distant Ávila, the era of the *patrones* there ended somewhat later. Roads did not penetrate this region until the 1980s.

14. *"Yanga tapa jundaranun, huangana, lumu cu- sahinu, cutu, paushi imata, yacami ima, yutu ima, mas jundarallapicaman, paiguna mitsas mana cachanun . . . yanga mitsanun."*

15. These included *sani—Picramnia sellowii* subsp. *spruceana* (Simaroubaceae)—which produced a dark blue color.

16. The estates with which the Ávila Runa had most contact were primarily those on the Napo River. For example, the wealthy hacienda La Armenia was known to employ many people from Ávila as well as from Loreto and San José in the first decades of the twentieth century (Gianotti 1997:44n33).

17. *Bulimus* spp. (Bulimulidae).

18. Among the Runa of Ávila and San José, resources that are collected in the forest such as snails and mushrooms are seen ambiguously as both delicious snacks and denigrated famine food; people enjoy these in the intimacy of their homes but are reluctant to share them with guests.

19. The Runa of the Archidona region, by contrast, owing to their proximity to administrative seats and their distance from the more easily navigable portions of the Napo River, were largely able to avoid enslavement in the rubber-boom era.

20. In Ávila the term *jiji* is used to refer to the order Orthoptera—that is, to the katydids, crickets, grasshoppers, and their ilk.

References

Castro, Eduardo Viveiros de. 1998. "Cosmological Deixis and Amerindian Perspectivism." *Journal of the Royal Anthropological Institute* 4:469–488.

Crumley, Carole L. 1994. "Historical Ecology: a Multidimensional Ecological Orientation." In *Historical Ecology: Cultural Knowledge and Changing Landscapes*, edited by Carole L. Crumley, 1–16. Santa Fe, N.M.: School of American Research Press.

Descola, Philippe. 1994. "Homeostasis as a Cultural System: The Jivaro Case." In *Amazonian Indians: From Prehistory to the Present*. Anna Roosevelt (ed.), 203–224. Tucson: University of Arizona Press.

———. 1996a. "Constructing Natures: Ecology and Social Practice." In *Nature and Society: Anthropological Perspectives*, edited by Philippe Descola and Gisli Pálsson, 84–102. New York: Routledge.

———. 1996b. *The Spears of Twilight: Life and Death in the Amazon Jungle*. Translated by Janet Lloyd. New York: New Press.

Fausto, Carlos. n.d. "Feasting on People: Eating Animals and Humans in Amazonia." *Current Anthropology*.

Gianotti, Emilio. 1997. *Viajes por el Napo: Cartas de un misionero (1924–1930)*. Translated by Maria Victoria de Vela. Quito: Abya-Yala.

Gonzalez Holguín, Diego. [1608] 1952. *Vocabulario de la lengua general de todo el Perú llamada lengua qquichua o del Inca*. Lima: Imprenta Santa María.

Gow, Peter. 2001. *An Amazonian Myth and Its History*. Oxford: Oxford University Press.

Hilty, Steven L., and William L. Brown. 1986. *A Guide to the Birds of Colombia*. Princeton, N.J.: Princeton University Press.

Hogue, Charles L. 1993. *Latin American Insects and Entomology*. Berkeley: University of California Press.

Hudelson, John Edwin. 1987. *La cultura quichua de transición: Su expansión y desarrollo en el Alto Amazonas*. Translated by Rosa Mercedes Polít. Guayaquil: Museo Antropológico del Banco Central del Ecuador; Quito: Abya-Yala.

Hugh-Jones, Stephen. 1989. "Wáríbi and the White Men: History and Myth in Northwest

Amazonia." In *History and Ethnicity*, edited by Elizabeth Tonkin, Maryon McDonald, and Malcolm Chapman, 53–70. London: Routledge.

Ingold, Tim. 2000. *Perception of the Environment: Essays on Livelihood, Dwelling, and Skill.* London: Routledge.

Kohn, Eduardo O. 2002a. *Natural Engagements and Ecological Aesthetics among the Ávila Runa of Amazonian Ecuador.* Ann Arbor, Michigan: University Microfilms.

———. 2002b. "Infidels, Virgins, and the Black-Robed Priest: A Backwoods History of Ecuador's Montaña Region." *Ethnohistory* 49(3):545–582.

———. 2005. "Runa Realism: Upper Amazonian Attitudes to Nature Knowing." *Ethnos* 70(2):171–196.

———. n.d. "Toward an Anthropology of Life: Amazonian Natures and the Politics of Trans-species Engagement." Manuscript.

Landázuri, Cristobal, ed. *La gobernación de los Quijos, 1559–1621.* Iquitos, Peru: IIAP-CETA.

Maroni, Pablo. [1738] 1988. *Noticias auténticas del famoso Río Marañon y misión apostólica de la Compañía de Jesús de la provincia de Quito en los dilatados bosques de dicho río, escribíalas por los años de 1738, un misionero de la misma compañía. Seguidas de las Relaciones de los P.P. A. de Zárate y J. Magnin (1735–1740).* Edited by Jean-Pierre Chaumeil. Iquitos, Peru: IIAP-CETA.

Martin, Bartolomé. [1563] 1989. "Provanza del Capitan Bartolome Martin." In Landázuri, *La gobernación de los Quijos,* 105–138.

Mercier, Juan Marcos. 1979. *Nosotros los Napu-Runas / Napu Runapa rimay: Mitos e historia.* Iquitos, Peru: Ceta.

Muratorio, Blanca. 1987. *Rucuyaya Alonso y la historia social y económica del Alto Napo 1850–1950.* Quito: Abya-Yala.

Oberem, Udo. 1967–68. "Un grupo de indígenas desaparecido del Oriente ecuatoriano." *Revista de Antropologia* (São Paulo) 15–16:149–170.

———. 1980. *Los Quijos: Historia de la transculturación de un grupo indígena en el Oriente ecuatoriano.* Otavalo, Ecuador: Instituto Otavaleño de Antropología.

Ordóñez de Cevallos, Pedro. [1614] 1989. "Historia y viaje del mundo." In Landázuri, *La gobernación de los Quijos,* 419–437.

Osculati, Gaetano. [1850] 1990. *Esplorazione delle regioni equatoriali lungo il Napo ed il fiume delle Amazzoni: Frammento di un viaggio fatto nelle due Americhe negli anni 1846–47–48.* Turin: Segnalibro.

Porras, Pedro I. 1979. "The Discovery in Rome of an Anonymous Document on the Quijo Indians of the Upper Napo, Eastern Ecuador." In *Peasants, Primitives, and Proletariats: The Struggle for Identity in South America*, edited by David L. Browman and Ronald A. Schwarz, 13–47. The Hague: Mouton.

Raffles, Hugh. 2002. *In Amazonia: A Natural History.* Princeton: Princeton University Press.

Ramírez Dávalos, Gil. 1989 [1559]. "Información hecha a pedimiento del procurador de la ciudad de Baeça . . ." In Landázuri, *La gobernación de los Quijos*, 33–78.

Rival, Laura. 1993. "The Growth of Family Trees: Understanding Huaorani Perceptions of the Forest." *Man* 28:635–652.

Taylor, Anne Christine. 1999. "The Western Margins of Amazonia from the Early Sixteenth to the Early Nineteenth Century." In *The Cambridge History of the Native Peoples of the Americas*, vol. 3, *South America*, edited by Frank Salomon and Stuart B. Schwartz, 2:188–256. Cambridge: Cambridge University Press.

Villavicencio, Manuel. [1858] 1984. *Geografía de la república del Ecuador*. Quito: Corporación Editora Nacional.

Wavrin, Robert. 1927. "Investigaciones etnográficas: Leyendas tradicionales de los indios del Oriente ecuatoriano." *Boletín de la Biblioteca Nacional* (Ecuador) 12:325–337.

Whitten, Norman E., Jr. 1976. *Sacha Runa: Ethnicity and Adaptation of Ecuadorian Jungle Quichua*. Urbana: University of Illinois Press.

II

Altering Bodies, Connecting Names

4

Sick of History

Contrasting Regimes of Historicity in the Upper Amazon

Anne-Christine Taylor

This chapter is about a regional system of the upper Amazon embracing the large ethnic ensemble of the Jivaro, their predominantly Quechua-speaking indigenous neighbors, and the white colonists settled throughout the area. It focuses on two contrasting ways of relating to change and to the narrative construction of history: the one favored by the Jivaroan Indians, centered on the intraethnic dialectics of vengeance and seemingly oblivious to the texture of interethnic relations, the other typical of the postconquest lowland Quechua formations and focused on their ethnogenesis as hybrid cultures. I will argue that these modes of construing the past are in fact interdependent, as are the cultures that produce them. The nature of Quechua societies is intimately tied to the existence both of colonist settlements and of "wild" Indian tribes, just as the persistence of the latter depends on the development of indigenous buffer groups mediating between them and non-Indian outsiders. Likewise, the kind of history experienced and told by Jivaroan speakers is tightly linked to the quite distinct history lived and narrated by the bearers of lowland Quechua culture; each one is sustained by the other. My aim is to present a brief outline of the system and dynamics underlying the play of these complementary regimes of historicity, as they existed between the late eighteenth century and the early 1980s. For reasons of space, I will not attempt here to deal with earlier or more recent developments.

Much recent work on Amerindian ways of construing the past, and in particular the history of relations with dominant non-Indian outsiders, focuses on the mimetic appropriation by Indian societies of elements of Western culture, and lays stress on the way processes of apparent "acculturation" come to form, and be seen as, indigenous tradition. This approach developed in reaction to a view—long entrenched in anthropology—of cultural change as loss of "authenticity," as a negative mode of alteration of a supposedly pristine way of life. Such a conception was open to criticism because it implied a static and essentializing vision of culture, and because it denied the Indians any form of historical agency. However, as Carlos Fausto points out in his contribution, the contemporary approach to Indian forms of historicity also feeds on the structuralist heritage, in particular on its emphasis on the assimilation of the Other as a mode of social reproduction.[1] From this latter perspective, the appropriation of various items of foreign culture as indigenous tradition can be seen as an extension of the principle of "ouverture à l'Autre" (Lévi-Strauss 1991) held to be a basic pattern of Amerindian cultures. Thus, Fausto suggests that the notion of "love"—apparently of Christian origin—that has become a central tenet of the traditional moral universe of the Guarani is in fact a structural transformation of the cannibal relation to the Enemy that formerly shaped many Tupian cultures, most notably that of the sixteenth-century coastal Tupinamba. Likewise, Aparecida Vilaça argues that the startling claim by the Wari' that they are whites rests precisely on their equating of whites to enemies, whose being and point of view can then be invested through shamanic modes of dual selfhood. The contributions of these authors, and of Fernando Santos-Granero, attest to a distinctively Indian way of being or becoming "white."

Against this background, the Jivaroans constitute an unusual case, though by no means a unique one. Rather than incorporating aspects of Western culture to maintain their own identity by changing, the Jivaro seem intent on insulating their tradition from outside influences, and on ignoring the history of their interactions with non-Jivaroans. Further, while social reproduction and the creation of proper Jivaroan selfhood are assuredly linked to a structural relation with enemy partners, these Others are internal: not whites, but fellow Jivaroans. Indeed, becoming another kind of "Other" is tantamount in their view to falling ill, to experiencing an unwanted metamorphosis of personhood. Yet such a negative state is also the gateway to a new identity and form of selfhood, premised on a distinctive way of representing and living the history of those interethnic relations so radically excluded from the Jivaroan view of the past. At the same time, this alternate identity and the culture in which it is embedded are entwined, both historically and structurally, with the Jivaroan societies. At one level, the "wild" Jivaro and their presumably "acculturated" Quechua-speaking neighbors are entirely separate and different social formations; at a deeper level, they are interdependent and mutually constitutive. "Being Jivaro" or "being Runa" (Quechua) are alternative choices, a matter of building up a certain kind of selfhood and engaging in the array of practices it is geared to, each one implying different ways of relating to the past.

Thus, while Jivaroan forms of historicity seem, if they are viewed in isolation from those prevalent among their indigenous neighbors, to belie the idea that Native American cultures thrive on change and the assimilation of traits of foreign origin, as soon as they are replaced within the regional system they belong to they clearly reveal their kinship to the configurations described by Fausto, Vilaça, Santos-Granero, and others. The originality of this model of alternate regimes of identity and historicity lies in the fact that it ultimately rests on a single variation within a restricted domain, in a context of shared cultural premises about modes of relating to nonselves. Each variant is made the core of a specific identity and elaborated in such a way that, by successive implication, it blossoms into a cultural universe quite distinct, in phenomenal terms, from that rooted in the other variant.

"Wild" Indians, "Tame" Indians, and Whites: Classificatory Practices in the Upper Amazon

The Jivaro, or more properly Shuar,[2] presently number some 80,000 to 90,000 people and straddle north-central Peru and southeast Ecuador. They are divided into several subgroups each claiming a specific identity. The two largest of these are the Shuar proper, most of whom live in the eastern foothills of the Ecuadorian Andes, and the Aguaruna (or Awajun), spread over the basins of the Marañon, the Cenepa, and the Rio Mayo. The Huambisa (Wampis) of the Santiago and Morona valleys are closely related to the Shuar in terms of language and social organization, but they now consider themselves a separate tribe. The Achuar dwell in the lowlands east of the Shuar and north of the Huambisa and are more or less evenly distributed between Ecuador and Peru. A smaller group known as the Shiwiar, located along the course of the Rio Corrientes in Peru and linguistically proximate to the Achuar, has emerged as a distinct subgroup within the last decades (Seymour-Smith 1988).[3] Finally, the Candoshi and Shapra of the lower Pastaza basin are now usually classified as Jivaroans: though their dialects, belonging to the Candoan subfamily, are quite distinct from those of the other Jivaroans, as is their kinship terminology, their cultural profile is virtually identical to that of the Achuar, Shuar, and Aguaruna (Payne 1981; Amadio 1985; Surrallés 1999).

It must be stressed that, apart from the case of the Shiwiar, the division of the Jivaroan ensemble as it stands today is not a recently evolved phenomenon. Border conflicts between the Andean nation-states, the spread of religious missions, and the wane of intertribal war and headhunting have certainly contributed to a stabilization of the frontiers between Jivaroan subgroups as well as to heightened tribal closure and self-definition, a process accentuated in recent years by the proliferation throughout western Amazonia of NGOs each in search of the proper kind of "tribal" clientele. Still, while tribal limits and territories have certainly shifted considerably over the past four centuries (Taylor 1986), as have tribal denominations, there is strong archival evidence that by the early eighteenth century at least there were already four or five clearly separate blocks of Jivaroan speakers corresponding roughly to the present Aguaruna, Shuar, Morona Huambisa, Achuar, and Candoshi.

This culturally homogeneous set of tribes is circumscribed by a belt of predominantly Quechua-speaking groups locally labeled—in contrast to the "fierce" or *auca* Jivaroans—as *indios mansos*, "tame Indians." *Auca* is a Quechua word meaning "wild, savage"; as used by the mestizo settlers of the upper Amazon, the term serves to designate any group of non-Christianized, purportedly hostile Indians,[4] as opposed to the "domesticated" or "civilized" Indians who observe elements of Christian practice and are subservient to whites. These circum-Jivaroan "tame Indian" groups are hybrid formations of multiethnic origin formed around small colonist settlements or Jesuit *reducciones* during the late seventeenth and eighteenth centuries. They developed as the remnants of distinct Indian tribes, decimated by epidemics and slave hunting and gathered at mission posts, came to share the common language, territoriality, sociopolitical organization, and mode of articulation to mestizo settlements imposed by the missionaries and by the secular colonial authorities. Examples of such societies are the Canelos Quechua of Ecuador, the Andoas (mission Indians of mixed Zaparoan and Jivaroan origin, now absorbed into Canelos society), the Lamistas of the lower Huallaga valley, and the Xeberos and Chayawita of the upper Marañon.

So-called *manso* Indian groups are not to be confused with the class of Amazonian inhabitants called mestizos or *ribereños* or, in Brazil, *caboclos*. The *mansos* are distinguished by their claim to a specific tribal identity, and by outsiders' recognition of this claim: "tame" Indians are seen to belong to a social entity bounded both in territorial and cultural terms, and clearly labeled as "Indian." In southeast Ecuador, there is no clear distinction between "whites" (Ecuadorian or foreign) and half-castes or mestizos. Amazonian non-Indians usually identify themselves simply as *blancos* (whites).[5] "Whiteness" has little to do with skin color: the defining characteristic of *blancos* is that they live in an urban environment, in *ciudades* (cities).[6] More recent and poorer immigrants, usually of Andean origin, call themselves *racionales* (rationals) and live in *centros*—towns in the making, as it were—connected to the "historic" cities founded in the nineteenth or, in a few cases, the sixteenth century. The important point is that there still are few non-Indian forest dwellers in this region. Consequently, there is no intermediate category between "tribal" Indians of the forest, whether wild or "domesticated," and city-dwelling "rational" whites.

Throughout the Peruvian Oriente, classificatory practices are more complex, because the social and spatial separation of the diverse types of Amazonian inhabitants is less clear-cut. The many settlers living in isolated homesteads along the riverbanks may identify themselves as *nativos* but are often labeled mestizos by outsiders because of their lack of tribal ascription (Gow 1991, 1993). In short, the far earlier and more dynamic expansion of the colonist frontier in this region has worked to produce a large body of mixed-blood forest dwellers poised between *nativo* and mestizo identities. Moreover, the pull toward the non-Indian pole of identity has until recently been much stronger in Peru than in Ecuador. The ancient ternary *racionales-mansos-aucas* classification forged in the early eighteenth century and still used in Ecuador has therefore modulated here toward an opposition between *blancos*, or *virachochas* in indigenous terms, who are urban-dwelling (the closer to the center of cities, the "whiter" their population), river-dwelling "mixed-bloods" (mestizo or *nativo*, according to context) and tribal *indios bravos* (fierce Indians) inhabiting the hinterland.

From the Indians' point of view, matters are more straightforward, at least at a superficial level.[7] Jivaroans , regardless of their tribal affiliation, refer to themselves as *shuar*, persons. Other Jivaroans are called either *shuar* or *shiwiar*, a term meaning "enemy Jivaroan." Or they may be designated by a place-name; for instance, *kapavinmaya* means "[person] from the Kapavi river." The same usage applies to non-Jivaroan Indians: they also are named either *shuar* or *aents* (person) along with a geographical specification, or simply referred to by a place-name followed by a suffix denoting origin; examples are *saracnumia*, "[person] from Sarayacu," and *puyunmaya*, "[person] from Puyo"—that is, Canelos Indians from Sarayacu or Puyo. More distant Indian groups, known by hearsay, are called by ethnonyms, including Kukam' (Cocama), Tawishiur (formerly the Zaparoans, now the Huaorani), and Ramista (Lamistas). All non-Indians (indeed, at a more inclusive level, all non-Jivaroans) are *apachi*, "grandfather" (lit., "little father," from Shuar and Achuar *apa*, "father" + dim. -*chi*). However, when contrasted to *kirinku* (gringo), *apach* denotes Ecuadorian or Peruvian nationals specifically.[8]

The polysemy and contextual lability of these modes of classification indicate that all these categories, both the Indians' and those used by non-Indian Amazonians, have little to do with objective, on-the-ground social groups. Rather than referring to fixed classes of beings, they designate positions, defined by cosmological, spatial, social, and economic correlates, within an integrated network of dependencies.[9] Thus, being an *auca* or *bravo* Indian is to be sited within a social and ecological environment (embedded in a web of kinship, inhabiting the interfluvial "deep" forest), to repel relations with outsiders, and to live on forest produce without producing wealth. Being a "tame" Indian or a *ribereño* is to domesticate this wildness by initiating its transformation into money and proper sociality, and to inhabit the loci—rivers and, increasingly, roads—that articulate forest and city spaces. Being "white," finally, is to be "urban," at a remove from the forest and its inhabitants, in a world where relations, including kinship, are entirely monetarized.[10]

The Genesis of "Tame" Indian Societies and Their Relation to "Wild" Indians

Although many Jivaroans, particularly the Shuar and the Aguaruna, have in fact been living close to colonists since at least the nineteenth century, the Jivaro are still considered by Amazonian whites and *manso* Indians as archetypal *aucas*. This is largely because, until very recently, the Jivaro did not interact with whites in ways that correspond to local definitions of a social relation. Contacts between the two groups were seen by both parties simply as a succession of random encounters, hopefully peaceful from the whites' point of view, hopefully productive of Western goods from the Indians' point of view. Fear, suspicion, and bravado formed the dominant tone of such interactions, because these were not integrated into the flow of a shaped and recursive type of relationship; they remained, in this sense, outside history. Social and economic ties between the *aucas* and the colonists were in fact almost entirely mediated by the *manso* Indians. A brief sketch of the genesis of these indigenous buffer groups will help understand the historical role they have played in the making of postconquest western Amazonia.

One typical example of such formations are the Canelos Quechua of Ecuador, a culture that emerged from the interaction of small groups of refugee Zaparoans, Andean Indians, Quijos (Napo Quechua), and Jivaroans loosely gravitating around the Dominican mission of Canelos founded in the late seventeenth century (Whitten 1976). By the mid-eighteenth century this small network, united by repeated intermarriage and a shared bond of nominal obeisance to the Dominicans, gained recognition by missionaries and colonial authorities as a distinct tribe. In the following decades it began to spread eastward, creating new settlements along the Bobonaza and Curaray rivers as it drew in more families or individuals of Napo Quechua, Achuar, or Zaparoan origin. Each new Canelos community eventually developed exclusive economic and pseudokinship ties with one or two mestizo families initially based in the historic frontier towns and dealing in forest products—gold dust, palm fiber, false cinnamon, various resins—collected by the Indians in exchange for paltry stocks of salt and manufactured goods, mainly tools, guns, ammunition, and cloth. Because of the Quechua's ramifying settlement pattern and their symbiotic links to white traders, the eastward spread of the Canelos carried with it an expansion of the colonist front: as Canelos kin groups branched out from their natal villages to found new settlements in uninhabited forest tracts, so too did the mestizo traders who exploited them.[11] This process lies at the origin of many of the towns founded since the nineteenth century in the northern upper Amazon. Until the 1970s the Canelos were the main source of Western goods for the Achuar, who acquired them either by taking over part of the debt in produce owed by a Quechua family—in exchange for a share of the latter's possessions—or by trade against traditional goods, such as blowguns, feather headdresses, hunting dogs, and curare, items sought after by the Canelos to maintain and reproduce the "forest Indian" facet of their identity. Quechua shamans also provided highly valued shamanic services to their *auca* neighbors, and built up powerful kin groups by attracting Achuar sons-in-law; reciprocally, Jivaroans occasionally served as contract killers for their Quechua kinsmen (Whitten 1976).

Another case of post-Columbian ethnogenesis as "tame" Indians is that of the Jeberos of Peru, a Cahuapanan group now known as the Shiwilu. An Indian group identified as Xeberos, neighbors of the (Jivaroan) Mayna and proto-Agua-runa of the upper Marañon, were "pacified" in the early seventeenth century by the colonists of Borja (Taylor 1986). The ethnic identity and linguistic affiliation of these Xeberos remains in dispute. Both their colonial name and the modern ethnonym they claim, Shiwilu, are close to Jivaroan names—Shiwilu sounds like a quechuized form of *shiwiru*, a possible corruption of *shiwiar*—and in fact these Indians have often been confused with the "Xibaro." The Shiwilu's own oral tradition hints insistently at a Jivaroan origin, despite the indisputably Cahuapanan affiliation of their language. Whoever they were, these Indians were first taken into the *encomiendas* of the local colonists before being settled by the Jesuits in a *reducción*, named Limpia Concepción de Xeberos, along with families of Coca-millas, Jivaro, Mayoruna, Cutinana, Parapurana, and Yameos. By the beginning of the eighteenth century, this mission post had become a large multiethnic village divided into distinct *barrios* or quarters, home to some 2,500 persons, most of whom spoke Quechua as well as Xebero. Famed throughout the Maynas mission for their docility and receptivity to evangelization, these hybrid Xeberos willingly served first as "ethnic soldiers" in apostolic *entradas* or civilian slave-hunting expeditions,[12] and later as guides, couriers, and oarsmen for colonial authorities or foreign visitors. The extensive traveling they undertook in the course of their duties provided the Xeberos with opportunities for developing trade relations with *auca* Indians, a practice in theory forbidden by the missionaries. After the expulsion of the Jesuits in 1767, and although the population of the former *reducción* sharply declined, the village remained closely linked to the local mestizo families, who routinely commandeered its labor force. Following the virtual disappearance of the Marañon colonist settlements by the end of the eighteenth century, the Xeberos fell prey to the *colonos* of Moyobamba, to whom they provided market-able forest products in exchange for Western goods and patronage. However, they also maintained and in fact intensified their relations with the Aguaruna and other "wild" Indians of the hinterland, offering their shamanic mastery as well as manufactured goods (Steward and Métraux 1948; Taylor 1986).

The highly dynamic Indian societies of colonial origin such as the Canelos and Shiwilu are relatively diverse both in their initial ethnic conformation and in their salient cultural traits. Nonetheless, they share a number of features that justify treating them as a single class. They are all built around the linkage between their dual "faces," the one they present to nonindigenous outsiders as "tame," Chris-tianized, "civilized" Indians (*alli runa*, in the idiom of the Canelos Quechua) and the one they present to their *auca* Indian neighbors as knowledgeable and powerful *sacha runa*, forest people[13] (Whitten 1976). Their major collective rituals, combining elements of Catholic liturgy and of the Andean system of *cargos*, are centered on the enactment of the mediating role that constitutes them as distinct societies with a specific identity. These rituals explore the tension between, on the one hand, the state of savagery incarnated by the *indios bravos*, who are also presented as a metaphor of the *mansos'* own past as projected in their historical discourse, and, on the other hand, the mechanized, predatory world of white men, representing an equally fearsome mythic future. Finally, all these "tame" groups have a highly developed shamanic complex. Their form of shamanism is of the "horizontal type," to borrow a term from Stephen Hugh-Jones (1994) for a kind of aggressive shamanism characterized by its practitioners' reputed ability to interact with foreign entities and enlist their help for offensive or defensive purposes, in contrast to a "vertical" shamanism emphasizing esoteric knowledge and ritual expertise in the reproduction of society. Among the Quechua, shamans (known as *yachaj*) are also the major political figures; it is they who, by balancing the threat of invisible aggression with the buildup of extensive affinal networks, give shape to the entire field of social relations.

Given the dual, quintessentially shamanic nature of these "tame Indian" societ-ies, the political preeminence of the *yachaj* is not surprising. It is directly linked to the pivotal role Quechua shamans play, by virtue of their professional cosmo-politism (both real and imaginary), in the process of regulated combination of wild, upriver jungle products and relations with those stemming from the "dark satanic mills" of the great Amazonian cities, the white man's heartland. Indeed, because of their ability to be at the same time a human and a nonhuman forest being (typically a game animal; see Vilaça, this volume), "horizontal" shamans are a condensed, metonymical expression of Janus-faced *manso* culture as a whole. By contrast, among the Jivaroans, as in many *auca* societies, the power of political leaders or "strong men" (*kakaram*, in Shuar and Achuar) rests on the repute they gain in warfare and hunting, fields of practice in which shamans are not actively or directly involved.[14]

All Jivaroan groups have over the centuries developed close connections with such "tame" Indian societies. The Achuar are closely tied to the Canelos Quechua of the Bobonaza-Curaray area, and until the 1920s they also interacted with the Andoas, as did the Candoshi. The Shiwiar and Candoshi, in turn, are linked to the Runa settled along the eastern tributaries of the Pastaza and the tributaries of the Napo River. The Aguaruna interact with the Lamistas and Xeberos and Chayawita (the latter another Cahuapanan-speaking group now known as the Shawi). The Shuar, in former times, were connected to Quechua-speaking groups made up of Andean Indian colonists settled along the upper Upano and Bomboiza valleys, and nowadays to Napo Quechua in whose traditional territory they have formed over the past decades several thriving colonies. Going further back, historical evidence suggests that the Jivaroans' practice of forming buffer groups along their frontiers, or at any rate of fostering peaceful relations of a distinctive kind with neighboring indigenous groups, may not be linked solely to the changes proceeding from the Spanish conquest. Certain ethnic groups who during Incaic and pre-Incaic times occupied the northern Peruvian Andes, namely the Guayacundos and Caxas, interacted with the Highland Paltas, a Jivaroan population still extant in the sixteenth century who inhabited the mountains south of Loja, in a manner highly reminiscent of the Achuar-Canelos association (Hocquenghem 1989, 1998; Taylor 1986, 1992b, 1994b).

The settlement patterns, kinship systems, political structures, and ritual performances of the *mansos* are quite distinct from those of the *aucas*. Yet while Jivaroans very rarely come to adopt a mestizo or non-Indian identity, they easily move in and out of neighboring "tame" Indian societies. Many Jivaroans, particularly along the periphery of the ensemble, are fluent in Quechua; some are married to incoming Quechua women; others have settled in Quechua groups and have adopted their identities, durably or temporarily. Young men and even children often spend several years among their Quechua relatives before returning to their own group. Even when they are not ostensibly bilingual or bicultural and disclaim prior familiarity with the language and manners of their "tame" neighbors, Jivaroan individuals seem to have no difficulty in adapting speedily to their new social environment. Finally, nearly all important Jivaroan shamans have, at some point in their careers, been in apprenticeship with Quechua shamans. In any case, their curing chants are invariably replete with oblique references to their mastery over the Quechua language,[15] and more generally over entities and techniques associated with Quechua shamanic practice.

The Jivaroans' ability to slide into an alien Indian identity and way of being, despite the ostensible difference between their own cultural background and that of the "tame" Quechua societies, is all the more striking as linguistic and social frontiers between the various Jivaroan subgroups are, contrary to those between Jivaro and Quechua, strongly emphasized. While it is true that, from an objective point of view, cultural variation between the Jivaroan tribes is slight, each group considers the others to be quite different from itself: the Achuar, for example, claim that the Shuar are non-kin and that their language is "unintelligible."[16] Thus, whereas Jivaroan tribal identities are mutually exclusive, dual macroethnic affiliations are not seen as contradictory; and whereas limits between Jivaroans are sharply asserted in terms of territory, language, kinship, and tribal "essence," frontiers between Jivaroans and Quechua are permeable, shifting, and generally downplayed.

Jivaroan History: The Outside View

Clearly, the Jivaro are by no means an isolated ethnic group only recently affected by the expansion of the colonization frontier. They have in fact been exposed to repeated attempts to conquer and "pacify" them ever since the time of the Incas. While the Tawantinsuyo's attempts to subdue the eastern montane Jivaroans met with resounding failure,[17] the Incas did effectively incorporate the Andean Jivaroans known as Paltas; as a consequence, these Indians had vanished as a distinct ethnic group by the end of the sixteenth century. By 1560 the western Jivaroans—the "Xibaros" and Bracamoros of the eastern Andean piedmont who had routed the Inca's armies, and the Marañon-Santiago Jivaro later known as the Aguaruna—were confronting an invasion of their montane territory by Spanish *capitanes* intent on carving out feudal domains for themselves. Hundreds of *encomiendas* were distributed in the course of these expeditions,[18] though most of them remained purely nominal, as their grantees had no means of effectively controlling their Indian *tributarios*. More worrisome to the indigenous population was the steady flow into their territory of foreigners—Europeans, half-castes, fugitive or displaced Andean Indians—intent on exploiting locally abundant gold placers and mines. This early gold boom collapsed by 1590, partly because of the discovery of far richer gold mines elsewhere in the Andes, partly because of a series of bloody local uprisings involving Jivaroan and Andean Indians as well as disgruntled mestizos. Nearly all the *encomenderos* and most of the floating population of outsiders drew back into the highlands, but the gold rush did leave in its wake a scattering of small, isolated urban settlements such as Macas, Borja, and Moyobamba, populated by a few dozen colonists.

Although the shriveled colonization front at the eastern foot of the equatorial

Andes remained fossilized until well into the nineteenth century, the Jivaroans had to contend, from the mid-sixteenth century on, with a new threat on their southeastern flank: the spread of the huge Jesuit Mainas mission, initially based in the town of Borja, on the banks of the Marañon. The Jesuits never succeeded in drawing the Jivaro into their network of *reducciones*, though several large, heavily armed apostolic *entradas* were launched against them, notably in 1690–91[19]; and by the middle of the eighteenth century the missionaries were in fact close to finally achieving the "pacification" of the Jivaro, with the help of a large group of Muratos (Candoshi) whom they had settled in a *reducción* in 1757 and who were expected to find and attract their more recalcitrant brethren (Veigl 1768; Jouanen 1941–43). The Jivaro—in this instance the Achuar—were saved by the abrupt expulsion of the Jesuits in 1767. From that date to the mid-nineteenth century, the Jivaro enjoyed a period of reprieve, though a few peaceful expeditions were sent into the western part of their territory in the late eighteenth century by Ecuadorian municipal authorities anxious to stimulate trade relations with lowland Indians. Around 1850, however, the colonization frontier in Peru began to expand rapidly, fueled by a series of extractive minibooms—of cinchona (quinine bark), of tagua (vegetal ivory), of sarsaparilla—and accompanied by military explorations, such as that of Raimondi along the Morona in 1860 (Raimondi [1876–80] 1905), and state-sponsored colonization projects (Santos-Granero and Barclay 1998). As a result, the southern and eastern Jivaro once again abandoned the major riverbanks and pulled back into the interfluvial hills.

This cycle of development culminated in the great rubber boom of 1880–1914. The frenzied exploitation of *hevea* sap and of the Indian labor needed to collect it did not affect the Jivaro as dramatically as it did other Indian groups in the western Amazon, partly thanks to their fearsome reputation, partly because there was little high-grade *hevea* in their territory. The Candoshi and Achuar did gather *balata*, a lower-grade rubber sap taken from the tree *Castilloa elastica*, for minor Peruvian bosses, but they did so more or less on their own terms, and they were not deported to work richer rubber fields. Still, the rubber boom marked the beginning of direct, sustained contact between white traders and Jivaroans. Caught up henceforth in the debt-and-credit system prevalent throughout the Amazon and locally known as *habilitación*,[20] the Jivaro (mainly the Candoshi and southern Achuar) turned from gathering balata to collecting pelts and smoked meat to trade for Western goods provided by their *habilitados*, and later to logging (Gippelhauser and Mader 1990; Mader and Gippelhauser 1984; Surrallés 1999). However, the hold of the *patrones* over the Jivaro always remained precarious. The only way of truly binding the Indians to their obligations was to establish close kin relations with them through in-marriage, but few *habilitados* dared to do this, for fear of becoming enmeshed in local feuding, an inevitable correlate of in-law status.[21]

Initially, the spread of the colonization frontier was limited to the south and southeast of Jivaroan territory, but in the wake of the rubber boom it extended rapidly northward, along with Peruvian influence, sanctioned by the much disputed border settlement of 1941 between Ecuador and Peru. As a result, the Ecuadorian frontier began to develop as well, and from the 1930s on, the Jivaro came under increasing pressure along both their northwestern and southeastern limits. Within the last decades, the habitat of the Shuar, Aguaruna, and southern Huambisa has been overrun by a steadily expanding population of Andean-based landless immigrants. Most Indian communities in this area now have collective rights over a portion of forest, but they share their former territory with colonists scattered along the riverbanks or gathered in *centros* accessible by road. More important, these Indians are almost fully integrated into the market economy; in some cases they have even lost their subsistence base and must either sell their labor—at best as bureaucrats, in indigenous federations or in municipal and regional administrations—or live off development schemes set up by NGOs.

The Resilience of Jivaroan Culture

Yet this centuries-long and conflictive cohabitation with non-Indians has not noticeably eroded the Jivaroans' distinctive way of relating to themselves and to others. Their culture has proved remarkably enduring and appears to have undergone relatively little change between the Spanish conquest and the middle of the twentieth century. Comparing early colonial accounts of the historic Jivaroans,[22] often quite detailed, with the writings of the first professional ethnographers of these Indians in the twentieth century—scientists such as Rafael Karsten (1935), Matthew Stirling (1938), or Günther Tessmann—one cannot fail to be impressed by the close fit between descriptions produced at an interval of close to four centuries, and relating to territorial implantation, settlement patterns, material culture, styles of warfare, appearance, and attitudes. In this respect the Jivaro contrast sharply with their Quechua-speaking neighbors, who not only emerged as distinct tribes from the colonial encounter but whose cultures are constantly adapting to social and economic transformation occurring in the dominant society they are articulated to. And whereas the latter Indians have built their identity on their very "mixedness," the Jivaro have always, throughout their engagement with outsiders, manifested a particularly strong and exclusive sense of ethnic belonging. Unlike, for example, the Wari' (see Vilaça, this volume), Jivaroans never claim to be "white," either in private or in public. To the contrary, the more involved they are in the economic, social, and political relations typical of the internal frontier zones of the Andean nation-states, the more militantly they defend their status as shuar, "Jivaroan persons." Even in their manner of adopting non-Indian objects, clothing, food, and behavior when in urban contexts, they affirm their ethnic personhood by competing with the whites at their own game. Thus, they make a point of being more elegantly and expensively dressed than the local mestizos, of speaking Spanish more fluently and with more authority, of spending more ostentatiously. In their view, being better at "whiteness" than the whites is just another way of being Shuar. Moreover, all the tribes have founded strong political organizations over the past thirty years to negotiate collectively the terms of their economic and political relation to the national society. They have built up their own systems of bilingual schooling and health care, contracted helpers to push through their land claims and set up economic development projects, and taken over many of the state's traditional administrative responsibilities. At the same time, these new forms of organization become contexts for reproducing key aspects of Jivaroan tradition, most notably the link between positions of social power and the disposition to engage in antagonistic relations, including homicide.[23]

The resilience of Jivaro society has little to do, however, with collective acts of armed resistance to encroaching whites. For all their fearsome reputation, the Jivaro did not in fact engage in concerted, organized warfare against non-Indian intruders. Their very real bellicosity is geared to internal conflict, in the shape of intratribal feuding and intertribal headhunting. In most cases, foreigners were (and are) peacefully received, and if they seemed threatening the most common reaction was flight, dispersion, and resettlement in more remote areas. This is not to say that the Jivaro never fought against aggressive colonizers. During the early colonial period and in the second half of the nineteenth century, frequent skirmishes opposed this or that local group to Spanish or Creole forces. However, such acts of warfare were purely local and occasional. Moreover, they concerned only whites; relations with non-Jivaroan Indians, and in particular with the neighboring lowland Quechua, were and remain ordinarily peaceful. This configuration—internal relations marked by mutual hostility versus external relations marked by a disposition to engage in peaceful trade—stands in sharp contrast to the pre-Andean Arawak system of relations, based on a strong prohibition of internal violence and a remarkable capacity to form extensive confederations ready to take up arms against invaders, as these Indians did, famously, during the eighteenth-century insurrection of Juan Santos Atahuallpa (Santos-Granero 1991, [1992?], 1993; Renard-Casevitz 1992). Contrary to expectation, however, the Jivaroans' disposition to fight each other rather than foreigners has not weakened them nor made them easy prey for colonists greedy for their land or labor force and for missionaries avid for their souls; rather, it has sustained their identity and the culture that feeds it.

Jivaroan Selfhood as a State of Health

The Jivaroans' pattern of being in and making history—predicated, as I will claim, on a distinctive way of defining what is to be remembered and forgotten and by whom—is a crucial factor in the persistence of Jivaroan culture. This form of historicity is in turn intimately linked to the production of certain states of selfhood considered fundamental to Jivaroan identity, as opposed to Quechua identity with its entirely different way of conceptualizing and living history.

Let me begin, then, by describing the subjective state of being defined by the Jivaro as both normally healthful and morally proper—that is, defined as characteristic of Jivaroan personhood. Among the features mentioned as constitutive of this state are a sense of physical strength and well-being, sharpness of mind and decisiveness, the capacity—indeed the urge—both to confront others and to shape their feelings with regard to oneself, and the ability to live correctly, to be or become aware of the rightness of values and norms perceived as specifically Jivaroan. Note that this subjective disposition is as much within the individual as outside, since it can be defined only in relational terms. This state of being and relating to the social environment is deemed "natural" in the sense that it is regarded as the proper Jivaroan "default state," but it is very far from being innate or given. Instead, it must be achieved.

Visionary experiences are a crucial factor in this process. Visions, obtained through fasting, dreaming, or consuming hallucinogenic drugs, are considered both health-giving and pedagogic, so that children, particularly boys, are encouraged to undergo these experiences and forced to if they persistently misbehave. There are many kinds of visions, but the most salient of these are encounters with an entity named *arutam*, literally "an old or used thing." *Arutam* are in fact avatars of the dead; they are what the recently deceased are transformed into by the process of funerary treatment and mourning (Taylor 1993b, 1998). During the ritually constructed encounter with this kind of ghost, the *arutam* transmits to the seeker a short verbal or visual message usually concerning the outcome of a conflict or of a planned raid, more generally the future relational status of the individual experiencing the vision. The content of this message as well as the identity of the dead Jivaroan who issued it must henceforth remain shrouded in utmost secrecy. The message is in effect a metonymical forecast of a significant destiny, and it imbues the receiver with a sense of invulnerability, heightened awareness of self, and a kind of energetic anger feeding an impulse to kill. In short, it confers on the seeker a strong sense of existential "health" and directionality. Most of these visionary experiences are built on a common scheme, in which a positive message, visual or verbal, concerning the life course of the seeker and delivered by the spiritual entity is framed by a traumatic and therefore highly memorable context of antagonistic confrontation. The confrontation is set up either between the seeker and the spirit—for instance, the *arutam* might appear as a threatening figure that must be approached and touched in order to receive the message—or between two "aspects" of the entity itself, perhaps taking the shape of two predators, such as jaguars or anacondas or harpy eagles, locked in mortal combat.[24]

Experiencing such visions is deemed vital for proper socialization, but it is also a cumulative process; men go on seeking visions throughout their lives in times of crises, in particular each time they actually do what the experience primes them to do, namely kill an opponent. Each killing causes a man to lose the force acquired from the previous one and therefore leads to further vision quests. Pragmatically, the kind of selfhood shaped by these experiences is manifested in heightened competence in the use of speech to persuade or exhibit power, and in particular to engage in full-blown ceremonial dialogue (another highly salient and valued ritualized agonistic relation), willingness to take up arms against whoever happens to be the focus of hostility at any given time, the adroit exercise of marriage strategies to establish relations with the right affines (which also means choosing the right enemies), and mastery at shaping others' attitudes (which also means the capacity to assume a leading role in organizing war parties). In sum, by highlighting the relation between exemplary destiny and agonistic stances, these experiences are instrumental in producing a disposition in which feelings of self, of worth, and of health, as well as a reflexive awareness of this state, are inextricably linked. The more you achieve in the game this complex is geared to, the greater the web of relations you vectorize, the more people you pull into your sphere of influence, and the more you kill, directly or by association; and as your repute as a "strong person" grows, so too does your sense of self, and the "angrier" you get. This mechanism is what shapes and defines a Jivaroan identity, and therefore the social and cultural system it is embedded in. Both for these Indians and for their indigenous and white neighbors, it underlies stereotypic views of what being a Jivaro is all about, though of course not everyone lives all the time in a condition of honed predatory intentionality.

History in the First Person

The state of being rooted in the relation between health, moral rightness, and bellicosity has another dimension. It is intimately tied to a discursive genre, namely autobiographical war stories, yet another instance of framing of adversarial relationships. The ability to tell such stories is of course a function of the kind of existential trajectory the narrator has forged; to become one's own historian, one has to have lived a life worthy of recounting. The telling of a full-blown biography of self as "strong man" (*kakaram*) is therefore limited to experienced older men with some repute as warriors.[25] Individuals claiming shamanic abilities do not engage in such narratives, any more than they participate in overt acts of war. To the contrary, shamans are ostensibly reticent to speak of their life history (Taylor 1993a); their version of autobiographical narrative is to be found in their curing chants, replete with oblique hints to the experiences of interethnic traveling underlying their shamanic capabilities. Women, on the other hand, do tell autobiographies, but their accounts differ sharply from those of *kakaram* in several aspects. First, feminine autobiographies are destined for a purely domestic audience—their own household—and they are recited in monologic form without any expectation of back-channel response, whereas men's accounts are typically delivered, in markedly dialogic form, during visiting sessions between households and local groups. Second, their dominant tonality is one of complaint; whatever the objective circumstances of their lives, women tend to speak of their past in terms of personal suffering, loss, and displacement (Juncosa 2000). Masculine stories, by contrast, stress the narrator's anger and fierceness; they are also rich in black humor, offering grimly ironical descriptions, and even imitations, of the fear and confusion felt by the narrator and others during the battle.

Autobiographies play a very important part in building up the Jivaroan regime of history. They constitute in fact the only kind of discourse in which experience of the past is given narrative shape.[26] The Jivaro do not tell stories about bygone collective exploits, like the pre-Andean Arawak (Renard-Casevitz 1992), or about dead heroes, like the Yagua (Chaumeil 1992, 1997). Among other reasons, this is because testimonial narration can only be in the first person. It is unthinkable to tell a story in the voice of someone else, or indeed about someone who is not the speaker. Segments of reported speech may occur in the narrative, but they are always brief and strongly marked with quotative indices, to avoid any hint of ambiguity as to speaker's identity.[27] The narrator's single voice remains clearly dominant throughout the telling. Moreover, these stories are invariably centered on warfare. Typically, they detail the narrator's reasons for taking up arms—usually a prior killing and the debt (*tumash*) this homicide entails for surviving close kin—and various or all episodes of the raids and counterraids in which the speaker participated as a result of this initial aggression.

War autobiographies are thus narrowly tied to the cycles of feuding and headhunting associated with intraethnic relations. They are not concerned with eventual acts of violence committed within the framework of interethnic relationships, because such events do not fit into the narrative scheme fueled by the momentum of reciprocal vengeance. For these reasons, the Jivaro preserve no oral record of the history of their relations with whites. More generally, the Jivaro tell almost no myths about whites or Western goods, with the exception—and this is a point I will return to—of those relating to shamanic capacities. Of course, myths do not relate to their "subject" in a transparent way, and therefore need not mention foreigners explicitly to be "about" whites and interethnic history (see Gow 2001 for a good example). Still, in such cases the connection between ostensible content and implicit meaning is often suggested by metonymy.[28] Thus, in the variants of an Andoke myth discussed by Landaburu (1993), the new name given by a narrator to a traditional mythic hero is understood by all (except the anthropologist) to refer to a white man, because it applies to a bird associated with a downriver location where Westerners are thought to reside. Jivaroan mythology, however, offers few clues that might point to an underlying discourse about relations with whites. To be more precise, while the processes inherent in such relations may be taken up in myth, the Jivaro seem to take great care to keep the terms of such relations as vaguely defined as possible, by expunging from their narratives any evocation of the whites, of their tools, of their gifts and threats. Even the pictures drawn by school-educated Jivaro to illustrate published editions of their mythology are devoid of the guns, dogs, poultry, and metal tools that have been for centuries part of the fabric of daily life (see, for example, García-Rendueles 1996).

In broader perspective, ties to past states of the Jivaroan collectivity are rarely objectified and recognized. Significantly, the archaeological remains found in abundance throughout Jivaroan territory are not considered to bear any relation to present society; they belong instead to hostile alien spirits (*iwia*). Collective history is a foreign country. Perhaps more important, links to the past are always translated into particularized relations to specific individuals.[29] This is the case both in ritual *arutam* quests and in mythic narration, wherein speakers invariably begin by naming the deceased relative who told them the story they are about to recount. At the same time, it is from the dead that the living Jivaro acquire both the unique bodily shapes they inhabit and their potential destiny or biography. However, the gift of reproduction can be obtained from the dead only by forgetting them, because human forms are finite in number and must be constantly recycled for new people to appear. This implies cleansing the recently deceased, through funerary treatment and mourning—a process of disremembering the dead and stripping them of any trace of evocability—of the shared affective memory that individualized or personalized the singular shape they acquired at conception. What remains of the dead is a kind of empty "memorability" devoid of any visual or biographical detail that would allow reminiscence (Taylor 1993b).

This memory of a memory is precisely what constitutes the *arutam* who confer on the living the ability to make history. The greater the repute of a person, the more arduous is the work of forgetting his appearance and his biography, and the more potent is the ghost he will become. Therefore the more compelling is the potential destiny he will hand down and the greater the capacity to make history and tell it. This is why one must not evoke one's own dead, and why one can speak only in first person, from one's own perspective.

Being Remembered by One's Foes

But this is not the whole story. While you must erase from memory your deceased relatives to go on living and producing children, you must never forget that they have been murdered. Whatever the cause of their death, it is always attributed to malignant human intention. Indeed, any and all acts of aggression committed by an individual are reactive, considered to be justified by the need to "defend" oneself and one's family, because enemies are a given in the texture of the world one comes into. This is precisely why one has to build up the kind of subjectivity I described initially. Thus autobiographies, at the same time that they recount the narrator's own feats, exhaustively detail the names and acts of his adversaries. In short, the explicit, socially circulated memory of one's own forgotten dead is delegated to one's enemies and kept alive in their perspective, as enemies, in a fashion reminiscent of the Tupinamba temporality of vengeance described by Manuela Carneiro da Cunha and Eduardo Viveiros de Castro. In the Jivaroan version of this mode of structuring history, individual memory is redistributed to build up a collective memory of adversarial relations, which means that one's enemies are reproduced at the same time as oneself. The end result is a highly self-centered form of history, oblivious to engagement with anything that does not feed it, and in particular with outsiders who do not enter into the proper adversarial relationship, or whom the Jivaro choose not to consider enemies.

Jivaroan naming practices closely mesh with this economy of memory. Persons receive a single name at birth, usually that of a recently deceased ascendant of one or the other parent. At the same time, great care is taken to avoid homonymy with any living individual belonging to the same neighborhood. However, adults are almost never addressed by their names: proper names are used only for young children and by their close relatives, or for adults by their enemies. In fact, the greater the repute of a man as a warrior, the more his name is spoken by his adversaries in their own autobiographies, and the less it is used by his own kin and allies. A sure sign of a man's status as a *kakaram* is the care taken by the members of his group to avoid mentioning his name even in his absence. His social weight is such that he becomes a nameless but ever-present delocutor for his kinsmen; meanwhile, his name crops up in more and more enemy war stories. Not surprisingly, it is considered a sign of weakness for a man to change his name during the course of his life.

The stability of Jivaroan culture, then, can be explained to a large extent by the fact that it is built around a tight set of linkages between identity as a certain kind of relational disposition and a distinctive way of organizing memory. It is, in a manner of speaking, carried forward by the history it is predicated on and produces. Thus, Jivaroan culture as tradition is not an objectified body of knowledge or set of explicitly held representations, nor is it concentrated in material things or institutions; it is primarily the means of achieving a certain kind of selfhood. This is why the Jivaro are, or rather were until recently, largely unconcerned about "losing their culture." So long as the confrontational stance they—and others—feel to be inherent in their identity finds contexts in which it can be activated, they will go on existing. To be a Jivaro, in short, all you need is to believe that the world contains figures intent on becoming enemies. Nor do these figures necessarily have to be "Jivaro" in the sense of belonging to a specific, bounded ethnic or cultural group; anybody willing to play the same game over a period of time sufficient to produce vindicatory memory becomes ipso facto Jivaroan.[30]

History as Illness

However, though Jivaroan culture as a system is extremely resilient, the state of being defined as paradigmatically Jivaro is fragile. As in any competitive social structure, the hierarchy of individuals is very unstable and their relative positions are constantly shifting. Jivaroan selfhood is thus highly vulnerable to erosion, through death or disaffection, of the web of relations that constitute it. Such a condition induces felt weakness, both social and physical—a kind of sociological anemia that translates into symptoms of illness and claims of being an orphan, a state that is tantamount to being sick.

This is where the history of interethnic relations comes back with a vengeance. As I stressed, none of this aspect of the past figures in the highly introverted Jivaroan forms of history I have dealt with so far. There is, however, one discursive register in which neighbors, whites, and foreigners in general figure prominently. This is the register of shamanic curing chants and the myths concerning the origins of shamanic power. In this type of discourse, foreigners as well as their objects and icons are very much foregrounded. Typically, the officiating shaman will describe himself as located in some markedly white location (a town, a military garrison, an air control towers), dressed in foreign attire (boots, uniform, helmet), speaking the foreigners' language and manipulating the most significant objects of their environment: pens, motors, books, swords, tanks. Likewise, the myths relating to the aquatic spirits named *tsunki* who are the ultimate source of shamanic techniques describe them as living in underwater cities and seated on turtles figured as cars (Pellizzaro 1978). The world that shamans build up through their healing songs is thus a strange, dreamlike bric-à-brac mixing elements of different times, types of outsiders, and ontological status. This is of course a feature of shamanic practice that has often been noted. Given the shamans' position as managers of alterity, the proliferation in their ritual chants of indices of their familiarity with the white man's world has often been interpreted as a symptom of a discourse of resistance to domination and cultural dissolution, through the mimetic appropriation of white power.[31] However, this understanding does not address the question of why this type of discourse is developed solely or primarily in the context of a therapeutic intervention, in the face of illness.

The answer is to be found not so much in shamanic discourse and practice per se as in the indigenous conceptualization of illness. Among the Jivaro, as in most lowland groups, illness is not seen as the reflection of an underlying cause. Instead, it is the experience of the symptoms themselves; it is suffering as such rather than its presumed cause. To this should be added that pain probably constitutes one of the most common perceptions of temporality as duration, of a time ordinarily fragmented in the unreflective chaining of daily activities and their qualitatively different rhythms—the more so as, among Jivaroans at any rate, illness manifests itself by a more or less acute state of prostration, a brutal disengagement from the world and from others. As I have already suggested, the suffering characteristic of the kind of illness requiring shamanic intervention—essentially diffuse internal pain, and more generally existential states of malaise that we would call anxiety or depression—is rooted in a degradation of the relations linking a person to his social environment and shaping him as a subject. Such a modification of selfhood is experienced as pathology. This means that illness is essentially a negative experience of qualitative change of selfhood. Indeed, it can be shown that the unwellness dealt with in the context of shamanic healing is a reversed image of the magnified sense of self brought on by the ritual encounter with the *arutam*. It is this unwanted metamorphosis—as opposed to the valued change induced by the encounter with a Jivaroan ghost—that brings on the transformation of the healing shaman into a polyglot generic foreigner.

I believe the reason for these parallel processes lies in the fact that the history of contacts with white men is itself conceptualized as a prolonged and painful process of transformation, and not at all as a series of "events" connected by a narrative thread. Rather than a series of causally linked delimited situations—"because the whites (under whatever guise) did this, we then did this," and so on—the history of interactions with Westerners is construed as a process of unwanted change, analogous to the transformation of the feeling of self brought on by illness. This view of history accords with the Jivaroans' emphasis on the achievement of enhanced individuality and with their "presentist" or, more accurately, forward-looking stance. The Jivaro do not see themselves as a "society" endowed with a durable identity or tradition, but as a collection of like but unique persons striving each to forge an exemplary life-course. Accomplishing this aim depends on men's ability to magnify their selves by killing enemies, and by absorbing lesser kinsmen's subjectivities into their own personhood through the social influence they wield. The capacity to be fully Jivaroan hinges in turn on encounters with *arutam*, forgotten, singular dead Indians, precisely the kind of spirits they will become posthumously, thus ensuring the transmission of new potentialities of making history in the Jivaroan manner. Given these Indians' preoccupation with the quality of selfhood, and with the threat of others' power to modify it by inducing unwanted change, the conceptual conflation of history and sickness is understandable: both modes of being are negative experiences of metamorphosis. History is the memory of repeated attempts at global conversion[32]—and not only in the religious sense—just as illness is the perception of an untrammeling of the tissue of relations underpinning healthy selfhood. In both cases, these shifts of selfhood are the consequence of deliberate malevolence. Enemy shamans and whites wreak their havoc in the same insidious, invisible way. For this reason, and because relations with whites have to do with qualitative, continuous processes of change rather than with discontinuous events, interethnic history cannot be encompassed by narrative. Social memory relating to it is instead encapsulated in the paradoxical images created by the shamans' ritual singing.

In this respect, the Jivaro closely resemble the Cuna of Panama, whose sense of history has been acutely analyzed by Carlo Severi. Like the Jivaro, these Indians have survived and actively resisted persecution by the whites for more than five centuries; like the Jivaro, the Cuna are both socially introverted, repelling sustained relations to outsiders, and fiercely attached to their ethnic identity. For them, post-Columbian history is a permanent nightmare heavy with the threat of loss of tradition. But it is not spoken about; rather, it is condensed in the "white" spirits evoked by shamans, pathogenic agents causing sickness and madness. Illness and spirits, according to the Cuna, share the same mode of being as entities whose presence is felt but remains invisible. By refashioning the supernatural world to include spirits of whites, Cuna shamans assimilate foreigners to maladies; conversely, to fall ill is to come under the shadow of history. Further, suffering bodies and the suffering world become interchangeable; thus, to experience pain is to perceive a shift in the texture of the world wherein the proper balance between the seen and the felt or heard is upset. By building up complex visual representations of this experience, Cuna shamans inscribe the trauma of history in a ritual tradition that is constantly reinforced by the very "illness" it is meant to deal with (Severi 1993, 2000).

In sum, for the Jivaro as for the Cuna, illness is the major mode of conceptualizing interethnic history, because it is a striking experience of painful temporality and because it involves the perception of a negative alteration of the web of relations underlying selfhood. This is why sickness triggers, in return, a specific kind of discourse on the history of interaction with foreigners. Taussig (1993) is surely mistaken, then, in asserting that Indians strive, through mimesis, to "become the Other." Clearly, neither the Jivaro nor the Cuna have any wish to become white; to the contrary, these Indians are deeply attached to a certain model of personhood and strongly resist forced conversion, which is to say, illness. But their adherence to a certain kind of selfhood is not antithetic to "being white" in an Indian way. As I have said, the Jivaro achieve this not by imitating but by competing with whites, a style of relation that is highly salient in the traditional mode of enhancement of selfhood. Like the Wari', the Jivaro see no contradiction between treating the whites as enemies and adding a "white skin" to their embodied selves. However, switching from an *auca* to a "tame Indian" identity is an entirely different matter.

The Taming of the Wild: Exiting from a Jivaroan Identity

I need not stress the obvious contrast between, on the one hand, the introverted, war-centered Jivaroan mode of making history, immune to change and linked to wellness of being, and, on the other hand, the shamanic mode of extroverted, transethnic history as a painful process linked to conditions defined as illness. What does need pointing out is that such states of unwellness are also the most common point of departure of a trajectory of transculturation, of moving out of a Jivaroan identity and into a neighboring Quechua identity.

Clearly, becoming and remaining an exemplary (and live) Jivaroan male is a demanding vocation. It is therefore not surprising that many individuals undergo occasional periods of breakdown, moments during which they feel unable to live up to the demands of their environment and hence disengage from their social ties. Persistent or repeated bouts of misfortune and depression, and the isolation they bring on, often lead to an exit from Jivaroan identity. Thus, when an Achuar man feels himself bereft of supportive social relations—therefore in deficit of selfhood and unable to defend his family—and he or his wives and children fall prey to chronic sickness, he will usually embark on a series of shamanic healing sessions, a course leading from one shaman to another and eventually to those shamans considered the most powerful, namely those outside Jivaroan culture and territory, more particularly the neighboring Quechua shamans. During his stay with one such healer, he may choose to start a shamanic apprenticeship and/or establish kin ties with the Quechua shaman's local group, often by marrying into it or by calling on previously established kin ties to settle with a given Quechua household. In short, from the Jivaroan point of view, moving into a "tame Indian" identity is a process of shifting from a position of sick patient to a position of actual or potential shaman. The connection established between illness and switches from auca to manso identities is not confined to the Jivaro and seems in fact to be widespread. Writing from the perspective of the Curaray (Canelos) Runa of Zaparoan descent, Mary-Elizabeth Reeve says that "the strategy always cited by Runa when they seek to explain the motive behind the desire of other peoples to "become" Runa is that of biological survival—to increase themselves following a period of devastating disease or intergroup warfare" (1993–94:20).

Whether a person opting out of an *auca* identity becomes a recognized shaman or not, moving into a so-called *manso* society is not just a matter of adopting a different set of cultural practices, of language use, of developing new kin ties or reactivating already established relationships. It is also, crucially, a matter of mastering and reproducing a type of historical discourse quite distinct from that of the Jivaro, and shifting into an equally distinct regime of historicity.

A remarkable trait of all these "domestic" circum-Jivaroan groups, however distant and different from each other they may be, is that all of them share a linear, periodized historical narrative structure, according to a ternary scheme dividing the past into sharply contrasted "times": a time of wildness, a more recent time of slavery, and a present time of "civilization" (Gow 1991; Muratorio 1987; Whitten 1976; Reeve 1988). The labeling of these periods varies somewhat from one group to another, but the threefold structure remains constant. Among the Curaray Canelos of Zaparoan origin, for example, the first period of history, that of being fully and exclusively Zaparoan, is called *unai*, glossed as "mythic time-space," a phase during which animals were human or consorted with humans by disguising themselves as such; the intervening *callari uras* or "times of beginning" (called "times of slavery" among the Peruvian *nativos* and "times of the grand-parents" among the Puyo-Bobonaza Canelos) corresponds to the period of the rubber boom and the demise of the Zaparo as a distinct ethnic group; "present times" refers to the Curaray Quechua's situation both as Quechua-speaking Runa linked by kinship to other Canelos subgroups, and as Zaparoans "hidden" among the Runa for purposes of survival (Reeve 1988, 1993–94:21).

Each of these periods can easily be related to actual phases of the historical past. However, as specialists in these eminently transformational societies have shown, this threefold structure also reflects a purely static view of states of imagined sociality. Thus, "times of wildness" can refer to a given tribal group—for example the Zaparoans before they were assimilated into *manso* culture—but at the same time it refers to a stereotypical vision of *auca* culture as marked by ignorance of the outside world, absence of proper mediation, chronic bellicosity, and extreme linguistic and social self-containment. Intermediate times or "times of slavery" refer usually to the rubber boom, or to the period during which *manso* groups were tied to lowland haciendas or *patrones*, but more generally it evokes the forced apprenticeship, under the rule of powerful white men, of ethnic mixity and of proper systems of production and consumption: for example, the exchange of forest products for manufactured goods and the right combination of imported and wild foods; the transition from bilateral, close cross-cousin marriage to distant marriage between unrelated people.[33] "Time of civilization," finally, denotes the living out, in conditions of individual freedom and political autonomy, of the henceforth internalized knowledge concerning the processes of interethnic and intercultural *mestizaje* (Gow 1991, 1993).

This type of historical narrative aptly illustrates the complex nature of these social formations, because such stories are both local traditions underpinning a particular tribal identity through shared reference—*nucanchij yachana*, "our cultural knowledge," as the Curaray Runa phrase it (Reeve 1993–94:21)—and a generalized discourse about processes of cultural hybridization common to a set of distant and unrelated *manso* cultures. In this respect, they clearly reveal the dual character of lowland Quechua groups as specific ethnic groups and, simultaneously, as general templates of change and transculturation. These narrative traditions also reproduce the Janus-faced character of such societies by setting up a dual reading of history, since they juxtapose an apparently Westernized (or at least Andeanized), chronologically linear register and an underlying register focusing on the process of change as such. This latter reading is much closer to the feeling of history as illness evoked in shamanic healing contexts among "wild" Indians, and it is also expressed and transmitted in ways similar to those current in auca cultures, being encoded in "commentary and allusion interspersed in conversation, in art forms, in ritual, in geography, in genealogies and in rights to territory" (Reeve 1993–94:22).

This is a crucial point, because there is a further dimension to these Quechua-style narratives. They are not only "phylogenetic" accounts, they are also ontogenetic accounts. In other words, they serve as templates for structuring an individual experience of transculturation. Because the states of sociality they describe can easily be mapped onto the phased experiences a person goes through when moving from an *auca* to a *manso* identity, these narratives of a collective history become at the same time the narrative of a personal history. Illness as weakness, disorientation, social isolation, communicative breakdown is thus easily woven into evocation of "wild" sociality, a markedly pathological state characterized by introversion, compulsive aggression, fear, and a limited range of interaction and communication; "times of slavery," insofar as they stress a position of positive and necessary subordination, come to frame not only the experience of being an incoming in-law—a highly asymmetric relation perfectly familiar both to Jivaroans and their Quechua neighbors—but also shamanic apprenticeship, another relationship in which pedagogy and asymmetry are sharply foregrounded. "Times of civilization," finally, serves as a metaphor both for the condition of being healed and for participation in the process of producing autonomously proper kinds of mediation; in short, for the state of being cured of history by history. Conversely, structuring one's personal trajectory in terms of this temporal framework also inherently carries with it adhesion to a type of social practice and discourse strongly marked in terms of ethnic identity, and closely bound with tradition as it is locally construed. The script underlying Quechua historical narrative, which is in fact poor in specific knowledge about the past and is essentially a framework that fosters and allows for the reorganization of elements of memory that are shared by everyone throughout this region, thus offers an idiom for constructing a representation of a trajectory of transculturation. At the same time, coming to use this idiom implies learning and reproducing a conceptualization of history that is a central feature of Quechua identity.

In short, chronic sickness as exit from a Jivaroan identity is also the gateway to a *manso* or dual Quechua identity, because the state of "orphanhood" implied by sickness as viewed from the Jivaroan perspective corresponds to, or at any rate easily translates into, a condition of sociality and postulated selfhood that, from the Quechua *manso* perspective, has to be absorbed into the civilizing process. At the same time, as it allows for this process since it is the starting point for a change of ethnic identity. To go on producing "civilization"—that is, being a proper forest Runa—you need sick wild *auca*, just as to go on being a *shuar* you need personal foes.

Conclusion

In synchronic as well as in diachronic terms, the Jivaro and their indigenous Quechua-speaking neighbors constitute mutually implicating cultures. The forms of selfhood as well as the kinds of memory that sustain their identities are closely connected and indeed interdependent. The "acculturated" *manso* groups are in some sense an organic extension of the *auca* societies; their persistence depends on the ongoing existence of "traditional" hinterland tribes. At the same time, the latter have remained "wild" only because of the development of these hybrid buffer groups, and their "traditionality" and postulated primitiveness are therefore shaped by the same historical forces that have fueled the ethnogenesis of the "domestic" indigenous societies of the upper Amazon.

This suggests that, in terms of what is usually defined as "culture," the two groups in fact share a great deal of common ground, a kind of "zero degree" of habitus, the commonality of which goes largely unperceived because it is, in a sense, meant to go unperceived: it is salient neither for the Indians nor for their ethnographers. This invisible backdrop of similar bodily techniques, work habits, mythic narratives, diets, ways of using and understanding language, and manners of interacting is what allows forest Quechua and Jivaroans to move in and out of each others' societies with such facility. Conversely, the differences between *auca* and "domestic" cultures are rooted in sharply contrasted ways of contextualizing and elaborating, in a few restricted domains, the same cultural stuff and the same sorts of knowledge.

The move from a Jivaroan to a Runa identity is, in essence, a shift from warriorhood to shamanic dual selfhood, through an intermediate state qualified as illness. The permeability between *auca* and *manso* identities clearly involves shared premises concerning the relational forms that underlie these kinds of personhood. Among the Jivaro, shamanic ways of relating to Others are opposed to, and largely insulated from, the "predatory stance" that lies at the core of their "ethnic" identity. In "tame Indian" cultures, by contrast, multiple selfhood is generalized: *yachaj* are merely exemplary or magnified versions of a type of selfhood common to all members of the society. At issue in these distinctive ways of framing identities is a hidden but decisive modulation in the relation to alterity constitutive of Self.

In the case of the Jivaraons, this basic relation is defined by a permanent tension between *ego* and an *alter* defined as "enemy"—that is to say, as maximally different from self. The axiomatic difference between the terms of the relation is both presupposed and reproduced by exacerbated antagonism. In abstract terms, "antagonism" is anti-identification, a process blocking the incorporation or assimilation of one term by the other: while the polarity of the relation is reversible—"killer" can become "prey" and vice versa, a transformation central to many Amazonian rituals[34]—neither of its terms can be subsumed in the other, short of annulling the relation. This is precisely the relational form designated by the concept of predation, as it has been defined by Eduardo Viveiros de Castro (1992,

1998), and further refined by Carlos Fausto (2001) through his exploration of the means whereby alterity is transmuted into sociality through the mechanism he calls "familiarization."

In the case of shamanic multiple selfhood, by contrast, the relation between *ego* and *alter* is predicated on a process of identification rather than on one of differentiating antagonism. In such a process of identification, each term of the constitutive relation is poised to subsume the other, instead of being opposed to it. "Self" can thus slide into an "alter" fragmented into a multiplicity of instantiations—animals, other humans, spirits—and become a congeries of "I's" since it is no longer dependent, to exist, on its continued predatory stance vis-à-vis a unified Other, the Enemy. Note, however, that the polarity of a process of identification is just as reversible as in differentiation: Self can either subsume or be subsumed by Alter; it may, in other words, become irrevocably "white" (or animal, or ghost) just as it may pull "whiteness" (or animality or ghostliness) into itself.

In light of this, it is easier to understand why sickness constitutes the no-man's-land an *auca* Jivaroan has to cross to become a *manso*. "Illness" is a hinge state between two ways of relating to Others. The enfeeblement of the "antagonistic" mode of relationship necessarily causes a diminishing of the self that is sustained by it: "social" weakness, conceptualized as orphanhood, and "existential" weakness are intimately connected. A diminished sense of self opens the way to identification with powerful others—that is, to the possibility of alienation. This, as I have shown, is what the Jivaro define as illness. Insofar as identification is intrinsically reversible, however, illness as a process of unwanted assimilation carries with it the shadow of its converse, the transformation of the Other into Self, namely shamanic mastery. Shamanism is the mirror image of alienation: it is the ability to control the polarity of the process of identification, and to suck foreign beings into one's own selfhood instead of the other way round. This is the source of the causal connection between states of illness and the move toward a kind of personhood epitomized by shamans but also intimately linked to a specific "ethnic" identity, that of *manso* Runa. Provided that a person's sense of worth and power has been restored through this process of transculturation, nothing then prevents him from reverting eventually to the "predatory" mode of relation that formerly shaped him, thereby assuming once again a Jivaroan identity.

Notes

1. The topic of "constitutive alterity" has within the last decades been amply explored and theorized by Amazonist ethnologists, most notably by Eduardo Viveiros de Castro (1992), Aparecida Vilaça (1992), Philippe Erikson (1993, 1996), and Carlos Fausto (2001).

2. The term *Jivaro* is a hispanicization of the vernacular word *shiwiar*, denoting roughly "enemies from another Jivaroan tribal group." Because of its Western origin and the heavy load of connotations it bears, most Indians belonging to the Jivaroan language family strongly object to being labeled as Jivaro. They refer to themselves instead as *shuar*, "persons" in most Jivaroan dialects. However, this usage conflicts both with contemporary tribal politics and with ethnographic habits. On the one hand, the word *shuar* is not used by some Jivaroan speakers, for example the Aguaruna; on the other hand, when used as an ethnic label it is often understood to refer to a specific subgroup, namely the "true" Shuar of the Ecuadorian and Peruvian montaña, a fact strongly resented by the Achuar and the Aguaruna. In short, there is no generally accepted term to designate the cultural unit formed by all these subgroups. Like most contemporary anthropologists, I have therefore chosen to restrict use of the term *Jivaro* to denote the ensemble—the set of peoples claiming use of a Jivaroan and/or Candoan dialect—as opposed to the tribal subgroups.

3. The Shiwiar emerged, as a Jivaroan tribe claiming a distinct identity, from the coalescence of a few Achuar families, separated since 1941 from the main body of this dialectal unit, and of other small groups of diverse origin: Andoas, Quechua, probably Candoshi, many of them uprooted and displaced during the rubber boom. Such loose admixtures of heterogeneous Indian groups, progressively unified by coresidence and a shared bond to a mestizo trader or a missionary organization, commonly adopt a Quechua *runa* identity (see below). That the Shiwiar gravitated toward a Jivaroan rather than a Quechua adscription can be explained partly by the active implication of the dominant Achuar component in the heavy feuding among the eastern Achuar throughout the 1960s and 1970s, and partly by the pull of the powerful Shuar Federation, the most important Indian political organization in the area until the early 1990s.

4. In Ecuador, the term *auca* was in fact widely used by non-Indians until recently as an ethnonym for the Huaorani, the epitome of Indian savagery since their "discovery" in the early 1950s.

5. During the 1970s and 1980s, nationalist-populist discourse in Ecuador extolled the virtues of *mestizaje* and insistently proclaimed, "Somos todos mestizos" (We [Ecuadorians] are all of hybrid origin). Paradoxically, proclaiming oneself a mestizo at that time was a way of claiming status as a white, because it demonstrated civic consciousness and a postulated degree of education (see Whitten 1985).

6. *Ciudades* and not *pueblos*, villages, though in fact many of these frontier settlements were until recently mud-ridden hamlets clustered around a central plaza heavily overlaid with cement, a major index of urbanness.

7. For a more detailed analysis of Jivaroan social classification, see Taylor 1985.

8. Ironically, *racionales* familiar with this Indian usage often understand it to mean that the *aucas* identify whites with the North American Apaches—"truly" fierce wild Indians.

9. In Peter Gow's words, "these classifications locate people in a particular vision of history, which is closely related to the particular system of commercial exchange that

dominates the economy of western Amazonia [i.e., the debt-and-credit system known as *habilitación*]. These are in turn related to a specific symbolism of space, with the forest at the center of the region and the industrialized Western nations on the outside" (1994:99).

10. For a Jivaroan view of this network, see Uriarte 1989; for a Canelos one, see Whitten 1976, 1985; on the *nativos*, see Gow 1991, also Chevalier 1982. On the social and economic history of the Peruvian Amazon, see especially Santos-Granero and Barclay 1998, 2000; on that of the Ecuadorian Oriente, see Taylor 1994, 1999.

11. The expansion of the colonist economic frontier is linked to the *purina* system and rooted in the following process: Quechua families would branch out from their original settlements on lengthy expeditions (*purina*) to hunt, collect, and gather produce owed to their boss. The seasonal camp set up on this occasion would after some years become the kin-group's permanent residence, and eventually grow into a village as in-laws and dependents of the pioneer household settled nearby. The new hamlet would then attract a mestizo trader, who would eventually settle in its midst, thereby pushing its Indian inhabitants toward the periphery and initiating a new cycle of settlement.

12. In the seventeenth century, according to Jesuit sources, the Xeberos often took heads during these forays (Figueroa 1986; Maroni [1738] 1988).

13. Both in discourse and in ceramic imagery, the Canelos depict themselves as "two-faced." The Achuar describe a mythic being named *jurijri*, dressed as a white and with two mouths, one hidden under its hair and devoted to cannibalizing overly greedy hunters. In other groups, the notion of dual appearance is less explicitly thematized, but it surfaces in ritual, in differential patterns of behavior according to the ethnic origin of the interlocutor, in settlement patterns and residential cycles. Among the *nativos* described by Gow (1994), the term *sacha runa* refers to powerful and potentially harmful forest spirits. *Nativos* express their dual nature by stressing their expertise in combining two opposed kinds of unmediated violence: that of the wild forest human and nonhuman peoples, and that of the invisible whites inhabiting the major urban centers.

14. Jivaroan individuals claiming shamanic mastery intervene in warfare by orienting armed aggression against suspected sorcerers, and by engaging in forms of divination before a war party is launched. But they do not shed real blood, either human or animal.

15. Beyond shamans' claim to mastery over foreign languages, explicitly stated in their curing chants, a study of their songs reveals a high degree of diglossia and a marked preference for Quechua words over their Jivaroan equivalents (for examples see Uriarte 1989, Pellizzaro 1978). From the Jivaro's point of view, rather than (or besides) being the language of a specific Indian group, Quechua is a kind of general purpose language, the functional equivalent of any and all foreign languages. There is good historical reason for this notion, in view of the Jesuits' use of Quechua as a standard language throughout the area covered by the Mainas mission.

16. Such claims of incomprehension are tantamount to defining interlocutors as *shiwiar*, Jivaroan enemies liable to headhunting raids (Harner 1972). Conversely, recognition

of a shared field of communication also implies recognition of kinship: kin are defined as people who talk in the same language. Objectively, differences between the Shuar and Achuar dialects are slight, and in contexts where partners wish to downplay their social distance, communication is perfectly fluid and unproblematic.

17. According to Cieza de León ([1550] 1947:228), "it is notorious among many *naturales* of these parts that Guayna Capac entered the land we call Bracamoros, but fled before the fury of its inhabitants" (my translation).

18. The largest and most famous of these *conquistas* were those led by H. de Benavente and A. Mercadillo in "Xibaro" land in 1550, those of Diego Palomino in the Chinchipe valley in 1549, those of J. de Salinas Loyola in 1557 and again in 1574 to the Santiago and upper Marañon valleys, that of Diego Vaca de Vega in 1618 in the same area, and finally that of the Martin de la Riva Herrera into the heartland of Jivaroan territory in 1656 (Taylor 1994b).

19. In the course of this expedition, nine hundred "Xibaros" were captured and deported to Borja; of these, more than eight hundred had died or fled by the following year (Maroni [1738] 1988, Jouanen 1941–43).

20. In the upper Amazon, this system rests on a lengthy chain of social and economic dependencies: a *patrón* located in one of the larger towns, such as Iquitos or Nauta, recruits a network of traders based in the smaller towns, and provides them, on credit, with manufactured goods in bulk. These petty merchants in turn furnish goods to *habilitados*, the *patrones* who regularly visit their Indian clientele and collect their produce, making sure the Indians' debt always exceeds their credit. This is just the skeleton of the system; in fact, the number of links between the two ends of the chain is usually far larger, including sub-*habilitados*, *regatones* (itinerant traders), and Indian intermediaries.

21. Eric B. Ross (1980) reports that in the 1960s, four mestizo loggers (*tronqueros*), married to Indian women, were killed by the Peruvian Achuar in these circumstances.

22. See for example the chronicles edited by Jiménez de la Espada ([1881] 1965) in the *Relaciones Geográficas de Indias*; also those edited by Taylor and Landázuri (1994), Pilar Ponce Leiva (1992), and Costales and Costales (1977, 1978), to name only a few of the major sources. For a useful synopsis of the data on Jivaroan "material culture" in early historical sources, see Wierhake 1985. For a synthetic treatment of Jivaroan history, see mainly Taylor 1986, 1994a.

23. The Shuar Federation is thus seen as an arena for the playing out of competitive power politics, and an instrument for the building of clientelist networks. The relationship between the Shuar and the Ecuadorian army during and since the war that opposed Peru and Ecuador in 1995 also illustrates the Jivaroans' adeptness at finding niches within the dominant society for pursuing traditional aims. While paying lip service to the pacifist attitudes expected by the NGOs funding the native federations, the Shuar were in fact eager to take up arms during the conflict: an Indian militia was set up with military support, and there was much talk of reactivating ritual vision quests and taking enemy heads. Having gained widespread sympathy for their patriotic fervor, the Shuar then sought to

persuade the army to set up military colleges in the lowlands to train Indian youths as officers, and to incorporate their militia as a regular battalion of professional soldiers, Gurkha-style.

24. On the subject of *arutam*, see Harner 1972; Mader 1999, Descola 1993, Brown 1978, 1986, Pellizzaro 1990.

25. See Hendricks 1993 for a usefully commented edition of a famous Shuar warrior's autobiography.

26. On the relation between time, memory, and narration, see especially Ricoeur 1983.

27. In shamanic chanted "autobiographies," to the contrary, singers omit or distort quotative marks and deliberately set up a complex polyphony of voices, in accordance with their multiple selfhood.

28. As Carlo Severi (2000) points out, representations of supernatural beings usually carry "realistic" indications, however oblique, pointing to their "true" or underlying nature.

29. It is true that in certain kinds of traditional discourse, such as ceremonial dialogue and early-morning lecturing of children, references to "our old ones" (*iinia uuntri* in Shuar and Achuar) are frequent. However, the expression does not refer to ancestors as such, but rather to seniors, alive or dead, taken as exemplars of normative behavior.

30. This is possibly what happened to the Candoshi, who are very like the Jivaro in most respects but whose language seems to be entirely unrelated to the Jivaroan family of dialect. Attempts to demonstrate a genetic relation between the two families have not proved conclusive (see Payne 1981). At the same time, Candoa seems to be unrelated to any other known linguistic stock, so it is impossible to determine whether the Candoshi originally belonged to a distinct ethnic group subsequently "jivaroanized" by its engagement in a sustained relationship of mutual enmity with the Jivaro proper, or whether they represent a sharply divergent branch of the Jivaro.

31. See, for example, Taussig 1993; Chevalier 1982; Santos-Granero, this volume. Countering this view, Gow (1994) has argued that the ayahuasca shamanism common to many Indian groups of the upper Amazon and to large sectors of the non-Indian local population actually originated among urban mestizos, as a metaphor of the historic and economic processes inherent to their own "ethnogenesis," and then spread to the Indians. I remain skeptical of this historical hypothesis, but I think Gow is right in assuming that the wide, transethnic diffusion of this kind of shamanism can be explained at least in part by its capacity to figuratively represent the basic processes underlying the political economy of western Amazonia, in particular the regional system of *habilitación*.

32. Unlike the "fickle" Tupi whose apparent receptivity to evangelization so gratified early missionaries (see Fausto, this volume; Castro 1993), the Jivaro were and are notoriously reticent to religious conversion. From the sixteenth century on, missionaries sent among them never ceased to complain of the Indians' crass materialism and "Voltairean" scepticism; they roundly declared the Jivaro to be "the most difficult mission in the world." On missionaries' views of the Jivaro, see Taylor 1983.

33. This view of ruthless ethnocidal exploitation as pedagogy is of course heartily endorsed by the *patrones*, who often present themselves as educators of the savage.

34. For excellent illustrations of this process, see in particular Castro 1992 and Albert 1985.

References

Albert, Bruce. 1985. "Temps du sang, temps des cendres: Représentation de la maladie, système rituel et espace politique chez les Yanomami du sud-est (Amazonie brésilienne)." Ph.D. diss., Université de Paris X–Nanterre.

Amadio, Massimo. 1985. "Los Muratos: Una sintesis historica." *Amazonia Peruana* 6(12):117–131.

Becquelin, Aurore, and Antoinette Molinié, eds. 1993. *Mémoire de la tradition.* Nanterre: Société d'Ethnologie.

Brown, Michael F. 1978. "From the Hero's Bones: Three Aguaruna Hallucinogens and Their Uses." In *The Nature and Status of Ethnobotany*, edited by Richard I. Ford, 119–136. Ann Arbor: Museum of Anthropology, University of Michigan.

———. 1986. *Tsewa's Gift: Magic and Meaning in an Amazonian Society.* Washington: Smithsonian Institution Press.

Castro, Eduardo Viveiros de. 1992. *From the Enemy's Point of View: Humanity and Divinity in an Amazonian Society.* Translated by Catherine V. Howard. Chicago: University of Chicago Press.

———. 1993. "Le Marbre et le myrte: De l'inconstance de l'âme sauvage." In Becquelin and Molinié, *Mémoire de la tradition*, 365–431.

———. 1998. "Cosmological Deixis and Amerindian Perspectivism." *Journal of the Royal Anthropological Institute* 4:469–488.

Castro, Eduardo Viveiros de, and Carlos Fausto. 1993. "La Puissance et l'acte: La Parenté dans les basses terres d'Amérique du Sud." *L'Homme* 33(126–128):141–170.

Chaumeil, Jean-Pierre. 1992. "La vida larga: Immortalidad y ancestralidad en la Amazonía." In *La muerte y el mas allá en las culturas indígenas latinoamericanas*, edited by María Susana Cipolletti and Esther Jean Langdon, 113–123. Quito: Abya-Yala.

———. 1997. "Les Os, les flûtes, les morts: Mémoire et traitement funéraire en Amazonie." *Journal de la Société des Américanistes* 83:83–110.

Chevalier, Jacques M. 1982. *Civilization and the Stolen Gift: Capital, Kin, and Cult in Eastern Peru.* Toronto: University of Toronto Press.

Cieza de León, Pedro de. [1550] 1947. *La Crónica del Perú.* In *Historiadores primitivos de Indias*, 2:359–458. Biblioteca de Autores Españoles 26. Madrid: Atlas.

Costales, Piedad, and Alfredo Costales. 1977. *La nación shuar.* Sucúa, Ecuador: Mundo Shuar.

————. 1978. *Los Shuar en la historia*. Sucúa, Ecuador: Mundo Shuar.

Cunha, Manuela Carneiro da, ed. 1992. *História dos índios no Brasil*. São Paulo: FAPESP, Companhia das Letras.

Cunha, Manuela Carneiro da, and Eduardo Viveiros de Castro. 1985. "Vingança e Temporalidade: os Tupinambas." *Journal de la Société des Américanistes* 71:191–208.

Descola, Philippe. 1993. *Les Lances du crépuscule: Relations jivaros, Haute Amazonie*. Paris: Plon.

Erikson, Philippe. 1993. "Une Nébuleuse Compacte: Le Macro-ensemble Pano." *L'Homme* 33(126–128):45–58.

————. 1996. *La Griffe des aïeux: Marquage du corps et démarquages ethniques chez les Matis d'Amazonie*. Paris: Peeters.

Fausto, Carlos. 2001. *Inimigos fiéis: História, guerra e xamanismo na Amazônia*. São Paulo: EdUSP.

Figueroa, Francisco de. [1661] 1986. "Ynforme de las misiones de la Compañia de Jesús en Marañon, Gran Parà o Río de las Amazonas." In *Informes de Jesuitas en el Amazonas, 1660–1684*, 143–209. Iquitos, Peru: IIAP-CETA.

García-Rendueles, Manuel, ed. 1996–99. *Yáunchuk—universo mítico de los Huambisas, Kanús (Río Santiago), Perú*. 2 vols. Iquitos, Peru: CAAAP.

Gippelhauser, Richard, and Elke Mader. 1990. *Die Achuara-Jivaro: Wirtschaftliche and soziale Organisationsformen am peruanischen Amazonas*. Vienna: Verlag des Österreichischen Akademie der Wissenschaften.

Gow, Peter. 1991. *Of Mixed Blood: Kinship and History in Peruvian Amazonia*. Oxford: Clarendon Press.

————. 1993. "Gringos and Wild Indians: Images of History in Western Amazonian Cultures." *L'Homme* 33(126–128):327–347.

————. 1994. "River People: Shamanism and History in Western Amazonia." In Thomas and Humphrey, *Shamanism, History and the State*, 90–113.

————. 2001. *An Amazonian Myth and Its History*. Oxford: Oxford University Press.

Harner, Michael J. 1972. *The Jívaro, People of the Sacred Waterfalls*. Garden City, New York: Doubleday, Natural History Press.

Hendricks, Janet Wall. 1993. *To Drink of Death: The Narrative of a Shuar Warrior*. Tucson: University of Arizona Press.

Hocquenghem, Anne-Marie. 1989. *Los Guayacundos de Caxas y la Sierra Piurana, siglos XV y XVI*. Lima: CIPCA/IFEA.

————. 1998. *Para vencer la muerte: Piura y Tumbes*. Paris: CNRS; Lima: IFEA/INCAH.

Hugh-Jones, Stephen. 1994. "Shamans, Prophets, Priests, and Pastors." In Thomas and Humphrey, *Shamanism, History and the State*, 32–75.

Jiménez de la Espada, Marcos, ed. [1881] 1965. *Relaciones Geográficas de Indias—Perú*. Biblioteca de Autores Españoles 185, vol. 3. Madrid: Atlas.

Jouanen, José. 1941–43. *Historia de la Compañía de Jesús en la antigua provincia de Quito, 1570–1773.* 2 vols. Quito: Editorial Ecuatoriana.

Juncosa, José E. 2000. *Etnografía de la comunicación verbal shuar.* Quito: Abya-Yala.

Karsten, Rafael. 1935. *The Head-Hunters of Western Amazonas: The Life and Culture of the Jíbaro Indians of Eastern Ecuador and Peru.* Helsinki: Societas Scientarum Fennica.

Landaburu, Jon. 1993. "Du changement de noms de certain dieux." In Becquelin and Molinié, *Mémoire de la tradition,* 145–160.

Lévi-Strauss, Claude. 1991. *Histoire de Lynx.* Paris: Plon.

Mader, Ernest. 1999. *Metamorfosis del Poder. Persona, mito y visión en la sociedad Shuar y Achuar (Ecuador, Peru).* Quito: Abya-Yala.

Mader, Elke, and Richard Gippelhauser. 1984. "Nuevas tendencias en la economía achuar." In *Relaciones interétnicas y adaptación cultural entre Shuar, Achuar, Aguaruna y Canelos Quichua,* edited by Michael Brown, 146–158. Quito: Abya-Yala.

Maroni, Pablo. [1738] 1988. *Noticias auténticas del famoso Río Marañón y misión apostólica de la Compañía de Jesús . . .* Edited by Jean-Pierre Chaumeil. Iquitos, Peru: IIAP-CETA.

Muratorio, Blanca. 1987. *Rucuyaya Alonso y la historia social y económica del Alto Napo 1850–1950.* Quito: Abya-Yala.

Payne, David. 1981. "Bosquejo fonológico del Proto-Shuar-Candoshi: Evidencia para una relación genética." *Revista del Museo Nacional de Lima* 45:323–377.

Pellizzaro, Siro. 1978. *El Uwishín: Mitos, ritos y cantos para propiciar a los espíritus.* Sucúa, Ecuador: Mundo Shuar.

———. 1990. *Arútam: Mitos y ritos para propiciar a los espíritus.* Quito: Abya-Yala.

Ponce Leiva, Pilar, ed. 1992. *Relaciones histórico-geográficas de la Audiencia de Quito, s. XVI–XIX.* Quito: Abya-Yala.

Raimondi, Antonio. [1876–80] 1905. "El Perú." In *Colección de leyes, decretos, resoluciones i otros documentos oficiales referentes al departamento de Loreto,* edited by Carlos Larrabure y Correa. Lima.

Reeve, Mary-Elizabeth. 1988. "*Cauchu Uras*: Lowland Quichua Histories of the Amazon Rubber Boom." In *Rethinking History and Myth: Indigenous South American Perspectives on the Past,* edited by Jonathan D. Hill, 19–34. Urbana: University of Illinois Press.

———. 1993–94. "Narratives of Catastrophe: The Zaparoan Experience in Amazonian Ecuador." *Société Suisse des Américanistes,* bulletin 57–58:17–24.

Renard-Casevitz, France-Marie. 1992. "História kampa, memória ashaninca." In Cunha, *História dos índios no Brasil,* 197–212.

Ricoeur, Paul. 1983.

Ross, Eric B. 1980. "Ecology and the Problem of the Tribe: A Critique of the Hobbesian Model of Preindustrial Warfare." In *Beyond the Myths of Culture: Essays in Cultural Materialism,* edited by Eric B. Ross, 33–60. New York: Academic Press.

Santos-Granero, Fernando. 1991. *The Power of Love: The Moral Use of Knowledge amongst the Amuesha of Central Peru*. London: Athlone.

———. [1992?]. *Etnohistoria de la Alta Amazonia: Siglo XV–XVIII*. Quito: Abya-Yala.

———. 1993. "From Prisoner of the Group to Darling of the Gods: An Approach to the Issue of Power in Lowland South America." *L'Homme* 33(126–128):213–230.

Santos-Granero, Fernando, and Frederica Barclay. 1998. *Selva Central: History, Economy, and Land Use in Peruvian Amazonia*. Translated by Elisabeth King. Washington, D.C.: Smithsonian Institution Press.

———. 2000. *Tamed Frontiers: Economy, Society, and Civil Rights in Upper Amazonia*. Boulder, Colorado: Westview.

Severi, Carlo. 1993. *La memoria rituale: Follia e immagine del bianco in una tradizione sciamanica amerindiana*. Florence: Nuova Italia.

———. 2000. "Cosmologia, crise e paradoxo: Da imagem de homens e mulheres brancos na tradição xamânica kuna." *Mana: Estudos de Antropologia Social* 6(2):121–155.

Seymour-Smith, Charlotte. 1988. *Shiwiar: Identidad étnica y cambio en el río Corrientes*. Quito: Abya-Yala; Lima: CAAAP.

Steward, Julian H., and Alfred Métraux. 1948. "Tribes of the Peruvian and Ecuadorian Montaña." In *Handbook of South American Indians*, vol. 3, *The Tropical Forest Tribes*, edited by Julian H. Steward, 535–656. Washington, D.C.: Smithsonian Institution, Bureau of American Ethnology.

Stirling, Matthew W. 1938. *Historical and Ethnographical Material on the Jivaro Indians*. Washington, D.C.: Smithsonian Institution.

Surrallés, Alexandre. 2003. *Au coeur du sens: Perception, affectivité, action chez les Candoshi*. Paris: Maisons des Sciences de l'Homme.

Taussig, Michael. 1993. *Mimesis and Alterity: A Particular History of the Senses*. New York: Routledge.

Taylor, Anne-Christine. 1983. "'Cette atroce république de la forêt': Les Origines du paradigme jivaro." *Gradhiva* 3:3–10.

———. 1985. "L'Art de la réduction." *Journal de la Société des Américanistes* 71:159–173.

———. 1986. "Les Versants orientaux des Andes septentrionales: Des Bracamoros aux Quijos." In *L'Inca, l'espagnol et les sauvages. Essai sur les relations entre les sociétés andines et amazoniennes, XV-XVI siècles*, edited by France-Marie Renard-Casevitz, Thierry Saignes, and Anne-Christine Taylor, 215–352. Paris: ADPF.

———. 1992a. "Historia pos-colombiana da alta Amazonia." In Cunha, *História dos índios no Brasil*, 213–238.

———. 1992b. "Les Paltas: Les Jivaro andins précolombiens à la lumière de l'ethnographie moderne." *Bulletin de l'Institut Français d'Etudes Andines* 20(2):439–459.

———. 1993a. "Des fantômes stupéfiants: Langage et croyance dans la pensée achuar." *L'Homme* 33(126–128):429–447.

———. 1993b. "Remembering to Forget: Identity, Mourning and Memory among the Jívaro." *Man* 28(4):653–678.

———. 1994a. "El Oriente ecuatoriano en el siglo XIX: 'El otro litoral.'" In *Historia y region en el Ecuador, 1830–1930*, edited by Juan Maiguashca, 17–67. Quito: Corporación Editora Nacional.

———. 1994b. "Estudio Introductorio." In Taylor and Landázuri, *Conquista de la región jivaro*, 1–32.

———. 1998. "Corps immortel, devoir d'oubli: Formes humaines et trajectoires de vie chez les Achuar." In *La Production du corps*, edited by Maurice Godelier and Michel Panoff, 317–338. Paris: Archives Contemporaines.

———. 1999. "The Western Margins of Amazonia from the Early Sixteenth to the Early Nineteenth Century." In *The Cambridge History of the Native Peoples of the Americas*, vol. 3, *South America*, edited by Frank Salomon and Stuart B. Schwartz, 2:188–256. Cambridge: Cambridge University Press.

Taylor, Anne Christine, and Cristóbal Landázuri, eds. 1994. *Conquista de la región jivaro, 1550–1650: Relación documental*. Quito: Abya-Yala.

Tessmann, Günther. 1930. *Die Indianer Nordost-Perus*. Hamburg: Harvey-Bassler Stiftung.

Thomas, Nicholas, and Caroline Humphrey, eds. 1994. *Shamanism, History, and the State*. Ann Arbor: University of Michigan Press.

Uriarte, Luis M. 1989. *Native Blowguns and National Guns: The Achuar Jivaroans and the Dialectics of Power in the Peruvian Amazon*. Ann Arbor, Michigan: University Microfilms.

Veigl, Franz Xavier. 1768. "Grundliche Nachrichten über die Verfassung des Landschaft von Maynas . . . bis zum Jahre 1768." In *Reisen einiger Missionarien des Gesellschaft Jesu in Amerika*. Nuremberg: C. G. von Murr.

Vilaça, Aparecida. 1992. *Comendo como gente: Formas do canibalismo wari'*. Rio de Janeiro: EdUFRJ.

Whitten, Norman E., Jr. 1976. *Sacha Runa: Ethnicity and Adaptation of Ecuadorian Jungle Quichua*. Urbana: University of Illinois Press.

———. 1985. *Sicuanga Runa: The Other Side of Development in Amazonian Ecuador*. Urbana: University of Illinois Press.

Wierhake, Gunda. 1985. *La cultura material shuar en la historia: Estudio de las fuentes del siglo XVI al XIX*. Quito: Abya-Yala.

5

Cultural Change as Body Metamorphosis

Aparecida Vilaça

The relationships between shamanism and Amerindian contact with the nonindigenous world are a recurrent theme in the ethnological literature. In general, what is emphasized is a one-way determining relationship: insertion in the Western world provokes either the end of shamanism or its effervescence—or occasionally both. This last case applies, for example, to a number of Tupi-Mondé groups of southern Amazonia: according to Brunelli (1996), shamanism disappeared from several of these groups soon after contact, only to be resumed some years later as a mark of ethnic identity. Elsewhere, J. Christopher Crocker (1985) records that among the Bororo, missionary influence was responsible for the disappearance of vertical shamanism—the shamanism of *aroe*—just as among various groups of the Tukano linguistic family, the experiences of contact and missionary work brought about the disappearance of jaguar shamanism (Hugh-Jones 1994). In contrast, among the Yagua the number of shamans has actually increased since contact (Chaumeil 1983:261).

There also exist accounts of the appropriation of Christian symbols by native shamans, the most famous being those describing the sixteenth-century Tupinambá. They are frequent in messianic movements such as those occurring in the upper Rio Negro, described by Hugh-Jones (1994), Wright (1981, 1996), and Wright and Hill (1986). Also well documented is a movement in the opposite direction—that is, the appropriation of native shamanic practices by mestizo populations (Chaumeil 1983, Gow 1994, Taussig 1986).[1]

My aim in this article is to analyze the relationship between shamanism and interethnic contact from another perspective, taking as my basis an ethnography of the Wari', a Chapakura-speaking group of southern Amazonia.[2] I intend to show that in place of a direct correspondence (positive or negative) between the intensity of shamanic practice and the degree of contact, or of an appropriation of Western religious and secular practices by shamans, what is striking among the

Wari' is that the process of contact with whites is conceived through the prism of shamanism. Just as shamans are simultaneously human and animal, the Wari' today possess a double identity: they are both Wari' and white.

A drawing (figure 5.1) made in 1987 by a Wari' man at my request reveals this double identity. In the picture, the figure of a Wari' man is formed through a double outline, in such a way that the Western-style clothing—such as that worn by the Wari' today—is superimposed over the body, but without concealing it. What can actually be seen are two simultaneous bodies, the white body on top and the Wari' body underneath. We find parallels to this drawing in various other ethnographic contexts. As one example I take the Kayapó of central Brazil, highly visible in the media in recent years: the Western clothes do not completely cover the body paintings, or else the latter are explicitly exhibited on the exposed parts of the body, displayed alongside shorts and long trousers. The late Xavante Mário Juruna—once a Brazilian federal deputy, and until today still the only Indian to have been elected for an important political office in Brazil—was renowned for matching feather head-dresses with suits and shirts.

Fig. 5.1. Wari' man, with Western clothing superimposed over the body without concealing it (drawing by Maxün Hat 1987).

Beth Conklin (1997) observes that until the 1980s Amazonian Indians used to wear full Western clothing, a consequence of their perception of the negative impact of their nude bodies and perforated lips and ears on nonindigenous people, from local rural populations to the inhabitants of large cities. Resorting to clothing was a way not only of being accepted but of being left in peace—to continue to live as before when far from the eyes of whites. Terence Turner (1991:289) makes similar comments concerning the Kayapó, who in 1962 were almost all clothed in Western fashion, while men had also removed their lip disks and cut their hair. For Conklin, the changes that took place from the 1980s onward, when the Indians began to display feathers and other adornments together with Western clothes, were related to the imposition on Indians of a specifically Western vision of aesthetics and authenticity, since

> the nature of contemporary eco-politics—especially its dependence on global media—intensifies pressures for Indian activists to conform to certain images. . . . Visual symbols are at the heart of this story because the politics of the Indian-environmentalist alliance is primarily a symbolic politics. . . . Symbols are important in all politics, but they are central in native Amazonian activism; in the absence of electoral clout or . . . economic influence, the "symbolic capital" . . . of cultural identity is one of Brazilian Indians' most important political resources. (1997:712–713)[3]

However, there is a question left unasked by Conklin, one concerning not indigenous regalia but their complement, Western clothing. If Indians resolved to change their presentation, mixing manufactured clothes with native painting and decorations (even where "untraditional") after becoming aware of a model of Indianness created in the modern West, why did they not completely refrain from the use of Western clothing? A good illustration is the case of the Nambikwara ritual cited by Conklin. When a filmmaker produced a video of a female initiation rite and then screened it for the participants, they were unhappy with their images, feeling they were overdressed. They decided to perform the rite anew for it to be refilmed. The men took off their T-shirts and put on smaller shorts, while the women—who had been in dresses, I imagine—wrapped sections of cloth around their waists like skirts (Conklin 1997:719). We know from the beautiful photos published by Lévi-Strauss in *Tristes tropiques* (1955) that the Nambikwara used to wear nothing. As well as absorbing the Western model of Indianness, had the Nambikwara introjected our notion of modesty so deeply that, despite knowing they would be more authentic, they could not bring themselves to appear completely naked? Perhaps if questioned about this, the Nambikwara would answer much as the Wari' did when I asked them why, if their memories of life in the forest before contact were so positive, they did not return there for good, abandoning the whites and all their things? "Because we are whites," they said. What does it mean to be white without relinquishing being Wari', and how does this double identity inscribe itself on the body?

Turner (1991) provides us with one means of reply. For him, the doubleness visible on Kayapó bodies expresses a compromise between an interest in a life integrated with the world of the whites, with easy access to coveted manufactured goods, and the struggle for autonomy. While in the 1960s the Kayapó looked for a kind of invisibility in contexts relating to Brazilian society, clothing themselves exactly like whites, with long trousers, shirts, shoes, and sunglasses, today they exhibit their ethnic identity with pride. What has emerged, according to Turner, is a new form of consciousness, resulting not from structuralist-type cognitive transformations but from the historical process of interethnic contact, in which "the household and the individual have likewise become double beings, diametrically divided between an internal, indigenous Kayapó core and an external façade composed wholly or in part of Brazilian goods and forms" (298).

Though the ambiguity or double nature of the clothing is undoubtedly a political option, reflecting not only an endogenous valorization of tradition but also a consciousness of the impact of visual symbols on whites who valorize authentic Indians, I do not think that reflection on confrontational processes exhausts the questions raised by such responses. In the Amerindian case, the choice of the body as a place for expressing this double identity is far from arbitrary. The hypothesis I shall develop here is that, for the Wari' at least, the external, Western face is not a façade covering a truer or more authentic interior, as Turner suggests for the Kayapó (1991:298).[4] It is equally authentic and exists simultaneously with the naked Wari' body.[5] As we shall see later, in being simultaneously Wari' and white, the Wari' undergo an experience analogous to that of shamans, who have both a human and an animal body. An analysis of the body's meaning in the Amerindian world is essential to understanding the role of Western clothes in the constitution of this double body.

The Amerindian Body

Almost thirty years ago, in an article that today remains a fundamental text on the notion of the person, Anthony Seeger, Roberto da Matta, and Eduardo Viveiros de Castro concluded that the body and its processes are central for Amerindians:

> the originality of Brazilian (and more widely, South American) tribal societies resides in a particularly rich elaboration of the notion of the person, with special reference to corporality as the focal symbolic idiom. Or, put

otherwise, we suggest that the notion of the person and a consideration of the place of the human body in the vision that indigenous societies produce of themselves are fundamental for an adequate comprehension of the social organization and cosmology of these societies. (1979:3)

As Joanna Overing had already remarked (1977a, 1977b), the structure of Amerindian societies was not found where the ethnologists had been searching, since the reference points were models imported from other regions: Asia, Africa, Melanesia. Faced with an absence of clans, lineages, and corporate groups, ethnologists postulated fluidity and a lack of integrating principles in these societies. Seeger, da Matta, and Castro, examining the work of some contemporary ethnographers— Christopher Crocker on the Bororo, Gerardo Reichel-Dolmatoff on the Desana of northwest Amazonia, Overing on the Piaroa of Venezuela—observed that each devoted a great deal of space to native ideologies of corporality: "theories of conception, the theory of illness, the role of body fluids in the general symbolism of society, alimentary prohibitions, body decoration" (1979:3). They felt that this was not accidental, nor a "product of a theoretical bias" (3), but a consequence of the centrality of questions relating to corporality in the structural definition of these societies, and that the problematic of sensible qualities raised by Lévi-Strauss on the basis of American myths, found in his monumental *Mythologiques* (1964, 1966, 1968, 1971), applied perfectly at the level of social organization.

Recently, Castro returned to the question of Amerindian corporality in search of a new synthesis, developing his theory of perspectivism or multinaturalism. For many Amerindian peoples, he wrote, "the world is inhabited by different sorts of subjects or persons, human and nonhuman, which apprehend reality from distinct points of view" relating to their bodies (1998:469; see also 1996, 2002). At issue is not what we know as multicultural relativism, which supposes

a diversity of subjective and partial representations, each striving to grasp an external and unified nature, which remains perfectly indifferent to those representations. Amerindian thought proposes the opposite: a representational or phenomenological unity . . . indifferently applied to a radically objective diversity. One single "culture," multiple "natures"—. . . A perspective is not a representation because representations are a property of the mind or spirit, whereas the point of view is located in the body. (478)

In place of a multiculturalism, therefore, we have a multinaturalism (477).

I turn now to the Wari' ethnography.

Among the Wari', the body (*kwere-*, always followed by a suffix indicating possession) is the location of the personality, and defines the person, animal, plant, or thing. Everything in existence has a body, the source of its own specific characteristics. The Wari' often say, "Je kwere" (My body is like this), which means "This is my style" or "I'm like this." The same applies when they refer to animals or things. If asked why white-lipped peccaries live in a herd, they would respond, "Je kwerein mijak" (The peccary's body is like that); if asked why water is cold, "Je kwerein kom" (That's what the water's body is like).

If everything has a body, only humans—which include the Wari', enemies, and various animals—possess a soul, which the Wari' call *jam-*. While the body differentiates species, the soul assimilates them as humans. In this sense, the Wari' constitute an exemplary case of Amerindian perspectival thinking. All humans share analogous cultural practices: they live in families, hunt, cook their food, consume fermented drinks, perform festivals, and so on. Different bodies, though, imply different forms of perceiving the same things. Both the Wari' and the jaguar drink maize beer, but the jaguar sees blood as beer in the same way that clay is beer for the tapir. Both jaguar and tapir conceive themselves to be humans, *wari'*, a term that signifies "people" or "us," and in turn they perceive the Wari' as nonhumans, preying on them as though they were game, injuring them with their arrows.

The Makuna, a Tukano-speaking people of the Colombian Vaupés, provide a clear illustration of this question of the humanity of animals:

> The fish are people. . . . The fruit trees that grow by the rivers are their swiddens, and the fruits their cultigens. . . . Just like humans, fish form communities. . . . In their underwater houses (invisible to normal human eyes), the fish store all their goods, tools, and instruments, identical to those we have in our houses. . . . When the fish spawn, they are dancing in their underwater houses. . . . The game animals are people. They have their own mind . . . and their own thoughts . . . the same as humans. (Århem 1993:112–113, 116)

The notion of the body as the location of difference is not limited just to interspecies relations. The Wari' think of society as a composition of corporal aggregates at various levels, their borders so variable that it actually becomes difficult to speak of a society.[6] Thus, near kin can become separated and, breaking contact, turn into enemies, beings ontologically identical to the Wari'. In the same way, enemies can be incorporated as kin through marriage, turning into Wari'.

It must be emphasized that the body is not conceived of as a genetic given, but is constructed throughout life by means of social relationships (Gow 1991; da Matta 1976:88). Among the Wari', the body of the child—constituted by a mixture of semen and menstrual blood—continues to be fabricated after birth through alimentation and the exchange of body fluids with parents, siblings, and other near kin. Adopted children, for example, are considered consubstantial with their adoptive parents and, in an analogous manner, husband and wife become consubstantial through the physical proximity consequent to marriage (see W. Crocker 1977 similarly on the Canela). Food is central to the constitution of physical identity, both of the Wari' and of animal species, as we shall see later in the case of shamans. In the first phase of my fieldwork, I repeatedly heard exclamations of the type "She isn't Wari', she doesn't eat grubs." When I finally swallowed some of these grubs in front of them, the news spread through the village that I had turned completely Wari'. The consubstantiality produced by physical relations and by commensality is just as effective as that attained by birth, so that those who live and eat together, or who share the same diet, become consubstantial over time, especially if they end up intermarrying.[7] More than simple physical substance, the body for the Amerindians is, as Castro has observed, "an assemblage of affects or ways of being that constitute a *habitus*" (1998:478).[8]

Returning to my earlier comments on the Wari' drawing and Kayapó clothing, we should emphasize that the body is not merely the location where social identity is expressed but the substrate where it is fabricated, so that adornments and clothes constitute less a "social skin," as Turner proposes (1971:104) for the Kayapó, which would externally socialize a naturally internal substrate, then the motor of a body process. My hypothesis is that there is no substantive difference between the animal clothes worn by shamans, those used by the animals themselves (when they reveal themselves to Indians), properly indigenous body decorations, and the manufactured clothes brought back to native settlements by Indians in contact with whites. They all equally count as resources for the differentiation and transformation of the body, and cannot be isolated from analogous resources such as alimentary practices and the exchange of substances through physical proximity. In a certain sense we could even say that the Western clothes worn by Indians are more traditional and authentic than the feather decorations juxtaposed with them, since *clothing is the indigenous way of being white*, a becoming anticipated by their conceptual system, while the feather decorations are *the way for whites to be Indian*, as Conklin suggests (1997).

In his same article on perspectivism, Castro calls attention to the fact that clothes, masks, and adornments are instruments and not costumes. Speaking of ritual paraphernalia, he writes: "We are dealing with societies which inscribe efficacious meanings onto the skin, and which use animal masks . . . endowed with the power metaphysically to transform the identities of those who wear them, if used in the appropriate ritual context" (1998:482). Among various examples, we have the Yagua of Venezuela, whose shamans utilize "clothing" that allows their transformation into animals (Chaumeil 1983:51, 66, 125); the Kogi of Colombia, who describe a mythic figure capable of transforming into a jaguar through ingestion of a hallucinogenic substance (in the form of a blue ball that he places in his mouth) and the use of a jaguar mask, thereby attaining the ability to "perceive things in a different way, the way in which the jaguar sees" (Reichel-Dolmatoff 1975:55, 58); the Baniwa of northwest Amazonia, who describe the transformation of a shaman into a jaguar as "wearing the jaguar's shirt" (Wright 1996:79); and the Desana, where the use of hides, masks, and other "disguises" characterizes the animals as such, but also allows the transformation of shamans into animals (Reichel-Dolmatoff 1975:99, 115, 120, 124, 125). In this sense, and contrary to Turner (1971:104), clothes, body painting, and masks are primarily a means of naturalizing undifferentiated cultural substrates (see Castro 1998:480) rather than a way of culturalizing an excessively natural body. Differentiation is given by naturalization, not by culturalization, since culture is common to all beings—precisely the feature that identifies them as human. The Makuna offer an excellent example of this body permutability:

> Although fish live in the river world, it is easy for them to convert into birds, small monkeys, rodents, peccaries, and other game animals that eat fruit. When river food is scarce, the fish turn into birds and terrestrial animals in order to search for food in the forest. (Århem 1993:115)

Here I can recall the Antillean anecdote provided by Lévi-Strauss in *Race et histoire* (1952) and cited by Castro (1998:475) as an illustration of perspectivism: while the Spanish investigated whether the Indians had a soul, the latter set themselves the task of drowning the whites in order to discover whether their cadavers were subject to putrification. In other words, the Indians wanted to know what type of human these whites were, and this knowledge became available to them only through studying the peculiarities of their bodies.

We can establish a continuity between this five-centuries-ago episode and recent events from the Brazilian eco-indigenous scene, reported by Conklin (1997:727) and relating directly to the question of body presentation we have been discussing. In 1984 the Pataxó Indians, inhabitants of the Bahia coast, were threatened by farmers who were claiming their lands, alleging that they were not authentic Indians. The Pataxó were visited by a delegation headed by the Xavante Mário Juruna, then a federal deputy. Juruna proposed that they abandon their lands. Expelled by the Pataxó, he returned to the city asserting that the reserve was "occupied by a majority of mestizos and only half a dozen true Indians" (CEDI 1984:293). A report on the episode in the *Folha da Tarde* of September 4, which scandalized defenders of indigenous rights, concluded: "Queried as to the indications that led him to cast doubt on the authenticity of the reserve's Indians, [Juruna] replied: Indians don't have beards, nor mustaches, nor hair on their chest" (cf. CEDI 1984:293; also see Conklin 1997:737).

More recently, in 1992 during the Earth Summit, an international ecological conference in Rio de Janeiro, native peoples organized parallel events, some of them inside a reproduction of an indigenous village especially constructed for the purpose. Assuming the role of hosts, the Kayapó ended up acting as doorkeepers, deciding who could and could not enter the houses. Apart from journalists and official organizers, the only people allowed admittance were those wearing exotic clothes and indigenous decorations. According to an anthropologist who related the episode to Conklin (1997:737), two North American Indians were barred after appearing in normal clothes, only to be admitted the following day when they returned with feather adornments.

Conklin (1997:727) interprets both these episodes as outcomes of the imposition on Indians of a Western model of Indianness focused on body aesthetics. Here I wish to call attention to the "authenticity" of this model, and to suggest that it is precisely because of its salience that the model was so rapidly accepted and incorporated by Indians. As I proposed concerning the relation between the Wari' and the Christianity of the New Tribes Mission (Vilaça 1996a, 1997), at work is a concurrence of ideologies: in Christian practice the Wari' found values from their own culture related to an ideal of generalized consanguinity, and one reason they became Christians was to experience this. It is necessary, therefore, to qualify Turner's observation (1991) on the impossibility of comprehending the adoption of double clothing as a structuralist-type cognitive transformation. If these transformations are the product of a political consciousness, they are only possible or only take place in this form as a result of their compatibility with structuring aspects of thought, such as the dualist logic that, according to Lévi-Strauss (1991), is related to the structural openness of Amerindians to the Other, and the notion of corporality as central to the constitution of the person. In relation to the first point, openness to the Other, we should note that—as becomes evident in these mixtures of clothing that express mixtures of identities—our exclusivist notion of tradition appears to be alien to various non-Western cultures. We shall return to this later.

First, though, we turn to shamans, for whom the possibility of corporal transformation constitutes the very essence of their activity. In the Wari' case, the similarity between transmutations relating to interethnic contact and those that connect the Wari' world with that of the animals has its primary basis in the equivalence between animals (*karawa*) and enemies (*wijam*), a category in which the Wari' locate whites. Both enemies and animals maintain a relationship with the Wari' that is characterized by warfare and predation. By means of these activities, a rupture is produced in the continuum of humanity, with predators defined as human, *wari'*, and prey as nonhuman, *karawa*—these positions being essentially reversible.

Shamans

The Wari' shaman (*ko tuku ninim*) is "the one who sees," a special being, part human, part animal. A shaman's career begins with a serious illness in which an animal afflicts the future shaman's spirit, with the intention of turning him into its companion, a member of its own species. The spirit of the afflicted Wari' arrives at the home of the animals of the relevant species, and is already able to see them as humans—or rather, he adopts the animals' point of view. They bathe him with lukewarm water and, in the manner of Wari' parents-in-law, offer him a girl who will be his future wife when, after dying, he becomes definitively animal. When the shaman is old, it is commonly said that his animal wife has already turned into a young woman, and that he will soon join up with her, consummating the marriage and his transformation into an animal. As in the context of the social relationships between the Wari', marriage is essential here to completing the transformation.

The future shaman also receives magic annatto and babaçu palm oil, emblematic body coverings that serve to characterize him as a member of the afflicting species, endowing him with the animal's point of view and the power to cure. From this point on, the man (female shamans are rare) has an active spirit, an animal double, which lives alongside its animal companions.[9] The Wari' say about the shaman's spirit (depending on the animal he "accompanies," by necessity an animal from a species possessing spirit): "He is completely peccary" (*Mijak pin na*) or "He went to the peccaries" (*Mao na jami mijak*) or "He is with the tapir" (*Peho non min*). I repeat here words spoken by Orowam, a Wari' shaman, in 1995:

> I'm a jaguar. I'm a real jaguar. I eat animals. When someone is ill, I go to see him and he gets well. An ill person has things in his heart. He cools down (gets well, feverless). I have babaçu palm oil and annatto. I go to the forest. I travel far and see other people. I see whites, I see everyone. I'm a true jaguar, not a false one.

Or, as the same shaman asserted some years earlier in 1987, "The jaguar is my true kin. My true body is jaguar. There is fur on my true body."

Identity is explicitly thought to be located in the body, and is related to kinship. As in the constitution of relationships of consubstantiality, commensality is fundamental to the shaman's definition as a member of a particular species, so that a shaman may "swap" species if he accompanies other animals. As well as roaming alongside them, this entails eating as and with them. The Wari' shamans usually say that there is no visual difference between animal species that possess spirit, since they perceive all of them in human form: what really differentiates them is their habits.

The inability to visually differentiate animal species, to perceive them in animal form, makes the shaman a poor hunter. Sharing the same identity makes predation and consumption unrealizable (Vilaça 1998, 2000a), not because of probable diseases resulting from eating a consubstantial, but because of the perception of identity. (For a description of several experiences of shamanic initiation, see Vilaça 1992.)

The shaman is characterized by possessing two simultaneous bodies: a human body visible to the Wari', which relates to them normally as a member of their society, and an animal body, which he perceives as human and which relates to all the other animals of that species as a member of their society too—a society identical to Wari' society. As the shaman Maxün Hat said, only his body remains in the village; his spirit is with the peccaries, day and night. Occasionally a type of short-circuit occurs: according to his wife, he sleeps badly at night, chomping his teeth as though he were eating fruit. The same occurs with the jaguar-shaman Orowam, who frightens his neighbors by roaring while he sleeps.

The shaman's presence at the heart of the group has two facets. The first is positive, acting in the alleviation and curing of illness. Like men in a war expedition, animal spirits may arrive at a Wari' village in a group, brought by the wind, shouting: "Let's shoot these enemies with our arrows!" Among these animals, there may also be a number of shamans, generally foreigners, members of other Wari' subgroups.[10] The local shamans can see them and immediately attempt to establish a dialogue, and thereby prevent the spirits of the Wari' from being attacked by their arrows and falling ill. They respond by forcing the animal spirits to view the world appropriately: "Look carefully, they're not animals, they're *wari*'! They're your kin!" The animals then recognize the Wari' as equals and retreat. Should somebody become sick, the shaman acts to prevent the victim transforming into an animal, removing all the residues left in the victim's body by the animal aggressor and—in cooperation with his animal companions—attempting to rescue the spirit already on its way to transforming into an animal. This transformation may be completed and lead to the body's death, or the uncured victim may continue to live, thereby becoming a shaman. In the case of death, the afflicted spirit will become part of the attacking species and associated with a new body. It is interesting to note here that in the case of deaths caused by enemies during warfare, the spirit of the dead Wari' becomes a member of the enemy group, gaining an enemy body and becoming unrecognizable to kinfolk who may happen to encounter him later.

The negative facet of shamanic agency concerns his capacity to turn into an enemy at any moment, attacking his own people and possibly causing death. Such action is unintentional, almost a "technical failure": the shaman's vision becomes deficient and he starts to see his kin as enemies or animal prey. The effect is as if his different bodies merge in such a way that he, as Wari', adopts the animal's point of view. And this happens not just to foreign shamans belonging to other Wari' subgroups; local shamans, classified by kinship terms as is customary among cohabitants, are also subject to these breakdowns, which are reminiscent of those of killers in a number of Tupi groups during the posthomicide period of seclusion (Castro 1995). I was once able to observe the shaman Orowam, whose spirit is a jaguar, preparing to attack the people around him, among them myself and his classificatory grandson. He rubbed his eyes and roared. Perceiving what was happening, his grandson spoke to him, reminding him that the people there were kin (kindly including me in this group).

The overall impression is of a mirror game: the shaman becomes animal, and as an animal he adopts the perspective of human beings, *wari'*, in turn seeing the Wari' as *karawa*, nonhumans. In this sense, the shaman provides Wari' society as a whole with the indirect experience of another point of view, the enemy's point of view: from *wari'* they shift to seeing themselves as prey, *karawa*, because they know that this is how the shaman sees them at that moment. A double inversion takes place: a man detaches himself from the group by becoming an animal and taking the position of a human (*wari'*); by doing so he makes it possible for the rest of the group to experience the animal's point of view.

If animals are potentially human, the Wari' are potentially prey, in such a way that humanity is not something inherent, but rather a position that must be fought for all the time. This sophisticated logic of double-handed predation has as its principal aim a profound reflection on humanity. The Wari' experience a constantly unstable situation, always risking living on the border between human and nonhuman—as though only by knowing what it is to be *karawa* can they experience what it really is to be human.

For a Physiology of Interethnic Contact

The conception of the shaman as "the one who sees," on the basis of various perspectives related to his body's doubleness, returns us once more to the initial observations on the Wari' drawing, which portrayed a man with two bodies, although one of them was not an animal body but a white body. What is striking about the Wari' representation of whites is that whites were from the beginning classified as an enemy, *wijam*, a category in which the Wari' also placed other Indians they would engage in warfare. In the beginning, the Wari' say, the whites were peaceful enemies, and only ended up becoming bellicose after being sub-jected to constant attacks by the Wari'. Historically, the first period corresponds to chance encounters between the Wari' and nonindigenous populations in the region at the start of the twentieth century. The second moment relates to the persecutions suffered by the Wari' at the hands of rubber tappers and other pros-pectors from the 1930s until the end of the 1950s, when pacification took place.[11]

Some years after pacification, the Wari' had already ceased to move around within the areas nominated as their territory. They constructed houses close to posts that the whites situated in places that they considered easier to access, near to the territory the Wari' formally occupied. In these new villages, they shared the land not only with whites and Indians from other ethnic populations but also with Wari' from other subgroups, foreigners who had previously occupied other nominated areas and other territories. However, whites are still referred to today as *wijam*.

To return to the question of living alongside foreign peoples, in relation to Indians from other ethnic groups the Wari' have pursued a process of incorpora-tion, seeking to turn them into affines and consanguines. Always constituting a minority in each village, these Indians marry with the Wari', eat their food, and speak their language. Though previously called *wijam*, enemies, these Indians are today in various contexts classified as Wari', especially when the desire is to dif-ferentiate them from whites.[12] As for the activities of the governmental organiza-tion for the protection of Indians, Funai (the National Indian Foundation), and of missionaries from the Indigenous Missionary Council (Cimi) toward shaping a panindigenous identity where all Indians would be equally Wari' in contraposi-tion to whites, the incorporation of enemies through marriage, physical proxim-ity, and sharing of food is inherent in Wari' culture. *Wari'* and *wijam* are above all positions, occupied by beings that are not ontologically distinct. This single on-tology has as its logical consequence the fact that every enemy is originally a Wari' who underwent a process of "becoming-enemy" determined by spatial dislocation and a break in the exchange of festivals and women. From this perspective, such a process of "becoming-enemy" is reversible, requiring only a resumption of geo-graphic proximity and the reestablishment of marriages.

There is a good example of this process of incorporating enemies. The OroWin—another Chapakuran people and their traditional enemies—were re-located by the Funai to the Negro-Ocaia post, previously inhabited exclusively by the Wari'. After some time, mixed marriages started to take place, which pro-duced children through which the Wari' could establish kinship ties with the OroWin. A Wari' woman told me that following the death of an OroWin man, the Wari', slightly constrained at first, felt themselves impelled to weep at the funeral, treating the deceased as a consanguine and using teknonyms to refer to him—the appropriate way of referring to a deceased person from the group during funeral singing.[13]

Nowadays, whites are the only ones to be insistently referred to as *wijam*, enemy, so that today *wijam* is a synonym for a white person. When the Wari' say that the *wijam* are arriving, they are not anticipating war, only the arrival of a few whites intent on visiting or selling their products. They are enemies lacking the relation of war, which allows the formulation of phrases once unthinkable, such as "I'm going to the *wijam*'s house to ask for fishhooks." They have become neighbors, but not affines or consubstantials like the other enemies.

We have seen that for the Wari', identity between two people or two groups is conceived as a relationship of consubstantiality, determined by physical proximity, whose direct consequence is the exchange of body substances and commensality. Marriage is such an essential part of the transformation process that, as I have mentioned, the Wari' say the shaman only becomes completely animal, turning into an effective member of the species that his spirit used to accompany, when he marries the animal-bride promised to him at the moment of initiation. This is when the shaman dies and ceases to be Wari'. When Wan e', a peccary shaman, was old, the Wari' used to say that his animal affines were calling him as it was time for him to consummate the alliance. When I arrived at the Negro-Ocaia village, already aware of the death of Wan e' whom I called father, the people tried to alleviate my sadness by saying that he was well, that he had already been seen by another shaman in his new house, and that he had formed a new family with his animal wife. The change in identity was characterized primarily as a change in nature.

The widespread diffusion of the Amerindian notion of relationship and transformation as exchanges of substance was identified by Seeger, da Matta, and Castro in their 1979 article:

> The vision of social structure that traditional anthropology has provided us is of a system of relations between groups. This vision is inadequate for South America. The continent's indigenous societies are structured in terms of logical categories that define relations and social positions based on an idiom of substance. (14)

It is paradoxical, therefore, that studies of so-called interethnic contact involving Amerindian groups usually focus attention on the relation between sociocultural entities—groups, institutions, and individuals as "social actors" or "historical subjects"—and not on the relation between corporal aggregates. From pioneering works following the acculturation studies line of the American culturalist school (see Baldus 1937; Wagley and Galvão [1949] 1961; Silva 1949; Oberg 1949; Galvão 1955, 1957), passing to the works of Darcy Ribeiro (1957, [1970] 1996) and those inspired by Balandier's notion of colonial situation (1951, 1971) and the situation studies of the Manchester School (Gluckman [1940] 1958), such as the works of Roberto Cardoso de Oliveira (1963, 1964, 1967), Melatti (1967), Laraia and da Matta (1967), and more recently Oliveira Filho (1988), what is emphasized is the encounter between entities defined a priori in terms of Western ontology, with a strong emphasis on the "representational" aspects of agency and society. As such, cultural features are seen to pass from one society to another, as in "acculturation studies," or alternatively concrete institutions and actors (but conceived in terms of "social roles") are seen to act as mediators of complex relations of confrontation between human groups that *conceive* themselves to be *culturally* distinct (without questioning what this "culturally" means), as in the studies of interethnic friction initiated by Cardoso de Oliveira in 1962 and continued, after successive reworkings, by Oliveira Filho (1988:54–59). My point is that these studies do not pay enough attention to the indigenous sociocosmic conceptions about the nature of these groupings—particularly how they conceive the distinction between groups, and how they understand the way in which *contact* takes place. What the recent ethnographies on Amazonian peoples reveal is that indigenous sociology is above all a "physiology," so that in place of "acculturation" or "friction," what we have is transubstantiation and metamorphosis.[14]

An exemplary case of the contact between Indians and whites imagined in terms of an exchange of body substances can be found among the Peruvian Piro studied by Gow (1991), who conceive themselves today as "people of mixed blood." As an example of the contrast between acculturation and transubstantiation, I return to the Pataxó case cited above. Galvão, in an article on cultural areas of Brazil written in the 1950s, claimed that Indians of the Northeast, including the Pataxó of Bahia, were "mixed," and pointed to the "loss of traditional cultural elements, including language" (1979:225). For the Xavante Indian Mário Juruna, as we saw, the evidence for the non-Indianness of the Pataxó lay in another place: on their bodies.

The "openness toward the Other" that, following Lévi-Strauss (1991:16), defines Amerindian thought is here a "physiological" openness. It is curious that although the native conception of society is not organic in a functionalist sense of the word, there exists a relation between body and society, which—in their enthusiasm to "deorganicize" society—modern processualist studies of contact have failed to perceive (see Oliveira Filho 1988:35, 54). If society is not an organism, in the sense of a conjunction of functionally differentiated parts, it is a somatic entity: a collective body formed from bodies, and not minds. The limits—situated at various levels, separating kin from non-kin, and the latter from enemies—are body limits, and the consubstantial group, a species of "biological" collective, exchanges with other units, similarly conceived, substances: foods, semen, sweat, blood, and human flesh (see Gow 1991:261 on the Piro; Seeger 1980:127–131 on the difference between corporation and corporality).

At this point, it is interesting to consider the meaning for Amerindians of what we usually term *tradition*. In an article on the concept of tradition among the Akha (Burma/Mianmar), Deborah Tooker (1992) observes that for them the term *zán*, which means "way of life," "the way of doing things," "customs," "tradition," is characterized as a set of practices, and conceived as a load to be carried in a basket. The idiom of tradition is, therefore, "exteriorizing," and runs in opposition to our idea of tradition as a set of internalized values that are adhered to—as Viveiros de Castro writes (1992:25)—as a system of beliefs, and that relate to our own "theological" conception of culture. (See also Boyer 1994:40 on the "theologistic bias" in cultural anthropology.)

Tooker begins her article by recounting the case of a Chinese family that decided to become Akha:

> They moved into an Akha village, built an Akha-style home-house with an Akha ancestral shrine, took on an Akha genealogy, spoke the Akha language, wore Akha clothes and became Akha. (1992:800)

Had they wanted to turn back into Chinese again, all that was needed was to take the reverse route, as an Akha couple did: after spending a few days in the city and becoming Christian, they returned to the village and "reconverted" to Akha customs (799).

I would say that for Amerindians the idiom of tradition is also exteriorizing, but it does not in this case involve a load—as a set of practices to be carried—because, as we have seen, all human beings possess the same practices: they drink manioc or maize beer, live in families, and make war. The difference between them is given by their point of view, which is determined by physical constitution. This being so, tradition is the body. We could even say that, in a certain sense, tradition is internalized, though not as belief or an attribute of spirit, but rather as food, as body liquids, and even as clothes, when we consider it as also constituting a body. While for the Akha to change tradition is to change load, for Amerindians it is to change body.

In an article on transformations of the notion of culture in northwest Amazonia (Tukano), Jean Jackson (1995:18) distances herself from a "biological" notion of culture, which, in her words, implies having culture in the way that animals have a pelt and claws, in favor of a more dynamic notion where culture is like a jazz musician's repertoire—that is, something more like the outcome of an improvisation. While we can concur with Jackson, as with Conklin (1997), in questioning the imposition on Indians of a notion of authenticity that is foreign to them, she seems to have missed an essential point in the example she chooses, much as the relation between body and society escaped the critics of the "naturalized" model of society, as I noted earlier. The conception of an animal pelt, if considered from the Indians' point of view, far from being a genetic conception, is in itself essentially dynamic, and as such is inappropriate as a metaphor for fixity. As Kaj Århem showed for another Tukano group, and as I have discussed, it is thought that animals can change pelts, thus transforming themselves into beings of other species. If "culture" turns into "nature," it becomes intrinsically mutable, just as the processualists would wish. It is not enough, therefore, to add a historical dimension to the old notion of culture. A radical dislocation of perspective is necessary, one possible only if we adopt the Indians' perspective.

Returning to the case of North American Indians barred by the Kayapó from the compound at the Earth Summit, it becomes comprehensible that visitors considered Indians one day later by the Kayapó doorkeepers had not been thought so a day earlier. It was not an equivocation resulting from a process of ideological oppression, as it may seem to our eyes: rather, it is probable that, to Kayapó eyes, on the day before when they appeared in full Western attire, the visiting North Americans were not Indians, despite being so the following day. Such an attitude would have, for the Kayapó, a meaning radically different from that which we would attribute to them, and perhaps closer to the case of the Chinese-turned-Akha described by Tooker. To advert once more to Chaumeil's ethnography, concerning the Yagua's resistance to the adoption of Western clothing: "to adopt whites' clothing is also, in a certain way, to become white oneself" (1983:157n11).

It is important to stress that although it may function as equipment, clothing cannot be dissociated from an entire context of transformation. Thus, when the Wari' say that they are turning into whites, they explain that today they eat rice and pasta, wear shorts, and wash with soap, in the same fashion that a jaguar-shaman knows himself to be a jaguar when he has fur on his body, eats raw animals, and roams in the company of other jaguars. Clothing is a constituent part of a set of habits forming the body.

An observation by Manuela Carneiro da Cunha (1998:12) on the importance of journeys in the shaman's training in western Amazonia provides an interesting illustration to our argument. She writes that Western-style spatial journeys, which imply stays in various towns and cities, are nowadays taken to be equivalent to the journeys of the soul, even favorably substituting for traditional apprenticeship in some contexts, such as among certain Pano groups.[15] She cites the case of

Crispim, a Jaminaua Indian who for decades was considered the most reputed shaman of the upper Juruá. He had been to the Brazilian cities of Ceará and Belém, where he had studied. In Cunha's opinion, the most significant aspect of these journeys was the opportunity they provided to learn about the world of whites. By uniting the global (the point of view of the towns and the whites) with the local, Crispim became a translator, a mediator between different worlds—itself an attribute central to the constitution of shamanic activity. But these journeys consist of what exactly? And what form does such "apprenticeship" in the white world take? Cunha's description provides us with a clue[16]: "As for his life, it is said that he was raised by a white adoptive father who took him to Ceará and, after a murder in which he dirtied his hands, to Belém where he studied, before returning to the Juruá" (12).

What this description suggests is that the journeys, far from constituting essentially visual excursions as for ourselves (visits to museums and other typical places), involve above all the establishment of intensive social relations, and cohabitation (peaceful or otherwise) with people from other worlds. This is exactly what the Wari' say when describing their trips to towns: they speak of the food they shared with whites, the physical aggression, and the cramped living in the same dwellings. In sum, apprenticeship derives from experiences linked to the body, and I would go so far as to say that it is exactly through constituting "bodily excursions" that these journeys to towns are for the Pano equivalent to shamanic journeys.

We can return now to the question of tradition. By saying that they are "completely white," the Wari' do not mean they are losing their traditions, or their culture, as we may think in seeing them drinking alcohol, eating rice, using rifles, or dancing forró. Rather, they now have the experience of another point of view. Just as the jaguar-shaman may see blood as beer, the Wari' know that manioc meal is the whites' maize paste, or forró is their *tamara*.[17]

As Paletó, a Wari' elder, taught me in Rio de Janeiro, it is necessary to know what the whites' beer is, or what real food is for whites. If from the relativist perspective the idiom of translation is one of culture, in Wari' "multinaturalism" (Castro 1996) the idiom is nature. During Paletó's first days in Rio, a friend invited us to a birthday party. As soon as we arrived, he offered us drinks, and Paletó accepted a cup of Coca-Cola. He downed it in one gulp, and our host, thinking that he was thirsty or that he had really enjoyed the drink, immediately offered him another full cup, which he again drank in one draught. It was only after the third or fourth cup, when Paletó began to belch, that I realized he was taking the Coca-Cola to be maize beer. In a situation much like the coincidences in Hawaii detailed by Marshall Sahlins (1981, 1985, 1995), which increasingly confirmed the

identity between Cook and Lono, my birthday party friend was comporting himself as a typical host of a Wari' festival, offering more and more drink to his guest.
Paletó, as guest, was obliged not only to down the cups in one but to drain all the
fresh cups offered to him. This is what he was doing—and would have continued
to do, vomiting to be able to drink more, if I had not intervened by asking: "Do
you want to stop drinking?" He replied: "I can?" The whites' maize beer festival
may use Coca-Cola, but what matters is that it cannot be anything other than a
maize beer festival.

Though it appears simple to understand why the Wari' say that they are becoming whites, it is strange that they do not want to "complete" the process, even
if we assume the possibility of reversion, which would occur if they distanced
themselves from whites and returned to the forest and to their own foods. I say
that they do not want to complete it because the Wari' insist on not marrying
whites—and as we know, it is marriage that finalizes a process of "change of
identity."[18] They do marry with Indians from other ethnic groups, but what ends
up happening is the incorporation of these into Wari' society. Where whites are
concerned, the Wari' are clearly uninterested in fully incorporating them, as they
refuse to give them women. There are few Wari' women married to whites, and
they openly criticize the attitude of those kinfolk who have allowed such marriages.

Exactly the opposite would be expected, that the Wari' would want to give
their women to whites, precisely in order to have them as real brothers-in-law and
sons-in-law, and to incorporate them as Wari'. However, they prefer to maintain
the whites as enemies, as they reveal by continuing to call us such. At the same
time, they do not relinquish their geographical proximity: the Wari' do not want
to return to "the forest," and they explain that being near the whites is their
choice.

I should again make it clear that I am not suggesting that material questions
are not fundamental to this choice; it is clear that the Wari' wish access to white
goods, axes, and medication for the illnesses that they now know are part of their
lives, as well as tape decks, electric typewriters, and the football matches and
"fight films" that appear on television, today present in each village. If they like
these so much, why not marry whites and mix with them for good? Why insist
on avoiding the only really effective means, apart from predation (today only
symbolic), of consummating the transformation?

I would say that the Wari' want to continue to be Wari' being whites, want
the two things at the same time—both points of view. Their other enemies, those
they took in, like the OroWin, quickly turned into Wari'. When proximity is
completed by marriage, the outcome is identity. As far as I can tell, the Wari' do

not want to be equal to whites, but wish to maintain them as enemies, preserving the difference while continuing to experience it. In this sense, their experience today is analogous to that of their shamans: they have two simultaneous bodies, which often become merged. Today they are Wari' and whites, sometimes both at the same time, as in the shamanic fits. If the Wari' previously had the indirect experience of another position, the position of the enemy, today they experience it in their own bodies.

Acknowledgments

Earlier versions of this article were published in French as "Devenir autre: Chamanisme et contact interethnique en Amazonie Brésilienne," in the *Journal de la Société des Américanistes* 85 (1999), and in Portuguese in the *Revista Brasileira de Ciências Sociais* 15, no. 44 (2000). I thank Eduardo Viveiros de Castro, Peter Gow, and Carlos Fausto for their comments and suggestions. Fieldwork among the Wari' was supported by the Wenner-Gren Foundation for Anthropological Research and by Finep (Financiadora de Estudos e Projetos). The translation into English is by David Rodgers.

Notes

1. Gow (1994) reveals, however, an unexpected complexity in this circuit of appropriations, showing that the ayahuasca shamanism of western Amazonia—considered "authentic" by ethnologists—most probably has its origin in the indigenous groups sheltered by Catholic missions during the seventeenth century.

2. The Wari' are also known in the literature as Pakaa Nova or Pacaas-Novos. The name *Wari'* originates from the native word *wari'*, which signifies "us" or "human being," and is nowadays the name they choose to be called by. Wari' will be used here as a synonym for Pakaa Nova, while the native term *wari'* will be written in italics.

3. On the relation between aesthetics and representation, see also Weiner 1997. For another analysis of the use of Western clothes by native people as a communicative device in the play of ethnic categories, see Veber (1992 and 1996) on the Peruvian Ashéninka.

4. I should make it clear that, in discussing the notion of authenticity, Turner does not refer specifically to clothes and adornments, but to houses constructed in the white regional style that are/would be "unreal," and to the "double" village of Gorotire, with some houses in a circle in traditional fashion and other houses in a row, along a road. According to Turner (1991:298), the part constituted by the circle of houses is called "authentic."

5. Perhaps because they traditionally wore nothing, there is no word for clothing in the Wari' lexicon. To designate Western clothes they use the term *awom*, "cotton," which they cultivated and utilized for decorations. When they refer to beings that are simultaneously

human and animal, as with particular animals and shamans, they say that they possess a human and an animal *kwere-*, "body."

6. See Gow 1991:264 for an analogous conception among the Piro; Seeger 1980:128–129 for the Suya; da Matta 1976:80–81 for the Apinayé.

7. On the importance of food in the constitution of identity, see the Piro material analyzed in Gow 1991; see also Baer 1994:88 for the Matsiguenga.

8. For further developments on the analysis of the Wari' body, see Vilaça 2002 and 2005.

9. I must clarify that for the Wari', healthy people do not have a spirit or soul (*jam-*). A soul comes into existence only when the integrity of the body is threatened by other persons—animals, spirits, witches—who attract and capture it. The soul is a body seen from the perspective of Others, or a body turned into Other (see Vilaça 2005 for the Wari' concept of the soul). This situation usually leads either to the death of the Wari' person or to his/her transformation into a shaman.

10. The Wari' divide into six subgroups, units with a strong territorial connotation and maintaining relationships of alliance.

11. For an analysis of the first contacts between the Wari' and the whites, see Vilaça 1996b and 2006.

12. Nevertheless, I should make it clear that the Wari' do not always classify the other Indians as Wari': this becomes clear in war narratives, when alien groups are called *wijam*, and even *iri wijam*, "real enemies."

13. The OroWin were in the process of being incorporated, or of "becoming-Wari'," when Funai transferred them to another post, far from the Negro-Ocaia. The geographic distance will certainly diminish the volume of matrimonial exchanges, but the OroWin left taking sons, daughters, and grandchildren of the Wari', which stimulates contact between them.

14. For an extensive critique of these studies, see Castro 1999.

15. Chaumeil (1983:317) notes this same type of equivalence among the Yagua: "these journeys beyond the known frontiers are also akin to the cosmic journeys made by the shaman." Also see p. 101.

16. Though Carneiro da Cunha attempts, in this article, to dissociate the shaman's position as mediator from the multiple or "mixed" constitution of his body, I refer specifically to the section in which she registers her divergence from Gow (1996), referring to the attribution of shamanic knowledge to so-called mestizos. According to her, "It is not so much miscegenation . . . which justifies a shaman's prestige, but his relative position in the river network—a metaphor for a relative position determining the degree of generalization afforded by a particular point of view" (1998:11).

17. *Tamara* is a Wari' ritual music.

18. Against the argument that it is probably the whites who do not want to marry them, I add that the Wari' assert that it is they who do not want to marry the whites. Although there have recently been a few white-Wari' marriages—four Wari' women and

two men out of three thousand people—these are strongly criticized, and in fact most of them failed because of the bad behavior of one of the partners (usually the white man).

References

Århem, Kaj. 1993. "Ecosofia makuna." In *La selva humanizada: Ecología alternativa en el trópico húmedo colombiano*, edited by François Correa, 109–126. Bogotá: Instituto Colombiano de Antropología/Fondo FEN Colombia/Fondo Editorial CEREC.

Baer, Gerhard. 1994. *Cosmología y shamanismo de los Matsiguenga: Perú oriental*. Translated by María Susana Cipolletti. Quito: Abya-Yala.

Balandier, Georges. 1951. "La Situation coloniale: Approche théorique." *Cahiers Internationaux de Sociologie* 11:44–79.

———. 1971. *Sociologie actuelle de l'Afrique noire*. 3rd ed. Paris: Presses Universitaires de France.

Baldus, Herbert. 1937. *Ensaios de Etnologia Brasileira*. São Paulo: Companhia Editora Nacional.

Boyer, Pascal. 1994. *The Naturalness of Religious Ideas*. Berkeley and Los Angeles: University of California Press.

Brunelli, Gilio. 1996. "Do xamanismo aos xamãs: Estratégias Tupi-Mondé frente à sociedade envolvente." In Langdon, *Xamanismo no Brasil*, 233–266.

Castro, Eduardo Viveiros de. 1992. "O mármore e a murta: Sobre a inconstância da alma selvagem." *Revista de Antropologia* 35:21–74.

———. 1995. "Le Meurtrier et son double chez les Araweté: Un exemple de fusion rituelle." In Destins de meurtriers," special issue, *Systèmes de Pensée en Afrique Noir* 14:77–104.

———. 1996. "Os pronomes cosmológicos e o perspectivismo ameríndio." *Mana: Estudos de Antropologia Social* 2(2):115–143.

———. 1998. "Cosmological Deixis and Amerindian Perspectivism." *Journal of the Royal Anthropological Institute* 4:469–488.

———. 1999. "Etnologia brasileira." In *O que ler na ciência social brasileira: 1970–1995*, edited by Sérgio Miceli, 1:109–224. São Paulo: Sumaré.

———. 2002. *A inconstância da alma selvagem, e outros ensaios de antropologia*. São Paulo: Cosac & Naify.

CEDI. 1984. "Povos Indígenas no Brasil/84." *Aconteceu Especial* 15. São Paulo: CEDI.

Chaumeil, Jean-Pierre. 1983. *Voir, savoir, pouvoir: Le Chamanisme chez les Yagua du nord-est péruvien*. Paris: Éditions de l'École des Hautes Études en Sciences Sociales.

Conklin, Beth A. 1997. "Body Paint, Feathers, and VCRs: Aesthetics and Authenticity in Amazonian Activism." *American Ethnologist* 24:711–737.

Crocker, Jon Christopher. 1985. *Vital Souls: Bororo Cosmology, Natural Symbolism, and Shamanism*. Tucson: University of Arizona Press.

Crocker, William H. 1977. "Canela 'Group' Recruitment and Perpetuity: Incipient 'Unilinearity'?" In Overing Kaplan, *Social Time and Social Space*, 259–275.

Cunha, Manuela Carneiro da. 1998. "Pontos de vista sobre a floresta amazônica: Xamanismo e tradução." *Mana: Estudos de Antropologia Social* 4(1):7–22.

da Matta, Roberto. 1976. *Um mundo dividido: A estrutura social dos índios apinayé.* Petrópolis, Brazil: Vozes.

Galvão, Eduardo. 1955. "Mudança cultural na região do rio Negro." *Anais do XXXI Congresso Internacional dos Americanistas* 1:313–319. São Paulo: Anhembi.

———. 1957. "Estudos sobre a aculturação dos grupos indígenas do Brasil." *Revista de Antropologia* 5(1):67–74.

———. 1979. *Encontro de Sociedades: Índios e brancos no Brasil.* Rio de Janeiro: Paz e Terra.

Gluckman, Max. [1940] 1958. *Analysis of a Social Situation in Modern Zululand.* Rhodes-Livingstone Papers 28. Manchester: Manchester University Press.

Gow, Peter. 1991. *Of Mixed Blood: Kinship and History in Peruvian Amazonia.* Oxford: Clarendon.

———. 1994. "River People: Shamanism and History in Western Amazonia." In Thomas and Humphrey, *Shamanism, History, and the State*, 90–113.

Hugh-Jones, Stephen. 1996. "Shamans, Prophets, Priests, and Pastors." In Thomas and Humphrey, *Shamanism, History, and the State*, 32–75.

Jackson, Jean E. 1995. "Culture, Genuine and Spurious: The Politics of Indianness in the Vaupés, Colombia." *American Ethnologist* 22:3–27.

Langdon, E. Jean Matteson, ed. *Xamanismo no Brasil: Novas perspectivas.* Florianópolis, Brazil: UFSC.

Laraia, Roque de Barros, and Roberto da Matta. 1967. *Índios e castanheiros: A emprêsa extrativa e os índios do médio Tocantins.* São Paulo: Difusão Européia do Livro.

Lévi-Strauss, Claude. 1952. *Race et histoire.* Paris: UNESCO.

———. 1955. *Tristes tropiques.* Paris: Plon.

———. 1964. *Le Cru et le cuit.* Paris: Plon.

———. 1966. *Du miel aux cendres.* Paris: Plon.

———. 1968. *L'Origine des manières de table.* Paris: Plon.

———. 1971. *L'Homme nu.* Paris: Plon.

———. 1991. *Histoire de Lynx.* Paris: Plon.

Melatti, Julio Cezar. 1967. *Índios e criadores: A situação dos Krahó na área pastoril do Tocantins.* Rio de Janeiro: Instituto de Ciências Sociais, Universidade Federal do Rio de Janeiro.

Oberg, Kalervo. 1949. *The Terena and the Caduveo of Southern Mato Grosso, Brazil.* Washington, D.C.: Smithsonian Institution.

Oliveira, Roberto Cardoso de. 1963. "Aculturação e fricção interétnica." *América Latina* 6(3):33–45.

————. 1964. *O indio e o mundo dos brancos*. Brasília: Editora da Universidade de Brasília.

————. 1967. "Problemas e hipóteses relativos à fricção interétnica: Sugestões para uma metodologia." *Revista do Instituto de Ciências Sociais* 4(1):41–91.

Oliveira Filho, João Pacheco de. 1988. *"O nosso governo": Os Ticuna e o regime tutelar*. São Paulo: Marco Zero.

Overing Kaplan, Joanna. 1977a. "Orientation for Paper Topics" and "Comments." In *Social Time and Social Space*, 2:9–10, 387–394.

————, ed. 1977b. *Social Time and Social Space in Lowland South American Societies*. Paris: Peeters.

Reichel-Dolmatoff, Gerardo. 1975. *The Shaman and the Jaguar: A Study of Narcotic Drugs among the Indians of Colombia*. Philadelphia: Temple University Press.

Ribeiro, Darcy. 1957. "Culturas e línguas indígenas do Brasil." *Educação e Ciências Sociais* 2(6):1–102.

————. [1970] 1996. *Os índios e a civilização: A integração das populações indígenas no Brasil moderno*. São Paulo: Companhia das Letras.

Sahlins, Marshall. 1981. *Historical Metaphors and Mythical Realities: Structure in the Early History of the Sandwich Islands Kingdom*. Ann Arbor: University of Michigan Press.

————. 1985. *Islands of History*. Chicago: University of Chicago Press.

————. 1995. *How "Natives" Think: About Captain Cook, for Example*. Chicago: University of Chicago Press.

Seeger, Anthony. 1980. *Os indios e nós: Estudos sobre sociedades tribais brasileiras*. Rio de Janeiro: Campus.

Seeger, Anthony, Roberto da Matta, and Eduardo Viveiros de Castro. 1979. "A construção da pessoa nas sociedades indígenas brasileiras." *Boletim do Museu Nacional* 32:2–19.

Silva, Fernando Altenfelder. 1949. "Mudança cultural terena." *Revista do Museu Paulista* 2:271–379.

Taussig, Michael. 1986. *Shamanism, Colonialism, and the Wild Man: A Study in Terror and Healing*. Chicago: University of Chicago Press.

Thomas, Nicholas, and Caroline Humphrey, eds. 1994. *Shamanism, History, and the State*. Ann Arbor: University of Michigan Press.

Tooker, Deborah. 1992. "Identity Systems in Highland Burma: 'Belief,' Akha Zan and a Critique of Interiorized Notions of Ethno-Religious Identity." *Man* 27:799–819.

Turner, Terence. 1971. "Cosmetics: The Language of Body Adornment." In *Conformity and Conflict: Readings in Cultural Anthropology*, edited by James P. Spradley and David W. McCurdy, 96–105. Boston: Little, Brown.

————. 1991. "Representing, Resisting, Rethinking: Historical Transformations of Kayapo Culture and Anthropological Consciousness." In *Colonial Situations: Essays on the Contextualization of Ethnographic Knowledge*, edited by George W. Stocking Jr., 285–313. Madison: University of Wisconsin Press.

Veber, Hanne. 1992. "Why Indians Wear Clothes: Managing Identity across an Ethnic Boundary." *Ethnos* 57(1–2):51–59.

———. 1996. "External Inducement and Non-Westernization in the Uses of the Ashéninka Cushma." *Journal of Material Culture* 1(2):155–182.

Vilaça, Aparecida. 1992. *Comendo como gente: Formas do canibalismo wari' (Pakaa Nova)*. Rio de Janeiro: EdUFRJ.

———. 1996a. "Cristãos sem fé: Alguns aspectos da conversão dos Wari' (Pakaa Nova)." *Mana: Estudos de Antropologia Social* 2(1):109–137.

———. 1996b. "Quem somos nós: Questões da alteridade no encontro dos Wari' com os brancos." Ph.D. diss., PPGAS/Museu Nacional, Universidade Federal do Rio de Janeiro.

———. 1997. "Christians without Faith: Some Aspects of the Conversion of the Wari' (Pakaa Nova)." *Ethnos* 62(1–2):91–115.

———. 1998. "Canibalismo e morte entre os Wari' à luz do perspectivismo." *Revista de Antropologia* 41(1):9–67.

———. 2000a. "Relations between Funerary Cannibalism and Warfare Cannibalism: The Question of Predation." *Ethnos* 65(1):83–106.

———. 2002. "Making kin out of others in Amazonia." *Journal of the Royal Anthropological Institute* (N.S) 8(2):347–365.

———. 2005. "Chronically Unstable Bodies: Reflections on Amazonian Corporalities." *Journal of the Royal Anthropological Institute* 11(3):445–464.

———. 2006. *Quem somos nós: Os Wari' encontram os brancos*. Rio de Janeiro: EdUFRJ.

Wagley, Charles, and Eduardo Galvão. [1949] 1961. *Os índios tenetehara: Uma cultura em transição*. Rio de Janeiro: Serviço de Comunicação, Ministério da Educação e Cultura.

Weiner, James F. 1997. "Televisualist Anthropology: Representation, Aesthetics, Politics." *Current Anthropology* 38(2):197–235.

Wright, Robin Michael. 1981. *The History and Religion of the Baniwa Peoples of the Upper Rio Negro Valley*. 2 vols. Ann Arbor, Michigan: University Microfilms.

———. 1996. "Os guardiões do cosmos: Pajés e profetas entre os Baniwa." In Langdon, *Xamanismo no Brasil*, 75–115.

Wright, Robin M., and Jonathan D. Hill. 1986. "History, Ritual, and Myth: Nineteenth Century Millenarian Movements in the Northwest Amazon." *Ethnohistory* 33(1):31–54.

6

"Ex-Cocama"

Transforming Identities in Peruvian Amazonia

Peter Gow

The book *The Upper Amazon* by the American archaeologist Donald Lathrap, published in 1970, was my first intellectual introduction to the Ucayali region of Peruvian Amazonia where I subsequently did fieldwork. It begins with this description of a dreary, if commonplace, phenomenon:

> On the lower Ucayali in eastern Peru there is a fast-growing town called Juancito. Most of the inhabitants still gain their livelihood by farming *chacras*, agricultural fields prepared by the slash-and-burn agricultural system, which lie a kilometre or so back in the surrounding jungle. Tobacco and rice are two of the most important cash crops. In matters of dress and custom the people are not noticeably different from the inhabitants of the two large cities of eastern Peru, Iquitos and Pucallpa. They consider themselves to be typical representatives of Peruvian culture and would be offended if called Indians. Yet, a generation ago most of the inhabitants of Juancito or their ancestors were classified as Cocamas, descendants of the great Tupían-speaking nation which dominated the mainstream of the Upper Amazon at the time of first European contact. A few of the women of Juancito still make pottery in a much debased style, which only dimly reflects the complex ceramic tradition of their ancestors; and in case of sickness a shaman who has conserved the religious and medicinal lore of the Cocama will be consulted. In spite of these vestiges of their old culture, or perhaps because of them, the townspeople of Juancito are even less tolerant of their Indian neighbours than is the average Peruvian citizen. (1970:17)

Seeking a shorthand term for this description, Lathrap coined the term *ex-Cocama*.

The "ex-Cocama" phenomenon is an example of stories familiar from all over Amazonia, and indeed the Americas more generally—here is yet another case of acculturation. As such, Lathrap's description is instantly recognizable to me, but I also find such recognition disquieting, given that the concept "acculturation" is alien to my intellectual toolbox as a social anthropologist. This concept derives from German cultural anthropology and its descendants in the United States and Brazil. It was cultural anthropologists who produced the initial accounts of indigenous Amazonian peoples, while social anthropologists really became interested in the area only through the work of Claude Lévi-Strauss, and have tended to follow his interests in their research. This being so, they have not looked at the sorts of problems raised by acculturation and phenomena like the "ex-Cocama."[1]

Undoubtedly the reason that social anthropologists have avoided the study of "acculturated" indigenous Amazonian peoples lies in their methodology. Social anthropologists are committed to finding, describing, and analyzing coherent systems of social relations, and have probably steered clear of phenomena like the "ex-Cocama" for fear that their study would not yield such coherence, or at least for fear that any coherent system found might be of such complexity as to defy currently available strategies of analysis. Cultural anthropologists, working with different methods and postulates, have had far less difficulty in dealing with such phenomena, and have, unlike the social anthropologists, proved capable of taking them as objects of enquiry. In the process, they have produced important ethnographic descriptions that can, I seek to demonstrate, be reread in a social anthropological manner. The goal is to extend the range and purchase of social anthropological analyses of indigenous Amazonian peoples into the ethnographic territory pioneered by cultural anthropology.

Therefore, I here analyze the ethnographic literature on the "ex-Cocama" using categories developed within the social anthropological literature on Amazonia, and in particular the literature on kinship. I want to show how "ex-Cocama" makes sense as a transformational variant of other indigenous Amazonian kinship systems, and I will argue that, because this is so, it is not evidence of the collapse of an indigenous social logic, but rather evidence of its ongoing transformation.[2] Further, insofar as the question of what Cocama people call themselves is a problem of naming, it is amenable to the sorts of structuralist analyses of onomastic systems inaugurated by Lévi-Strauss's *The Savage Mind* (1966).

Here I look anew at ethnographic data generated within another strand of anthropological questionings to see whether that data can be rethought, and whether phenomena such as "ex-Cocama" can be given a new positivity. Obviously, this essay offers no new ethnography or history; it simply takes on a literature that already exists but remains largely unaddressed by social anthropologists. That said, I believe the present experiment is important for two reasons. Firstly, one of the main values of ethnography is that it is written precisely to be reread and reinterpreted in the light of new findings, and I try to show that the ethnographers of the "ex-Cocama," through the sheer quality of their work, have given us insight into a fascinating social world, even if they themselves would never have produced the account of that social world that I give here. Secondly, if I can show that the "ex-Cocama," supposedly rendered uninteresting to us by their acculturation, are actually a remarkable transformational variant of social forms more familiar to us, then this in turn suggests important questions about the past of the region, and about how its present came in to being. Throughout, the reader should bear in mind that my analysis here is constantly in implicit comparison with my work on the indigenous people of the Bajo Urubamba, some of whom are Cocama or descended from them (see Gow 1991, 2001 and the explicit comparison in 1993). I begin with my own experience with one Cocama/"ex-Cocama" community, San Pablo de Tushmo.

A Night and a Day in Tushmo

The first time I saw San Pablo de Tushmo was by night. Before going to the Bajo Urubamba for the first time, I was staying in the house of the sculptor Don Agustín Rivas on the lake called Yarinacocha near Pucallpa, with a motley crew of other people: some tourists, a poet from Ayacucho, and a very strange Dutchman who was so convinced that the world was about to end in nuclear conflagration that he burned his passport in front of us. We would hang out with some forestry engineers from Lima, and one of these, one evening, told us there was a festival in a local community. We set out in the dark, along the banks of the lake, through the main settlement of Puerto Callao, and further on to a part of the lake I did not know. On and on we walked in the darkness, then inland, until we finally arrived in a settlement of houses laid out in streets, filled with people. These people did not look much different from the mestizo inhabitants of Puerto Callao, and were clearly different from the Shipibo people living around Yarinacocha.

It was the eighth of December, and the festival turned out to be a celebration of the Feast of the Immaculate Conception. I had never seen anything like it. The local people were happy to see us, and quickly plied us with manioc beer, maize beer, rum, and a variety of local foods. We were invited into the house of the owner of the festival, where a table had been set up as an altar, with an image of the Virgin Mary surrounded by candles. In front of this altar, men and women danced backward and forward, with their arms raised and hands stretched upward. A band was playing, drums and a flute, in a style of music I had never heard before. It was only later, after months on the Bajo Urubamba, that I discovered that the dancing style is called *danzar*, and the music called *bombo*, after the name of the drum. People on the Bajo Urubamba told me that these styles of dancing and music were distinctive of *bajo ucayalinos*, people of the Bajo Ucayali, such as residents of Pucallpa and its environs. The villagers were so friendly and the festival so enjoyable that we visitors were thoroughly charmed. I, at least, was reminded of what I had read about the Jesuit and Franciscan missions of colonial Peruvian Amazonia, and felt that I had been magically transported into a distant past.

The second time I saw San Pablo de Tushmo was by day, and in very different circumstances and with very different results. It was almost two years later, at the end of my first fieldwork on the Bajo Urubamba. This time I had a definite purpose in Tushmo. My Cocama compadre Julio Shahuano from Sepahua on the Bajo Urubamba had given me a letter for his brother Juan, who continued to live in Julio's home village of Tushmo. Julio had described Tushmo to me as a Cocama community, and told me that his father was a well-known ayahuasquero shaman there. He said that many sick people from Sepahua took advantage of missionary-financed trips to the famous Hospital Amazónico on Yarinacocha to simultaneously consult Cocama shamans like his father, consultations that they did not tell the missionaries about. Julio explained to me how to reach Tushmo from Pucallpa. So, on a very hot day in the dry season, I took the bus to Puerto Callao and began to walk along the road that leads toward the Summer Institute of Linguistics (SIL) base further down the lake. It was almost midday, and there was no shade on the road. Eventually I found Tushmo, which looked strangely familiar. I realized that this had been the locale of the festival long before.

In the heat, there were few people about. I asked a man if he knew where Julio Shahuano's brother lived, explaining that I was Julio's compadre, and was bringing a letter from him. The man looked at me suspiciously and denied knowing anything about any such people. I asked anyone else I could find as I wandered about the village, and consistently met the same reaction: suspicion and denial of knowledge. Since they agreed that I was indeed in Tushmo, I knew that they were lying to me. By then I also knew that lying is not held in the same dismal regard in Peruvian Amazonia as in my own society. It rapidly dawned on me that they, in turn, thought that I was lying about the letter and about being Julio's compadre, and that I was doubtless searching for Juan Shahuano for some malign purpose of my own. They were protecting him. Eventually I found an old man, who on hearing my request, laughed and said, "Oh, everyone is called Shahuano here! You'll never find him!" Having said that, however, he pointed me to a particular house, and suggested there they might know the man I was looking for. At that house the owner, like the others, denied knowing Juan Shahuano, but he invited me to sit down in the shade. His wife brought me some juice to drink, for which I was very grateful. They were friendly enough, but off-putting about my project. Finally, when I despairingly asked what on earth I was going to do with Julio's letter, the man smiled and said, "Just give it to me, I'll make sure this Juan Shahuano gets it, whoever he might be." Handing the letter to him, I was filled with the certainty that I had completed my appointed task: this man was Juan Shahuano! But he gave no further information, while remaining hospitable. I made my excuses and left, utterly mystified by the reaction to my visit.

I was mystified because I could not understand why the people of Tushmo, so friendly to me when I was a total stranger at their festival, were so evasive when I came at the behest of a kinsman living in a distant community. Their dissembling seemed to be a reaction to the urgency and specificity of my mission: to find this specific person who was related in this way to that other specific person and to myself. My diurnal visit seemed to violate a possible rhythm of polite interaction. What the people of Tushmo rejected was any sense that knowing people's names and knowing named people's relations to each other gave me any direct lien on their relationships, including their relationships to myself. Such knowledge could not short-circuit their rhythms of relationship. As I show, names matter to these people, as do the temporal aspects of relationships.

Peruvian Amazonia

Peruvian Amazonia makes up 37 percent of the territory of Peru, and has a population of just over a million people, largely concentrated in the two main cities of Iquitos on the Amazon River and Pucallpa on the Ucayali. Since the mid-nineteenth century, this region has been economically dominated by a commercial sector of mercantile extractivism—the exportation of primary products of the natural environment and the importation of manufactured goods. This commercial sector is complemented by a subsistence sector, upon which most of the poor local people are dependent most of the time. The commercial sector is characterized by dramatic boom-and-bust cycles: at their height, the boom phases absorb almost all the local labor power and subsistence production all but ceases, while in the bust phases, most labor is absorbed into subsistence production. The area has very little industry, so there is nothing like an urban proletariat, and until very recently there was nothing that could be described as a peasantry. (For more detailed descriptions of the region, see San Roman 1975; Regan 1993; Santos-Granero and Barclay 2000.)

The region's economy has its symbolic armature in an ideology of race, whereby the commercial sector is strongly associated with being "white"—that is, of foreign ancestry—while the subsistence economy is strongly associated with being "indigenous," or of local ancestry (see Gow 1994). "White people" and "indigenous people" are the local poles of a continuum mediated by "mixed-blood people," those of both white and indigenous ancestry, whether claimed or attributed. "Mixed-blood people" are associated with both commercial and subsistence production. The racial ideology has two external poles: "wild Indian people" who do not engage in any commercial production or exchange, and "real foreigners," those who live outside the region and are the target of exports and the source of manufactured imports. The existence of these external poles can also be used to render all local people (excluding the "wild Indian people") as more or less "of mixed blood."

The "Ex-Cocama"

In what follows, I use the term *Cocama* in two senses. The first sense refers directly to the Cocama proper, *la gran cocama*, "the Big Cocama," while the second sense is a cover term for the combined "Big Cocama" and "Little Cocama," the Cocamilla. I apologize for any confusion this causes. The division is an old one, although the two peoples seem to have always been virtually identical in language and customs. The Cocamilla or "Little Cocama" are concentrated in one area of the Marañon valleys, and especially on the lower Huallaga River. The Cocama are found along the Marañon, Ucayali, and Amazon rivers, stretching down along the Amazon into Brazil. Many live in the towns of the region, including big cities like Pucallpa and Iquitos, and even Belem do Pará at the mouth of the Amazon. The Cocama population in Peru is hard to guess, for reasons that will become obvious. In the 1996 census more than 10,000 people recorded themselves as Cocama or Cocamilla (Brack Egg, n.d.), but this is likely to be a rather small proportion of the true number. Their population is expanding rapidly; more than half are under fifteen years old, and infant mortality is fairly low. This has been true since the early twentieth century, when the Augustinian priest Lucas Espinosa (1935) gave the same population estimate of 10,000. That such rapid and sustained growth is associated with a stable population suggests that a lot of Cocama people are, indeed, going missing.

I have quoted what Lathrap said about the people of Juancito, but he is not a lone voice. His student Peter Roe, discussing the situation on Lake Yarinacocha, a suburb of the city of Pucallpa, states that "the now-Europeanized ex-Cocama, as rural mixed-blood people, are aggrandizing their land holdings in the name of expanding civilization against the still visibly Indian Shipibo-Conibo" (1982:81).

Anthony Stocks, author of the important ethnography of the Cocamilla community of Achual Tipishca (1981), does not use the term *ex-Cocama* in his writings. However, his concern with the same or a parallel problem is indicated by the title he gave to that study, *Los nativos invisibles*, and in a general article on the Tupi people of Peruvian Amazonia, the Omagua, Cocama, and Cocamilla, he wrote:

> It is difficult to know to what point the Tupi peoples have maintained a distinct body of customs. Accounts differ, and the most probable interpretation is that the extent to which such customs are maintained varies broadly over the large region in which the Tupi peoples are found today. The Cocama, in the most urbanized areas such as Pucallpa, Iquitos, and Requena, no longer consider themselves indigenous in any way, and to treat them or . refer to them as Cocama would be an insult. By contrast, the indigenous Cocamilla people who have been living for a long time near Catholic missions on the Huallaga and Marañon rivers have maintained a definite sense of "ethnicity," and one often hears a Cocamilla man distinguish himself from the "white people." This occurs despite the apparent similarity in way of life of the Cocamilla and other riverine people (1977:60).

Stocks does not use the term *ex-Cocama*, but the utility of this term can be appreciated in the incoherence of his sentence "The Cocama, in the most urbanized areas such as Pucallpa, Iquitos, and Requena, no longer consider themselves indigenous in any way, and to treat them or refer to them as Cocama would be an insult." Is this sentence, which affirms only to deny, in itself an insult to many inhabitants of Pucallpa, Iquitos, and Requena? And what could it possibly mean to no longer consider oneself indigenous?

Oscar Agüero, in a study of Cocama involvement in the Hermandad de la Cruz, a millenarian movement founded by the Brazilian Francisco da Cruz, wrote:

> The Tupí-Cocama . . . do not consider themselves natives anymore, but *peruanos*. There is a particular type of concealment of their proper identity due to the historic situation of contact between the White/Mestizo society that they conceive of as adverse. . . . because of this they try to change their socio-economic organization according to the standard of White society. (1992:33)

Agüero's position is also a little paradoxical: Why do the Cocama accommodate themselves to the way of life of those they call "the Peruvians," when he shows that that is precisely what they call themselves?

Jaime Regan, Jesuit priest and anthropologist, and the coordinator of a ethnographic project on popular religion and social conditions in Peruvian Amazon, writes, of Cocama informants' reports of being mistreated by what they call "middle-class people":

> The Cocama try in various ways to free themselves from this kind of treat-
> ment. They dress like everyone else, they go to school, they consider them-
> selves to be mixed-blood people or riverine people, they do not speak their
> language in front of outsiders, and at times they change their surnames. In
> general the Cocama try to present themselves like the thousands of other
> mestizos of Peruvian Amazonia who have indigenous ancestors, but they
> suffer because of their surnames. An informant said: "Those who have for-
> eign names humiliate those of us who have Peruvian names." (1993:111)

Regan's account provides us with a hint of what might underlie the unwilling-ness of Cocama people to openly admit to being Cocama, or at least their refusal to identify themselves as indigenous. We may imagine that being indigenous is a low-status or even potentially dangerous kind of identity to have in Peruvian Amazonia, and hence that those who might possibly escape it try to do so. The model here would be "passing" in the United States, where black people who look white deny their black identities and operate as if they were white. It may be significant here that most of the writers on this aspect of the Cocama are Americans themselves.

The problem here is who the Cocama might be trying to "pass" for. Regan notes that they "try to present themselves like the thousands of other mesti-zos of Peruvian Amazonia who have indigenous ancestors." But who are these thousands of other mixed-blood people? As Santos-Granero and Barclay noted in their important recent study of Peruvian Amazonia (2000), the concept of a riverine mixed-blood population is a twentieth-century one, and began to be widely recognized after the 1940s. As I discuss further in the conclusion below, the post–Second World War period was one of profound socioeconomic transforma-tion in Peruvian Amazonia, and this transformation included schemes of social classification.

This means that it is entirely possible that the Cocama or "ex-Cocama" are not seeking to transform from one established identity into another established identity, on the model of passing in the United States. Instead, the despecification of the Cocama has been occurring in precisely the same context in which a new specification, that of riverine mixed-blood peasants, was emerging. It is even pos-sible that these new people are the Cocama, and that the "ex-Cocama" concept simply records their changing name. In challenge to that possibility, however, Regan notes that what distinguishes the Cocama from these other mixed-blood people, and what causes them to suffer, is their surnames. The informant said:

"Those who have foreign names humiliate those of us who have Peruvian names." It is to the meanings of surnames, foreign or Peruvian, that I turn next.

Cocama Onomastics

The significance of surnames is an important theme in the available ethnography. People in the Amazon, Marañon, and Ucayali valleys distinguish between *apellidos humildes* (humble surnames) and *apellidos altos* (high surnames) or *apellidos de wirakocha* (white people's surnames) (Stocks 1981:140–141; see also Gow 1991 and Chibnik 1994). As throughout the Spanish-speaking world, a person is identified by a given name and the paternal surnames of the father and the mother. Since men transmit paternal surnames continuously across generations while women transmit them for only one generation, maternal transmission of paternal surnames encodes the individuality of sibling groups. Further, surnames provide a global system for the identification of any given person in relation to any other.

What do surnames actually mean to Cocama people? Here I use as a model Stocks's study of the Cocamilla of Achual Tipishca (1981).[3] Stocks shows that surnames in Achual Tipishca are markers of what the Cocamilla call *sangres*, bloods. Blood is transmitted from a man to his children, and is marked by the transmission of surnames. These named blood groups establish the limits of incest and are, in effect, exogamous patrilineal descent groups linked by an ideal of bilateral cross-cousin marriage. It is clear that what the Cocamilla mean by "blood" is not the biogenetic substance imaged by Europeans and North Americans, but rather a corporeal substance transmitted, along with its attendant name, by men to their children. The logic of the naming system would suggest that women also transmit paternal blood, but only for one generation: the available ethnography is unfortunately silent on this point.

The division between "humble" and "high" surnames is an important form of social differentiation through class. I have quoted Regan's account of Cocama informants' reports of being mistreated by "middle-class" people, and he gives an example. Rosa Arcelia da Silva from Requena said of her hometown: "There are mixed-blood people and Cocama people. No others. They get along well. They are marked off, however, by their surnames. It is not the same to be called da Silva as to be called Manuyama" (Regan 1993:112). Manuyama is a distinctively Cocama name, while da Silva is distinctively Brazilian—and Brazilian tends to mean high status in Peruvian Amazonia. From a Cocamilla perspective, and one almost certainly shared by this woman, surnames like da Silva would encode the transmission of high-status Brazilian blood, while Manuyama would encode the transmission of low-status Cocama blood. Such transmitted blood would also be associated with bodily features, and one young man included in Regan's study said: "About the relation between the different social classes, there is often a very subtle scorn on the part of those who think that they are better, because they are mixed-blood people, or a bit white, with light-colored eyes, and who want to run things" (110–111).

However, as I noted above, Regan also claimed that Cocama people sometimes seek to change their surnames. This claim raises a key problem: If surnames encode the cross generational transmission of blood, and if blood is associated with readily visible bodily features, merely changing one's surname would not help very much if one was seeking to overcome prejudice of this sort.

Regan provides no concrete cases of name changing other than quoting one José Chota Magipo from Ollanta, who said:

> Some families believe that by changing their surnames they will make themselves better. This is what happened to one family who think themselves very superior and who say they wouldn't marry anyone from here because they say they are fine people, and in everything they are really troublesome. The people know them as bad elements, and they never stop gossiping about their neighbors. They are the only ones who think they know everything, and without even recognizing the surname of their parents they're always fighting, they fight among brothers, with neighbors, et cetera. Poor people are always totally simple. You can work with them. (1993:111–112)

Without knowing more about José Chota Magipo and the state of social relations in Ollanta, it is difficult to be sure about this case. However, the tenor of his statement suggests to me that the family in question are trying to act as bosses and to treat their coresidents as workers, rather than accepting that they are actually kin. To use an expression frequently heard on the Bajo Urubamba, Chota's statement is the accusation that these people have "stolen their surname" (Gow 1991:256n1). This is not the claim that the Manuyamas might decide one day to become da Silvas, but that the self-proclaimed da Silvas might actually be Manuyamas in stolen finery. Name changing would therefore be an accusation, not necessarily a social process.

Stocks, however, does give concrete cases of changes of surname—and, interestingly enough, these turn out to be gendered. He writes that "many young girls, who leave to work as domestic servants in white/mestizo houses, change their surnames after leaving their first job, in order to disguise their native identity; for example, although the surname *Pereyra* is historically Brazilian, it is so strongly associated with the Cocamilla in the local context that in one of these cases it was changed to Perea" (1981:141).

What would be the logic of changing their surnames? What advantage might be sought? The obvious candidate, given that these are young unmarried women, would be marriage to someone with a "high" surname. Now, on the face of it, it is highly unlikely that these young women think that changing their surnames will of itself change their visible bodily features. So the advantage of the change must lie elsewhere. The disadvantage to these young women of having Cocamilla surnames cannot be that these names publicly encode their blood and hence visible bodily attributes, but rather that their surnames hint at ongoing social relations that their potential husbands might not want. That is, the ex-Pereyra-now-Perea girl is openly asserting that her high-status husband will not be expected to have ongoing affinal ties with Cocamilla people, ties that, given the linkage of surnames and class, will involve a largely unidirectional flow of resources from the husband to his Cocamilla affines. By changing their surnames the girls are not disguising their identities but, I suggest, signaling that they are abandoning their kin ties as ongoing projects. I suspect that something very similar occurred in the case described by José Chota of Ollanta.

That said, there may indeed be a sense in which these young women would hold that their blood and bodily features had changed. Ever since the seminal work of Seeger, da Matta, and Castro (1979), we have known that throughout indigenous Amazonia the body is imaged as the target of social action, and that its attributes are socially produced. Bodies are made, not given, in indigenous Amazonia, and ethnography after ethnography shows how bodies are built up and transformed in ongoing sharing of such things as food, speech, and illnesses. Young women who have lived as domestic workers in white/mestizo houses would indeed have changed their bodies through such intimate daily contact with white/mestizo people, at least in their own and their kin's eyes. The change of surname would express this bodily change in the onomastic register.

Of course, such name changing would likely be viewed as illegitimate by the sort of white/mestizo people who can afford domestic servants, for they operate with strongly innatist views of race and visible bodily features. Even they, however, would accept that the young woman's name change signaled an unwillingness to have further contact with her kin, and hence be a sign of her increasing "civilization" and acceptability as a potential spouse by "fine people."

These data from northern Peruvian Amazonia suggest a broad similarity to my own ethnography of the Bajo Urubamba, five hundred miles to the south. There, the possession of high surnames encodes membership in the widely ramifying network of *confianza*, or trustworthiness, that defines the actual and potential circulation of credit in the commercial sector of the economy. The possession of humble surnames encodes membership in the widely ramifying parallel network of *paisanos*—compatriots, kinfolk—that defines the circulation of food and labor in the subsistence sector of the economy. That this same kind of logic is operating in the north is suggested by Rosa Lomas Pacaya of Requena, quoted by Regan: "There is some disdain because of surnames or money. Sometimes the people with low surnames, if they are professionals, are better than those with high surnames. There's disdain toward tribal people. . . . the poor people don't help out the rich people. They don't get together" (1993:112).

That the poor people don't help the rich people is due, I suggest, to the fact that the rich people would neither need nor want the help of poor people. "Help" is an idiom of kinship relations, and the whole point about being rich is making sure that you are not so related to poor people.

Foreigners and Tribals

Thus far, it might seem that surnames are self-evidently humble or high in this region, but in fact this turns out to be more complicated. Stocks notes that the word *Cocamilla* is used very seldom in Achual Tipishca, and then only in two contexts. One is when talking about language, as in "the Cocamilla language," which has very few speakers, and the other is when talking about surnames. Certain surnames are strongly associated with being Cocamilla, but this, oddly enough, includes surnames that are simultaneously defined as "foreign." For example, a Brazilian man called Pereyra married a Cocamilla woman in the nineteenth century and had many living descendants in Achual Tipishca, and so the surname *Pereyra* is now, in the Bajo Huallaga area, strongly associated with Cocamilla people. Similarly, the Spanish-Basque name *Olórtegui* is also considered Cocamilla, but, Stocks notes, "in this case the identification is not complete, and the majority of the Olórteguis who used to live in Tipishca when the white/mestizo people lived there have moved to their own community to avoid being identified as Cocamilla" (1981:141).

Given the importance of the contrast between humble and high surnames, and given that high surnames are foreign and humble ones are local, what conceptualizations of social process can lead a high surname to become a humble one?

Having noted that the Cocamilla very seldom refer to themselves as Cocamilla in everyday life, Stocks goes on to quote a discussion with two informants:

> When we spoke of the origin of surnames like Mashigashi in Esperanza, [José] said, "Yes, Mashigashi is Aguaruna. It is a *tribu* like the Cocama. There are Cocama and Little Cocama. My surname, Curitama, for example, is not Cocamilla but really Cocama. We Curitamas are all from the Big Cocama. Efraín and Froilán, they are both Lamista, but they live here now, exactly like the Cocamilla. Wilfredo here is properly Brazilian. His grandfather . . . came and left him here, growing like a tree. He sows a seed and

look today, what do you find? A whole tree, full of Pereyras." Wilfredo smiled openly and affirmed that his grandfather "left us here as Cocamilla." (1981:141)

Stocks glosses *tribu* as "'tribal' or relatively unacculturated native people" (1981:163) and, following the passage just quoted, goes on to discuss the extreme hostility of the Cocamilla to any suggestion that they might be tribal people like the Aguaruna. What then are we to make of José Curitama's overt claim that his surname is Cocama, and that the Cocama are tribal people like the Aguaruna?

José's apparently contradictory claim does make sense if we differentiate between Cocama as tribal in the past and Cocamilla as tribal in the present. Just as Wilfredo Pereyra is "properly Brazilian" but was "left here as Cocamilla," so too the Curitamas originated as tribal but are no longer such. I have discussed this elsewhere, focusing on Cocamilla notions of transformations over time (Gow 1993), but here want to note another dimension. Surnames encode processes by which originary separate peoples come together through intermarriage to form a new people. Historically, tribals, Lamista Quechua from the upper Huallaga, Brazilians, and so forth intermarry and found a new set of communities and people. However, the originary state of differentiation must be retained as a trace via the surnames, for it is these that allow for ongoing intermarriage, through the differentiation of "bloods."

This image is a familiar one to students of indigenous Amazonian societies ever since it was first enunciated by Joanna Overing. She argued that these societies are characterized by the subtly achieved mixture of dangerous but fertile difference with safe but sterile sameness. In a comparison of indigenous societies from the Guianas, central Brazil, and the northwest Amazon, she wrote: "Society can only exist as long as there is contact and proper mixing between entities and forces that are different from one another. . . . social existence is associated with both difference and danger, and asocial existence is associated with identity and safety" (1983–84:333).

Clearly the Cocamilla of Achual Tipishca also see themselves as precisely the result of such a process of achieved mixture, where the potentially dangerous differentiation of their ancestors, which caused warfare or exploitation, is domesticated via intermarriage. Similarly, the potentially dangerous indifferentiation of their ancestors, which led to incest (see below), is neutralized by the ongoing transmission of original differences as surnames.

This might also allow a slightly more charitable interpretation of the action of the Olórteguis: perhaps unable to live well with their coresidents in Achual Tipishca, they leave to found their own community. The Pereyras, with just as good a claim to a "high surname," are happy to have been "left as Cocamilla," and stay.

Kin, Affines, and Foreigners

The Cocama perspective on sameness and difference comes up very clearly in one account by a Cocama informant quoted by Regan. In telling a myth about the flood, when the raft carrying the survivors had reached dry land, Alfonso Amia Ahuanari of Indiana continues, "and we are from that family. We have become many from their daughters-in-law, their sons-in-law, not from one father like those from before who were all just kin. Afterwards the foreigners from other countries arrived to separate that family, and they introduced the surnames to distinguish us" (1993:111).

The story is a bit cryptic, and Regan does not publish the full text of this version,[4] but the implication would seem to be that before the flood, people married among close kin, children of one father, then after the flood real affinity got going, such that contemporary Cocama are descended from the multiplicity of the survivors' affinal alliances.

This story would seem, on the face of it, to contradict the problem of "humble surnames." Surely the problem of the humble surnames, like Manuyama, is that they are of self-evident local origin? What kind of sense does it make to say that "the foreigners from other countries" brought Cocama surnames to Cocama people? One could, conceivably, argue that the narrator is referring to, and perhaps even resisting, the well-known colonial imposition of order on indigenous Amazonian chaos. Maybe so, but the story follows a distinctively indigenous Amazonian social logic: names, even when they refer to autochthonous differences, come from other people.

Eduardo Viveiros de Castro, in his rethinking of the so-called Dravidian kinship systems of Amazonia, has argued for the centrality within them of what he calls potential affinity. He notes that real affinity is consistently erased in these systems, by its assimilation to consanguinity—over time, real affines are consanguinized. In these systems, the place of affinity as otherness is most plainly marked by the potential affine, those people with whom one does not exchange spouses, but rather spouse-hypostases: "The true affine is the one with whom one does not exchange women, but rather other things: dead people and rituals, goods and names, souls and heads. The actual affine is his weakened variant, impure and local, truly or virtually contaminated by consanguinity; the potential affine is the global, the classical, the prototypic affine" (1993:179).

What does the Cocama myth say? "Afterwards the foreigners from other countries arrived to separate that family, and they introduced the surnames to distinguish us." That is, after affinal relationships have succeeded incestuous relations, along come potential affines who give not spouses but surnames. These names mark the fact of real affinity in its nonincestuous aspect, and guarantee its reality by reference to the potential affine par excellence, the foreigner.

It should be clear by now that the key contrast on which Cocama people base their model of social life is not between the biogenetic and the cultural but between *tribu* and *extranjero*, the originary differentiation of tribals and foreigners. A proper social life is constituted by the safe mixture of these dangerous differences. But mixture of differences does not equate with erasure of differences, for these must be maintained on the edges of the system to generate its ongoing dynamics.

This analysis explains what it means to be "ex-Cocama." "Ex-Cocama" are those people who have Cocama surnames but are not Cocama in the sense of tribal people. Tribal Cocama existed in the past, and were the ancestors of contemporary people with Cocama surnames, but that fact does not necessarily make these contemporary people Cocama. Located between tribal people and foreigners, these contemporary people are neither.

Roe, as I noted, considered the Cocama "Europeanized," but I do not think that the historical precedents of contemporary Cocama social life lie in Europe. Instead, as I have shown here, contemporary Cocama social life appears to be a variant of a general indigenous Amazonian social logic, and its origins are almost certainly local. There is good evidence that this kind of social logic is ancient, and very distinctive to the Americas. In a classic article on trade and war in South America, Lévi-Strauss pointed out:

> Further, it is beyond doubt that since the discovery of the Antilles, inhabited in the sixteenth century by Caribs, whose wives bore witness still, by their special language, to their Arawak origin, processes of social assimilation and dissimilation are not incompatible with the functioning of Central and South American societies. . . . But, as in the case of the relations between war and trade, the concrete mechanisms of these articulations remained unnoticed for a long time (1976:338).

That contemporary Cocama use terms like "foreigners" and "tribals" to generate their social relations reflects the historically contingent fact that these are terms that lie easily to hand in the social environment in which they currently find themselves.

Lévi-Strauss did not invoke the very early colonial period in the Caribbean because it has any specific historical or analytical priority as a very early colonial period.[5] He invoked it as an exemplar of a failure of European sociological imagination, which recognized very early the ethnographic fact that Island Carib women spoke Arawak, but failed to draw the requisite conclusion that it was now on very unfamiliar sociological terrain. The significance of these facts, so long known, can be understood only through ethnographic contact with their transformational variants among the Nambikwara or Tupi-Cawahib. Anthropological enquiry starts from ethnography, and this is true even of anthropological interest in the historical archive (Lévi-Strauss 1948; Gow 2001).

My focus here has been on history as Cocama people understand it, as it is set forth in myths and in accounts of personal and communal origins in the activities of ancestors and associated with the transmission of surnames. This is "history-for-the-Cocama" (see Gow 1991). I have not attempted an analysis of "history-of-the-Cocama," the sort of history that we could reconstruct of ongoing social transformations from critical attention to the documentary archive (for an excellent summary, see Stocks 1981).

At most, I want to look briefly at some evidence to suggest that "ex-Cocama" is an ancient phenomenon among these people. In 1845 Paul Marcoy visited the Cocama. Marcoy was an excellent observer, and through his eyes we definitely see the Cocama people in all their ancestral splendor. He wrote:

> We have said that all the individuals of the Cocama race, long since baptized and pretty much Christians, have changed their costume along with their beliefs, and wear European shirts and trousers. Further, absolutely nothing is left of the ancient customs of this nation, and its current representatives have so far erased their memory that it is impossible for me to give any idea of them. The language of their parents is the sole evidence of the past that the Cocama have conserved, and this language, already altered by daily contact with Brazilians to the east and Peruvians to the west, threatens to disappear like everything else (1869:2:230).

Some 120 years divide Marcoy's observations from those of Lathrap, and 120 years is, by most standards, a pretty long time. The imminent vanishing of the Cocama therefore looks less like a late-twentieth-century phenomenon and paradoxically more like a structure of *la longue durée*.

It might be argued that there is a key change over those 120 years: the wide-spread abandonment of the Cocama language. This change is real, and I would not deny it for a moment. There has, however, been a recent development in the field of linguistics. The Cocama language has always been a embarrassment to students of Amazonian languages, for it is clearly very closely related to Tupinambá, the dominant language of the Brazilian coast in the early colonial period. Why should the closest linguistic relative of Tupinambá be spoken so very far to the west in Peruvian Amazonia? The Tupinambá moved about a lot, but nobody has ever thought that they could have moved that far.

Greg Urban (1996) has proposed an intriguing solution to this problem. He suggests that the Cocama language that began to disappear between the nineteenth and twentieth centuries was not the original Cocama language at all, but actually *was* Tupinambá. He argues that in the late sixteenth and early seventeenth centuries the Cocama adopted Tupinambá as a trade language, and Cocama is therefore the first dialect of Lingoa Geral, the Tupinambá-based trade language of the Brazilian Amazon. In the Cocama case, this trade language later took over and became the maternal language. Urban's hypothesis is entirely reasonable and, if correct, suggests that "ex-Cocama," as a late-twentieth-century process of transformation, is a kind of social process shared with their remote ancestors.

Peruvians

In coining the term *ex-Cocama*, Lathrap pointed to an important and real social phenomenon in Peruvian Amazonia. Cocama people operate a distinctive social logic that both asserts that they are descended from "tribal" ancestors and denies that they are indigenous today. What has struck many writers about them as a self-hating denial of an obvious indigenous identity can be rethought, as I have done here, as the common-sense application of their own social logic onto how they identify themselves to specific outsiders. Identifications are never context-free, and have ongoing implications for the identified and the identifiers. Because Cocama/"ex-Cocama" people's claim that their ancestors were Cocama but that they are not does not make a great deal of sense to us, we are left with a key onomastic problem: what to call these people. Lathrap nimbly invented "ex-Cocama," which allows ethnography to be written but looks a little uncomfortable. I conclude by looking more closely at what the Cocama people call themselves.

Lathrap said of the Cocama people of Juancito, "They consider themselves to be typical representatives of Peruvian culture and would be offended if called Indians." I cannot imagine anyone in Peruvian Amazonia actually saying anything like "We are typical representatives of Peruvian culture." I can, however, imagine this scenario: An American anthropologist asks the people of Juancito if they are indigenous, and they deny it. He then asks what kind of people they are ("¿Qué clase de gente son Vds., entonces?"), and they reply, "Somos peruanos no más" (We're just Peruvians). This would accord with Agüero's report quoted above.

A statement such as "We're just Peruvians" has a pragmatic obviousness to it in context. Contemporary Cocama people would hear any term for "indigenous" as "tribal," a category to which they cannot logically belong as contemporary people. Given that "foreigners," as I have shown, have a high social salience for the Cocama, Lathrap's Americanness would have interested them. If you were born and raised on the Ucayali River, calling yourself "Peruvian" in response to a query by an American is hardly very surprising. And if you don't want to be offended by further questions about being "tribal," you might as well say that you are "just Peruvian."

There is, however, a deeper point here concerning the recent historical context of the "ex-Cocama," which has to do with the relationship of these people to the Peruvian state. Lathrap was describing a period in which the categories of American cultural anthropology were becoming of direct material significance to Cocama people through the activities of a North American missionary organization, the Summer Institute of Linguistics (SIL). In the late 1940s the Peruvian state, for complicated geopolitical reasons, effectively handed control over almost all aspects of its relations with indigenous people in Amazonia to this missionary organization. The SIL, in return for permission to work with and translate the Bible into all indigenous languages in the area, agreed to educate indigenous people and especially to educate them as Peruvian citizens (see Stoll 1982).

The SIL had their own agenda, which was the translation of the Bible into every known human language. The SIL understood this odd commission in terms affected by American cultural anthropology: a language implied a distinct people with a distinct culture. According to the SIL definition, "the term 'language group' [*grupo idiomático*] refers to an ethnic group whose language differs from the rest (a) because it is not comprehensible to the speakers of other languages, or (b) because its phonological system demands a distinct alphabet" (Shell and Wise 1971:9).

The Cocama presented a problem, given that few people spoke the language other than older illiterate people. The SIL decided it was not worth translating the Bible into this language. Equally, the Cocama had no interest in bilingual education.[6] In the political conditions of the 1950s and 1960s, the Cocama, despite being among the largest indigenous populations in the region, lacked SIL—and hence state—recognition of indigenous status.

I most certainly do not want to suggest that either the SIL or the Peruvian nation-state is able to interpellate the Cocama as "ex-Cocama," to use the Althusserian categories that seem to unconsciously underlie so many of the supposedly Foucauldian discussions of identity in anthropology. Instead, I believe that the terms and relations implied in such institutional interpellations must always intersect with the terms and relations that their targets find meaningful in their own lives. In the present case, institutional interpellations by the SIL and the state would have intersected strongly with Cocama people's categories in ways that would have been unexpected by those organizations.

In particular, it would have been clear to Cocama people that SIL and state recognition of indigenous people coincided exactly with their own category of "tribal people," which, as we have seen, can be a category of Cocama ancestors but cannot contain contemporary Cocama people. Every exemplar of SIL- and state-recognized "indigenous people," like the Conibo or the Aguaruna, would have been a "tribal people" to Cocama eyes. Every attempt by the Peruvian state or by anthropologists or missionaries to get the Cocama to reassert their indigenous identities became a dialogue of the deaf. The anthropologists and missionaries interpreted the Cocama refusal of indigenous identity as bad-faith attempts at passing, while the Cocama must have heard those suggestions as claims that they were "tribal" and that their history of community-building had not, in fact, happened (see Stocks 1981 and discussion of the Cocamilla case in Gow 1993).

In this new battle over identifications, the Cocama seem, however, to have gone on the offensive. Constantly pressured to define themselves and very reluctant to become "indigenous/tribal people" and so forget their history, they have taken possession of a new name for themselves, *peruanos*, "Peruvians." As we have seen, names matter in Peruvian Amazonia, and social relations in the region can be characterized as an endemic onomastic warfare, with surnames suffering the process of losing rank as associations of "foreignness" are contaminated with associations of autochthonous origin. White people maintain the "height" of their names by asserting the purity of their foreignness. This, of course, exposes them to the charge that they are, in fact, basically "foreign" in the new and dangerous sense of "not really Peruvian." Being "not really Peruvian" would be an uncomfortable position in the period of heightened nationalization of everyday life in late-twentieth-century Peruvian Amazonia.

As the Peruvian state increased its concern for making its Amazonian citizens into good Peruvians, it provided a chance for people with "humble surnames" to open a new round in the onomastic warfare, reconfiguring their humble surnames as Peruvian names, and hence themselves as the real Peruvians. As Regan reported, an informant said, "Those who have foreign names humiliate those of us who have Peruvian names." It is a clever argument, which the people with high surnames would have the greatest difficulty refuting, given the importance they place on their foreign origins. Here what was once a "foreign" name, "Peruvians," is incorporated into the self as its transparent specification. The "ex-Cocama" are in the process of stealing the most important identity position in the region for themselves.

I should stress that my analysis is largely based on ethnographic data collected from the 1960s to the early 1980s, and is thus specific to that historical period. Fernando Santos-Granero, in a letter commenting on an earlier version of this essay, has pointed out that many Cocama people in Peru experienced profound social and political transformations during the 1990s, which has lead to an increased interest in indigenous identity mediated by forms of political representation, legal recognition, and educational policies. As he pointed out, however, such later transformations do not invalidate my analysis here, and raise interesting questions about what it might mean to reassert a Cocama identity in the twenty-first century. Similarly, Natalie Petesch has told me that while Peruvian Cocama consider themselves to be "just Peruvian," Cocama people in Colombia and Brazil assert themselves to be Cocama precisely to avoid being identified as "Peruvians" and hence as alien nationals. She notes, however, that these Cocama people deny being like the "real Cocama" of the past, a way of being associated by them with the Peruvian Cocama. Clearly, in their ongoing transformations, Cocama people continue to generate images of themselves that follow a distinctive logic that confounds what powerful outsiders insist they should be.

Lathrap began *The Upper Amazon* with his account of the "ex-Cocama" of Juancito for a reason. He was concerned to show how contemporary ethnographies of Amazonia could be linked to archaeological data to reveal continuous and uniform cultural processes in the region over several thousand years. Behind their appearance of acculturation, Lathrap argued, the "ex-Cocama" were continuing a struggle for good agricultural land several millennia old. While I am not sure of the specific content of Lathrap's analysis, I agree with the scope of it. The phenomenon of the "ex-Cocama" and this new identity as "just Peruvians" is a continuous and uniform social process of transforming of the other into the self that is at least five hundred years old in Peruvian Amazonia, and doubtless very much older.

Acknowledgments

Without the work of the various ethnographers of the Cocama, my own reinterpretation would have been impossible. My debt to them is clear, even where my analysis of their materials differs notably from their own. I also thank Eduardo Viveiros de Castro, Edward Simpson, Fernando Santos-Granero, Carlos Fausto, Natalie Petesch, Roxane Rivas, and the participants in the seminars of the Department of Anthropology of the London School of Economics and PPGAS in the Museu Nacional/UFRJ for comments on this essay. An earlier version was published in Portuguese in *Mana: Estudos de Antropologia Social* 9, no. 1 (2003:57–59). Translations of texts in languages other than English are my own, as are all errors.

Notes

1. Exceptions would be Gow 1991 and Taylor 1999.

2. The present essay extends the analysis of indigenous Amazonian societies as histori-cally transformational systems developed at greater length in Gow 2001.

3. It should be noted that Achual Tipishca is a highly atypical community by Co-cama/Cocamilla standards. It has no non-Cocamilla permanent residents and it is largely endogamous.

4. Regan publishes another version (1993:124–125) that does not refer to this episode.

5. See Hill and Santos-Granero 2002 for recent perspectives on these peoples.

6. Stocks's ethnography (1981:143) suggests a further possible dimension for resistance to the SII project, when he notes that the Cocamilla language is associated with shamanic song and action.

References

Agüero, Oscar Alfredo. 1992. *El milenio en la Amazonía: Mito-utopía tupí-cocama, o la subversión del orden simbólico* (Lima: CAAAP; Quito: Abya-Yala, 1994).

Brack Egg, Antonio, ed. n.d. *Amazonía: Biodiversidad, Comunidades y Desarrollo*. www.regionloreto.gob.pe/amazonia/tca/menu.htm.

Castro, Eduardo Viveiros de. 1993. "Alguns aspectos da afinidade no dravidianato amazôni-co." In *Amazônia: Etnologia e história indígena*, edited by Eduardo Viveiros de Castro and Manuela Carneiro da Cunha, 149–210. São Paulo: NHII-USP/FAPESP.

Chibnik, Michael. 1994. *Risky Rivers: The Economics and Politics of Floodplain Farming in Amazonia*. Tucson: University of Arizona Press.

Espinosa, Lucas. 1935. *Los Tupí del Oriente peruano: Estudio lingüístico y etnográfico*. Ma-drid: Hernando.

Gow, Peter. 1991. *Of Mixed Blood: Kinship and History in Peruvian Amazonia*. Oxford: Clarendon Press.

———. 1993. "Gringos and Wild Indians: Images of History in Western Amazonian Cultures." *L'Homme* 33(126–128):327–347.

———. 1994. "River People: Shamanism and History in Western Amazonia." In *Sha-manism, History, and the State*, edited by Nicholas Thomas and Caroline Humphrey, 90–113. Ann Arbor: University of Michigan Press.

———. 2001. *An Amazonian Myth and Its History*. Oxford: Oxford University Press.

Hill, Jonathan D., and Fernando Santos-Granero, eds. 2002. *Comparative Arawakan His-tories: Rethinking Language Family and Culture Area in Amazonia*. Urbana: University of Illinois Press.

Lathrap, Donald W. 1970. *The Upper Amazon*. London: Thames and Hudson.

Lévi-Strauss, Claude. 1948. "La Vie familiale et sociale des indiens nambikwara." *Journal de la Société des Américanistes* 37:1–131.

————. 1966. *The Savage Mind*. London: Weidenfeld and Nicolson.

————. 1976. "Guerra e comércio entre os índios da América do Sul." In *Leituras de etnologia brasileira*, edited by Egon Schaden, 325–339. São Paulo: Nacional.

Marcoy, Paul. 1869. *Voyage à travers l'Amérique du Sud, de l'Océan Pacifique à l'Océan Atlantique*. 2 vols. Paris: Hachette.

Overing, Joanna. 1983–84. "Elementary Structures of Reciprocity: A Comparative Note on Guianese, Central Brazilian, and North-West Amazon Socio-political Thought." *Antropológica* 59–62:331–348.

Regan, Jaime. 1993. *Hacia la Tierra sin Mal: La religión del pueblo en la Amazonía*. 2nd ed. Iquitos, Peru: CETA.

Roe, Peter G. 1982. *The Cosmic Zygote: Cosmology in the Amazon Basin*. New Brunswick, New Jersey: Rutgers University Press.

San Roman, Jesús Víctor. 1975. *Perfiles históricos de la Amazonía peruana*. Lima: Ediciones Paulinas.

Santos-Granero, Fernando, and Frederica Barclay. 2000. *Tamed Frontiers: Economy, Society, and Civil Rights in Upper Amazonia*. Boulder, Colorado: Westview.

Seeger, Anthony, Roberto da Matta, and Eduardo Viveiros de Castro. 1979. "A construção da pessoa nas sociedades indígenas brasileiras." *Boletim do Museu Nacional* 32:2–19.

Shell R., Olive A., and Mary Ruth Wise S. 1971. *Grupos idiomáticos del Perú*. 2nd ed. Lima: Universidad Nacional Mayor de San Marcos/Instituto Lingüístico de Verano.

Stocks, Anthony Wayne. 1977. "Notas sobre Los Tupí del Perú." *Amazonía Peruana* 1(1):59–72.

————. 1981. *Los nativos invisibles: Notas sobre la historia y realidad actual de los Cocamilla del río Huallaga, Perú*. Lima: CAAAP.

Stoll, David. 1982. *Fishers of Men or Founders of Empire? The Wycliffe Bible Translators in Latin America*. London: Zed.

Taylor, Anne Christine. 1999. "The Western Margins of Amazonia from the Early Sixteenth to the Early Nineteenth Century." In *The Cambridge History of the Native Peoples of the Americas*, vol. 3, *South America*, edited by Frank Salomon and Stuart B. Schwartz, 2:188–256. Cambridge: Cambridge University Press.

Urban, Greg. 1996. "On the Geographical Origins and Dispersions of Tupian Languages." *Revista de Antropologia* 39(2):61–104.

III

Remembering Ancestrality

7

Faces from the Past

Just How "Ancestral" Are Matis "Ancestor Spirit" Masks?

Philippe Erikson

Throughout the ethnographic literature so far dedicated to the Matis, a Pano people from the Brazilian Amazon, the masked figures they call *mariwin* have been depicted as the representation of "ancestral" spirits. In the light of new fieldwork material, my aim in the following pages is to provide a closer definition of what "ancestral" means in this Amazonian context. More precisely, I intend to show that the *mariwin* achieve the paradoxical feat of embodying values associated with ancestrality while nonetheless being denied the status of kin, since discourses and practices connected to them ostensibly reject the idea of filiation per se.

Following a discussion of the ceremonial aspect of the masquerades and an examination of the ontological traits imputed to the *mariwin*, I will support the notion that these beings never cease to appear as virtual affines, despite their close association with the group's dead, preceding generations, and self-identity. As we proceed, it will become clear that the affinity associated with these emanations of a past age can actually be located within a specific time and place, since it suggests the existence of past but nonetheless highly significant links with a neighboring ethnic group: the Katukina-Kanamari. I therefore hope to shed new light on the conceptions of temporality and generational succession typical of Western Amazonian systems of thought.

The *Mariwin*: Ritual Aspects

The *mariwin* appear during masquerades when men embody the spirits by smearing their bodies with mud (sometimes tinted with charcoal), wrapping themselves in ferns, and covering their faces with elegant clay masks (Erikson 2002). They carry bundles of long fronds taken from *daratsintuk* palms (*Astrocaryum muru muru*), which are used to whip children, and shuffle about on their haunches, adopting a highly conventionalized set of vocalizations, mimicries, and postures. Although nowadays the ludic (not to say touristic) aspect of the masquerades seems to be growing in importance, embodying the *mariwin* by donning a mask still amounts to a serious act. In fact, the person is supposed to be very literally transformed into a spirit, and the linguistic expression in this context, *tsusin impak-*, "become a spirit," is the same used to refer to the postmortem fate of someone who has recently died. Making oneself up as a *mariwin*, at least from a traditional point of view, is not without risk for the actor—a danger eliciting a certain number of ritual precautions connected especially to the gaze (Erikson 2001).

The *mariwin* visit humans in sporadic fashion without any fixed periodicity, aside from the fact that their visits normally coincide with the maize season. They arrive in small groups of two or three when the aim is simply to punish disobedient children, which is one of their functions, but in larger numbers during important rituals, in particular when initiates are tattooed. On these solemn occasions, which I have never had the chance to witness, the group of *mariwin* rise up to sing instead of simply squatting and grunting as they normally do. *Mariwin* and tattoos are systematically associated in Matis discourse—people never miss a chance to remark that the exuberant ornamentation of the masks, equipped with numerous kapok labrets and macaw feathers, provides a model they themselves strive to imitate through their own decorative practices. Although unexpected to children, the arrival of the *mariwin* is, of course, foreseen and even choreographed by adults. Women summon them by using highly codified shrill cries, while men summon them by playing the *masën*, a lateral globular clay flute specially designed for this purpose. The Matis claim this musical instrument—the only one they possess—should be played only when meat is abundant, doubtless because without meat, social life comes to a standstill. In the past when the Matis still lived in dispersed groups, the *masën* likewise served to invite the denizens of other villages. This implies that, although not offered food, the *mariwin* enjoy the status of guests.

The *mariwin*'s main function involves whipping children, adolescents, and pregnant women, whose unborn offspring benefit metonymically from the lashes. Far from implying mere punishment, the lashes are presented as a way of transferring energy (*sho*) to those on their receiving end. Although they do indeed serve to discipline misbehaving youngsters, the lashes are mainly perceived as a method of stimulating growth and curing laziness. Indeed, in contrast to the younger children who have to be constrained, adolescents very willingly expose themselves to the *mariwin*. However, despite being used as de facto whips—an undeniable fact in view of the marks they leave on the skin—the *mariwin* canes are said to be effective essentially because of the innumerable tiny spines covering the palm fronds they are made of. These multiple prickles enable the "spirits" to inject—in the most literal sense of the term—a portion of their energy (*sho*) into the recipients. Before using the palm fronds, the *mariwin* sometimes coat them with a little of their sweat, a concrete materialization of the energy they wish to transmit.[1] We may also note that in order to ensure their effectiveness, the canes must absolutely be obtained by uprooting them bare-handed, a sweaty job, rather than simply cutting them with a machete.

During the masquerades, while still crouched on their haunches and moving about with their typical swaying gait, the *mariwin* twitch the base of the canes abruptly, signaling their intention to "sting" (*sek*) the children. It should be noted that there is no gesture likewise signifying their intention to "whip" (*kwesek*) them, additional proof that the logic involved here is one of "acupuncture" (see figures 7.1 and 7.2). The children are able to observe these stereotypical gestures, which could readily be described as a form of dance. They can also witness the pantomime performed by the *mariwin* as they respond to the more or less absurd questions put to them by grown-ups, a farce provoking general amusement. In

Fig. 7.1. Yellow-ochre *mariwin* in action (photo by Philippe Erikson).

Fig. 7.2. Stereotyped threatening posture of the *mariwin* (photo by Philippe Erikson).

contrast, when the ceremony reaches its climax, adults frequently remind children that they should avoid looking at the spirits, in particular at the critical moment when the whip is poised to strike the base of their spine or the upper part of their thighs. This precaution is obviously justified as a way of protecting the children from being struck in the eye by a whip. However, it is impossible to avoid comparing this ocular ban with the symmetrically inverse visual constraint imposed on the *mariwin*, who must keep an eye on the children. When their visit is over, they leave the house backward to keep the children continually within their sight. This important point evokes certain Pano beliefs relating to the immaterial components of the deceased, in particular the so-called eye-spirit.

Rather than being whipped, the youngest children simply have their feet stroked with a small bundle of medicinal plants called *bwate*. This is meant to encourage them to learn to walk. The practice leads to insistent comments on the endurance of the *mariwin*, who come from very far away, either from the old swiddens of now abandoned villages or from cliffs located downstream on the banks of rivers. Elsewhere I have shown that downriver represents a direction systematically associated with death, alterity, and the past (Erikson 1989).

Women and especially children are supposedly unaware that the masked figures who visit the village are disguised humans rather than "true" *mariwin*. However, adult women—in particular those from the category of *macho* (postmenopausal women)—only pretend to be duped, since their involvement is in fact an essential part of the ritual. These women are the ones who make the ceramic bases on which men create facial features to transform the pottery into masks. Women also intervene during the masquerades by emitting ritually performative cries, analysis of which clearly indicates that the women are perfectly aware of what is going on (Erikson 2000a).

Today, with the large number of ad hoc performances held to indulge the curiosity of occasional visitors—filmmakers, tourists, agents from Funai or various NGOs—the *mariwin* appearances are evidently on the way to becoming a folkloric show with all the inevitable consequences. Children are no longer tricked, and the actors are ever younger, while various innovations have affected the form of the masks, the nature of the growling, and the actual organization of the show. The differences between what I observed in the mid-1980s and the displays recently staged for and shown by Discovery Channel, TV Globo, RAI Uno, Fuji Television, or Canal Plus confirm this.[2] The *mariwin* are no longer a secret except perhaps to ethnology. As far as the rest of the world is concerned, Matis children and Western television viewers alike know more than ever about them. Until the end of the 1980s, the Matis jealously hid their masks. Today they manufacture them in large quantities for sale, while some informants go so far as to deny the existence of "true" *mariwin* except as humans in disguise (although everyone staunchly believes in the existence of *maru* spirits, beings we shall discuss below). Yet while the ritual associated with them has been slightly degraded of late, the underlying cosmological beliefs regarding the *mariwin* remain vivid. Let us now focus on this conceptual dimension of the *mariwin* that appears to be resisting modernization far better than its ritual counterpart.

The *Mariwin*: Ontological Dimensions

The Matis distinguish three kinds of *mariwin*, each associated with a color, a bird, and a specific ecotype: the *mariwin kuru* (yellow-ochre), the *mariwin put* (red), and the *mariwin wisu* (black). The first are also called *shiashkegit*, while the latter two, especially the black variant, may also be called *winu winu tsusi*, an expression that can be translated as "spirits of the *Bactris* palm wood instruments." A woman known as Chiampi Teshkam once told me that the black and red *mariwin* are in fact *chuka*, namesakes: in other words, as the relation of homonymy has great significance among the Matis (see Erikson 1993), they belong to the same category. I was also told that the red *mariwin* are younger than the black ones, which is confirmed by the symbolism of the colors, since black connotes antiquity for the Matis, while red is associated with all that is new. Since I learned about the existence of the *mariwin kuru* (ochre) only in 1996, I failed to distinguish them from the *mariwin put* (red) in many of my earlier publications, in which I also claimed that the red ones live in the palm groves of abandoned villages, while the black ones live in steep riverbanks. Further investigation is needed to ascertain whether it is the ochre rather than red *mariwin* who live in the derelict swiddens. Whatever the case, the *mariwin* are each associated with a different type of macaw parrot of which they are said to be *kurasek*, a term that may generally be translated as "jealous," but that in this instance has the particular meaning "to maintain a privileged relationship"—a condition obviously not incompatible with jealousy. As would be expected, the ochre *mariwin* are *kurasek* of the yellow macaws, the red ones of the red macaws, and the black ones of the blue macaws.

Notwithstanding their differences, the three kinds of *mariwin* display a certain number of common characteristics, relating to their dietary preferences, their mode of perception, and their morphology. The *mariwin* in fact feed entirely on macaws—more to the point, on young macaws, I was told. They hunt with blowpipes, as they possess no bows, and savor their favorite fowl meat served with *mamõ*, a type of resin.[3] However, in one of those perceptual havocs that have amply interested Amazonian ethnology in recent years, the *mariwin* consider the resin, which is black, to be sweet manioc, which is white, and the macaws, whose flesh is dark and tough, to be *kwëbu* guans (*Penelope jacquacu*, the Spix's guan), a bird whose flesh is white and tender. This can be interpreted either as a perspectival effect or as the indigenous avatar of a structural opposition. Regardless, what is black and tough to humans seems white and tender in the eyes of spirits. This simply means that what connotes old age for mere mortals connotes by contrast youthfulness for these beings who, in terms of seniority, are obviously very much older—in fact, ancient enough to connote ancestrality (more on this later). What may appear very old to the young may appear very young to the old. It is therefore no surprise that this translates into the chromatic code used to speak about the hyper-old *mariwin*.

From a viewpoint that complements rather than competes with the first, it is equally possible to interpret these perceptual paradoxes as deriving from a principle of inversion. The *mariwin*—beings of the infraworld since they come from underground—see things in a way that is in fact readily presented as the opposite, if not the negative, of our own familiar view of the world.[4] Descriptions of their morphology confirm this, since one of the *mariwin*'s main characteristics is precisely that their bodies are both back-to-front and inside-out. Apart from frequently shuffling backward during rituals, the *mariwin* are also said to possess, unlike humans, their *winte* ("heart" or "pulse") at the rear of their skulls, meaning they can be killed if struck there. Their faces are, in contrast, extremely tough; indeed, the mask covers only the face, being simply tied with a string at the back of the head. Their numerous labrets allegedly pierce their bones directly, rather than their skin and flesh, as though their bone structure were external, like a shell. Here again, the *mariwin* are obviously in complete contrast to humans, whose ornaments are stuck through the soft parts of the body rather than through the actual skeleton.[5]

Finally, although the teeth of the *mariwin* appear on the mask—as their labrets, in fact—they are also thought to possess a true set of teeth deep inside their head (*ukëmuruk*), located on what could be called their underface. Though sometimes represented on certain atypical masks by peccary teeth, these "true teeth" are more usually compared with those of caimans and unanimously described as *isamarap*, hideous. In place of salient teeth projecting outward—the appropriate form for these tools of predation—the *mariwin* thus have "interiorized" teeth.[6]

Among the traits common to all *mariwin*, whatever their color, one of the most prominent is that they are all very closely associated with maize and the *Bactris* palms, the association being merely proximal in the first case and openly symbiotic in the second. Elsewhere I have shown the almost consubstantial nature of the relation that links *Bactris* palm trees—the very last plant a swidden yields—and the *mariwin* spirits (Erikson 2001). Their relationship with maize, a crop also harvested in the middle of the rainy season, is of a different nature: this plant in fact represents youthfulness, a role to which it is marvelously suited, since it is the very first to be produced by a new swidden and is cultivated only when rituals are planned. In addition, sowing takes place in a ritual atmosphere. The Matis sometimes say that the *mariwin* are *tsari kurasek*, "maize jealous/close." Tumi Preto explained to me one day that this frequently heard expression simply means that the *mariwin* would become vexed if the humans failed to finish all the maize they produce in their gardens, and would therefore strike even more strongly as a result. He went on to say that the *mariwin* live in their own swiddens on the banks of rivers, but regularly come to visit the gardens of humans, where they are found especially often at the foot of burnt trees (which happens to be precisely where saplings of the *Bactris* palms are planted). Their presence ensures that the maize flourishes: its growth is hindered if they do not come. Here we can clearly see yet another illustration of the omnipresent parallel in

Matis ritual symbolism between the biological destiny of the maize and that of the candidates for tattooing, whose growth is likewise an outcome of a ceremony, the success of which depends on the arrival of many *mariwin*. Tumi then told me that the mariwin come in large numbers provided that the women look at the tops rather than the roots when they harvest the maize. Sometimes, though, the women (or children) discover a mask in an abandoned or recently scorched garden. This is then said to be the remains of a *mariwin* who perished in a fire, since the *mariwin* are mortal in their own way, capable of reproducing just like people. A twelve-year-old girl once told me the *mariwin* do not come during the dry season because there is no maize and they are dead. Although the opinion was by no means that of an expert, it is nonetheless striking for its congruence with everything else known about these spirits.

Having gained a better idea of what the *mariwin* are, let us now see what they are not—in other words, how they seem to represent the perfect antithesis of spirits known as the *maru*.

The *Maru/Mariwin* Opposition

Matis typology of beings, which is thoroughly dualist, rests on a series of oppositions oscillating between two poles, *ayakobo* and *tsasibo*, the former connoting alterity and the latter interiority. Although its sociological yield is extremely slight today, this polarity is reminiscent of a moiety system, of which countless examples can be found throughout the Pano area, where an "inside" moiety is frequently opposed to an "outside" moiety (Townsley 1987). Numerous clues from various areas of representation point to the notion that a dualist system of this kind still operated among the Matis in the relatively recent past (Erikson 1996/1999). From this perspective, the *mariwin* category, which falls within the *tsasibo* (inside moiety), is opposed to that of the *maru*, which comes under *ayakobo* (outside moiety).

At first glance—though it will become clear this proposition needs to be qualified—the contrast between *mariwin* and *maru* is total, these two types of spirits opposing each other as the social and the asocial, the visible and the invisible, the hairy and the hairless, the beneficent and the maleficent, to select just some of the oppositions I have examined in more detail previously (Erikson 1996/1999). While the *mariwin* prototypically embody Matis values—endurance, generosity, lack of slothfulness, a strong amount of *sho*—and exhibit a body ornamentation that can be termed *hyperbolic*, the *maru* are by contrast typified by their malignity (they display a propensity for leading people astray in the forest) and a total absence of ornamentation and body hair, features that supposedly make them invisible. The former represent a kind of model that contemporary generations strive in vain to equal, while the latter—more often ridiculous than truly detestable, and readily compared with the *curupira* in conversations with neo-Brazilians—appear instead as a foil.[7]

At first, the *maru/mariwin* opposition indisputably evokes the contrast between *ayakobo* and *tsasibo*. However, as is almost invariably the case in indigenous America, one dualism conceals another; this is very much the case here, since the different categories of *mariwin* are themselves also divided into *ayakobo* and *tsasibo*. More precisely, the black and red *mariwin* are *tsasibo*, while the yellow *mariwin* (*mariwin kuru*) are *ayakobo*. We are obviously in the presence of one of those forms of reduplicative dualism, like a Russian doll, a phenomenon frequently described in the Andean area but with equivalents also in the lowlands (Molinié 1988). This slight touch of *ayakobo* found among the *mariwin* naturally evokes that other aberration comprised by the grotesque aspect of certain rare *mariwin* masks endowed with "ugly" teeth (atypical artifacts mentioned above; for illustrations see Erikson 1996:276; 1999:340). These facts suggest a paradoxical conjunction between the otherwise opposed categories of *mariwin* and *maru*—yet another example, were one needed, of the very un-Manichean character of Amerindian dualism. *Mariwin* and *maru* exclude, suppose, and define each other—one in relation to the other but not one without the other.

The *maru* undoubtedly have an asocial dimension, even an antisocial one, but—to follow a lead suggested by Bidou (1999:80) in a text dedicated to this category of spirits in northwestern Amazonia—it is equally possible to conceive them as essentially "presocial" beings, envious of humans since they are like infants who have yet to receive a body. In fact, among the Matis, newborns are often compared to these spirits: insofar as they too are hairless and still lacking in ornaments, they are spontaneously said to be *maru maru pa*, "similar to the *maru*." In addition to this fact, it is notable that many elements resembling the products of human activity but lacking any practical use are attributed to the *maru*, in particular a large number of wild plant species recalling human artifacts or cultivated plants. Patches of forest flattened by gales are called *marun maë* (*maru* swiddens), wild bananalike plants are called *marun tsinkwin* (*maru* bananas), the large white mushrooms that cover decomposing trees are called *marun paut* (*maru* ear pendants),[8] and so on. With the exception—predictably enough—of maize, practically all cultivated plants have a wild counterpart imputed to the *maru*. All these products are clearly characterized by being imperfect and/or unproductive, underlining the idea that the *maru* verge on humanity without ever fully attaining it.

The dance in which Matis men imitate the *maru* provides a variation on this theme. Armed with crude sticks supposed to represent giant knives, the dancers in fact take a wicked delight in destroying everything inside the communal house (pottery in particular) as they attempt to sharpen their entirely useless wooden "blades." As they do so, they sing in the esoteric mumbo jumbo imputed to the *maru*: "tambos menas, shëpi menas, kwen mas menas, awane menas," which, according to the glosses conveyed to me, means that their axes are blunt and they are therefore really bad at cutting trees. And in fact while the *mariwin* maintain a close relationship with human swiddens, the "*maru* swiddens" are no more than small clearings in which trees were knocked down by high winds (a reminder of the close relationship between the *maru* and the wind).

Although the *maru* are theoretically invisible, Iba Shono and his brother Kwini were nonetheless able to describe them to me one day in minute detail, after telling me that other Matis, in particular the late Dani-Macho, had actually encountered them. The *maru* have a human form; their bodies are black except for the stomach, which is white, and their skins are covered with stinging caterpillars. To crown it all, these figures lack an anus but are endowed with an immensely long penis—so long that they have to carry it tied up in a knot (a classic theme in Pano mythology). Their feet are so tough that thorns (*musha*) never get in, a fact that—to use a small dose of structuralist imagination—reinforces the idea that they embody the antithesis of the *mariwin*, since we know that the *mariwin*, far from being insensitive to them, are systematically associated with thorns, whether those of the *daratsintuk* palm (*Astrocaryum muru muru*), which they use as whips, or those of the *wani* palm (*Bactris gasipaes*) in their plantations, by means of which tattooing is carried out in their presence. Indeed, tattoos are also designated by the term *musha*.

In terms of originality, the *maru*'s technology surpasses even their morphology, since they use stingrays (*ihi*) as plates (*ancha*), caimans (*kapët*) as seats (*tsate*), and electric eels (*dendu*) as digging sticks (*mekte*). As well as these fairly unusual auxiliary animals, the *maru* menagerie also includes marmosets (*sipi*) and Spix's guans (*kwëbu*).[9] The *maru* also raise jaguars (*kamun*), which a perspectival illusion leads them to perceive as white-lipped peccaries (*chawa*).[10] These swine-felines prove to be so docile and tame that one can touch their teeth. However, the *maru*'s main domestic animal (*wiwa*) is the collared peccary (*unkin*), since they are said to see it as a dog (*wapa*). On the other hand, I was explicitly informed that these spirits do not raise "true" white-lipped peccaries (*chawa*), doubtless because their place is already held by jaguars (*kamun*). Indeed, if *kamun* are already their *chawa*, what place could they grant the true *chawa*?

The special bond between the *maru* and collared peccaries, combined with the explicit denial of any real relation between these beings and white-lipped peccaries, points to the notion that an equally close bond may very well unite the latter with the *mariwin*. This would be on one hand fully compliant with the principle of complementary distribution that orders the relations between the two spiritual entities, and on the other hand compatible with the image of white-lipped peccaries as an associated benefit (or a derivative) of human mortality. The idea that these animals are in one way or another a positive outcome of deaths arising in their own ethnic group—or sometimes among their neighbors—seems in fact to be very widespread in Amazonia (including among the Kulina, whom we shall discuss later; cf. Pollock 1993). From this viewpoint jaguars, who stand as white-lipped peccaries for the *maru*, should conversely evoke the themes of premature death and the negative aspects of reincarnation.[11] The Matis, for their part, associate their dead with white-lipped peccaries in claiming that those (supposedly the majority) who die during the rainy season (which is also the *mariwin* season) live in a subworld where such animals are abundant. Finally we may note that the image of the collared peccary as a faint double or weak avatar of the white-lipped peccary is very much a classic theme of Amazonian mythology (Calavia Sáez 2001), so the fact this pattern comes to overlap the *maru/mariwin* opposition is far from surprising.

A final characteristic of the *maru* deserves our attention. The powder obtained from their calcined bones is held to confer magical powers, allowing any object one might desire to disappear from its original owner's possession and reappear in one's own. A person who chances to kill a *maru*, or collect one of their bodies, can thus acquire these beings' ability to "make things disappear" by concocting a remedy from the ashes of their bones. I have elsewhere (Erikson 1996:231; 1999:295) cited other examples of readaptation for social purposes (albeit selfish) of the normally harmful properties of the *maru*, including their use within the repertoire of body decoration.[12] The only exceptional thing, therefore, about this powder is that it provides yet another cryptic bridge between the *maru* and the *mariwin*, whose masks (read: bones) are also occasionally found burnt (in swiddens). The proximity is all the more striking since the ashes deriving from the cremation of spiritual entities often appear in western Amazonia as the mythic origin of numerous medicinal plants. These spiritual beings—such as the Shipibo *yoshin shëtaya*, to pick out just one example—are very clearly akin to the *maru* and/or *mariwin*. This no doubt sheds further light on certain practices such as Shipibo phanerocannibalism (a custom that involves burning the deceased's hair and consuming the ashes), or the fact that the ferns that cover the bodies of the *mariwin* are called their *dawë*, their "plant remedy."

To summarize, the *mariwin* can be said to be opposed to the *maru* as fertile seniority to sterile immaturity, or the superhuman to the subhuman. Transposed onto an ontological plane, these features appear to embody two opposed poles as a "forelife" and an "afterlife," in effect symbolically framing the temporal development of human existence. The similarities between *mariwin* and *maru* can therefore be explained by the fact that both equally belong to the universe of the "nonliving," whether by excess or deficit. Leaving the *maru*, these incarnations of unfulfilled destinies, to their sad fate, I wish to consider now the extent to which the very opposite characteristics of the *mariwin* endow them with properties that amount to a poignant metaphor of a highly idealized past—in other words, an image of ancestrality.

Mariwin and Ancestrality

The clues supporting the notion that the *mariwin* represent an incarnation of ancestrality are many and congruent. First, that the *mariwin* are dead is quite clear. They emerge from under the earth covered in dirt, like freshly unearthed corpses, and they lack *piskare* collars, ornaments that, as I have shown elsewhere, are associated with sexual maturity and membership in the community of the living (Erikson 1996/1999). Ascertaining whether the *mariwin* more specifically represent deceased forebears is a trickier question, one to which we shall return. However, we can at once note that dead kin are placed in the same category as the *mariwin* and the *maru*. Indeed, all three types of beings are the main addressees of the highly stylized cries frequently emitted by postmenopausal women (see Erikson 2000a). Dead kin are therefore addressed in exactly the same way as the *mariwin* (and the *maru*). This practice clearly exposes a symmetry in which the pole opposite to the *maru* is no longer occupied by the *mariwin*, as is more usually the case, but instead by the deceased. The *maru* are summoned to repel thunderstorms, whereas the dead are called upon when rain is desired.[13] The dead and the *mariwin* thus seem to be interchangeable in acting as a structural counterpart to the *maru*.

From a comparative point of view, the "ancestral" character of the *mariwin* equally stems from their resemblance to categories of spirits found among their neighbors, which are explicitly presented by these peoples as emanations of their own ancestors. I am thinking in particular of the mythic founders of Marubo sections, whose resemblance to the *mariwin* has been closely analyzed by Melatti (1992), or to the *noshman* ghosts of the Matsés.[14] Another category of spirits widely found throughout the entire Pano area, the "eye spirits" (*bëro yushin* and other names), may no doubt be cited too. These beings—which can be found among the Shipibo as well as the Cashinahua, the Yaminahua, the Marubo, and the Katukina, to mention just a few examples—make up one eternal component of the person who continues to watch over their descendants from the world beyond. Although they have no true equivalent among the Matis, it is worth noting how insistently they emphasize the remarkable brightness of the eyes behind the *mariwin* masks, as well as the fact that these spirits are said to fix their gaze constantly on the young during their visits. Finally, the *mariwin* in many ways resemble a "walking exoskeleton," a motif that, even in Amazonia, is not without echoes of intergenerational continuity, in particular when we encounter this figure in a context of patrifiliation (Chaumeil 1997). And indeed, the northern Pano social systems present a fairly pronounced patrilineal inflection (Erikson 1996/1999 chap. 6).[15]

The *mariwin* maintain an almost consubstantial link with the elder people of the group, further underlining the idea that they represent the conclusion of the aging process. Matis discourses insist on the fact that they are elders (*darasibo*), even superlative elders (*darasibo kimo*, "paradigmatic elders"). The *mariwin* are also qualified as *tsusi*, a term that may be translated as "spirit" but also serves to designate shadows and in particular elderly people. This elderly quality is an essential aspect inasmuch as the transmission of energy via injection is always carried out from elder to younger. For example, when men whip each other in order to improve their hunting prowess, it is always the two oldest men who wield the whips, transferring energy (*sho*) to their younger companions before whipping each other in turn. To do this they use the same canes (*kweste*) from the *daratsintuk* palm used by the *mariwin*, behaving in a way akin to the spirits.

Another clue to the convergence between old people and the *mariwin* can be seen in the belief that only the absolute elder of a village (the oldest man, *darasibo kimo*) can safely invite the *mariwin* to visit the humans by intoning the chant *kanchi buntak*, "young pineapple shoot."[16] Any man can invite the *mariwin* with a *masën* flute, but should a younger man decide to do so by singing, he risks being bitten by a snake in the forest—a risk further increased, I was told, by the fact the young hunt much more often than the old. This slightly utilitarian interpretation of the belief need not prevent us from surmising that the oldest man naturally finds himself "closer" to the *mariwin* than his companions with fewer years, from the simple fact of the proximity of death increasing as one becomes older. Elders are, so to speak, the "already-dead living"—also called *tsusi*, as mentioned, as if they were already ghosts—while *mariwin* are kinds of "still-living dead." Their trajectories merge.

The resemblance between old people and spirits also stands out as we observe food prohibitions. Once the young have been tattooed, they must gradually reintroduce the different meats into their diet in a fixed and immutable order. While most game fairly rapidly becomes permissible once again, macaw meat—the *mar-*

iwin's favorite dish—becomes accessible only when the person reaches seniority, since it may be eaten only by those whose tattoos are so old that they seem to have disappeared.[17]

The link between the *mariwin* and macaws may be explained in part by the latter's longevity, and by the fact that they hang around the same places as the spirits, namely old swiddens and river bluffs. The link is also borne out by the fact Matis tattoos bear a strong resemblance to the facial marking of these birds, a similarity that at least one of my consultants made explicit (Erikson 2002). If the *mariwin* never come in such large numbers as during the tattoo ceremonies, doubtless this is because they are, as we have noted, *kwenat kurasek*, "macaw-jealous."

The Matis ceaselessly repeat that their impressive facial ornamentation has the main function of increasing their likeness to the *mariwin*, proclaiming that their ornaments allow them to resemble both these spirits and their ancestors (*darasibo*) who themselves resembled the *mariwin* even more than the contemporary Matis. Moreover, during the tattoo ceremonies, emphasis is laid on imitating the ancestors and on the succession of generations. Before being tattooed, the youths must ask the performer under the watchful gaze of the *mariwin*: "Tattoo me now, just as you were tattooed in the past" (*mibi paren enden shebondash, eobi akta, nebi*) (Erikson 2003). It seems possible to conclude, therefore, that the Matis have their faces tattooed in order to resemble their ancestors and that this resemblance is mediated by the spirits. However, as I have mentioned, the paradoxical fact remains that the tattoos are by no means the main ornament of the *mariwin*, since their mask actually emphasizes the innumerable labrets that surround the circumference of the mouth and the long macaw rectrices that emerge from the upper lip. This is particularly puzzling since, as I have shown elsewhere (Erikson 1996/1999), whereas tattooing clearly connotes alliance, the labrets, in particular those on the top part of the face, refer to issues of consanguinity; they stand in opposition in the same way that what originates from the maternal uncle stands in opposition to what originates from the father. It is notable that while the *mariwin* are mobilized for a celebration of alliance—the tattoo ceremony in new swiddens—the decorative features they display primarily connote consanguinity. Thus, although the pretext for the *mariwin*'s visit is a ritual centered on bonds of affinity, it is nonetheless strongly inflected by a logic resting primarily on the principles of patrilineal continuity.

Belonging to the category of *tsusi*—which, depending on the context, means "shadow" or "spirit" or "elder"—the *mariwin* are intimately associated with themes of death, ancient times, and the perpetuation of collective identities by way of imitating a highly respected primogenitors. It is said these beings haunt abandoned swiddens—in other words, the sites occupied by past generations—and they play a prominent role during the rites of passage. The notion of resurrection, linked in particular to the agricultural cycle, predominates in the discourse relating to them, in which imitating the ancestors and the succession of generations are emphasized. Thus it seems that all the requirements are met for the *mariwin* to qualify as ancestors. Yet this interpretation faces a major obstacle. Indeed, the Matis explicitly deny that the *mariwin* are their kin, presenting them instead as what they call their *tawari*. Let us now see what this term delineates.

Our Friends the *Tawari*

Tawari is the term systematically used by the spirits, in the reported speech attributed to them, to refer to the Matis. When the *mariwin* visit the humans, the growls they emit on their arrival are said to mean *nukun tawari eombi isek*, "I've come to see my *tawari*," and when they ceased to come after the postcontact epidemics, this was because, so people say, they were grieved for their *tawari* and their *tawarin baku*, the children of their *tawari*. Tumi Preto told me one day that it would be more appropriate for the *mariwin* to call the Matis *nukun igbo*, "my masters," rather than *nukun tawari*, "my *tawari*." But *tawari* nonetheless remains the word they are said to use.

Explaining the meaning of this term to me, Matis friends suggested a close relationship between people who resemble and respect each other, but without being related as kin. The links that brought me together with an English film-maker during the shooting of a documentary—ironically entitled *Return of the Ancestors*—was cited as an example. The Matis knew that our homes and mother tongues were different, but they also saw that we spent most of the daylight hours working together. We were therefore *tawari* to each other.

At first sight, then, *tawari* can be translated as "friend," with the proviso that it refers exclusively to a relation between people who are not previously related and who belong to different groups. Those among the Matis who get along particularly well are not described as *tawari*. On the other hand, during the first peaceful contacts with Funai in the mid-1970s, the very first phrase addressed to a functionary after he arrived back from the river was *autsi korokanon mimbi wakarapa wek, tawari*? (What are you going to cook with that water you just fetched, *tawari*?).

The *mariwin* are therefore certainly friends, but also strangers rather than kindred. Moreover, this is perfectly coherent with the fact that the whip blows dispensed to increase fertility are, as a general rule, administered by affines, in particular the maternal uncle (who whips women at the time of their menopause, for example). We may further note that certain men when they embody the *mariwin* refuse to whip children to whom they are very close, concentrating instead on their cross-kin. The Matis *mariwin* are perhaps best characterized by oxymorons such as "ancestors-in-law" or "ancestors by adoption" or—in a nod to the "foreign" nature of these spirits—the no less paradoxical "naturalized ancestors."

To date, I have found only one occurrence of the word *tawari* in other Pano languages. In a text called "Uma guerra" [A war], Brazilian historian João Capistrano de Abreu (1914:64, sent. 491) depicts a Cashinahua warrior calling his Cutanauá opponent "tawarî." Abreu's informant translated this as *inimigo*, enemy, but the term also very probably had appeasing connotations, since it was used in an attempt to pacify (and/or deceive) the opponent: "inimigo, eu te atirei não, me atira não!" (enemy, I didn't shoot you, don't shoot me!). *Tawari* here appears as a mitigating alternative to more hostile-sounding Cashinahua terms such as *txai* (brother-in-law) or *nawa* (stranger). In other words, it might have been better translated by "friend" than by "enemy."

If rare in Pano languages, *tawari* is nonetheless frequent in languages of the neighboring Katukina family, where it means the exact opposite of "enemy." In Kanamari, for instance, *tawari* means "friend" and can also be used in certain contexts to refer to local groups (*djapa*) considered close (Reesink 1993:26). This homology may be the result of mere chance, given the aleatory nature of phonological combinations. Nonetheless, the hypothesis that the term was borrowed from the Kanamari-Katukina calls for careful thought, since it allows us to explain the following enigma: Of all the western Amazonian masks, the only ones that look like those of the Matis are the Katukina's (see Harcourt 1948; Labiak 1997) (see figures 7.3 and 7.4). Indeed, these masks' traits suggest harmony, being endowed with beautiful teeth and ornaments, in contrast to those of the Pano (the Matis excepted), which represent grotesque hairy beings with terrifying dentition. Thus while the Matis masks seem to work systematically as an exact opposite to those of other Pano (Erikson 2002), on the other hand they present striking resemblance to those of the Katukina.

The little ethnohistorical material available to us is perfectly compatible with the facts cited above. Marcoy (1867:116) tells us that the Mayoruna of the Javari—probable ancestors, among others, of the contemporary Matis—had "friendly relations" with various (non-Pano) ethnic groups who occupied the region situated between the Jandiatuba and the Jutahy, which allowed them to move about freely. The iconography also indicates that these populations had very elaborate mouth ornaments. Marcoy mentions only the Culinos, the Marahuas, and the Huaraycus, but the Catukina (Katukina) must have inhabited the region as well. Furthermore, among the Katukina-speaking groups, Métraux (1948:663) men-

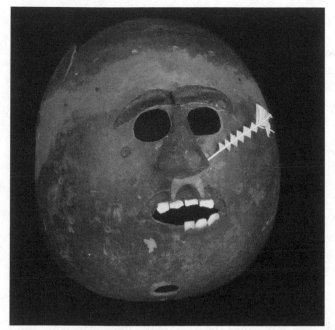

Fig. 7.3. Katukina mask of calabash, resin, feather, mother-of-pearl, and brass, collected by Constant Tastevin, early twentieth century.

Fig. 7.4. Matis mask of clay, macaw feathers, kapok, and ferns.

tions the Tawari, who were located "between the headwaters of the Jutaí River and San Felipe on the Juruá River (lat. 6°30'S, long. 70°W)"—in other words, immediately to the east of the territory traditionally occupied by the Matis. Anthropologist Jeremy Deturche has told me that Kanamari "workers" were forcibly sent to the Javari during the rubber boom, and Constant Tastevin (1924:423) mentions the existence of several Katukina (probably Kanamari) clans, one called Tawari (which he translates as "comrades"), another being the Ben-dyapa, "who used to live on the right bank or the affluents of the Itecoahy, itself a tributary of the Javary." The odds that they met ancestors of the Matis or the Korubo in such a place are obviously quite high. Let us also note that no fewer than three of the four words of "Canawary" registered by Chandless (1866:118) are obviously Panoan: *warí* for sun, *chi-i* for fire, and *wáka* for water. The Panoan and Kanamari-Katukina languages being otherwise totally distinct, this strongly suggests close contact. All this encourages us to think that the ancestors of the Matis could very well have known a time when visits of their "*tawari* friends" were not necessarily masquerades.

It is of course impossible, in retrospect, to precisely define the nature of the relationship suggested above. The design of the Matis masks might have come from the Katukina, who in former times might even have physically attended Matis initiations. But one could just as reasonably suppose that, in the past, "other" ethnic groups were present only in image form, as masks. All we can do is point out the striking similarities between Matis and Katukina ritual terminology and paraphernalia.

Conclusion

The Matis would be surprised, and probably indignant, to hear me suggest that their masks may reflect a period when the initiation of youngsters called upon relations of interethnic alliance rather than the endotic logic that seems to prevail today. (Their bewilderment would no doubt be shared by the Kulina, who whip their consanguines in order to transform them into affines; see Pollock 1985). Nevertheless, if we take this hypothesis seriously, it becomes apparent that from the Matis point of view the *mariwin* would amount to "descendants of the formal friends of our ancestors," rather than directly "our ancestors." Perhaps this is why contemporary humans are not expected to become *mariwin* after their death, whereas I was told the humans of the past did undergo this transformation.[18] Be that as it may, the *mariwin* finally stand out as a focal point for a discourse on consanguinity pieced together on the basis of relations of affinity, further illustrating the primacy of the latter category in Amazonian social logics, in which affinity seems indeed to constitute the nonmarked pole against which consanguinity is continually forced to reconstruct itself (Castro 2000). Let us note that the Matis are far from being the only native Amazonians to use the idiom of contemporary affinity to make statements about their past. The same play between spatial and temporal gaps has been finely analyzed by Howard (1993) among the Waiwai, for instance.

Attachment to the past, continued relationship with the dead, longing to look like the ascendants, insistence on the continuity between generations. Admittedly, all the requirements appear to be met to ensure the emergence among the Matis of "ancestors" in the full anthropological sense of the term. The notions of constitutive alterity and ontological rupture between the living and the dead—notions whose importance is well known in an Amazonian context—have nonetheless tinged their conceptualization of the past sufficiently to carry it in a very different direction, in which ancestrality to some extent finds itself subsumed by the remains of alliances. Thus the *mariwin* are less like ancestors in the strict sense of the term than a kind of residual emanation of the social life of previous generations. While their link with the ascendants of the contemporary Matis is not in doubt—explaining the paradoxical emphasis on their labrets rather than their tattoos—they are nonetheless formally excluded from the sphere of consanguinity. In other words, the *mariwin* seem to personify a form of mediated ancestrality that, in a typically Amazonian fashion, is defined less in terms of descent than of ceremonial friendship and alliance. If this were to be done all over again, I would no doubt look for a more Amazonian title than *La Griffe des aïeux* [The mark of the ancestors] for the monograph I devoted to my Matis *tawari*.

Acknowledgments

The main part of my ethnographic material was gathered in 1985–86 in the course of a twelve-month field trip funded by a research award from the Ministère de la Recherche, a grant from the Fondation Fyssen, and funds from the Centre National pour la Recherche Scientifique. Three shorter trips, just over four months in total, were made in 1996, 1998, and 2000 as part of the crew for film documentaries. These stays afforded the information presented here, which supplements the previous publications dedicated to the *mariwin* (Erikson 1990a, 1990b, 1992, 1996/1999, 2000a, 2001). A French version of this article was published in the *Journal de la Société des Américanistes* 90–91 (2004). The present version was translated by David Rodgers.

Notes

1. According to Romanoff (1984:237), "sweat" and "heat" are, among the Matsés, synonyms for this form of "energy," which humans can transmit by means of substances such as frog skin emetics or tobacco powder.

2. A relatively exhaustive filmography can be found in Erikson 2000b:285–287. As in a smorgasbord, the representations made for camera generally involve several types of *mariwin* at the same time—one ochre plus two black, for instance—thereby providing a more representative sample instead of complying with traditional practices. Much time has passed since the Matis could say that the *mariwin* wore no shorts as they were unaware of whites!

3. Contrary to what I published erroneously in the past (Erikson 1996:224; 1999:286), the resin in question is that burnt in torches and not that used to coat blowpipes, the confusion deriving from the fact both are called by the generic term *mamõ*.

4. According to Needham (1967:230–231), the conception of death as a state of reversal (up becomes down, front becomes back, etc.) is widespread: "there are many reports [from Indonesia and Africa] of the belief that the state of death is in various particulars a continuation of life under an opposite sign."

5. Tumi Preto, who told me this, also remarked that the skulls of white-lipped peccaries—who, he had said, were formerly human—are naturally provided with two small holes on either side of the top of the skull, which may be readily compared to the orifices of the *mariwin* masks as well as, of course, to the foramina of the maxillary bones of humans, which happen to be located just beneath the labrets of the upper lip of humans.

6. We may note in passing that this undeniably helps reinsert the *mariwin* in the wider complex of West Amazonian masquerades, since the presence of impressive teeth seems to be one of the main characteristics of the masks of other Arawak and Pano groups from the region, to the extent of appearing in the actual name for the *munti xëtaya* (toothed gourd) mask of the Cashinahua (Kensinger 1975) or the *yoshin shëtaya* (toothed spirit) mask of the Shipibo, the latter also having the particularity of being hairless, like the *maru* discussed below (Loriot et al. 1993; Baer 1993).

7. *Curupira* is "a fantastic being that, according to popular belief, inhabits the forests and appears as an Indian whose feet display the ankle facing forwards and the toes facing backwards" (*Dicionário Aurélio da Língua Portuguesa*). It passed into Brazilian popular culture from a similar belief held by the Tupi-Guarani peoples that inhabited the Atlantic coast at the beginning of colonization.

8. The Matis ear pendants are white and round in shape, which effectively makes them look like certain kinds of mushrooms. On the tendency to associate wild fungi and asocial spirits, consult Blust 2000.

9. The description given to me of the *maru* as possessors of a black body but a white stomach recalls a number of *sipi* tamarins. David Fleck informs me that the Matsés distinguish four species of *sipi*, one of which just happens to be called the "maru" monkey

(*madun sipi,* "demon's tamarin," *Cebuella pygmaea*: pygmy marmoset, *tití, leoncito, sói*). The Matis also mention an animal they call *marun sipi*, rarely seen and characterized by its great "tameness" rather by its morphology. Furthermore, the emphasis on the taming of true *kwëbu* by the *maru* becomes doubly interesting when we recall that it is this very bird that the *mariwin* see in their avian doubles, the macaws. Had we not already known, we could have guessed that the *kwëbu* is the first bird introduced into the diet, while the macaw is the last.

10. Some of the optical illusions to which the *maru* succumb clearly relate to what has recently become known as perspectivism (Castro 1996). It may be noted, though, that some of the practices imputed to the *maru* defy not only ordinary human understanding but also the laws of physics. Since it is not just the gaze but also the bottom of the *maru* that is thought to rest on the caiman seat, it is not just the way of perceiving but also the actual functioning of the world that is called into question here—a multinaturalist hypothesis pushed to an extreme. To be sure, it may simply be a way of emphasizing, with a fair dose of humor, the basic impotence characterizing the *maru* (see below) through the easily imagined paltry results obtained with their completely soft "digging stick."

11. Among the Capanahua, according to Loos (1960), it is the souls of evil shamans that transform into jaguars. Although the Matis, who no longer have any recognized shamans, do not share this belief, we might nonetheless note that in the weeks that followed the accidental death (by snakebite) of one of their most influential leaders, numerous jaguar traces began to be discovered on the periphery of the village.

12. Men disguise themselves as *maru* by taking off all their body ornaments and painting themselves black, in particular before war expeditions. This is reminiscent of the Desana warriors' former practice of preventing enemy reaction by painting crosses on their faces with "violence powder"—ashes collected where the culture hero Yurupari is said to have been cremated (Dominique Buchillet, personal communication).

13. The Matis say that the rain is sent to them by the dead so they can drink and bathe. This runs in parallel with the idea that the rain is beneficial, providing endurance. The *maru* for their part are summoned by older women when thunderstorms approach. They are asked to dispel the rain—to make it lose its way—just as they lead people astray in forest. The dead are therefore believed to bring what the *maru* take away: rain.

14. The *noshman*, which Fields (1973) defines as ghosts reincarnating the group's dead and who arrive to initiate the young, present stunning resemblance to the Matis *mariwin*, but it would be risky to associate them completely, since the Matis also recognize another category of spirits, distinct from the *mariwin*, who they say call themselves by the term *noshoman*, though humans call them *kushana*.

15. In relation to this question, we should note that the most likely etymology for the term *darasibo*, which designates the elderly, could in fact be summarized as "purely masculine." For its part, the name of the palm tree from which the whips and *piskaré* collars are taken and in which one deposits the umbilical cords of newborns is called *daratsintuk*, a term that can be interpreted as "naked man."

16. Concerning this song, see Erikson 1996:264; 1999:332.

17. This undoubtedly is one clue to explaining why tattoos so rarely feature on the *mariwin* masks: among the several dozen masks I have seen, there was only one such occurrence. This might also be linked with the acknowledged fact that tattoos tend to become ever fainter with age.

18. As previously noted, the same expression, *tsusin impak-*, "become/embody a spirit," is used to refer both to wearing a mask and to being deceased.

References

Abreu, João Capistrano de. 1914. *Rã-txa hu-ní ku-{i}, a língua dos Caxinauás do rio Ibuaçu, afluente do Muru (prefeitura de Tarauacá)*. Rio de Janeiro: Typographia Leuzinger.

Baer, Gerhard. 1993. "Para o melhor entendimento das máscaras sul-américanas." In *Karl von den Steinen: Um século de antropologia no Xingu*, edited by Vera Penteado Coelho, 289–309. São Paulo: EdUSP.

Bidou, Patrice. 1999. "Des fantômes et des hommes: Une topologie amazonienne de l'inconscient." *L'Homme* 149:73–82.

Blust, Robert. 2000. "Rat Ears, Tree Ears, Ghost Ears and Thunder Ears." *Bijdragen tot de Taal-, Land- en Volkenkunde* 1156(4):687–706.

Calavia Sáez, Oscar. 2001. "El rastro de los pecaríes: Variaciones míticas, variaciones cosmológicas e identidades étnicas en la etnologia pano." *Journal de la Société des Américanistes* 87:161–176.

Castro, Eduardo Viveiros de. 1996. "Os pronomes cosmológicos e o perspectivismo ameríndio." *Mana: Estudos de Antropologia Social* 2(2):115–144. In English as "Cosmological Deixis and Amerindian Perspectivism," *Journal of the Royal Anthropological Institute* 4(1998):469–488.

———. 2000. "Atualização e contra-efetuação do virtual na socialidade amazônica: o processo de parentesco." *Ilha* 2(1):5–46.

Castro, Eduardo Viveiros de, and Manuela Carneiro da Cunha, eds. 1993. *Amazônia: Etnologia e história indígena*. São Paulo: NHII-USP/FAPESP.

Chandless, William. 1866. "Ascent of the River Purus." *Journal of the Royal Geographical Society* 35:86–118.

Chaumeil, Jean-Pierre. 1997. "Les Os, les flûtes, les morts: Mémoire et traitement funéraire en Amazonie." *Journal de la Société des Américanistes* 83:83–110.

Erikson, Philippe. 1989. "Les Matis de la tête aux pieds et du nez aux fesses." In *Les Figures du corps*, edited by Marie-Lise Beffa and Roberte Hamayon, 287–295. Nanterre, France: Société d'Ethnologie.

———. 1990a. "How Crude Is Mayoruna Pottery?." *Journal of Latin American Lore* 16(1):47–68.

———. 1990b. "Near Beer of the Amazon." *Natural History* 8(90):52–61.

———. 1992. "Poils et barbes en Amazonie indigène: Légendes et réalités." *Annales de la Fondation Fyssen* 7:83–91.

———. 1993. "A onomástica matis é amazônica?" In Castro and Cunha, *Amazônia*, 323–338.

———. 1996. *La Griffe des aïeux: Marquage du corps et démarquages ethniques chez les Matis d'Amazonie.* Paris: Peeters.

———. 1999. *El sello de los antepasados: Marcado del cuerpo y demarcación étnica entre los Matis de la Amazonía.* Quito: Abya-Yala; Lima: Institut Français d'Études Andines.

———. 2000a. "'I,' 'Uuu,' 'Shhh': Gritos, sexos e metamorfoses entre os Matis (Amazônia brasileira)." *Mana: Estudos de Antropologia Social* 6(2):37–64. In French in *Insularités: Hommage à Henri Lavondès*, edited by Alain Babadzan, 197–228. Nanterre, France: Société d'Ethnologie, 2003.

———. 2000b. "Bibliografía anotada de fuentes con interés para la etnología y ethnohistoria de los Pano septentrionales (Matses, Matis, Korubo . . .)." *Amazonía Peruana* 27:231–287.

———. 2001. "Myth and Material Culture: Matis Blowguns, Palm Trees, and Ancestor Spirits." In *Beyond the Visible and the Material: The Amerindianization of Society in the Work of Peter Rivière*, edited by Laura Rival and Neil Whitehead, 101–121. Oxford: Oxford University Press.

———. 2002. "Le Masque matis: Matière à réflexion, réflexion sur la matière." *L'Homme* 161:149–164.

———. 2003. "'Comme à toi jadis on l'a fait, fais-le moi à présent . . .': Cycle de vie et ornementation corporelle chez les Matis (Amazonas, Brésil)." *L'Homme* 167–168:129–152.

Fields, Harriet. 1973. "Notes on the 'Singing People' Ceremony." *Información de Campo*, no. 131, pt. d.

Harcourt, Raoul d'. 1948. *Arts de l'Amérique.* Paris: Chêne.

Howard, Catherine. 1993. "Pawana: A farsa dos visitantes." In Castro and Cunha, *Amazônia*, 229–264.

Kensinger, Kenneth M. 1975. "Studying the Cashinahua." In *The Cashinahua of Eastern Peru*, edited by Jane Powell Dwyer, 9–85. Providence, Rhode Island: Haffenreffer Museum of Anthropology, Brown University.

Labiak, Araci Maria. 1997. "'Frutos do céu' e 'frutos da terra': Aspectos da cosmologia kanamari no WARAPEKOM." Master's thesis, Universidade Federal de Santa Catarina.

Loos, Eugene. 1960. "Capanahua Patrilineality and Matrilocality." *Información de Campo*, no. 67.

Loriot, James, Erwin Lauriault, and Dwight Day. 1993. *Diccionario shipibo-castellano.* Pucallpa, Peru: Instituto Lingüístico de Verano.

Marcoy, Paul. 1867. "Voyage de l'Océan Pacifique à l'Océan Atlantique à travers l'Amérique du Sud: Douzième étape, de Tabatinga à Santa Maria de Belen do Para." In *Le Tour du Monde, Nouveau Journal des Voyages*, edited by Edouard Charton, 15:97–160. Paris: Hachette.

Melatti, Julio Cezar. 1992. "Enigmas do corpo e soluções dos Panos." In *Roberto Cardoso de Oliveira, Homenagem*, edited by Mariza Corrêa and Roque Laraia, 143–166. Campinas, Brazil: UNICAMP.

Métraux, Alfred. 1948. "Tribes of the Juruá-Purus Basins." In *Handbook of South American Indians*, edited by Julian H. Steward, 3:657–686. Washington, D.C.: Smithsonian Institute.

Molinié, Antoinette. 1988. "Sanglantes et fertiles frontières: À propos des batailles rituelles andines." *Journal de la Société des Américanistes* 74:49–70.

Needham, Rodney. 1967. "Right and Left in Nyoro Symbolic Classification." *Africa* 37:425–451.

Pollock, Donald K. 1985. "Looking for a Sister: Culina Siblingship and Affinity." In *The Sibling Relationship in Lowland South America*, edited by Kenneth M. Kensinger, 8–15. Working Papers on South American Indians, 7. Bennington, Vermont: Bennington College.

———. 1993. "Death and the Afterdeath among the Kulina." *Latin American Anthropology Review* 5(2):61–64.

Reesink, Edwin Boudewijn. 1993. "Imago Mundi Kanamari." Ph.D. diss., UFRJ/MN/PPGAS.

Romanoff, Steven. 1984. *Matses Adaptations in the Peruvian Amazon*. Ann Arbor, Michigan: University Microfilms.

Tastevin, Constant. 1924. "Les Études ethnographiques et linguistiques du P. Tastevin en Amazonie." *Journal de la Société des Américanistes* 16:421–425.

Townsley, Graham. 1987. "The Outside Overwhelms: Yaminahua Dual Organization and Its Decline." In *Natives and Neighbors in South America*, edited by Harald O. Skar and Frank Salomon, 355–376. Göteborg, Sweden: Göteborgs Etnografiska Museum.

8

Bones, Flutes, and the Dead

Memory and Funerary Treatments in Amazonia

Jean-Pierre Chaumeil

Amazonian ethnology has displayed considerable interest in recent years in forms of mourning among lowland South American societies. The region in fact presents us with a puzzling contrast when we turn to this topic: the extreme complexity of representations and discourses relating to death appears to be balanced by a relative simplicity—not to say a real scarcity—in mortuary practices. Commentators have frequently evoked the absence of cults, cemeteries, or even visible places associated with the dead, as well as the shallow depth of genealogical memory among these populations, the widespread forgetting of the dead, or the taboos placed on their names, in order to refute the idea of any predisposition toward the dead in the Amazonian region. This apparent disinterest in the deceased and the lack of visibility at the level of practice is thus seen to be compensated by a rare complexity in the metaphysical constructions concerning death.

Without contesting this very real wealth of symbolism, a close examination of the empirical data nonetheless raises a number of questions concerning the supposed paucity of Amazonian mortuary practices. The works available to us on this theme actually reveal a more nuanced and varied panorama, a fact I intend to highlight by focusing on the material aspects of the funerary rituals and the mechanisms for remember the dead. I shall therefore leave aside for now indigenous discourses on death—the topic of another study—as well as practices reserved specifically for the remains of enemies or strangers, especially in the form of trophies, despite the evident difficulty in disassociating the two phenomena in any categorical fashion. Certain societies indeed tend to treat their dead relatives (or some of them) as strangers, and perform apparently similar funerary rites for them both. While in a general fashion relics are thought to perpetuate the continuity of the group, trophies extracted from enemies were often invested with analogous properties, to the point of appearing equally essential to social repro-duction (see the discussion below on "constitutive alterity" as an indispensable element in the definition of self in numerous lowland cultures). However, a dis-tinction observable throughout Amazonia seems to separate relics from trophies properly speaking. The latter, which are often abandoned or even sold after use, are rarely made the object of "double funerals," whereas relics are generally stored at home or reburied. This may help to explain the relative ease with which cer-tain nineteenth-century travelers were able to acquire enemies' remains through simple trading, while those of dead relatives were much more difficult to obtain.

This said, it makes sense to adopt some basic precautions when talking about funerary practices. It is in fact rare to encounter a uniform treatment of everyone within a given culture. The dead are not all in the same boat: their destiny var-ies greatly according to their age, sex, social status, place of death, and manner of dying (at home/elsewhere, slow/violent, and so on). As we know, disposing of an entire body or one of its parts modifies the performance of the funerary ritual itself and the type of relationship that will be established with the deceased. Certain kinds of violent death accentuate the rupture of this relationship, while others tend to minimize it. When the whole corpse cannot be recovered, an en-deavor will be made to take home a part of it or—should this too prove impos-sible—some kind of substitute in order to carry out the "funeral." It can thus be seen how difficult it is in some cases for one form to prevail over another.

Relations between the Living and the Dead: The Question of Alterity

What do comparative studies tell us in this respect? It makes methodological sense to distinguish from the outset two phases in the approach to funeral modes in Amazonia. The first phase, from the 1920s to the 1960s, primarily strove to compile an inventory of funerary processes, placing an emphasis on the diversity of the practices and the possible links of continuity with the dead resulting from certain sociocultural features of the groups concerned. The second, from the 1970s onward, involved a switch in perspective by posing an ontological discontinuity or rupture between the living and the dead as the predominant mortuary form in the South American lowlands. Let us examine these two sequences more closely.

The first study available to us, by Walter Roth (1924), was dedicated to the Guianas and provided a survey of the wide range of funeral modes in this re-gion: endocannibalism, direct burial or burial in urns (primary or secondary), cremation, certain forms of mummification, and preservation of bones—whether stored inside funerary baskets, deposited in rock shelters, or distributed among the kin of the deceased in a mode recalling the practices of dividing up the flesh or ashes in exocannibalism and endocannibalism. (Roth's work can be compared with the more recent study by Rostain in 1994 on the same region.) A few years later, Sigvald Linné (1929) focused more specifically on endocannibalistic practices in South America, a subject he maps out in detail. These pioneering works were later completed by Alfred Métraux (1947) in a now classic essay where he underscores the widespread diffusion of secondary burial in urns in South America. Guided by his research on the Guarani, Métraux pays special attention to the treatment of human bones. Adopting a more sociological approach, the later studies by Luis Boglar (1958a, 1958b, 1959) and Otto Zerries (1960) examine in particular the relations between funerary rituals and other sociocultural practices. Thus Boglar associates endocannibalism with the practice of burning clearings for swiddens—an "agricultural" treatment of the body. However, many present-day swidden cultivators in the lowlands do not explicitly practice this type of funeral. Zerries pushes the analogy even further by linking endocannibalism with the Yurupari ritual familiar to Amazonianists. According to a version widespread in the mythologies of northwestern Amazonia, Yurupari is the name of a culture hero sacrificed by fire, then resuscitated from his ashes (calcined bones) in the form of "sacred" flutes. These in turn are likened to Yurupari's "bones." Subject to a variety of interdictions, these flutes are utilized during initiation rituals, food exchanges, or funeral ceremonies in many societies of northwestern Amazonia (Århem 1980). Zerries's hypothesis thus suggests a link between an object (the "bone-flute") incarnating a dead ancestor and the funerary practice of recovering the bones, whether through double funerals (whole bones) or through endocannibalism (pulverized and ingested bones). Indeed, some ethnologists including Louis-Vincent Thomas (1980) have shown the close proximity between these funeral forms at the conceptual level. This is a topic to which we shall return later.

Although stimulating, these contributions did not really provided an adequate response to the question of mourning in the lowlands at a moment when ethnological discourse as a whole was still dominated by a model—developed in particular by Africanists—of society closed in on itself, possessing an intrinsic identity, and turned to its ancestors. Ethnology had to await the works of Hélène Clastres and above all those of Manuela Carneiro da Cunha on the Jê in order to break with this model, one of little applicability in Amazonia, and pose the relationship to the dead in other terms. Amazonian studies have in fact revealed the determining weight of affinity—in detriment to genealogical ties—and the structuring function of alterity in the construction of Amerindian identities and social systems, a mechanism denominated by some as "constitutive alterity" (Erikson 1996) or "familiarizing predation" (Fausto 2001). These expressions designate the process, typically Amazonian, of incorporation of the other—the affine, enemy, or stranger—as a necessary condition for the construction of the self. This has given rise to a problematic of funerals in the lowlands that associates the dead with this figure of the stranger, a kind of "anti-ancestor" excluded from the sphere of the living, as Hélène Clastres (1968) showed in her study of Guayaki funeral rituals. Whether they eat the flesh (rather than the bones) of dead relatives or bury them, the Guayaki adopt a common attitude vis-à-vis the dead: they treat them as enemies. Based on her analysis of the Krahó materials, Cunha (1977, 1978) confirms this separation between the living and the dead, and proposes its overall dominance in the Amazonian world. In this conception, she writes (1977:292), "there exists no place for the ancestors in the society of the living." The widely revealed absence, at least in canonical form, of ancestor cults in Amazonia would thus find verification in the character of alterity acquired by the deceased. For his part, Pierre Clastres (1980) returns to the notion of ancestrality in order to explore the distance separating Andean thought linked to the cult of the dead and Amazonian thought seeking above all to abolish the dead—an analysis taken up recently by Claude Gélinas (1996). A specialist in the Guarani, Clastres does, however, make a couple of exceptions: the corpses of the ancient Tupi-Guarani chiefs, which were subject to double funerals in urns, and above all the bones of great shamans, apparently the objects of very elaborate cults in the past. Eduardo Viveiros de Castro (1992) likewise qualifies the equation of the dead with enemies among the ancient Tupinambá by showing that it applied only to a single class of death: that of deaths at home, adorned moreover with attributes otherwise used for enemies. Deaths elsewhere, "among the enemies of their enemies" in Castro's expression, were venerated as heroic since they alone had achieved the "beautiful" death—which is to say, in the stomach of enemies. The interpretation of cannibalism as a central element of the funerary system among the Tupi-Guarani is no longer in any doubt. But is it necessary to establish a link, as Combès does (1992), between the cannibal act and the theme of "lightening" the corpse—conserving the skeleton unencumbered by the weight of the flesh—as a condition for the voyage to the Land-without-Evil? The sources do not allow us to make such a claim with any certainty, though we do know the importance of the theme of recovering the bones as a potential form of resurrection in the cosmological thought of these peoples (Allard 2000; Fausto 2001). Whatever the case, exploring the parallels between cannibal and funerary practices as alterity *en devenir* can only stimulate analysis of these cultural phenomena in nonsubstantivist terms—that is, in terms of relations or of the acquisition of positions rather than substances. Witness the widely reported desire of these peoples to forget or efface all material traces of the dead, to avoid all direct contact with corpses converted into "partners," slightly unusual ones since they theoretically occupy the position taken by enemies. Anne-Christine Taylor (1993) illustrates this idea in a study dedicated to Jivaro mourning as a mechanism for forgetting the recent dead. Here the physical treatment of the deceased appears secondary to their spiritual "materialization" in the form of *arutam*, the vision of which, for the Achuar, is supposed to reveal the destiny or trajectory of an individual's life. The author argues that the *arutam* transmit nothing concrete of a "substantial" kind, but rather virtualities of existence. (See, however, the discussion in Fausto 2001:465–466 on the transmission of the *arutam* among the Achuar as a possible recycling of life potentials and identities within the same kindreds; Descola 1993:185 sees continuity comparable to a "true principle of exofiliation.") According to Perrin (1979:119), the Guajiro think that the dead whose remains are mixed with ancient bones in the collective urns serving as cemeteries lose all individuality in returning in the form of rainfall and sickness. Many other contemporary examples would confirm the thesis of the radical alterity assigned to the dead (see among others Coffaci de Lima 2000, Fausto 2001, and Vilaça 1992 on the Katukina, Parakanã, and Wari' respectively).

Still, the figure of the deceased-enemy expelled from the memory of the living as a general paradigm of mourning in the South American lowlands does not really fit with a range of practices still observable today. Indeed, although speaking of a predominant funerary model in Amazonia on the basis of an examination of contemporary situations is fully justified and its use has proved highly productive, this procedure also has a downside: it tends to flatten the diversity of the funerary practices, just as it fails to take sufficiently into account those of the past revealed by recent developments in Amazonian archaeology (see below). For example, the global interpretation given by Philippe Erikson (1986) of Pano endocannibalism as a formula for retaining the deceased (only close kin eat the pulverized bones) seems to contradict the notion of the dead person's radical alterity. See also Cecilia McCallum's interpretation (1996) of Cashinahua "cannibalism" as an act of compassion and homage toward the dead: according to her, the body's consumption constitutes kinship rather than involving a question of alterity and predation—an argument disputed by Aparecida Vilaça (1998, 2000). Erikson moreover notes the far from negligible ideological function accorded to the "ancestors" among certain Pano groups who do not necessarily assign a dangerous character to their dead. In his contribution to the present volume, Erikson speaks of "mediated ancestrality" or "ancestors by alliance" in relation to the Matis *mariwin* spirits, an idea indicating that ancestrality in Amazonia, if it exists, does so only by means of a detour via affinity. Nonetheless, the deeper question is—as Thomas (1980) proposes—whether endocannibalism should be treated as a rite of destruction, effacing all traces of the deceased, or as conservation of the remains, through absorption of the deceased's attributes. Viveiros de Castro (1992) for his part observes that although the Araweté, of Tupi origin, assimilate their recent dead to the enemies, they feel no desire to forget them, nor even to efface the material traces—the graves and skeletons—that could recall them to the memory of the living. Their names are evoked, while their personal belongings are not destroyed but inherited. In this case, we could suggest that the remembrance of the deceased, achieved via the permanence of the name and inherited goods, lessens the rupture conferring the condition of stranger or enemy. Kaj Århem (1980) observes, in turn, that while the Makuna are supposed to forget their dead, the dead are in reality remembered many years after the funerals. He establishes a principle of spiritual continuity between the living and the dead in this society—and in a classic fashion in the Tukano systems—for the recycling of the souls of the dead, in the form of names, in the second-generation descendants. The Xavante, a Jê people of central Brazil studied by Laura Graham (1995), fully incorporate their dead, called "immortals," in the system of life-cycle age classes. Xavante society thus integrates the living and the dead within its whole. Furthermore, the dead are not feared, in apparent contrast to the prevailing mood among other Gê groups. In addition, the individual memory of certain eminent "immortals," the great leaders, encounters a form of perpetuation in the Xavante creation tales. I have also shown the double movement of the dead toward affinity and ancestrality among the Yagua of Peru depending on the kinds of death and burial (Chaumeil 1992). It seems to me to provide evidence of a process of "ancestralization" reserved in this society for important figures, notably the great warriors whose names are immortalized in a particular genre of epic tale still occasionally told today. The notion of ancestrality must be taken here in a flexible sense insofar as the permanence of these beings from the past does not necessarily imply the recognition of precise genealogical links. In any event, the funerary treatments of these individuals contrast strongly with those of common people, who are submitted to a recycling of their vital elements and destined for a sort of anonymity. Heckenberger (2005 and this volume) equally shows the importance of ancestrality in the rituals of homage paid to great leaders and in certain funerary ceremonies of the upper Xingu.

Taking all the above into account, the panorama appears more complex and diversified than usually postulated, and does not really conform, to put it mildly, to the single model of a radical discontinuity between the living and the dead. I shall attempt to account for this in the remainder of the chapter by reexamining several types of funerary practice, past and present—each of which may be potentially combined with one or more other types in the same society—in order to reveal more clearly the practices left unexplained by this model. Abandonment of the corpse as the main funerary mode has been attributed to very few groups; it applies more widely to those individuals accused of sorcery. For example, as France-Marie Renard-Casevitz tells me, the Matsiguenga of Peru often abandon their deceased on flimsy skiffs left to float downriver, but they also practice direct inhumation. In any case, we can assume that abandonment of the corpse expresses a radical break with the dead. Immersion of the body, practiced at the end of complex funerals by the Bororo and the ancient Saliva, otherwise seems to be little represented in the South American lowlands.

Inhumation

A funerary procedure extremely widespread in the area that concerns us, inhumation may be single in kind (burial in earth or in urns) or double (a first burial followed after a lapse of time by a second and definitive burial).

Direct inhumation in earth, with the body usually wrapped in a length of fabric or the deceased's hammock, is reported among a number of Tupi and Carib groups. It takes place in the house (often but not always abandoned), on the village plaza, or in the forest, where a miniature hut sometimes marks the site of the tomb. The ancient Tupinambá combined two modes of burial, one directly in the earth, the other in urns. In the first case, a funerary chamber was built to prevent the earth weighing directly on the corpse, thereby evoking the principle of urn burial. When they abandoned their villages, the Tupinambá had the habit, according to Jean de Léry ([1580] 1992), of leaving *pindo* palm leaves on the tombs so that the site would be recognizable and the memory of the dead conserved: "les passants, par ce moyen, y reconnaissent forme de cimetière, . . . aussi quand les femmes s'y rencontrent, . . . si elles se ressouviennent de leurs feus maris, ce sera, faisant les regrets accoutumés, à hurler de telle façon qu'elles se font ouïr de demi-lieue" (186) [the passers-by can thus recognize the location of a cemetery, and when the women meet there, . . . if they remember their dead husbands, they will break out into their customary lamentations, and howl to be heard half a league away]. It is equally possible to argue, as Fausto does of the Parakanã practice of temporarily abandoning their village site when one of their own dies (2001:407–408), that this comprises a way of maintaining a distance from the burial spot, a place thought of as potentially dangerous, at least until the flesh has completely decomposed.

The custom of direct burial in urns is common to the Guarani, a people often said to lie at the origin of this funerary mode. This custom is equally frequent in the Chaco and among numerous groups of Amazonia (Nordenskiöld 1920; Boglar 1958a). The Chiriguano of the Chaco bury their dead in this fashion inside dwellings that they continue to inhabit afterward. It may be thought that peoples who bury their dead inside inhabited houses cultivate a very different relationship from those who destroy or definitively abandon their dwellings after inhumation. We should note, though, that residential permanence after inhumation need not indicate links of continuity with the dead: certain groups, such as the Parakanã, who do not share this conception, used to reoccupy their past dwellings after temporary abandonment once the corpse was deemed "inoffensive," that is to say, rid of its flesh (Fausto 2001). According to Curt Nimuendajú (1952), until the end of the nineteenth century the Ticuna of the Amazon used to practice primary burial in urns—sometimes decorated with necklaces of human teeth, trophies taken from enemies—which they visited regularly. Numerous funerary urns have also been discovered on the Japurá River. These are likely remains of ancient cemeteries (Métraux 1930). The Cocama of the upper Amazon combined direct burial in urns with secondary funerals in smaller urns, containing the bones of certain classes of dead people (Figueroa [1661] 1986; Maroni [1738] 1988). Other peoples, such as the Cubeo of northwestern Amazonia, have progressively abandoned urns in favor of coffins made from old pirogues. Although the nature of the container has changed, the principle of protecting the corpse remains identical.

Double Funerals

Double inhumation in urns is typical especially of Arawakan groups—Antilles, Orinoco, north and south of the Amazon, Jurua-Purus, Mojo—but is also found with numerous variations elsewhere (Métraux 1947). The bones, whole or reduced to ashes, are either reburied or deposited in urns or funerary baskets. In the latter two cases, they are generally kept in the house of the deceased or placed in communal cemeteries. Like many other ancestral practices, the domestic conservation of the bones of the deceased has become increasingly rare, replaced by Christian burial in individual graves. Funerary baskets have been reported among the Warao of the Orinoco delta and the ancient Carib (Gumilla 1758). Certain Arawakan and Cariban groups of the Guianas preferred to distribute the bones among the kin of the deceased in order for them to be kept separately. The conservation of bones in urns or in wrapped bundles was also very widespread, in particular the long bones and the skull, which were often painted with annatto dye, for instance among the Guahibo of the Colombian savanna. The Yuko, Caribs of the Sierra de Perijá, have a complex funerary ritual detailed by Reichel-Dolmatoff (1945): the corpse is firstly mummified over a fire, then buried in the house, which is abandoned. The body is exhumed some two years later, when the mummy is cleaned, wrapped in new straw mats, and transported with great pomp into the village.

There a dance is celebrated in its honor, with the deceased's kin dancing with the mummified corpse. The day after, a close kinsman suspends the mummy in the roof of his dwelling, storing it there for several weeks; it is then passed on to another member of the family, and so on. At the end of this familial "voyage," the mummy is deposited in a cave-cemetery where hundreds of other mummies rest. The presence of cave necropolises in this part of northern South America aroused the interest of the first European travelers—but so too that of grave robbers.

Cemeteries

Contrary to popular opinion, the existence of indigenous cemeteries predating the colonial period is less rare than supposed and will probably become even less so after numerous archaeological sites, particularly in the Guianas, have been subjected to systematic excavation (Rostain 1994). In addition to the Yuko case mentioned above, ancient "necropolises" have been documented along the coasts of the Guianas and Amapá, on the shores of the Maracá River (Guapindaia 2001), on Marajó Island (Meggers and Evans 1957; Roosevelt 1993; Schaan 2001), in the region surrounding Manaus (see the Anthonay collection, 1897, Musée du quai Branly, Paris), on the Japurá and Atures rivers (Scaramelli and Tarble 2000), along the middle Ucayali, among the Guajiro, among the Karajá of the Araguaia River, and finally, further south, among the Caingang (Métraux 1946), the Mbayá, and the Guaicuru of the Chaco (Métraux 1947).

The use of caves as funerary sites was extremely common along the middle Orinoco throughout the eighteenth and nineteenth centuries, and probably at much earlier dates (Scaramelli and Tarble 2000). In 1800, at the time of his famous exploration, Humboldt visited the Ataruipe cavern near Atures, where he counted numerous skeletons painted with annatto dye or coated in resin and stored in baskets and urns. Jules Crevaux, followed by Chaffanjon (1889), later examined other necropolises in the same region and ascribed them to the ancient Atures. Not far from there, the Piaroa also until recently followed the custom of depositing their dead in caverns or rock shelters distant from their dwelling places (Mansutti 2002). However, abandonment of the sites was compulsory—less, it seems, to flee from memories of the deceased than to elude the much more menacing reprisals of their aggressors, often identified with enemy shamans.

In addition to the presence of cemeteries discovered on Marajó Island and in the regions around Cunani and especially Maracá (containing tubular urns representing imposing human figures: see Guapindaia 2001), several Arawakan groups were acquainted with this mode of collective burial. In the middle of the nineteenth century, Paul Marcoy (1869) described the site of ancient open tombs close to the modern city of Manaus that had belonged to the ancient Manao and Baré. These same cemeteries were visited some years later by Keller-Leuzinger (1874), who counted several hundred urns buried in alignment at a shallow depth and containing whole skeletons placed in a crouching position. Métraux (1930) thought that all these funerary remains of the middle Amazon were the work of Arawak populations. (Concerning the Manao and the circuits of Arawak expansion on the Rio Negro at the start of the colonial period, see Vidal 2000.) The chain of urns extends as far as the upper Amazon with the Omágua and Cocama, Tupi peoples, while it is broken in the direction of the lower Amazon at the height of Santarém where, despite Nimuendajú's excavations (Linné 1928), no presence of urns has been found, suggesting that the Tapajó practiced endocannibalism as their main funerary mode. Further to the north, the Palikur of the Oyapock River maintained clan cemeteries until recent times. The bones were prepared either by boiling or smoking, or by putrefaction in a first burial, then deposited in a second urn after a period of storage with the deceased's family (Grenand and Grenand 1987).

Like many of their neighbors from the Jê family, the Bororo of central Brazil practice double funerals but, as far as we can tell, following two different modalities, depending on the status of the deceased. The relics of important figures, especially *bari* shamans, are immersed at the bottom of a lagoon, while those of common folk are buried in the ground (Viertler 1991). There is evidence that during an earlier period the funerary baskets containing richly decorated bones were stored in cave-cemeteries beneath cliffs, but their constant profanation by grave robbers undoubtedly led to their abandonment, forcing the Bororo to modify their funerary practice (Albisetti and Venturelli 1962). In any event, Bororo funerals are performed following a very elaborate ritual, one of whose specific features involves the practice of "substituting the deceased." Buried in the village's central plaza, the corpse is submitted to rapid putrefaction by being soaked copiously in water. The bones are then exhumed, cleaned, painted, decorated with feathers, and placed in funerary baskets, first exposed and then immersed according to current practice. The end of the funerary cycle is marked by incinerating all the goods belonging to the deceased—who, by contrast, does not disappear from the world of the living since s/he is subject to a ritual substitution in the shape of a formal companion or friend who, after the funeral and for life, represents the deceased in this world. Belonging to the moiety opposite to the deceased's, he must, among other tasks, hunt down a replacement animal, generally a jaguar, to serve as a metaphoric equivalent of the dead person, and prepare the funerary basket (Crocker 1977; Viertler 1991). According to Renate Viertler, the replacement animals' hide and teeth, strung in necklaces, represent a repayment sent by

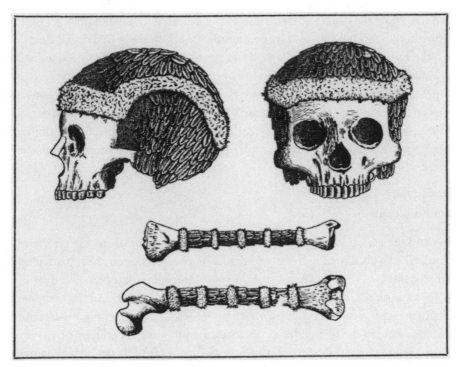

Fig. 8.1. Decorated Bororo bones (after *Enciclopedia Bororo*, vol. 1, 1962).

the dead to their kinsfolk for the heavy investments occasioned by their funerals. Here, rather than being feared, the dead appear as a source of peace and harmony for the living, the Bororo's greatest fear being precisely that no "substitute" from the other moiety will take care of their bones after death.

Still in Brazil, the Karajá of the Araguaia performed their entire funerary cycle in cemeteries located, in precontact times, outside their villages (Ehrenreich 1948; Pétesch 2000). The funerals were carried out in two phases under the responsibility of the deceased's affines—a procedure nowadays abandoned. According to Nathalie Pétesch, the relationship between the living and the dead is not broken here, since the dead maintain a constant presence in the day-to-day life of the Karajá, especially during hunting. In approaching this theme, Pétesch makes a comparison between Jê, Bororo, and Karajá funerals. Whereas some Jê peoples reintroduce the bones of the dead buried outside the village back into social space, the Bororo in effect practice the inverse, with the bones circulating from the village plaza to the rivers or rocky shelters. As for the Karajá, they maintain a close parallelism between the social space of the dead (the cemetery) and that of the living (the village). In the first case, we could propose that the principle of rupture with the community of the dead is lessened by the "return" of the bones, in the second by the ritual representation of the deceased by a living member of the other moiety, and in the third by communication with the spirits of the dead.

The Kaingang, a Jê people of southern Brazil, also interred their dead in kinds of cemeteries made up of several tumuli in which funerary chambers were erected. Such tumuli have been reported since the eighteenth century among the ancestors of the Kaingang. The extreme care with which they constructed these conical tombs testifies to the importance accorded to the dead in their society (Métraux 1946; see Crépeau 1999 on the complexity and central character of the funerary ritual among the Kaingang).

Incineration

Beyond the partial incineration associated with endocannibalism, simple cremation was practiced predominantly to the north of the Amazon river, particularly among the Carib of the Guianas. A funerary procedure that has nowadays become exceptional, it was once commonplace among the Wayana except for their shamans, who were buried. Other societies proceeded in precisely the opposite fashion. Among the Aparai, for example, cremation was the exclusive privilege of shamans and chiefs (Linné 1929). Only the bodies of the most renowned shamans were incinerated among the Cashinahua, the other dead being either consumed or, if they were without close kin, simply buried (McCallum 1996). The ashes were most often interred, piled on the ground or placed in a small hut specially built on the cremation site, or alternatively kept with the remains of the calcined bones in pottery or baskets stored in the houses, enabling them to be transported when the people relocated. It may be seen that cremation, like endocannibalism, is a procedure in perfect congruity with the theory of double funerals. It is above all an antiputrefaction process, diametrically opposed to the exposed or abandoned body. For Thomas (1980:179), burning is centered less on destruction than on conservation, since the fire simply accelerates the dissolution of the body's soft parts so as to be left with the "remains."

Mummification

A very important aspect of Andean cultures, mummification was a funerary procedure likewise practiced in the lowlands, essentially on the Amazon and to the north as far as the Darien peninsula in preconquest times and during the colonial period. Thereafter it became more infrequent. More than any other funerary mode, it involved a selective procedure applied primarily to eminent figures—chiefs, great warriors, shamans. Mummification could be achieved through drying in the sun or by fire, or through embalming using plant resins. It was often combined with urn burial or raised exposure. The desiccation of corpses by means of smoking is practiced or was observable until a relatively recent date among several indigenous societies both of Venezuela (see the Yuko above) and of Brazil, including the Maué, the Apiaká, the Mundurucu, the Puri-Coroado, and the ancient Tapajó. Concerning the latter, Nimuendajú (1949) turns to the missionaries João Felipe Betendorf and João Daniel for reports made during the second half of the seventeenth century—we may presume that Father Daniel, whose mission was later in the second half of the seventeenth century, refers to these same events—about a supposed "cult of dried corpses." According to the missionaries who set fire to this "tribal sanctuary" in 1682, some of the mummies had been venerated for many years and were honored by dances and offerings. These practices of mummification reserved for important persons may have been coupled with funerary endocannibalism, a hypothesis put forward by Erland Nordenskiöld (1930) in part to explain the absence of any evidence of tombs in the region. On the other hand Denise Gomes (2001), noting the visual aspect of the mummified bodies, establishes an archaeological parallel with the Maracá funerary urns. These were not buried, but were deposited on the ground at sites relatively close to the places of habitation, thus destined to be seen and visited, probably indicating the closeness of the ties uniting the living and the dead in these cultures (Guapindaia 2001).

According to Debret (1834–39), the ancient "Puri-Coroado" of Brazil stored the mummified remains of their chiefs in impressive urns buried at the foot of certain large trees. Decorated with the most beautiful ornaments, of which charming specimens were still to be found at the start of the nineteenth century, these mummies present a striking likeness to those of the ancient Peruvians—though this is undoubtedly due to Debret's artistic talent.

Drying corpses by fire was also practiced by the Maué of the Amazon until quite recently (Pereira 1954). The Mundurucu in the same manner conserved the mummified heads of enemies and those of their kin killed in battle—or, lacking the head, an arm or leg—which they kept for a period of five or four years respectively; in contrast, those dying at home were given an urn funeral (Tocantins 1877; Ihering 1907; Menget 1993). Nevertheless, once the years had gone by, the heads taken from the enemy were abandoned, while the others were buried at home. The analogy between the treatment of kin killed among enemies and the enemies themselves is therefore not absolute. The final inhumation reintroduces the former within the sphere of kin, while abandonment places the latter outside kinship. The direction taken by the dead is inverse. While the figure of the dead person as an enemy cannot be applied in full to the Mundurucu case, we can still

Fig. 8.2. Mummy conserved in an urn (after Debret 1834–39).

observe a correspondence between the active phase of the recovered remains and that of enemy trophies. The reader will have been reminded of certain funerary mechanisms of the ancient Tupinambá, with the difference that here it is those dying in warfare, and not those dying at home, who are endowed with attributes reserved for enemies.

Raised Exposure

The exposure of corpses on raised platforms is a practice closely akin to natural mummification. Generally combined with other funerary modes, aerial tombs have been reported among numerous peoples, including the Warao, the Yukpa, the Siriono, several groups from the Chaco (the Mataco, for example), and the Jivaro. Among these last, the raised exposure of a corpse is achieved with the aid of a platform, or in a hollow trunk suspended from the roof of a house, or beneath a shelter at some distance from the place of habitation. Today the dead are more usually buried in the dwelling, which is abandoned only after the death of its owner. The use of urns is confined to the corpses of children, although it is not implausible that this funerary mode was more widespread in the past, especially if we take into account the hollow trunk–urn association. The great warriors received a specific funerary treatment closely akin to natural mummification: dressed in his most beautiful adornments and his weapons, the warrior was left on his own stool, his back supported by the center pole of the dwelling, protected from predators by two palisades. If these facts are accurate, the Jivaro were familiar with at least two funerary modes: single burial, either in earth or in urns, and raised exposure, the latter sometimes accompanied by double burial, according to Stirling (1938) and Eichenberger (1961) on the Aguaruna. Harner (1977) on the other hand notes the possibility for a great Jivaro warrior to communicate to his sons his wish to transmit to each of them one of the *arutam* could forming at his death. (See Fausto 2001 on the transmission of *arutam* among the Achuar as a kind of internal recycling of life principles.) A host of elements that do not really lend credence to the idea of a radical rupture with the dead and contrasting with the recent works of Taylor (1993, 1998).

If raised exposure was the main funerary mode of the Jivaro before the impact of missionaries, it was doubtless not the most efficient means of lessening the physical presence of the dead. The treatment of the deceased among the neighboring Candoshi, belonging to the Jivaro-Candoa complex, would seem to confirm this impression (Surrallés 2000). Their mortuary platforms are built in the immediate vicinity of the dwelling houses. Over the first weeks, the body drips with the liquids exuded by putrefaction of the flesh. This fails, though, to prevent kin from taking care of the deceased, visiting daily in a display of affection and speaking with the corpse to provide assurance that he or she is well there. The second funeral takes place after one or several years with the burial of the bones in a pit under the floor of the house. Surrallés notes that the force of a great warrior can be recuperated by his descendants at the moment of his demise so that they themselves may flourish, a mechanism recalling that described by Harner apropos of the *arutam* among the Jivaro. The attitude shown to individuals struck down by a *male-mort*, or violent death, is very different: such people are avoided and feared as purveyors of sickness, thereby constituting a category apart.

Funerary Cannibalism (Flesh and Bone)

The funerary mode of endocannibalism, involving the consumption of all or part of the bodies of the deceased—sometimes coupled with exocannibalism or "warfare cannibalism," the ingestion of the flesh of killed enemies—has been the object of several comparative studies attesting to its antiquity and its great diffusion in South America (see Zerries 1960; Conklin 2001). It has been reported from the Atlantic coast and the Caribbean islands in the north as far south as Paraguay and, in the twentieth century, particularly in western Amazonia along the border between Brazil, Peru, and Bolivia among Panoan and Chapakuran groups (Conklin 2001:xxiv). We should note, though, that the classical distinction made by ethnologists between exocannibalism and endocannibalism loses its pertinence here if we accept the general thesis of the dead person as an enemy. In this sense, funerary cannibalism closely resembles a kind of warfare cannibalism (Vilaça 2000)—which does not mean, however, that the actions implied in either of the two cases would be equivalent from the point of view of the interested parties—as Beth Conklin aptly remarks (2001:xxiii).

Generally speaking, funerary cannibalism may take two forms in Amazonia: consumption of the flesh or of the calcined bones (osteophagy), distinct procedures that may however be combined in certain societies such as the Cashinahua or the Wari'.

Of the two practices, osteophagy is incontestably the more widespread in the South American lowlands. Its area of distribution covers the north of Brazil, the upper Orinoco, and the northwest and upper Amazon. The rite consists of reducing to powder the calcined bones of the deceased—and sometimes the hair, implying in this case phanerocannibalism (see Erikson, this volume)—so that they may be absorbed subsequently in the form of a drink by more or less close kin. The bones are generally obtained by partial cremation, though they may also be garnered through decomposition of the flesh on a platform, or by single burial if following the principle of double funerals. Ingestion of the ashes may take place immediately or may be delayed for several years, in which case the bone powder is kept in baskets or funerary gourds, as is done among the Yanomami of Brazil and Venezuela.

The second type, flesh cannibalism, is less frequent in South America. It can be found primarily among the Guayaki of Paraguay (see above), among some Pano groups in Peru, such as the Cashinahua, who practice it only for certain individu als (McCallum 1996), and among the Wari', who until recently combined all three forms of cannibalism. In the case of the Wari', the cooked flesh of the deceased was partially consumed in small morsels, while the calcined bones were mixed with honey to be ingested by the deceased's entourages, generally composed of their affines.

This being said, Amazonian studies have supplied two different interpretations for funerary cannibalism, construing it either as a mechanism for absorbing certain attributes of the dead or, conversely, as a procedure for eradicating them. The first position has been most notably defended by McCallum (1996), for whom Cashinahua endocannibalism is primarily an act of compassion toward the dead, aiming to retain them in some form within the bodies of the living—effectively a way of conserving or memorizing the dead by consuming them. Adherents of the second interpretation, notably Vilaça (1998, 2000) based on her analysis of the Wari' materials, contend that conceptions of death in the lowlands are primarily a question of predation, understood here as a relationship between predator and prey in which eating is an act of depersonalization/dehumanization and transformation of the deceased into a preylike condition.

The recent study by Conklin (2001) on the same Wari' qualifies this position by assigning to funerary cannibalism a double function, both destructive and generative, necessary to the perpetuation of the group. The author takes the notion of cannibalism as an act of respect and compassion for the dead and their families. Making corpses disappear by eating them is indeed a way of eliminating them from the living's memory, with the aim of lessening the latter's suffering. Yet it is also a way of reproducing a cycle of transformation and exchange between the living and the dead via the spirits of animals: the Wari' hold, in fact, that their dead join the domain of the animal spirits, where they transform into white-lipped peccaries. These in turn will become the game of hunters. In Conklin's view, the members of this group thereby enact a double endocannibalism in consuming the flesh of their dead, firstly as a human body (funerals), secondly as game (hunting). The Kulina, an Arawá people studied by Donald Pollock (1993), possess an analogous system of reciprocal predation between the living and the dead: here the flesh of peccary-ancestors forms the souls of the newborn. Endocannibalism in this case is perceived to be less an incorporation of the qualities of the deceased than a transformation of bodies and souls between the living and the dead within the parameters of a wider sociocosmological dynamic. At the same time, it amounts to a process of forgetting aimed at the dissolution of the dead person's social identity. This would imply that it is attachment to the dead, not rejection, that forces the Wari' to eradicate them from memory by consuming them. Either way, death is not seen here just as a discontinuity: it is also a transformation essential for the continuation of social life (Conklin 2001). Furthermore, this process of forgetting the dead and inserting them within broader cosmological conceptions has numerous parallels in Amazonia (Oakdale 2001).

The Yanomami, who practice osteophagy exclusively, also strive to efface all material trace of the dead (Clastres and Lizot 1978; Albert 1985). Nevertheless, the memory of the dead seems to survive the disappearance of their bodies, especially if the dead person was highly skilled or a courageous warrior killed in combat. The pulverized bones are kept in funerary gourds and gradually absorbed by the person's relatives, including affines, over periods that, Bruce Albert tells me, sometimes exceed ten or fifteen years, depending on the duration of revenge preparations. Thus, far from being a total effacement, the rite attempts to achieve a difficult balance between remembering and forgetting (Clastres and Lizot 1978).

Funerary Substitution

Occasionally we find that the dead are represented by parts of the body (tufts of hair, teeth, nails), by objects (figurines, posts, trunks of wood), or even by living persons, as in the Bororo case where a formal friend belonging to the other moiety serves lifelong in the condition of ritual substitute of the deceased (Viertler 1991). The existence of statues that had to be "fed" or anthropomorphic figurines containing mortuary remains was apparently common among the Arawak of the islands and coast at the time of conquest (Rouse 1992). Such objects have also been reported at different periods in several lowland regions—unfortunately without attracting much attention from the researchers involved. Today there are few possibilities of observing these forms of funerary substitution. It seems the Uni, a Cashibo people of Peru, still fabricate wooden statues representing the dead during a ceremony for lifting mourning, celebrated when the nostalgia experienced by certain persons for the dead proves too intense (Frank 1994). Bundles of hair belonging to the dead, usually kept in pendants around the necks of kinfolk, are draped at this point on the statue, which is carried in procession to the village and then destroyed. The "return" of the dead person or dead people (depending on the number of bundles attached) can therefore be interpreted as a form of double funeral: once the funerary substitutes are destroyed, the memory of the dead is felt to diminish in intensity. The Guahibo also resorted to this kind of funerary substitution. Nails and clumps of hair were carefully kept—not this time by kin but by the shaman, who regularly consulted the relic bundles to discover the origin of the deceased, an indispensable prelude to the performance of second funerals in urns the following year (Chaffanjon 1889). It has been hypothesized that the tree trunks used in the famous log races connected to funerals in certain Jê societies represent the dead (Stahle 1971–72; Pétesch 1983, 2000). Among the eastern Timbira, the logs are actually called "logs of the deceased." According to Vera-Dagny Stahle, the log races had an initial function of placing the living in regular contact with the dead. Finally, we can evoke the *kuarup* funerary complex of the upper Xingu, celebrated in honor of dead chiefs. The term *kuarup*—of Tupi origin, with a Carib equivalent in *egitsï*—may designate a tree or, as here, a section of trunk or post, decorated and planted in the ground, that is supposed to represent the spirit of dead chiefs (Carneiro 1993; Heckenberger 1999). According to Michael Heckenberger (1999 and this volume), the Kuikuro conceive the *kuarup* trunk as a representation of the past, which links the living not only with recently deceased leaders whose power has passed to current ones but, through them, with ancestral chiefly lines extending metaphorically back to the "divine" ancestors, since the wood from which the divine mother was originally carved was the *kuarup* tree. A number of Kalapalo myths also tell how the illustrious dead represented by the posts transform in the course of the ritual into "living persons" whom the shamans must contain through abundant fumigations of tobacco (Basso 1973). The difficulty here lies in comprehending the indigenous concept of representation. Carlos Fausto tells me that the Kuikuro term for designating the trunk is *hutoto*, "image," preceded by the name of the commemorated person. This term is applied to certain types of pictures or to photos, and can indicate a relation of figurative resemblance between an image and its referent. A more generic and "musical" form of representing the dead by ritual objects may perhaps be found in the complex of scared flutes, which we shall examine later on.

Bones and the Memory of the Dead

The present exercise has brought to light two series of funerary treatments. While some groups make efforts to erase all traces and memory of the dead, others seek to conserve their memory and maintain a continuity between the living and the dead, notably through the use of bones. Little examined by Amazonian ethnology, this second series commands our attention here. It may be noted, however, that the two series are by no means exclusive and may perfectly well coexist within the same group, as Olivier Allard (2000) endeavors to show in the case of the Guarani.

The custom of preserving the bones of the dead for more or less lengthy periods is in fact confirmed in many Amazonian societies from the Guianas and the Chaco. Among these groups, the Guarani displayed a very specific interest in the relics that they occasionally transported, assembled in bundles, on their seasonal migrations (Vignati 1941–46). Dobrizhoffer ([1783] 1822) claimed to have seen non-Christianized Guarani carrying on their treks small boxes containing the bones of their shamans, in which they placed many of their hopes. The Mbyá also preserved the bones of their dead—not just their shamans—over periods lasting many years. These remains were kept in wooden containers placed in the center of the ritual house and were not disposed of until a message from the gods declared they would not come back to life (Cadogan 1950; H. Clastres 1975:570). Various authors have mentioned the theme of potential resurrection via bones among the Tupi-Guarani. These different rituals recall another that Ruiz de Montoya observed in the seventeenth century among the Guarani of Paraguay. In deep forest the missionary discovered kinds of "temples" housing the dried bones of great shamans, which were consulted as oracles. Sometimes extremely ancient and richly adorned, the relics would reply, and complete trust was accorded to their prophecies: they were thought to assure good planting and a fertile and prosperous year ahead. As Métraux remarks (1928b:93), "These illustrious dead would resuscitate and live in flesh and blood on certain occasions." Combès (1992) locates this cult within the Tupi-Guarani tradition of resurrecting the flesh from the bones. The antiquity of this rite can be questioned, of course, since it occurred at a time when the rivalry between shamans and missionaries was rife, and we know all too well the importance of the theme of bodily resurrection in Christianity and the power of attraction missionary sanctuaries were able to exercise on indigenous leaders in order to eliminate completely the latter's influence (Menget 1999b). Nothing proves, though, that these conceptions did not preexist in the indigenous cultures and that there had not been rather a convergence between two sets of beliefs and practices (Fausto 2002 and this volume). Concerning this "war of relics" between missionaries and Indians, we may also recall the case of the Jesuit Franciso Pinto described by Castelnau-L'Estoile (2000). Father Pinto's bones, carefully preserved by the Tupi of Ibiapaba, brought rain or sunshine on demand. When the Portuguese sent an expedition to retrieve them, the Indians categorically refused to relinquish the remains of this "master of the rain," as they had baptized him; exhuming and hiding the missionary's skeleton, they obliged the Portuguese to return empty-handed. Among some other societies, such as the Juruna and the Apiaka or certain Arawakan groups of the Purus, the practice of conserving the bones applied, it seems, to the majority of the deceased.

Far from being reserved for shamans and leaders, the use of bones equally applied to another class of the dead: warriors killed in battle, even those who had died far from home. A very widespread procedure in the lowlands, the recovery of a part of the deceased's body underlines the importance accorded to the natal territory as a place of return for those dying in foreign lands. It is quite difficult to see any manifestation of a radical rupture with the dead in this practice. Father Fauque ([1736] 1843) in the middle of the seventeenth century left an important testimony on the modalities of recovering remains among the Palikur of Guyana. We find an identical usage at the other end of the subcontinent, among the Abipones of Paraguay, who carried the bones of the dead by horseback over great distances in order to deposit them in family tombs. The Mundurucu likewise used to pay funeral homage to warriors killed among enemies by retrieving at least the head or the humerus when unable to recover the whole body. Responsibility for this operation fell to a compatriot belonging to the opposite moiety: he would take great care of his charge, sleeping with it "as if it were a child" (Murphy 1958). Subjected to natural mummification, the remains became the focus of ceremonies honoring the dead over the next four years. During these manifestations, where sacred flutes were played, the widow or mother or sister of the deceased displayed the remains around her neck. These were finally buried in the house of the deceased, differentiating them from the war trophies generally abandoned after a period of five years. Thus the relics of warriors were kept by the opposite moiety and then buried at home, while the war trophies were kept at home and then exteriorized. The first case involved reconsanguinizing a temporarily "affinized" dead kinsman, while the second case involved expelling a previously "consanguinized" dead enemy.

The Ipurina of the Purus River used to perform an elaborate ceremony during which a kinsman recalled the warrior exploits of the deceased while brandishing one of his bones. The case of the Siriono of eastern Bolivia provides an even better illustration of this relation of quasi-intimacy between the living and the dead through the interposition of human bones. According to Alicia Fernández Distel (1984–85), the Siriono have employed three successive funerary modes: (1) transportation of the skeleton during their seasonal nomadism (the most ancient procedure), (2) double burials in earth, and (3) direct burial (a recent introduction). In the first case—of primary interest to us here—the body was exposed to a low fire on a funerary platform, following a number of modalities that varied according to the status of the deceased. The encampment was deserted but the platform regularly visited so as to tend the fire. Afterward the dried skeleton was placed in a large basket. Thenceforth the bones shared, so to speak, the life of the members of the group, who spoke to them and transported them during their seasonal treks. The bones of the dead brought good luck in hunting, while the skulls—especially those of important people, inherited by the oldest son—healed the more serious illnesses. Put simply, the dead ensured protection for the living, while the living repaid the dead with marks of respect and trust. With the introduction of the practice of double earth burials, only the skull was kept for

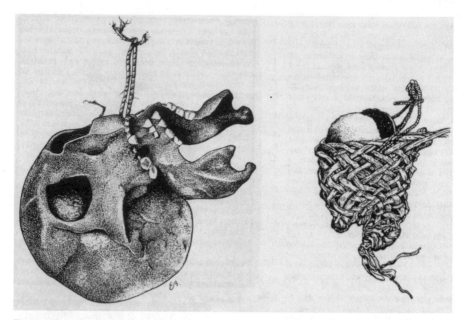

Fig. 8.3. Siriono relics transported during seasonal migrations (after Fernández Distel 1984–85).

its therapeutic virtues. The other remains were burned and interred. If the data are accurate, the Siriono had perfected an original system of relations with the dead, based on reciprocal protection and not on the idea of rupture.

The "Sacred" Flutes Complex

At the start of this chapter, if the reader recalls, I raised the possibility of a connection between the treatment of bones and the Amazonian complex of "sacred" flutes whose blowing, musical sound or even visual appearance alone sometimes has, like Siriono skulls, the power to attract game or to cure serious afflictions. Porro (1996) provides several historical references to these rituals, notably the Yurimagua cult of Guaricaya where we find the key elements of the rituals today known by the name of Yurupari. (See also Gomes 2001 for treatment of this theme and the association of flutes with certain topoynms.) In this part I shall therefore seek to explain the link between possession of these instruments, the conservation of bones, and the memory of the dead.

The Amazonian literature uses the term *sacred flutes*—called Yurupari in northwestern Amazonia—to designate a variety of musical instruments played exclusively in a ritual context: male initiation, seasonal rituals of food exchange, therapeutic or funerary ceremonies. These flutes may represent either ancestral entities (mythic or clanic) or nonhuman entities (bird spirits, for example), and incarnate their voice and bones, or sometimes a part of their body. Among most of the Tukano and Arawak groups of northwest Amazonia, the flutes represent the bones of eponymous ancestors of the clans, who are treated on these occasions as though they were living beings. In other cases, as among the Yagua and Mundurucu, they shelter or symbolize the voice and bones of certain categories of ancestral spirits associated with game. Although not amounting to a general rule as such, the frequency of such associations allows us to postulate, I think, the existence of a relationship between these flutes and bones. Furthermore, the instrumental ensemble they form is subject to a heavy visual interdiction of women and the noninitiated under penalty of death, rape, or serious illness. The prohibition may be total or partial depending on the case; for example, certain details of the fabrication of flutes may be banned to view. Defined in this way, the sacred flutes can be compared with another very ancient instrument in Amazonia, the bullroarers. Allard (2000) has suggested that these aerophones, present especially in the east of Brazil and in the sub-Andean region of Peru, occupy an "inverse" position to the flutes that many societies make from the bones of enemies: while the first type of flute involves the ancestors "giving voice," the second type involves dead enemies being "made to sing."

Today the area of distribution of this musical complex is concentrated in western Amazonia, the middle Orinoco, and central Brazil, notably the upper Xingu region. In the past it extended along the length of the Amazon, to the Colombian llanos and the vast region running from the Purus to the Mojos savannas (see map, figure 8.4).

Among Arawakan groups—to whom the origin of this complex is generally attributed—these instruments may be found among the Curripaco (associated with male initiation and food gathering rites), the Yukuna (male initiation), and the Achagua of Colombia (funerary ceremonies). Over in Venezuelan and Brazilian territories, they are present among the Warekena, the Wakuénai, the Baniwa, and the Baré of the upper Rio Negro, where they are associated with initiation and food exchange rituals. In the upper Xingu region, the Mehinaku, the Waura, and the Yawalapiti keep these sacred flutes with the bullroarers in the men's house. According to much older documents, the "Mojo," Bauré, Manasi, and Paressi—all once powerful and hierarchical Arawak societies—used to keep their sacred instruments in "temples."

The sacred flutes complex also occupies a central place in the religion of the Tukano of the Vaupès—Desana, Barasana, Makuna, Cubeo, and so on—although it is absent among the western Tukano. Here the pairs of instruments are placed in correspondence with the different levels of clan-type social segmentation (Hugh-

Fig. 8.4. Area of the "sacred" flutes.

Fig. 8.5. Saliva funerals (after Gumilla 1758).

Jones 1979; Århem 1980). The Maku may have lent the Tukano their flutes along with their system of social segmentation. Such flutes were also signaled among the Yurimagua and Omágua, ancient Tupi of central Amazonia, by the first chroniclers, and they are still in use among the Mundurucu of the Tapajós, who employ them during hunting to seduce the spirits of game, somewhat in the manner of head trophies. The Piaroa of Venezuela, in the Saliva linguistic family, possess one of the most complete panoplies of sacred instruments, played at the performance of the great *sari* or *warime* rituals, an instrumental ensemble

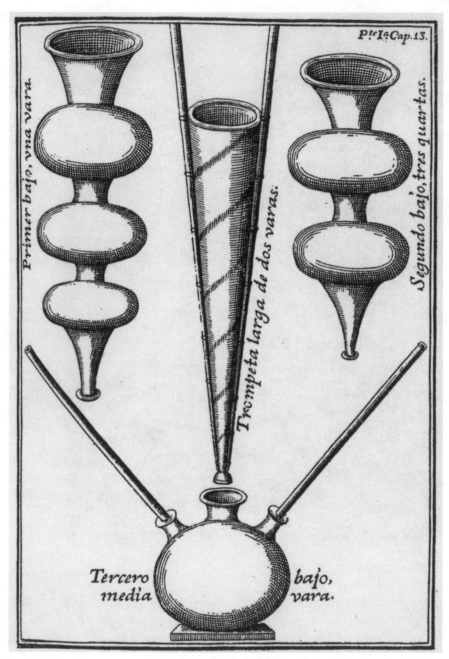

Fig. 8.6. Sacred instruments of the Saliva used in funerary ceremonies (after Gumilla 1758).

recalling that of the ancient Saliva described by Father Gumilla in the middle of the eighteenth century.

On the Amazon, the Ticuna and the Yagua also manufacture these kinds of instruments in connection with initiations and large collective hunts. Construction of the large communal houses among the Witoto, Bora, and Ocaina, may also give rise to the celebration of a ritual of the same kind. Among the Carib, in contrast, the complex of sacred flutes seems to be little developed except by the Carijona, who were exposed to the double influence of the Tukano and Witoto, and by the Kalapalo and Kuikuro, who belong to the upper Xingu cultural nexus.

At an organological level, this musical assembly comprises several classes of wind instruments (trumpets, pipes, and flutes) generally played in pairs following different formulas (older/younger, male/female, long/short) and sometimes placed in hierarchical relationship (trumpets superior to flutes, or vice versa) depending on the importance of the entities being represented. Their fabrication is the responsibility of initiated men according to their clan affiliation, although they may also be the work of specialists, as among the Mehinaku (Gregor 1979:255). In such cases the flutes fetch a high price, and their acquisition requires the supply of high-value exchange goods. The instruments are then kept in the "flute house" or placed in the care of a guardian. Elsewhere, the instruments are destroyed or abandoned once the rituals have been held, except for one part, usually the imperishable wooden tip of the trumpets or the body of the flutes, which is carefully kept from one ritual to the next, wrapped in bark and concealed in deep forest or at the source of streams, a little bit as though it were a relic. The guardian, "he who takes care of the flutes" in the expression of the Desana of Brazil as I am told by Dominique Buchillet, will then periodically remove the "body" of the instrument from the water or earth to ensure its perfect conservation until the day when it will be used again to make new flutes for the approaching rituals. This practice evokes the principle of successive double funerals—and recalls the proposed relationship between the flutes and the bones of the ancient dead. The fairly widespread custom of "feeding" the flutes with drinks or tobacco can be interpreted in this context as a way of giving back flesh to the "bones" of the ancestors; in other words, it is a means of bringing them to life, as though this periodic "resurrection" is meant to mark a link between the living and the dead, a continuity across the generations. As it happens, many of the societies possessing the sacred flute complex perform, or used to perform, double funerals in urns (whole bones) or endocannibalism (pulverized bones)—two funerary modes in perfect harmony, I believe, with the theory of conserving remains. The myths from western Amazonia on the origin of flutes moreover echo these two funerary forms. According to the most common version, it was the calcined bones of the mythic hero that gave birth to the *paxiuba* palm (*Iriartea* sp.) used to make the flutes, his relics in this world (Hugh-Jones 1979). This episode of his resurrection via ashes is found in more or less transmuted form in numerous flute origin myths and suggests an association with the practice of osteophagy. In other versions, though, such as those of the Yagua, the episode with the ashes is missing; instead, the hero reaches the sky by extracting a liana vine from his navel and immediately sends his bones to earth for people to make the flutes. Additionally, the Yagua say that in the past the instruments were made from bones and not wood as today. In the mythology, the first flutes acquired by the twins came from the bones of their dead kin, in particular their father. Such instruments were distinct from trophy flutes, which the Yagua once fabricated from the humeri of enemies killed in combat and which served exclusively as weapons of war (Chaumeil 2001). In fact, as far as we know, the Yagua did not practice endocannibalism but favored double funerals in urns, at least for important figures. We could thus risk the hypothesis of a double correspondence between (a) the "bone" version of the myth and double funerals, and (b) the "ash" version and endocannibalism.

As a link between generations, the sacred flutes also bind the living and the dead, a relationship strengthened by the material entering into their fabrication. Several species of palm with very hard wood (*Iriartea* sp., *Bactris* sp.) are used for both the body of the flutes and the tip of trumpets. These same species also serve in the manufacture of arms among a large number of Amazonian peoples. *Bactris* in particular—which has been domesticated by indigenous peoples and is the result of crossing two wild species—grows very slowly and reproduces on the same site over many generations. In order to harvest the fruits or exploit the wood, the societies cultivating it must therefore return periodically to the old clearings close to the places occupied by the dead. Moreover, certain groups such as the Yagua or the Mayoruna explicitly associate the *Bactris* palm with the "ancestors." Erikson (1996 and this volume) has underlined the almost consubstantial link that unites this palm with the ancestral spirits of the Matis, guardians of the fallow grounds where the *Bactris* grows. This observation provides the basis for his hypothesis that the groups cultivating the *Bactris* palm or proximate species have "a relation of ancestrality very different from that of the majority of groups in Amazonia, for whom death alienates, provoking an abrupt shift into alterity" (1996:188–189). Laura Rival (1993) develops a parallel argument about the Huaorani of Ecuador: for this indigenous group, the colonies of *Bactris* express slow growth, generational continuity, and the memory of the dead. Far from being a gift of the forest, the palm's racemes are in fact seen by the people as the product of the work of past generations. When they cross zones populated by *Bactris* palm, the Huaorani remember particular people who have died, related to the members of the group who exploited these particular palm stands. It seems, then, that the sacred flutes make up part of a broad western Amazonian cultural complex, linking together these palm trees, ancient groves, and the "ancestors."

Moreover, we can note that most of the groups of western Amazonia possessing sacred flutes also have a system of lineage-type social segmentation, clanic or similar, with an emphasis on patrilineal filiation, in contrast with the cognatic kinship prevalent elsewhere in Amazonia. With the exception of Reichel-Dolmatoff (1989), the authors focusing on this question have unanimously associated the flutes with a "male cult," some of them going as far as to speak of an "ancestor cult." There is no reason to conclude, though, that the Yurupari rituals are performed only in connection with filiation: they also produce full-scale alliance through ceremonial exchanges. In this sense, the sacred flutes undoubtedly achieve the articulation of the principles of filiation and alliance in equal measure, although the filiation side is more explicitly pronounced (Århem 1981). With this in mind, Hugh-Jones (1993) proposes the introduction of the notion "house society" to characterize this type of social organization, much closer in his view to indigenous practices and conceptions than reference to the notion of unifiliation alone. True, but what then to make of the Piaroa or the upper Xingu societies that possess the flutes but not, as far as we can tell, any form of social segmentation of this kind? An intriguing point in the Piaroa case concerns the existence of mortuary clans, a theme developed by Overing (1993): Although operating little in daily life, they are still used today in classical fashion in the actions involving territorial claims. Further back in the past, it seems, these funerary clans, each reuniting dead members of the same "filiation group" in the next world, were linked to precise local geographic referents that could indicate potential rights over using space. In a recent thesis, Alex Mansutti (2002) has shown the crucial role of toponymy in the construction and appropriation of space among the Piaroa and how this code of concrete reference points can serve as a support for producing history in this society. The possible association of the flutes and the dead is even more enticing here since the ancient Saliva associated the sacred instruments with their funerary ceremonies. In the case of the upper Xingu, the institution common to the area of "men's houses"—where the flutes were and still are stored—may also provide an interesting lead for further exploration. Egon Schaden (1959) had already emphasized the potential interest of studying the "Yurupari religion" in conjunction with the institution of men's houses in South America. Future research will say whether these remarks are pertinent. For now, the indications are that there is indeed a strong link between the possession of instruments, the conservation of bones, the memory of the dead, and a "unilinear" conception of society.

Memory and Cumulative Historical Knowledge

The expression of a continuity, of a permanence beyond the succeeding generations, through mortuary remains and sacred flutes (with their successive "double funerals" after each ritual) prompts us to consider the production of a form of memory in these societies clearly somewhat different from that present in those other Amazonian groups more concerned with erasing all reference to the dead. Perhaps these contrasting forms of relationship to the dead allow us to discern a shift from a cyclic temporality to a more cumulative conception of time—not truly historical in the sense we commonly understand, but one where the elements layer on top of each other. An indigenous kind of "chronology," in other words. In fact, it has often been claimed that Amazonian societies show little concern in establishing a chronology of past events, even relative, that would lead from a point of departure to the present, whether through oral tradition—which more often utilizes the forms of mythic narration—or the mostly rare transmission of objects and attributes (Menget 1999a). Symbolic objects as important as the trophies were seldom kept, but were rather abandoned because their value was held to decrease over time. Yet among the Yagua exactly the opposite took place: the trophies of human teeth were almost the only items the warriors passed down before their death to their male descendants. This was done in the hope of assuring them prosperity, strength, and longevity; at the same time they comprised a kind of living memory of killed enemies, as such necklaces were sometimes kept within families for three or four generations. Apparently similar procedures were reported on the Amazon in the middle of the eighteenth century by the missionary João Daniel (Chaumeil 2002). It is also known that many societies of the Guianas, the middle Amazon, and the Rio Negro used or still use various mnemonic systems, especially in the shape of knotted cords, which some authors have likened to rudimentary quipus. These were used not only to transmit messages, as Vidal (2000) indicates of the Warekena, but as marks or "calendars" for determining the dates for celebrating particular rituals or fixing the chronology of certain events (Chaumeil 2002). Much research remains to be conducted on these different indigenous systems of computation and memorization, which seem to imply a particular idea of chronology. Other societies have sought to preserve their historical memory by inscribing it in the landscape by way of myths and rituals (Santos-Granero 1998; Mansutti 2002; Wright 1993; Vidal 2000). All these authors have in fact stressed the importance in various groups including the Piaroa, Wakuénai, Warekena, Yanesha, and Paez of toponymy and particularly specific places—the famous "sacred spaces" or "topograms" in Santos-Granero's expression—in fixing and transmitting historical memory. Writing more specifically about the Yanesha, Santos-Granero has shown that the epic "voyage" of the solar divinity Yompor Ror retraces in close detail what we know today of the historical migration and settlement of Yanesha populations; equivalents may be found in the mythic "journeys" of Wajari among the Piaroa or Kuwai among the Baniwa. Such "topographic writing" shared by several Amerindian societies may be seen, then, as an important means of preserving historical memory in these oral cultures—in sum, a specifically indigenous mode of manipulating the past. Santos-Granero, however, detects an Andean influence in this process. This makes perfect sense in terms of the Yanesha, living at the base of the Andean mountains, but is less clear for the groups of the Rio Negro. These examples in any case tend to show that the idea of a chronology applied to certain facts of the past is not perhaps as absent in Amazonian as was thought.

Returning to the "sacred" musical instruments of more direct interest to us here, Robin Wright (1993; see also Vidal 2000 on the Warekena and Baré, and Hill 1993 on the Wakuénai) has explored a very similar idea in relation to the Baniwa of the Rio Negro in an article describing the mythic journeys of the cultural hero Kuwai in search of flutes (which incarnate his own body) stolen by women. In his quest, the hero geographically describes an immense territory based around a place of emergence common to numerous Arawakan groups in the region: the Isana River. Wright argues that these "journeys," punctuated by the flutes, retrace the ancient migrations and networks of intertribal exchange typical of the Arawak of northwest Amazonia at the time of contact; the Manoa, for example, were inserted in exchanges connecting the upper Rio Negro and the upper Amazon, an intermediate position that the Achagua similarly occupied between the Colombian llanos and the Antilles. The sites of the flutes may in this sense indicate territorial marks or legitimacy, serving as a topographical memory of ancient circuits. At a wider level, the journeys of Kuwai (or Wajari) perhaps express a form of cumulative historical knowledge, registering past experiences while remaining open to events. This explains why the Baniwa consider the old Brazilian capital of Rio de Janeiro a site of the hero Kuwai, since the chimneys of nuclear power stations they saw close to the city were for them a representation of Kuwai's flutes! (Wright 1993:24). Resumption of the sacred flutes ritual after a partial abandonment—a phenomenon observable among several groups of northwestern Amazonia as an emblem of ethnocultural revival—doubtless arises from this logic of reifying ancestral lines by legitimizing a presence or a territory.

This is also the case with the Asurini (Müller 1992). Confronting the construction of a hydroelectric plant on the Xingu that threatened to flood part of their territory, they indicated the presence in the area of a number of "cemeteries," the ancient graves of warriors, evoking for them the memory of the dead. Among the Mapoyo of Venezuela, a Carib group once thought to be on the brink of extinction, it has likewise been shown (Scaramelli and Tarble 2000) that the change in funerary modes—reoccupation of the ancient cave-cemeteries—corresponds to their return in force on the Venezuelan political scene at the moment of the discovery and exploration of a deposit of bauxite on their territory. The use of the past to defend or justify cultural or territorial rights is, as we know, a general phenomenon in Amazonia (and elsewhere) and probably existed well before the present (Vidal 2000). With this in mind, it would certainly be intriguing to study the numerous messianic movements that have convulsed the Arawak cultures of the Amazon and Rio Negro from the middle of the eighteenth century onward, invariably interpreted as a form of resistance against colonial domination. These complex questions and the different processes they imply would obviously demand a study in itself. For now I simply wish to underline the idea that relations to time and history among societies that conserve their dead or reembody them in ritual objects are different from those relations among societies that strive to make the dead vanish as quickly as possible. In place of an exocentric definition of society, where alterity acts as a strong encompassing value, we find another definition, centered much more on the self, on generational continuity, and on relations between the living and the dead, where the cult of sacred flutes occupies a central role. (See the centrifugal/centripetal distinction proposed by Fausto 2001 as a way of characterizing these two sociocosmological regimes, as well as the logical and historical possibilities of shifting from one to the other.) If the above is correct, this instrumental ensemble would not only have an ultimate function of incarnating the dead but also perhaps the primary function of perpetuating memory over the generations. More than a ritual object of substitution, the flute complex would comprise a cognitive operator allowing society to be imagined in continuity with its own dead.

Conclusion

Our rapid examination of these topics does not, therefore, provide total confirmation of the thesis that the archetypical form of mourning in the South American lowlands rests essentially on a relation of exclusion vis-à-vis the dead, transforming the latter within paradigms of alterity whereby no one would dream of consecrating a specific place to them or of fixing them in their memories. Although a large amount of empirical data can be cited to support this thesis, an equally large amount contradicts it—a fact borne out by the two series of funerary treatments highlighted in this text. Rather than the *socius* being collectively defined in relation to the exterior by treating its own dead as strangers, the aim is to avoid losses by conserving the dead "at home." However, far from excluding each other, the two scenarios may perfectly well coexist within the same culture. The majority of Amazonian groups possess several funerary modes, depending, among other factors, on the type of death involved or the status of the person who died. The present text has particularly sought to emphasize the importance of the conservation of bones in various different forms (as relics, substitutes, flutes, and so on, the question of osteophagy remaining open) as part of the process of continuity and remembrance of the dead—or at least some of them, generally the most eminent persons: the chiefs, shamans, great warriors, or combatants felled in foreign lands. In sum, it is more a question of creating an adequate distance from or relation to the dead than of systematically obliterating them via a collective amnesia. At the same time, analysis of these materials forces us to reflect on the production of different forms of historical memory in these societies.

Questioning the degree of complexity of funerals in the lowlands is one thing; inquiring into the type of memorization put into action in these contexts is another. Everything depends on whether the mortuary memory concerns the individuality of the deceased, set to become an "ancestor," or the anonymous collective represented by the community of the dead, with no prospect for individual survival. In this case too, the two scenarios coexist, but with the detail that, as a whole, explicit genealogical references are maintained only for important dead figures, whose names and exploits are often immortalized in particular genres of biographic or epic tales, as reported among the Xavante, the Yagua, or certain groups of the upper Xingu. Moreover, it perhaps makes more sense to qualify these figures as "immortals" than as "ancestors." In any event, the "sacred" flutes that have retained much of our attention in this work may perhaps occupy an intermediary position between these two poles, between the "ancestors" and the anonymous collective representing the community of the dead.

One thing in any case seems certain. The differential or selective treatments reserved to the dead in numerous Amazonian societies imply the existence of forms of internal social differentiation much more pronounced than previously thought—a fact corroborated by recent archaeological research. They also reveal funerary practices that are infinitely more varied and elaborate than those more generally presented to characterize lowlands societies.

Acknowledgments

This article is a modified and updated version of "Les os, les flûtes, les morts: Mémoire et traitement funéraire en Amazonie," published in *Journal de la Société des Américanistes* 83 (1997). I warmly thank Carlos Fausto for his comments and valuable suggestions.

References

Albert, Bruce. 1985. "Temps du sang, temps des cendres: Représentation de la maladie, système rituel et espace politique chez les Yanomami du sud-est (Amazonie brésilienne)." Ph.D. diss., Université de Paris X–Nanterre.

Albisetti, César, and Angelo Jayme Venturelli. 1962. *Enciclopédia bororo*, vol. 1. Campo Grande, Brazil: Museu Regional Dom Bosco.

Allard, Olivier. 2000. *Passé/présent des rites funéraires guarani*. Master's thesis, Université de Paris X–Nanterre.

Anônimo. 1865. "Memoria sobre os usos, costumes e linguagem dos Appiacás, e descobrimento de novas minas na Provincia de Mato Grosso." *Revista de Historia e Geographia do Instituto Histórico e Geographico Brasileiro* 6:305–318.

Århem, Kaj. 1980. "Observations on Life Cycle Rituals among the Makuna: Birth, Initiation, Death." Göteborgs Ethnografiska Museum, Annual Report for 1978:10–47.

————. 1981. *Makuna Social Organization: A Study in Descent, Alliance and the Formation of Corporate Groups in the North-Western Amazon*. Uppsala: Almquist and Wiksell International.

Baldus, Herbert. 1937. "O culto aos mortos entre os Kaingang de Palmas." In *Ensaios de etnologia brasileira*, 8–33. São Paulo: Companhia Editora Nacional.

Basso, Ellen B. 1973. *The Kalapalo Indians of Central Brazil*. New York: Holt, Rinehart and Winston.

Boglar, Luis. 1958a. "Urn Burial of the Brazilian Indians." *Acta Ethnographica* 6(3–4):347–355.

————. 1958b. "Ein endokannibalischer Ritus in Südamerika." In *Miscellanea Paul Rivet, octogenario dicata*, 2:67–85. México: Universidad Nacional Autónoma de México.

————. 1959. "Some Notes to Burial Forms of the Brazilian Indians." In *Opuscula Ethnologica Memoriae Ludovici Biro Sacra*, edited by Tibor Bodrogi and Luis Boglar, 159–163. Budapest: Akademiai Kiado.

Cadogan, León. 1950. "La encarnación y la concepción: La muerte y la resurrección en la poesía sagrada 'esotérica' de los Jeguaká-va Tenondé Porä-Güé (Mbyá-Guaraní) del Guairá, Paraguay." *Revista do Museu Paulista* (São Paulo) 4:233–246.

Carneiro, Robert. 1993. "Quarup: A festa dos mortos no alto Xingu." In *Karl von den*

Steinen: Um século de antropologia no Xingu, edited by Vera Penteado Coelho, 405–429. São Paulo: EdUSP.

Castelnau-L'Estoile, Charlotte. 2000. "Un maître de la parole indienne: Francisco Pinto (1552–1608), missionnaire jésuite au Brésil." *Arquivos do Centro Cultural Calouste Gulbenkian* 39:45–60.

Castro, Eduardo Viveiros de. 1992. *From the Enemy's Point of View: Humanity and Divinity in an Amazonian Society*. Translated by Catherine V. Howard. Chicago: University of Chicago Press.

———. 1996. "Os pronomes cosmológicos e o perspectivismo ameríndio." *Mana: Estudos de Antropologia Social* 2(2):115–143.

Cipolletti, María Susana, and Esther Jean Langdon, eds. 1992. *La muerte y el más allá en las culturas indígenas latinoamericanas*. Quito: Abya-Yala.

Chaffanjon, Jean. 1889. *L'Orénoque et le Caura*. Paris: Hachette.

Chaumeil, Jean-Pierre. 1992. "La vida larga: Inmortalidad y ancestralidad en la Amazonia." In Cipolletti and Langdon, *La muerte y el más allá*, 113–124.

———. 2001. "The Blowpipe Indians: Variations on the Theme of Blowpipe and Tube among the Yagua Indians of the Peruvian Amazon." In *Beyond the Visible and the Material: The Amerindianization of Society in the Work of Peter Rivière*, edited by Laura Rival and Neil Whitehead, 81–99. Oxford: Oxford University Press.

———. 2002. "Armados hasta los dientes: Los trofeos de dientes humanos en la Amazonia." In *Artifacts and Society in Amazonia*, edited by Thomas P. Myers and María Susana Cipolletti, 115–126. Markt Schwaben, Germany: Verlag Anton Saurwein.

Clastres, Hélène. 1968. "Rites funéraires Guayaki." *Journal de la Société des Américanistes* 57:63–72.

———. 1975. *La Terre sans mal: Le Prophétisme Tupi-Guarani*. Paris: Seuil.

Clastres, Hélène, and Jacques Lizot. 1978. "La Part du feu: Rites et discours de la mort chez les Yanomami." *Libre* 3:103–133.

Clastres, Pierre. 1980. "Mythes et rites des Indiens d'Amérique du Sud." In *Recherches d'anthropologie politique*, 59–101. Paris: éd. du Seuil

Coffaci de Lima, Edilene. 2000. "Com os olhos da serpente: Homens, animais e espíritos nas concepções Katukina sobre a natureza." Postgraduate thesis, Universidade de São Paulo.

Combès, Isabelle. 1992. *La Tragédie cannibale chez les anciens Tupi-Guarani*. Paris: Presses Universitaires de France.

Conklin, Beth A. 1995. "'Thus are our bodies, thus was our custom': Mortuary Cannibalism in an Amazonian Society." *American Ethnologist* 22(1):75–101.

———. 2001. *Consuming Grief: Compassionate Cannibalism in an Amazonian Society*. Austin: University of Texas Press.

Crépeau, Robert. 1999. "Rôle et signification des funérailles chez les Kaingang de Xapeco, Brésil." Actes du Colloque "Anthropologie et la mort," 28–33. Université de Montréal.

Crocker, Jon Christopher. 1977. "Les Réflexions du soi." In *L'Identité: Séminaire interdisciplinaire dirigé par Claude Lévi-Strauss*, edited by Jean-Marie Benoist, 157–184. Paris: Grasset.

Cunha, Manuela Carneiro da. 1977. "Espace funéraire, eschatologie et culte des ancêtres: Encore le problème des paradigmes africains." In *Social Time and Social Space in Lowland South American Societies*, edited by Joanna Overing Kaplan, 2:277–295. Paris: Peeters.

———. 1978. *Os mortos e os outros: Uma análise do sistema funerário e da noção de pessoa entre os índios Krahó*. São Paulo: Hucitec.

Debret, Jean-Baptiste. 1834–39. *Voyage pittoresque et historique au Brésil*. 3 vols. Paris: Firmin-Didot.

Descola, Philippe. 1993. "Les Affinités sélectives: Alliance, guerre et prédation dans l'ensemble jivaro." *L'Homme* 33(126–128):171–190.

Dobrizhoffer, Martin. [1783] 1822. *An Account of the Abipones, an Equestrian People of Paraguay*, vol. 2. London: John Murray.

Ehrenreich, Paul. 1948. "Contribuições para a etnologia do Brasil." *Revista do Museu Paulista* 2:7–135.

Eichenberger, Ralph. 1961. "Nacimiento, vida y muerte en la selva." *Perú Indígena* 9(20–21):51–65.

Erikson, Philippe. 1986. "Alterité, tatouage et anthropophagie chez les Pano: La Belliqueuse Quête de soi." *Journal de la Société des Américanistes* 72:185–210.

———. 1996. *La Griffe des aïeux: Marquage du corps et démarquages ethniques chez les Matis d'Amazonie*. Paris: Peeters.

Fauque, Père. [1736] 1843. "Excursion dans les terres entre l'Ouyapoc et le fleuve des Amazones." In *Lettres édifiantes et curieuses concernant l'Asie, l'Afrique et l'Amérique*, edited by M. L. Aimé-Martin, 24–29. Paris: Société du Panthéon Littéraire.

Fausto, Carlos. 2001. *Inimigos fiéis: História, guerra e xamanismo na Amazônia*. São Paulo: EdUSP.

———. 2002. "The Bones Affair: Knowledge Practices in Contact Situations Seen from an Amazonian Case." *Journal of the Royal Anthropological Institute* 8(4):669–690.

Fernández Distel, Alicia. 1984–85. "Hábitos funerarios de los Siriono (Oriente de Bolivia)." *Acta Praehistorica et Archaeologica* 16/17:159–182.

Figueroa, Francisco de. [1661] 1986. *Informes de Jesuitas en el Amazonas*. Iquitos, Peru: IIAP-CETA.

Frank, Erwin. 1994. "Los Uni." In *Guía Etnográfica de la Alta Amazonia*, edited by Fernando Santos and Frederica Barclay, 2:129–237. Quito: FLACSO; Lima: IFEA

Gélinas, Claude. 1996–67. "Eschatologie et configuration des rituels funéraires sud-américains: L'Importance du rapport d'identité entre les vivants et les morts." *Recherches Amérindiennes au Québec* 26(3–4):55–64.

Gomes, Denise. 2001. "Santarém: Symbolism and Power in the Tropical Forest." In McEwan, Barreto, and Neves, *Unknown Amazon*, 134–155.

Graham, Laura R. 1995. *Performing Dreams: Discourses of Immortality among the Xavante of Central Brazil.* Austin: University of Texas Press.

Gregor, Thomas. 1979. "Secrets, Exclusions, and the Dramatization of Men's Roles." In *Brazil, Anthropological Perspectives: Essays in Honor of Charles Wagley*, edited by Maxine L. Margolis and William E. Carter, 250–269. New York: Columbia University Press.

Grenand, Françoise, and Pierre Grenand. 1987. "La Côte d'Amapa, de la bouche de l'Amazone à la baie d'Oyapock, à travers la tradition orale Palikur." *Boletim do Museu Paraense Emilio Goeldi* 3(1):1–76.

Guapindaia, Vera. 2001. "Encountering the Ancestors: The Maracá Urns." In McEwan, Barreto, and Neves, *Unknown Amazon*, 156–173.

Gumilla, Joseph. 1758. *Histoire naturelle, civile et géographique de l'Orénoque*, vol. 1. Avignon: Jean Mossy.

Harner, Michael J. 1972. *The Jívaro, People of the Sacred Waterfalls.* Garden City, New York: Doubleday, Natural History Press.

Heckenberger, Michael. 1999. "O enigma das grandes cidades: Corpo privado e estado na Amazônia." In Novaes, *A outra margem do ocidente*, 125–152.

———. 2005. *The Ecology of Power: Culture, Place, and Personhood in the Southern Amazon, A.D. 1000–2000.* New York: Routledge.

Hill, Jonathan. 1993. *Keepers of the Sacred Chants: The Poetics of Ritual Power in an Amazonian Society.* Tucson: The University of Arizona Press.

Hugh-Jones, Stephen. 1979. *The Palm and the Pleiades: Initiation and Cosmology in Northwest Amazonia.* Cambridge: Cambridge University Press.

———. 1993. "Clear Descent or Ambiguous Houses? A Re-Examination of Tukanoan Social Organisation." *L'Homme* 33(126–128):95–120.

Ihering, Hermann von. 1907. "As cabeças mumificadas pelos indios mundurucus." *Revista do Museu Paulista* 7:179–201.

Keller-Leuzinger, Franz. 1874. *The Amazon and Madeira Rivers.* London: Chapman and Hall.

Léry, Jean de. [1580] 1992. *Histoire d'un voyage fait en la terre du Brésil—1557.* Montpellier: Max Chaleil. Translated by Janet Whatley as *History of a Voyage to the Land of Brazil, Otherwise Called America* (Berkeley and Los Angeles: University of California Press, 1990).

Linné, Sigvald. 1928. "Les Recherches archéologiques de Nimuendajú au Brésil." *Journal de la Société des Américanistes* 20:71–91.

———. 1929. *Darien in the Past.* Göteborg: Elanders.

Mansutti, Alex. 2002. "Le Parcours des créatures de Wajari: Socialisation du milieu naturel, système régional et migrations chez les Piaroa du Vénézuéla." Ph.D. diss., EHESS, Paris.

Marcoy, Paul. 1869. *Voyage à travers l'Amérique du Sud, de l'Océan Pacifique à l'Océan Atlantique.* 2 vols. Paris: Hachette.

Maroni, Pablo. [1738] 1988. *Noticias auténticas del famoso río Marañón.* Edited by Jean-Pierre Chaumeil. Monumenta Amazónica B4. Iquitos, Peru: IIAP/CETA.

McCallum, Cecilia. 1996. "Morte e pessoa entre os Kaxinawa." *Mana: Estudos de Antropologia Social* 2(2):49–84.

McEwan, Colin, Cristiana Barreto, and Eduardo Neves, eds. 2001. *Unknown Amazon: Culture in Nature in Ancient Brazil.* London: British Museum Press.

Meggers, Betty J., and Clifford Evans. 1957. *Archeological Investigations at the Mouth of the Amazon.* Washington, D.C.: Smithsonian Institution, Bureau of American Ethnology.

Menget, Patrick. 1993. "Notas sobre as cabeças Mundurucu." In *Amazônia: Etnologia e historia indígena,* edited by Eduardo Viveiros de Castro and Manuela Carneiro da Cunha, 311–321. São Paulo: NHII-USP, FAPESP.

———. 1999a. "Entre memória e história." In Novaes, *A outra margem do ocidente,* 153–165.

———. 1999b. "A política do espirito." In Novaes, *A outra margem do ocidente,* 167–180.

Métraux, Alfred. 1928a. *La Civilisation matérielle des tribus Tupi-Guarani.* Paris: Paul Geuthner.

———. 1928b. *La Religion des Tupinamba et ses rapports avec celle des autres tribus Tupi-Guarani.* Paris: Ernest Leroux.

———. 1930. "Contribution à l'étude de l'archéologie du cours supérieur et moyen de l'Amazone." *Revista del Museo de La Plata* 32:145–185.

———. 1946. "The Caingang." In *Handbook of South American Indians,* edited by Julian H. Steward, 1:445–475. Washington, D.C.: Smithsonian Institution, Bureau of American Ethnology.

———. 1947. "Mourning Rites and Burial Forms of the South American Indians." *América Indigena* 7(1):7–44.

Müller, Regina. 1992. "Muertos y seres sobrenaturales, separación y convivencia: Principios cosmológicos en la concepción asurini de la muerte." In Cipolletti and Langdon, *La muerte y el más allá,* 77–90.

Murphy, Robert F. 1958. *Mundurucu Religion.* Berkeley and Los Angeles: University of California Press.

Nimuendajú, Curt. 1949. "Os Tapajó." *Boletim do Museu Paraense Emilio Goeldi* 10:93–106.

————. 1952. *The Tukuna*. Translated by William D. Hohenthal. Berkeley and Los Angeles: University of California Press.

Nordenskiöld, Erland. 1920. *The Changes in the Material Culture of Two Indian Tribes under the Influence of New Surroundings*. Göteborg, Sweden: Elanders.

————. 1930. *L'Archéologie du bassin de l'Amazone*. Paris: G. Van Oest.

Novaes, Adauto, ed. 1999. *A outra margem do ocidente*. São Paulo: Companhia das Letras.

Oakdale, Suzanne. 2001. "History and Forgetting in an Indigenous Amazonian Community." *Ethnohistory* 48(3):381–401.

Overing, Joanna. 1993. "Death and the Loss of Civilized Predation among the Piaroa of the Orinoco Basin." *L'Homme* 33(126–128):191–211.

Palavecino, Enrique. 1944. "Practicas funerarias norteñas: Las de los indios del Chaco." *Relaciones de la Sociedad Argentina de Antropologia* 4:85–91.

Pereira, Manuel Nunes. 1954. *Os indios Maués*. Rio de Janeiro: Organização Simões.

Perrin, Michel. 1979. "Il aura un bel enterrement. . . Mort et funérailles Guajiro." In *Les Hommes et la mort: Rituels funéraires à travers le monde*, edited by Jean Guiart, 113–125. Paris: Le Sycomore.

Pétesch, Nathalie. 1983. "La Mort et l'identité sociale en Amazonie: Les Mécanismes de reproduction sociale des sociétés Gê et Bororo." Master's thesis, Université de Paris X.

————. 2000. *La Pirogue de sable: Pérennité cosmique et mutation sociale chez les Karaja du Brésil central*. Paris: Peeters.

Pollock, Donald. 1993. "Death and the Afterdeath among the Kulina." *Latin American Anthropology Review* 5(2):61–64.

Porro, Antonio. 1996. *O povo das águas: Ensaios de etno-história amazônica*. Petrópolis, Brazil: Vozes/EdUSP.

Reichel-Dolmatoff, Gerardo. 1945. "Los indios Motilones." *Revista del Instituto Etnológico Nacional* 2(1):15–115.

————. 1989. "Biological and Social Aspects of the Yurupari Complex of the Colombian Vaupés Territory." *Journal of Latin American Lore* 15(1):95–135.

Rival, Laura. 1993. "The Growth of Family Trees: Understanding Huaorani Perceptions of the Forest." *Man* 28:636–652.

Roosevelt, Anna C. 1993. "The Rise and Fall of the Amazon Chiefdoms." *L'Homme* 33(126–128):255–283.

Rostain, Stéphen. 1994. "La Mort amérindienne: Une Synthèse ethnohistorique." In *L'Occupation amérindienne ancienne du littoral de Guyane*, 2:637–668. Paris: ORSTOM.

Roth, Walter Edmund. 1924. *An Introductory Study of the Arts, Crafts, and Customs of the Guiana Indians*. Washington, D.C.: Smithsonian Institution.

Rouse, Irving. 1992. *The Tainos.* New Haven, Connecticut: Yale University Press.

Santos-Granero, Fernando. 1998. "Writing History into the Landscape: Space, Myth, and Ritual in Contemporary Amazonia." *American Ethnologist* 25(2):128–148.

Scaramelli, Franz, and Kay Tarble. 2000. "Cultural Change and Identity in Mapoyo Burial Practice in the Middle Orinoco, Venezuela." *Ethnohistory* 47(3–4):705–729.

Schaan, Denise. 2001. "Into the Labyrinths of Marajoara Pottery: Status and Cultural Identity in an Amazonian Complex Society." In McEwan, Barreto, and Neves, *Unknown Amazon,* 108–133.

Schaden, Egon. 1959. *A mitologia heróica de tribos indígenas do Brasil.* Rio de Janeiro: Ministério da Educação e Cultura.

Silva, Alcionilio Brüzzi Alves da. 1955. "Os ritos fúnebres entre as tribos do Uaupés (Amazones)." *Anthropos* 50:593–601.

Stahle, Vera-Dagny. 1971–72. "Carreras ceremoniales con troncos entre Indios brasileños." *Folklore Americano,* 17:117–124.

Stirling, Matthew W. 1938. *Historical and Ethnographical Material on the Jivaro Indians.* Washington, D.C.: Smithsonian Institution.

Surrallés, Alexandre. 2000. "Passion, mort et maladie dans une culture amazonienne." In *En substances: Textes pour Françoise Héritier,* edited by Jean-Luc Jamard, Emmanuel Terray, and Margarita Xanthakou, 387–396. Paris: Fayard.

Taylor, Anne-Christine. 1993. "Remembering to Forget: Identity, Mourning and Memory among the Jívaro." *Man* 28(4):653–678.

———. 1996. "Une Courte histoire de l'oubli: Perspectives jivaro sur la mémoire des morts et la destinée des vivants." *Ateliers* 17:79–88.

———. 1998. "Corps immortel, devoir d'oubli: Formes humaines et trajectoires de vie chez les Achuar." In *La Production du corps,* edited by Maurice Godelier and Michel Panoff, 317–338. Paris: Archives Contemporaines.

Thomas, Louis-Vincent. 1980. *Le Cadavre: De la biologie à l'anthropologie.* Paris: Complexe.

Tocantins, Antonio Manoel. 1877. "Estudos sobre a tribu mundurucu." *Revista do Instituto Histórico e Geográfico Brasileiro* 40(2):73–161.

Vidal, Silvia. 2000. "Kuwé Duwakalumi: The Arawak Sacred Routes of Migration, Trade, and Resistance." *Ethnohistory* 47(3–4):635–667.

Viertler, Renate Brigitte. 1991. *A refeição das almas: Uma interpretação etnológica do funeral dos índios Bororo—Mato Grosso.* São Paulo: Hucitec/EdUSP.

Vignati, Milciades Alejo. 1941–46. "Censo óseo de paquetes funerarios de origen guarani." *Revista del Museo de La Plata* 2(9):1–11.

Vilaça, Aparecida. 1992. *Comendo como gente: Formas do canibalismo wari'.* Rio de Janeiro: EdUFRJ.

———. 1998. "Fazendo corpos: Reflexões sobre morte e canibalismo entre os Wari' à luz do perspectivismo." *Revista de Antropologia* 41(1):9–67.

———. 2000. "Relations between Funerary Cannibalism and Warfare Cannibalism: The Question of Predation." *Ethnos* 65(1):83–106.

Wright, Robin M. 1993. "Pursuing the Spirit: Semantic Construction in Hohodene Kalidzamai Chants for Initiation." *Amerindia* 18:1–39.

Zerries, Otto. 1960. "El endocanibalismo en la America del Sur." *Revista do Museu Paulista* 12:125–175.

9

Xinguano Heroes, Ancestors, and Others

Materializing the Past in Chiefly Bodies, Ritual Space, and Landscape

Michael Heckenberger

> Memory is life, borne by living societies founded in its name. . . .
> History, on the other hand, is the reconstruction, always problematic
> and incomplete, of what is no longer. Memory is a perpetually actual
> phenomenon, a bond tying us to the eternal present: history is a
> representation of the past.
>
> Pierre Nora, "Between Memory and History"

This chapter explores aspects of cultural memory as expressed in discourse, material culture, and the built environment among Xinguano peoples of northern Mato Grosso state, Brazil. Xinguano refers to a plural society of closely related communities who occupy the basin created by the headwaters of the Xingu River, one of the principal southern tributaries of the Amazon. Today most of their traditional territories are included in the Parque Indígena do Xingu (PIX). Since the nineteenth century, when Karl von den Steinen (1886, 1894) first described the region, Xinguano or Upper Xingu society has been composed of nine or more single or multiple-settlement communities. This essay focuses on one community, the Kuikuro, but describes features generally shared by other Xinguano communities, which include three other dialect communities of Carib speakers (the Kalapalo, Matipu, and Nafuqua), three Arawak-speaking communities, and two Tupi-speaking communities.[1]

The Kuikuro have much in common with other Amazonian peoples, as amply documented in recent (post-1880s) ethnographic history: they are fisherfolk and manioc farmers, supplementing these staples with a diverse range of other managed and cultivated plants; they have a general worldview that fits well within what is described as Amazonian animism; they bedeck themselves with few "clothes," favoring instead body decoration and colorful "accessories"; they dwell in large pole-and-thatch houses, in settlements generally lacking any permanent standing structures.

Archaeology suggests that many basic elements of agricultural and fishing technology, house manufacture, and village configuration have ancient roots and were characteristic throughout the past millennium. Correlating archaeology and indigenous history also enables accurate placement of many of the ancient settlements mentioned in Kuikuro histories radiocarbon-dated to the sixteenth century and soon after. When considered over the long term, the Kuikuro exhibit a variety of features considered common if not typical of small-to-medium-sized complex societies elsewhere in the world, although these features are underemphasized and underrepresented in twentieth-century ethnography. They live in permanent, structurally elaborate settlement areas. They are densely settled throughout much of the basin, and supported by a productive agricultural and wetland management system. They have a sociopolitical structure that is dominated or "topped" by a hereditary hierarchy. This hierarchy extends across the region within a peer society of hereditary chiefs who engage in formal exchange, intermarriage, and co-participation in chiefly rites of passage, all of which creates substantial differences in symbolic capital in the local and regional political economy. Hereditary chiefs not only mediate these rituals but, in so doing, often amass large surpluses of food stuffs and wealth for ritual payments.[2]

Xinguanos, in general, are thus notable among ethnographically known Amazonian peoples for the degree to which the ritual construction of persons is tied to real or imagined genealogy. History and cultural memory are activated, so to speak, by genealogy, specifically through performance of mortuary feasts and other chiefly rites of passage, which make present cultural memories of founding ancestors and "sediment" them in place. Not surprisingly, ancestor recognition and commemoration, or simply "ancestrality," is a keystone characteristic of social and symbolic reproduction and the transmission of political power. Sociality is rooted in internal hierarchies based on hereditary rank, which are legitimized within a regional structure of exchange, and local history takes on a hagiographic quality. Ranking leaders are thus current "reproductions" of recent and distant ancestors, expressed through name transmission and exclusive control over ritual narrative and performance that invokes in diverse ways more distant founding ancestors and ancient culture heroes.[3]

This personification of the past links living human subjects, and specifically, the hereditary chiefs, individuals marked as being *aneti*, or "chiefly," and ancient human ancestors (past *aneti*). This line extends back in time to the creation of humans by the human-form creators, who later transformed themselves into the Sun and Moon, from the first human family (and first *anetï*, chiefs, who founded a special lineage, which corresponds to the *anetau* [plural] elite and their personal histories). It is also unusual in regional ethnology in the degree to which the past is "privatized," or, in other words, ancestors are exclusive "property" of living chiefly individuals. Hereditary leaders are thus uniquely historical, the products and producers of history, since they embody collective histories, identities, and cultural memory in a particularly direct way (Sahlins 1985). These patterns, although uncommon ethnographically in many parts of the Amazon, holds important clues to understanding the nature of large, settled populations scattered widely throughout the region centuries ago. This essay briefly explores two aspects of cultural memory: (1) historicity (indigenous views on history) and, in particular, how chiefly subjects are constructed both as individuals and as model persons, living exemplars or iterations of ancestors, past chiefs, and therefore stand in a sense between humans and ancestors; and (2) temporality (the way history and time are remembered or "felt" in nondiscursive ways) and, specifically, how material culture, ritual performance, and the built environment make the past present and visible as cultural memory.

Making History

The Kuikuro have diverse forms of narrative, as well as myriad ways in which daily and ritual practice are sedimented in material culture and the built environment. Therefore substantial contextual variation exists in how the passage of time and cultural memory, including narrative histories, are experienced. To some degree, narrative moods or genres reflect different conceptions of time. There are narratives internally marked as historical gravitating around historical personages, whereas others are marked as myths of "dawn time" people. Although both of them are categorized as "real narratives" (*akiña hekugu*), they are distinguished by a contrast between a time "when we were already people" (*kugei leha kukatamini*) and a time "when we were all still spiritual beings" (*itsekei gele kukatamini*) (see Fausto et al., forthcoming). Other verbal genres contain a sense both of linear and of cyclical time. A notable example is the formal discourse (*anetâ itaríñu*) used by chiefs when receiving foreign visitors. This discourse recounts collective founder genealogies that include elements of cosmogonic myths, but also the relations between language groups, through reference to common ancestors, the founders of the local group (*otomo*), and their chiefly peers in older times, who represent the ancestors of other *otomo*, as well as many specific features of landscape, social and ritual life, and nonhuman beings.[4]

Xinguano ritual cycles also reflect different conception of time. Many performances are geared toward communication with spirits, as in the case of *unduhe* masking rituals; others, like the chiefly rites of passage, notably initiations and mortuary feasts, reenact genealogical time and a relation with immediate ancestor figures (Franchetto 2001, 2003). Historical changes are also clear, particularly in recent times, as historical consciousness was piqued by contact with national society (see Turner 1991, 1993). Archaeology and early ethnohistory suggest that precolonial indigenous history was punctuated with large-sale, dynamic changes, as was true throughout the colonial and national periods. Certain aspects of historical consciousness, which have been part and parcel of Xinguano historicity and temporality throughout their history are "hot" (dynamic and historical) and/or "cold" (cyclical and mythic) depending on context and perspective (Hill 1988). Persons and their moods change as they pass through events and places and contexts, punctuating history and giving it a dynamic or deictic quality, within an overall theory of history that itself is context- or mood-oriented (Basso 2005).

Basso (1985:61) neatly captures critical elements of indigenous Xinguano history:

> history [is] a cultural form that combines narrative discourse with a theory of past events. . . . the Kalapalo sense of history is based as much upon ideas about actors, their moods, motivations, and goals, as upon events. Moreover, actors are treated in terms of their relationships to one another, the feelings they provoke within each other and the motives arising from these feelings. It is this focus that gives Kalapalo historical narrative a distinctly different character from that of contemporary European scholarship, in which personal motivation is subservient to generalized processes, forces, ideas, or interests that are held to exist in the abstract, independently of individuals. It is similar to the "Great Man" view of history, which stresses personal motivations as pivotal, but the Kalapalo emphasis upon interpersonal processes suggests that even this European view of history, like more modern ones, is concerned with different problems and manifests differing ideas of causality.

All cultural forms of memory are also structured by basic differences between groups, whether within a community, between communities (*otomo*), or between Xinguanos (*kuge*) and more distant "others," including other indigenous people (*ngikogo*) or whites (*kagaiha*) (Basso 1995; Ireland 1988, 2001). One of the most critical dimensions of Xinguano constructions of history, memory, and identity is social alterity based on rank-based distinctions. There are thus also aspects of Xinguano historicity that are deeply inflected by hierarchical notions of personhood, specifically of chiefs as remade ancestors. In this case, history is a mode of generalized communication or exchange not only between living persons but between types of persons, ancestors and descendants, within an ideology rooted in concepts of founder's or first-occupant identities. Although not conforming exactly to the old-style Great Man view of history, as Basso notes, this aspect of history conforms to that type of great-person history that Sahlins (1985) has aptly called "heroic history." It is this aspect of local conceptions of history, the past as embodied in high-ranking persons and places of the present, that is the focus here.

History and Hierarchy: Personifying and Privatizing the Past

Histories are good to hear, and every Kuikuro has at least some anecdotal knowledge of history, but knowing the details of group history is the business of the chiefs. As living extensions of other chiefly persons, who are remembered in histories, they stand in a special relation to creation stories, histories of founding ancestors and their deeds. The chiefly hierarchy itself is history—defined in terms of social and spatial relations within chiefly kindreds, between rival chiefly kindreds within and between communities, and between chiefs and commoners. It is clearly marked by the transmission of names, titles, ritualized dispositions, and places—that is to say, heritable "properties"—across generations. Hereditary leaders are like living ancestors, precisely because they have genealogies and, through these, come to legitimately embody founding ancestors of the group.

History is therefore not only a critical element of sociality but an important element of political strategy and power relations among the living, since the knowledge of and right to recount group histories is a critical element in political action and rivalry. As noted, Xinguano theories of history focus on both nonlinear (cyclical or so-called structural, ecological, or mythical) and linear (genealogical and historical) conceptions of time, depending on perspective or context. Thus it is critically important to see how historical subjects, persons, are constructed in ritual and daily life and, particularly, how some maintain control over ritual spaces and elite goods—symbolic and economic capital. The question is not simply how society at large conceives of history, as a collective pool of memory and experience, but also of who history is about, who is interested in it or controls it, and how it is deployed.

The formal speech of chiefs draws its force from the legitimacy of the past and the historical relations of the people and things contained in narratives. This is a special kind of history, which focuses attention on specific individual humans, notably chiefly persons, and how they encompass larger historical personages or larger segments of society: the sum of the social "bodies" subordinate to them, framed in an idiom of descent from founding ancestors. This can be cast as a question of how high or deeply one can engage group genealogy, within a regional society of chiefs that has come down through time since the creation of humans.

In *anetï itarïñu*, which is spoken only by primary titular chiefs in ritual events, the *otomo* (entire local group) is referred to as "children" (*kangamuke*), a use that reciprocally defines chiefs as group fathers. *Anetï itarïñu* deals specifically with named ancestors, but also with relations between generations, such as inheritance of substances, places, and things, which become indelibly attached to certain individual and aggregate persons, constituting the basis of the "cosmological authentication" of social hierarchies (Weiner 1992). Through the stanzas of chiefly discourse, a series of eight founding ancestors are invoked and ultimately linked to the three chiefs that created the Kuhikugu *otomo*, a single-village community existing at the time Karl von den Steinen first recorded Upper Xingu society around 1880. The ancestors named in one sequence of the *anetï itarïñu* belonged to ancient houses of Oti *otomo*, a large village predating the foundation of Kuhikugu *otomo*, the ancestral origin place of the contemporary Kuikuro (see Franchetto 1992).[5] The names recounted in these narratives, at least the final three, founders of Kuhikugu, remain in the Kuikuro pool of chiefly names, although the ranking family through much of the twentieth century was marked by other names (perhaps one day becoming the next in this list of specific Kuikuro ancestors).

In this formalized discourse, the nature of supralocal social relations is also specified, phrased in terms of special gifting relations to other *otomo*, specifically in terms of the unique village specialties including shell necklaces, ceramics, prized woods, salt, and other items used by Xinguanos as prestations and barter items during ritual occasions related to interactions between local groups (Franchetto 2003).

In various ways, such as by reference to and transmission of names, prestations, and place, as well as by the speech and gestures of living chiefs and by their positions in specific places (houses, villages, regions) at specific times, chiefs are linked to ancestral Kuikuro lines leading back to founding creator beings. Specifically, contemporary chiefs come to stand for, in the place of, the eight original founding chiefs of the Kuikuro who "are no more," as they say in the formal discourse, creating a past that is isomorphic with their person and "codified through the poetic resources of the *anetï itarïñu*" (Franchetto 1993:95; see also 2001). This genealogy of chiefs provides the grammar for the ritual legitimization of chiefly ancestors, a form of communication between humans and ancestors, but also crystallizes the social relation between and within groups based on actual social relations between the speaker (one of principal chiefs) and listeners (the local group and representative chiefs of other *otomo*).

The primary ritual context is the sequence leading up to the mortuary feast (*egitsï*, or more generally known by the gloss *kuarup*, the Kamayurá (Tupi-Guarani Xinguano) word for feast and special wood of ceremonial trunks (made of wood of the divine human grandmother, who was created of this wood by her father, the first ancestor of the human line). This ritual sequence is catalyzed by the death of a senior *anetï* and takes months to cycle through fully. The deceased *anetï* is typically closely related to the speaker, who is the sponsor or "owner" (*oto*) of the ritual. The ritual series confirms the high rank of *egitsï oto* and creates a metaphorical and narrative link between the living chiefs, the recently deceased Kuikuro *anetï* going back to the immediate ancestors of the group at Kuhikugu, and more ancient culture heroes, principally Taogi, the creator or father of Xinguanos and other humans. At various stages, kin relations between deceased and living *anetï* are reaffirmed, for instance in formal wailing where mourners call out their kin relation, as children, siblings, parents, grandparents, or affines, which are then mapped onto space in ranked arrangements keyed to the movements and actions of living persons, their dwelling in space.

Prismatic History and the Dawn Time

Histories of heroes and other ancestors are not only or even primarily about chronological marking, nor do they necessarily follow a precise sequencing of events, places, and personages. Nonetheless, these discourses are imbued with a linear, temporal quality in which reference to specific events and people is critical. Even if it is not the central message in much indigenous historicity, there is an obvious linear feel to much of history, both in genealogical and settlement history. In ritual performance of the *anetï itaríñu*, genealogical elements dominate not only the narrative structure but performance overall, including ritual and bodily orientations. Poetic speech and formalized actions in life crisis rituals bring about a metaphorical shift, a "prismatic effect," to a higher level of cyclical or social time.

Several major moments and performative episodes are noted that specify relations between humans and ancestors. At these times, this metaphorical "prismatic" effect turns one type of person, at least briefly, into another. Chiefly ancestors and their immediate descendants undergo a process of "transcorporeality," whereby they come to stand for specified others: as immediate ancestors of future *anetï ekugu* and as bearers of certain goods (craft specializations) that mark basic distinctions of rank and community affiliation. Ancestors thus have agency upon the living, or social relations, in the same way spirits do in a kind of "mirror world," since it is the histories of which they form a part that provide the script for the living, for ritualized performance and daily practice. These histories provide a bridge to even older ancestors, culture heroes (ancient chiefs), back to the dawn of time, since the central ceremony of Xinguanos, what distinguishes them as *kuge*, the people, was given to them by Taogi.

In the beginning, when Taogi created humans, just prior to transforming himself into the sun and lighting the world, he and his twin brother, Alukuma, later the moon, took down the mummified body of their dead mother, Hsangitsegu, hanging in the rafters and brought her back into the world of the living, just for a day, before she was allowed to die definitively, marking the first death in the ancestral line of humans. Upon her bodily transformation she became *añá*, a spirit, and founded the village in the sky where all Kuikuro ancestors go after death (see Carneiro 1989).[6] This death and rebirth of the divine grandmother of humanity was the beginning of the *egitsï* cycle. She was commemorated in the first *egitsï* ritual.

Hsangitsegu and her younger sister were made from *kuarup* wood (*uengifï* in Kuikuro) and animated by her creator and father, the cultural hero Kwantingï (Mavutsinin, in Kamayurá), who was himself half tree and half bat in parentage. Hsangitsegu was made to be given in marriage to the chief of the jaguars, Nitsuegï, who fathered her offspring, the twins Taogi and Alukuma. Through the coupling of the sun with his mother's sister, the great-great-grandparents of contemporary chiefs were born. Taogi made Xinguanos in the image of himself and his maternal family, and gave them their material culture, adornments, dances, and especially the great mortuary feasts, which made them human, *kuge*. This ritual complex of chiefly prerogatives and personhood is today the exclusive preserve of chiefs. Subsequently the twins transformed themselves into the sun (Giti) and moon (Ngune), not only providing light to the dawn-time world but also creating the origin point or birth of historical times, the age of *kuge*, which is marked by the first death, Hsangitsegu, after which things could die. It was also the first *egitsï*.

Making Chiefs

Hierarchical conceptions of social relations, dependent as they are on legitimate ties with ancestors, are inevitably tied to issues of history, the inheritance of the past. As earthly manifestations of ancestral lines of power, chiefs link contemporary individuals with collective history and ultimately with the founding ancestors of Xinguano society itself. All Kuikuro have ancestors, to the extent that recent forebears are remembered in one way or another, but some can be described as ancestors themselves, not only parents and grandparents but apical figures through which group genealogy is remembered. As apical descendants of previous chiefs, the firstborns of firstborns, *aneti ekugu* are apical ancestors of the living groups, and collective history becomes situationally isomorphic with chiefs, as aggregate subjects. History *and* subjectivity are constructed through the *anetau* (plural of *aneti*) and the social linkages they embody.

Public or group memory is enacted in ritual performance, spatial orientations, and practice, though the mediums of the human body and material culture, as much or more than it is remembered in discourse. Temporality, in large part, refers to how history and time are remembered or "felt" in nondiscursive ways or ways not explicitly conceived as history. It insinuates itself into every aspect of life as well, in elements of feeling, dwelling, and perception. Material culture, ritual performance, and the built environment all make the past present and visible as cultural memory, and ritual contexts are "turned on," so to speak, by the certain individuals who animate and are animated by the major ritual events.

In a local sense, space and society come to a point in many ritual occasions, the center of a concentric circle (the plaza), the *axis mundi* and center of public life, and the tip of a pyramid embodied in the great chiefs. As I have argued, this interplay creates historical links between current and ancient chiefs, the symbolic rebirth of Xinguano society, which mythically "naturalizes" hierarchical social relations. It does so by bringing the historical process under direct scrutiny in the context of "making" chiefly sons and daughters into chiefs and chiefs into ancestors. These ritualized actions reproduce and redefine space through the structured movements of people, and notably those of high rank; specific places are personified, and the people who occupy them become, or come to stand for, fathers, representatives, ancestors—in other words, founders—as well as leaders; the words and bodily deployments of the chief's performance draw history onto their person; there are no other great chiefs, they are all gone, as the *aneti itaríñu* states of recent ancestors, so that just the speaker remains, in place, the chiefly or "heroic" I (Franchetto 1993, 1996a, 1996b; see also Rumsey 1999; Sahlins 1985).

Changes of body or person, social and symbolic construction, are most directly at issue. In the case of high-ranking persons, this includes not only direct exchange between things and persons of similar proportions but also more generalized exchange between social beings of all kinds, including ancestors, other human communities, and nonhuman beings. The interactions between past and present ancestors, like that between the generations of parents and children in initiations, involve the "replacement" of old ancestors (older chiefs) with new ones. The immediate sons and daughters of the founding Kuikuro chiefs—and, through them, of the founding Xinguano ancestors—are the *anetï ekugu*, the "true" male chiefs, and the *itankgo* (singular and plural), or high-ranking women.

Of Heroes and Houses

In complex Kuikuro conceptions of personhood, hierarchy is rooted in the distinction of seniority, temporal precedence. In social settings, this distinction is often expressed as "shame" (*hïsene*), being in a state of humility, deference, or respect to a social superior (elder): to parents, older siblings, and chiefs, as well as affines.[7] This extends to the temporal sequence, encoded in the complicated Xinguano naming systems, which sequentially juxtaposes parents, children, grandparents, and grandchildren. These names embody not only individuals but social personages.

Formalized rank distinctions and defined elite status, wherever they are widely recognized as legitimate, depend to a large degree on actual genealogy. Social rank is framed in an idiom of descent, but requires little depth of actual genealogical knowledge: legitimacy is tied to specific recent ancestors. In these societies, descent—being one step closer to founding ancestors—becomes a primary dimension in the definition of social identities and boundaries. Actual genealogical links are often lost after three or four generations, but only the relationships with immediate predecessors are needed to establish linkages with deeper genealogies, which over time are pruned down to a few critical individuals, as is common among societies without written records.[8]

Individuals reckon descent differently based on their position in the existing chiefly hierarchies: high-ranking individuals place far greater emphasis on issues of genealogy and birth order than do most people, and are able to recount genealogical relations to specific chiefly figures going back more than a hundred years (Franchetto 1992; Ireland 1996). Lower-ranking individuals often place so little emphasis on genealogy as to be characterized by a "genealogical amnesia" (Gregor 1977). The historical result on the ground is the definition of a hierarchy of individuals of greater and lesser substance—great chiefs, recognized already as part of a historical "society" of chiefs; other chiefly persons, who may be inaugurated based on relations to the great chiefs; and commoners. One step closer to true ancestors thus means that chiefs are the ancestors of the local group, and through them more comprehensive sociohistorical partitioning is mapped over communities.

The pyramidal structure, although complex in terms of historical performances and social dynamics, can be viewed as an extension over time and space of a simple separation of elder (superior) and younger (inferior) siblings, based on primogeniture, since strong *anetï* are ideally the firstborn sons and daughters of firstborn parents, traced cognatically. The hierarchy thus relates to the depth one engages history as expressed in group genealogy (the founder's principle). This is defined by who can know, speak, and perform histories. Thus, an older sibling is closer to forebears than a junior and a senior line (firstborns) closer than a junior line, leading back to the founders of the village, the local group, and broader population clusters. This temporal succession is also implied in spatial and ritual arrangements of houses, settlements, and small regions.

This creates an upper tier of high-ranking individuals, a peer community of men and women who are unquestionably strong in chiefly blood and are separated (*aneti*) from the rest of society. These individuals inherit names and positions directly from ancestors and, through the course of their lives, come to "own" communal and sacred things—objects, structures, spaces, ritual knowledge, language—as they attain political stature. Principal among titled or "sitting" chiefs are *anetï ekugu* ("true" or "great" chiefs; and female *itankgo*), notably named "owners" (*oto*), the *hugogó òto* (the "owner of the middle") and the *eté òto* (the "owner of the village"), and, by extension, their heirs and coleaders: younger brothers, nephews, and especially sons and daughters. These men should have mastery of the full complement of chiefly knowledge and demeanor and be able to conduct the principal chiefly rituals; those who have learned to perform the chiefly discourse (*anetï itaríñu*) have to formally receive the messengers of peer communities.

A second tier is composed of weaker and ascendant political figures, "smaller" chiefs (*anetï insoño*) who, while having special rights and prerogatives—sponsoring rituals, labor projects, oration—are subordinate to primary chiefs. These secondary figures achieve prominence and move toward greatness (*anetï ekugu*) by acting as the temporary sponsors of lesser rituals such as men's masking and flute rituals, and female rituals, based on the inclusive hierarchy, including men and women, that relates to the strength of one's claims to *anetï* status.

Birth order is critical in households, composed of "heads" and their local kindred ("bodies"), or what Seeger (1977) termed *corporeal descent groups*: "substance lines" based on parentage and residence. Birth order is itself a form of temporal marking, which over time exalts certain "lines," but these do not correspond to a narrow definition of lineages, nor do they depend entirely (nor even closely in some contexts) on actual biological relatedness. Such social logic or configurations are more commonly known today as House societies, following Lévi-Strauss (e.g., 1987; see Carsten and Hugh-Jones 1995).

The chiefly House is organized around a core group of high-ranking men and women linked through common descent, which men and women share equally although they differ significantly in political and economic terms. Hierarchical relations are based on the bilateral (cognatic) transmission of names, titles, and ritual prerogatives. In the Xinguano case, titles and prerogatives are not controlled by individual *aneti* families, but can pass between high-ranking families, depending on actual social relations and who holds power and authority at any given time. Over the long term, there is no single dominant lineage, but instead competing Houses that at any moment in time are themselves reoriented into internally hierarchical social bodies.

In the present case, this has added significance in light of the regional and hierarchical nature of descent of all kinds: the self-scaling and metonymical qualities of Xinguano social formations, or, in other words, the iteration of cultural systems through time or across space. Thus we find households combined into Houses, which compose parts of peer communities that are still greater Houses, extending on up to the whole of the Xinguano people, the maximal "moral person," which is thus organized on basic principles grounded in family and domestic life.

At one level, the chief is primus inter pares among the household heads of multiple, chiefly nonchiefly, Houses, but at a higher communal level, the chief is symbolically situated at the apex of a pyramid, as head of the village, village clusters, or even the region, within a society of chiefs that includes all apical ancestors (founders), including the first (dawn-time) kindred.[9] While the local group (*otomo*) is the equivalent of the chief's maximal house, it is also highly factionalized and multicentric. Thus, what at one level or in one context seems fairly crystalline, pyramidal, and centric evaporates into a more amorphous, multicentric, and "flat" arena of competing interests and interests groups by changing the scale, perspective, and time frame. This does not negate, however, the underlying hierarchical organization of social relations.

The Mortuary Feasts

People are not simply born into or positioned along a developmental line, but are socially constructed through discourse and performance. People are reborn or "grow" by dwelling in and animating certain spaces and objects, and high-ranking people in particular are specially marked through chiefly life-crisis rituals, exclusive to the *aneti* and conducted each year. The process of chief-making and the reproduction of hierarchy begins through birthright, but it is in ritualized actions that hierarchy is most clearly expressed and negotiated—in ornamentation, bodily and spatial orientations, and demeanor. History is most visibly "calibrated" to changing contemporary social and political conditions and group composition through the performance of chiefs in rituals, particularly those that commemorate or "replace" ancestors (see Wagner 1989). Individual status is constructed or augmented in an indelible way. Exclusive wealth items, including objects, designs, spaces, structures, narratives, chiefly dialect, and even corporeal dispositions in formal settings, become the property of specific persons, in their lifetimes, and are exclusive to the *anetau* elite. These items become inalienable possessions of chiefs that both represent and perpetuate social hierarchies, which are reinvented, although not "zeroed," with each passing, each ritual birth and death.

In ritualized discourse, as noted, at certain moments in the ritual cycle the founding ancestors are invoked as key founding figures when chiefs literally come to stand in their places—in houses, villages, and ritual spatial organizations—and speak for or represent them. As community "representatives" they form or embody a critical strand of composite history, being seldom absent from discursive and spatial group memories, and history is a primary focus of their knowledge. They are specialists in group history and the conduct of rituals that reproduce the collectivity, since it represents their legacy and the reason they deserve to have one in the first place. In the most exemplary of these rituals, chiefly mortuary feasts (*egitsi*) and initiations (*tiponhi*), distinctions of rank and ancestry are emphatically and graphically represented throughout the year-long cycle.

Chiefly performance is as much corporeal and spatial as spoken, and combines diverse repetitive and serial elements (see Bourdieu 1977). This materiality focuses attention on successive reorientations of specific social bodies in place and material culture, particularly when the social body itself is rejuvenated in rites of passage, particularly the death of chiefs. In the *kuarup*, history is literally written onto the bodies, choreographed by and embodied in chiefs and their movements and actions in structured space—or, in other words, how they dwell in or inhabit the world. In fact, chiefs are paraded before all. The old chiefs (now true ancestors) and the living chiefs (newer versions of the deceased ancestors) are situated in ritual spatially and socially. A temporal order, a procession of "owners" (the founders of the *otomo*) represented as owners (*oto*) of rites of passage, is also perpetuated, as is the geography of the spaces through which they flow. These spaces, in turn, can be defined by successional "offices" that chiefs hold through their lives, including being *oto* of formal structures, such as major roads, bridges, communal weirs, the doors of the ceremonial house and the central house, the plaza center, the chief's house, and the village itself.

The principle of centrism permeates all ritual arrangements. Take, for instance, the benches stretched in a line when the kindred of deceased chiefs, for whom a *kuarup* is called, are bathed by the community to wash away the sadness of the death, thus releasing the community from formal mourning. The principal or principals sit in the middle, with the ranked order of their kindred(s) on either side, an order that will be duplicated in the placement of the *kuarup* trunks, with the one or two principals in the middle and a ranked order on either side. This order is also replicated in the order of boys' initiation. In the *tiponhï*, boys sit on stools, oriented hierarchically out from a center, proportioned to their social "size." They wear the *oinlape* and full-feather headdresses, unlike the rest of their cohort of initiates. These headdresses, the sunlike yellow and red diadems, and the *oinlape* are also placed atop the *kuarup* trunk representing deceased chiefs. The resemblance between the initiate chiefs and the initiate ancestor (the decorated *kuarup* trunk) is striking, and in these rituals of passage these hierarchies are inscribed on the ground and in materials, perhaps the most graphic being the form, size, and uniqueness of the things placed on and around chiefly bodies. An example is the set of small, medium, and large *yanapï*, ceremonial pots used in the ear-piercing festival among the Waura, Arawak-speaking Xinguano. Similarly, the three benches of chiefs that sit before their people, the guest *otomo*, during the culminating wrestling matches, are a graphic representation of hierarchy. In short, the deployment of chiefly bodies and, through them, all other bodies is always a critical aspect of the rituals. The sites of these rituals, of social and symbolic reproduction, are critical nodes not only of space but of cultural memory, as places.

The way visiting participants in these rites are also precisely partitioned into pie-shaped configurations around the plaza circle is another example of how social relations are inscribed in place, in this case reflecting the necessarily supralocal (inter-*otomo*) character of these rituals. The outside is taken here to have diverse meanings: ancestors and their in-laws, other Xinguano groups, or potentially even more distant "others," meaning "fierce Indians" and, today, "white people" (who have diversified extensively over the past two centuries and include numerous and varied members of nonindigenous cultures). Gifting is an important element of these diverse external relations, and chiefs also mediate the outside through gift-giving. Ritual or economic exchanges of prestige goods, including necklaces, headdresses, benches, and particularly such chiefly trappings as jaguarotooth necklaces, jaguar-skin diadems, certain special earrings, and communal symbols like the blackwood bow, are a critical manifestation of chiefly authority and political power.

Today the wood idols stand above the recently buried chiefs. They are dressed as living *kuge* should also be, wearing belts, necklaces, headdresses, and paints, and they are given food, participating one last time in the world of the living. The body of the divine mother, so to speak, is consumed productively by each subsequent generation not only through the *kuarup* idol, occupied briefly (one night) at the culmination of the *egitse*, but in all chiefly constructions, including the men's house and particularly the house of the chief (*tajïhe*) and the house of the dead (*tafïte*), an hourglass-shaped structure over the special grave, which itself contains diverse symbols of chiefly rank. Chiefs bring certain objects and

Fig. 9.1. *Kuarup* trunk idol of recently deceased chief in mortuary feast.

substances onto themselves, which reflect an ancestral power that only chiefs can use. Chiefs are positioned in the place of these ancestral beings, and exclusively use not only the *kuarup* wood but also the body parts of jaguars, the paternal kin of the creators, as well as the spaces where these things are placed.

In Xinguano society, wealth items are generally not passed from generation to generation as heirlooms, and thus hierarchical kin relations are defined, as often as not, by inheritance of the past (history) rather than vice versa—that is, by who actually inherits general chiefly prerogatives, such as objects, spaces, ritual orientations, and manners of speaking, rather than who could or should. In performance, and through objects and body design as well as names and allusion to founding ancestors of the local group, and through exclusive use of ritual knowledge and objects handed down from ancient ancestors and ultimately from creator beings, high-ranking persons come to embody ancestors. What is privatized, however, is not things but historical persons and living individuals who, through social and spatial proximity, come to control or otherwise occupy chiefly status in the historical group of "great chiefs."

Access to wealth is a function of prestige, first and foremost, and diverse specialists are required to meet the demands of ritual and daily consumption, including not only chiefs (*aneti*) but shamans (*hïati*), artists and skilled crafts-men (*ologi*), singers, dancers, and others. However, without a surplus of symbolic capital, inalienable properties such as names, titles, and esoteric knowledge, it is impossible to command or even strongly influence the primary cycles of socio-symbolic reproduction, and thus the collective identity and memory. Specialties can provide the means to mobilize alternative political strategies, but these must be legitimized through ritual recognition of degrees of chiefliness to enter into the dominant political flows of competing houses. Wealth items, especially pres-tige goods, are not the exclusive property of elite persons, only rotating between ranked chiefs, but clearly chiefs have an advantage in the quantities and qualities of goods they control. We can expect that even greater exclusivity was present in the past, in both spatial and material dimensions, given the much larger popula-tions and the lack of industrial tools, notably metal, guns, bikes, and motors, among other modern luxury items.

It is not only in the context of chiefly life-crisis rituals that these distinctions are important. The chief also delivers hortatory discourses, meant to cajole or praise basic Kuikuro values, which are not so much preached as performed through appropriate deployment of his body and his voice—for instance, late at night in the plaza, all alone, when only he can be heard. The commanding directionality of political oration and the authority of myth-history most eloquently express themselves, discursively, in chief's language and, corporeally, in ritual orchestra-tion (Franchetto 1993, 1996a, 1996b, 2001). Ancestors thus ultimately define what are traditional values, or the "right" and "wrong" way to be a person, since chiefs are refractions of ancestors who act the way they do because important personages did so in the past.

Making Landscapes

The way corporeal, social, ecological, cosmological, and ritual time combine to precipitate cultural memory is both situational and structured by tradition. It involves both present actions and their articulation with the residues of past ac-tion (material culture and built environment). Extending histories beyond the specific memories of living persons hinges on questions of practice and landscape. In this scale, the focus changes from what is said to what people do, to their lived experience. This temporality is suggested in Seeger's 1977 benchmark article on

Suyá conceptions of space and time, framing the issue of personhood in ways not anticipated by either the eco-functionalist or the structuralist tendencies that had dominated regional anthropology. In particular Seeger points to the contextual, processual, and historical elements of the built environment and, notably, suggests the importance of "body language" or corporeal deixis. Specifically, he notes situationally different actions in ceremonial settings and at nonceremonial times when divisions of space exercise less rigid control over individual activities. This cartography graphically represents a unique cultural history (Santos-Granero 1998). As Seeger recounts, part of being educated as a novice was to learn the names of the places he visited (1977). This knowledge is learned as much from dwelling as from hearing, and common experience links people (including researchers) with other people, from any time.

The present case resonates particularly strongly with the Suyá, not just because southern Arawak and Gê speakers share central plaza organization, generically, but since the Suyá are ao geographically and historically close. Among Xinguanos, specifically, Basso notes: "Stories about ancestors and ancestral places constitute a narrative bridge leading from actual experiences in recent times to the stories of the very distant past" (2001:296, my translation). The split that gave rise to the Kuikuro, for instance, is well remembered in a variety of stories, some of which are related to chiefs named in chiefly discourse. Other chiefly names pertain to older times, in the mid-eighteenth century, when the white men were "ferocious" and attacked various Xinguano settlements ancestral to the Kuikuro, and others go back yet farther, to the sixteenth and seventeenth centuries, when even older ancestral villages were occupied and abandoned (see Franchetto 2001; Heckenberger 2005). These names of persons and places not only are recounted in the chiefly discourse, the *aneti itaríñu*, but are permanent markers of past settlements, whereby the memory of the settlement is, to some degree, isomorphic with the major chiefs of that place. These stories and names from the past also form a pool of historical resources that chiefs draw from to make points about the past.

Ancestral places and the historical figures and events they emplace not only frame historical consciousness but also constitute a kind of cultural language of history, analogous to the utterances, stanzas, and sequences of narrative history. In Xinguano systems of language and knowledge production, one can get virtually anywhere, and by extension to anyone, by following out the logic and architecture of landscape. History is thus expressed, produced, and reproduced in a historically defined landscape of greater and lesser places, special settings, and locales, tied together through time and space by the specifiable actions of discrete human and other beings.

Social relations are not based only on who persons are but also, and perhaps more importantly, on who they were, where they came from in terms of ancestors, and what places they've been. Equally critical is who they will be, or should become, because of how they replace, fall short of, or exceed the ancestors of old, preserved in narrative memory: chiefs, shamans, bowmasters, and other great persons. Chiefs in particular are always remembered in place, like creation-story heroes. Chiefs are chiefs precisely because they are *oto*, owners of public architecture and works and ritual, and because they are in or even "of" these special, ritualized places—the *tajïfe*, the *kuakutu*, the *hugogo*, the *kuarup* wood trunk—where they are legitimized and divided further by use or not of special ornaments and designs such as the blackwood bows, the jaguar-claw necklaces, and jaguar-skin and sunlike feather diadems.

The plaza settlement is the most explicit text or manual of group history and its making, as the positions manifested by different social bodies define history to make it conform, in fairly exact terms, to the relations between the living. The places of ancient occupations are remembered, not only by physical relationships, nor by the communities who inhabit them, but particularly by the critical events and individuals who lived there, remembered in chiefly discourse and narratives (see Basso 1995). The greatest among these places, these passages of Xinguano history, are the plaza villages, remembered by the chiefs who reigned and died there, the chiefs for whom the elaborate mortuary feasts are held.

Hierarchy, in particular, is always linked to spatial distributions, such as where one walks, talks, sits, sleeps, or eats. Like persons, not all houses are constructed the same: some are larger, more finely constructed, and more elaborate. Design decisions have much to do with personal preferences or motivations, as well as the support available to any individual building a house. Not surprisingly, however, the houses of principal chiefly families, headed by the primary village chiefs, are typically bigger and better. They are also positioned in key areas of the domestic ring, corresponding to cardinal points and the orientation of the plaza and its formal causeways. This is important because positioning is as much a community as a personal decision.

The Xinguano "true" house (*üne*) is also a history, and it is made according to very exacting building standards: each space, each post, beam, stave, and door has a name, and each is positioned in a highly standardized way. The layout of a true house likewise follows a highly regular pattern, with specific domains marked according to gender and functional differences, notably a central public area and a peripheral domestic area. It also marks the hierarchical relations that characterize all houses, expressed in where one sleeps or stores one's things. The hammock of the highest-ranking individual in each of two household divisions is situated along the long axis of the house; the one on the right, as one comes though the front door, is the higher ranking of the two—the house "owner" (*üné òto*).

The village is highly differentiated and oriented to these selfsame principles: as noted, the most sacred of all village space is the plaza core (*hugogo*), which, insofar as it is "owned" by a single chief, can be seen as an incarnation of that individual(the *hugogó òto*) and more importantly of the office he represents. In other words, the plaza, men's house, and cemetery are institutions representing central and established practices, relationships, or organizations of society; they are also monuments to chiefs, both to living chiefs who own them and to the chiefly rank itself. Plazas are not only models of society and complex mnemonic devices that preserve knowledge of diverse sorts, they are also metaphors of chiefs, or chiefliness.

Villages are laid out according to a very clear design, an architectural grammar, based on widely shared meanings regarding spatial orientations. In other words, architecture and spatial organization encode much about society, about aesthetics, political organization, cosmology, gender relations. Villages are metaphors for society, as Lévi-Strauss and those influenced by him have so eloquently shown. As noted, Xinguanos have a keen awareness of geometry, that is to say of points, lines, and areas and their properties, measurement, and relations in space. This became clearly apparent as I was conducting my own mapping, with Kuikuro assistants, of the places, houses, villages, and archaeological sites that make up their territory. Xinguanos, although lacking a quantified system of measurement, have a sophisticated system of reproducing distances and angles, which, when combined with their developed system of counting, provides the ready means for highly precise architecture and engineering.

Like spaces within domestic units and houses, village spaces are allotted systematically to different kin groups based on their positions in the social hierarchy, with the primary chiefly individuals generally living at cardinal points opposite each other. There is no doubt, in other words, as to who's who in a village: the chief's house has roots coming out of the ends, it is usually bigger, and it always sits at one of the cardinal points. In the Kuikuro village, the kindred of the *hugogó òto* are at the south point, and his family has maintained this position for at least the last six decades. The village itself is thus an observatory—not only a cosmological observatory, oriented as it is to cardinal points, but also an observatory for the social relations of the villagers.

Spacing is always a critical aspect of ritual identities. Bodily indexicality or deixis refers to this material, gestural, and spatial staging of ceremonies and daily life. Importantly, it refers to the fact that elements of the built environment, and particularly ritual spaces, are situationally activated or animated by the people who are in them and what they are doing; in other words, they are "turned on" or "turned off" in different contexts.[10] Some perspectives are thus clearly marked and graphically represent conceptual categories, refractions of cultural notions of, for instance, place and the cosmos. When the chiefs of peer communities are sitting before their respective peoples, with the highest-ranking in the center and facing their host peers (the "owners" of the *kuarup*), the whole social and cosmological world is to some degree laid bare before their eyes, even though getting there was every bit as much about contingency and strategy as about tradition and replication. They not only interact with each other as individual human actors, they do so as "aggregate agents" operating simultaneously and expressing collective "agency."

Cultural and political history is "sedimented" in broader landscapes, once again organized according to the same sociospatial logic as houses and villages (see figure 9.2). Landscapes, as we have noted, are peopled with memories, histories, stories of the past, which also represent and perpetuate contemporary conditions of territory and property. Although actual land ownership beyond the village is primarily based on usufruct, continuity in land tenure is maintained between generations, since manioc gardens turn into piqui groves "owned" and inheritable among closely related kin within the context of long-term field rotation patterns. Relations that empower some and exclude others are diverse, but symbolic and economic capital are highly concentrated in the hands of hereditary chiefs. It is

Fig. 9.2. Aerial photograph of Kuikuro village, 2003.

easy to envision that, in the past, prime lands and resources, as well as labor and the flow of material wealth, would have been more tightly controlled by elite groups, creating the conditions for a fully political economy.

That time, space, and elements of personhood are inscribed in spatial organization and landscape, and in very precise ways, does not require that there be formalized units of measurement. The focus on material culture and the built environment is thus strategic, since these are essential if we wish to validly assign meaning to the archaeological past. The house, the mortuary feast, or the village is an iteration of this materiality, each choreographed with meticulous attention to partitioning space—who sits, sleeps, walks, and talks where, and with whom—creating a map of the Xinguano landscape of great detail, infusing the landscape and ethnocartographies with self-scaling cultural properties in diverse ways. Everywhere one looks, one sees pattern and regularity, the reproduction of relationship and proportion as well as distance and angle.[11] For instance, the way rafters are twined, the "weave" of the house, like that of the hammock, net, and basket, or the common linear and geometric designs, all encode mathematical and social principles.

Discussion

Although beyond the scope of this essay, which, in keeping with other volume contributions, focuses on ethnographic patterns, a look farther into the past suggests that the patterns noted here of exclusivity and power would likely have been even more rigidly defined and enforced, making the gap between elite and common all the more obvious and difficult to resist. While change occurred, the highly repetitive and precise orientations of east-west, right-left, center of a circle, and center of a line, bespeak a discipline associated with the movements of the body in ritual and domestic life that are also clearly visible in archaeological contexts. Large and densely distributed settlements of the deep past, some more than ten times the size of current villages, make likely that many of the relations described here were more accentuated and elaborated. Likewise, there were at least eight times as many of them, ordered by a clear, almost crystalline division into graded centers or nodes.

Xinguano communities and regional clusters are hierarchically ordered, according to genealogy, works, gender, and age, and we see that ancestors or, more precisely, ancestral places are likewise arranged according to these social principles. The regular placement of settlements, of central plazas, of all the residential areas, houses, roads, gardens, of all the estates across the region, only dissipates any lingering doubt that ethnophysics was every bit as complicated as ethnoecology among Amazonians. The historical outcome is both a hitherto unsuspected

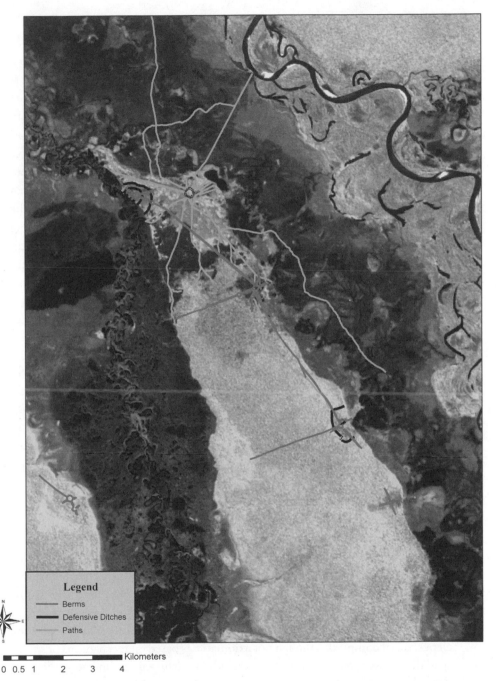

Fig. 9.3. Overview of Kuikuro village area in the Parque Indígena do Xingu (PIX), Mato Grosso, Brazil. *Note:* Overlain on Landsat 7, 8/03, with high-resolution contemporary community of Ipatse with radial roads/paths leading from it in upper right (light-colored) and prehistoric towns and road systems (darker) lines based on detailed ("real-time") GPS satellite image survey.

complexity of human cultural variation in the region, to match the enormous biodiversity, and the grim reality that much is a "widowed land."

When diverse and dynamic forms of cultural memory are considered, it becomes clear that Xinguano peoples do not deny history, nor do they wait for it expectantly or fatalistically, nor do they attempt to precipitate change, any more than most people, at least in the non-Western and particularly Native American world (Hill 1988). Their history is interesting in regional ethnology, however, in the attention placed on specific ancestors, and in how persons, things, and places come to stand for them in ritual. Such a history is, however, written on human bodies, dwellings, communal spaces, and the broader built environment, as much or even more than it is narrated. History is marked, punctuated, according to the life histories of specific places, people, and events, historical personages of varying sizes and ages, all ranked according to precise sociohistorical orders. Social replication—the "replacement" of ancestors—is a critical dimension, if not the leitmotif, of this cultural heritage, and draws our attention to the transposable and transcorporeal, or metonymical, nature of history, particularly in mortuary feasts.

In the Upper Xingu, when taking on past persona, taking them into oneself through the manipulation and exchange of ritual substances, one comes to "embody" larger families: one's House (minimal *otomo*), the local plaza settlement (typical *otomo*), or the "nation" (maximal *otomo*)—that is, the community or "moral person" at large, each with a specified territory. As is true of many small-to-medium-sized complex societies that are both regionally integrated and hierarchical, clear notions of genealogy, ancestral substance, and cosubstantiality of residence are critical. But the question remains: How can we observe these sociohistorical enchainments, the specific links between different types of histories and historicities?

Many authors have noted similar features—the personification of history, the focus and exaltation of certain persons in history, and the importance of ritual, in particular spectacular feasts—and their correlation with changes in sociopolitical organization, namely the emergence and persistence of hierarchical complex societies (Scarre 2005). This is not to say that Amazonian societies followed a pathway to complexity like other world areas defined before (see McIntosh 1999), but merely that when we consider the likely range of variation of past Amazonian peoples, their history was not entirely dissimilar either. In many early complex societies, social complexity, though not axiomatic, is based on mechanisms of social, spatial, and symbolic simplification, including partitioning, mnemonic devices, and self-scaling properties. The Xinguano conception of history, as contained in diverse forms of cultural memory, may in fact be one of the few living legacies of a modality of historical consciousness much more widespread in past (precolonial) times, one of large, settled agro-fisherpeople who were integrated in hierarchical regional polities.

Acknowledgments

Nearly two years of primary research in the Kuikuro village between 1992 and 2006 has been funded by the National Science Foundation, the Social Science Research Council, and the William T. Hillman Foundation. Special thanks to Bruna Franchetto and Carlos Fausto of the Museu Nacional, Rio de Janeiro, collaborators whose discussions and writings have inspired or inflected virtually every aspect of my Xinguano research. Ellen Basso's work over the past several decades has also inspired many of the ideas summarized here. Above all, I owe deep gratitude to the Kuikuro, and especially the principal chief, Afukaka.

Notes

1. The acculturation of outsiders into regional society—"becoming human," as Coelho (2001) puts it, paraphrasing an Aweti chief whose people had, in fact, been acculturated into Xinguano society some centuries ago—and permeable cultural boundaries have characterized regional interaction into recent times. Since the beginning of the nineteenth century the Bakairi (Carib), Trumai, Suyá (northern Gê), Ikpeng, and others have become enmeshed in the sociopolitical orbit of the Xinguano nation. The nation of related Xinguano peoples has included peripheral groups who have come into the now PIX territory within the past century or so and entered into relations with established or "core" communities who have traditionally occupied the headwater basin of the Xingu River, or upper Xingu, since at least 1,250 years ago (see Franchetto and Heckenberger 2001).

2. Certain characteristic features widely agreed upon by specialists, notably regional sociopolitical integration, hereditary leaders and social hierarchy, settled village life in plaza communities of numerous large longhouses, and productive agriculture and fishing technologies, can be inferred from archaeological data leading back a thousand years or more. These features are similar to those of culturally related Arawakan societies along the southern margins of the forested Amazon basin and beyond (Heckenberger 1996, 2005; Hill and Santos-Granero 2002).

3. See Foster 1995 and Wagner 1989 for an interesting comparative example from New Ireland. In the present case, names are transmitted from grandparents to grandchildren, along gender and age lines, and include several names for each person, related to the mother's and father's affinal name restrictions (and the ban on speaking names), but also related to life histories. Cycling names across generations is an ongoing process, and the current chief has already cycled through several names, although he retains the name of his own grandfather as his primary name in supralocal public interactions.

4. See Franchetto 1986, 1992, 1993, 1996a, 1996b, 2001, 2003 for definitive descriptions of historical and temporal cycles and forms among the Kuikuro from ethnolinguistic research conducted since 1975; see also Basso 1973, 1985, 1995, 2001 on the closely related Kalapalo dialect of upper-Xingu Carib, which she has studied since the late 1960s.

5. Amatuagu, one of the eight Oti *otomo* chiefs who helped found Kuhikugu *otomo*—the Kuikuro, ancestors of the current village of Ipatse *otomo*—was also a chief of an even more ancient, seventeenth- or eighteenth-century community, Tafununu, of ancestral Carib sites around the largest lake (*ipa*) in the region, also called Tafununu, the Ipa *otomo* (see Basso 1995).

6. Carneiro's 1993 article on the *kuarup* ceremony touches upon many things mentioned here, and Agostinho's (1974) and Basso's (1973, 1985) descriptions give further detail and variation on the ritual. The author has participated in six *kuarup*, once (1994) as an adopted kinsmen, two other times in the Kuikuro village (2001, 2003), and, as a visitor camped out with the Kuikuro contingent, twice in the Yawalapiti village (1993, 2003) and once (1993) in the Kamayura village.

7. *Hïsene* is the Kuikuro variant of a term that has equivalents in the other Xinguano languages. *Kamaga*, to refer to nonchiefly individuals, is likely derived from the Brazilian word *camarada*, but the critical issue is that elite status, high rank, is marked and named.

8. Adams and Kasakoff (1986:61) note that oral societies seldom "record reasonably full genealogies back more than three generations" and those that do go back farther in time are/were "invariably of the descendants of a tribal hero or demigod, pruned of any links that were not necessary to tie the living into a web of nameable relationships."

9. This is shown when representatives are chosen from the *anetï* ranks to mediate or participate in chiefly rituals, which marks them graphically. In a recent "democratic" move, the kindred hierarchy of the principal chief was reproduced in the recently formed community organization: the eldest brother (1), who is the principal chief, became honorary president; the second-eldest brother (2) became president; their brother-in-law became vice president; the youngest brother (half brother to 1 and 2) became secretary; and the eldest son of 2, the oldest male child of 1 and 2 combined, became treasurer.

10. Ellen Basso's discussions (1985, 2005) of discourse, performance, and specifically "deixis" are particularly critical here, since the Kalapalo are members of the same language "cluster" in the regional Xinguano culture/nation. See also Franchetto 1986, 1993, 2001.

11. It is often difficult to elicit a concrete answer, let alone a formula or formalized unit, regarding the designs on bodies, and things, and across places that instantiate Xinguano mathematics. The principles are, however, encoded in virtually everything: counting lines, making tokens, wefts, house posts, carefully measured distances the size of a blade of grass, an arrow cane, or even a long, extended cord, which may then be graduated by the measured distance from chest to outstretched hand of the person responsible for doing this: the chiefly "cubit."

References

Adams, John W., and Alice B. Kasakoff. 1986. "Anthropology, Genealogy, and History: A Research Log." In *Generations and Change: Genealogical Perspectives in Social History*, edited by Robert M. Taylor Jr. and Ralph J. Crandall, 53–78. Macon, Georgia: Mercer University Press.

Agostinho da Silva, Pedro. 1974. *Kwarup: Mito e ritual no alto Xingu*. São Paulo: EdUSP.

Basso, Ellen B. 1973. *The Kalapalo Indians of Central Brazil*. New York: Holt, Rinehart and Winston.

———. 1985. *A Musical View of the Universe: Kalapalo Myth and Ritual Performance*. Philadelphia: University of Pennsylvania Press.

———. 1995. *The Last Cannibals: A South American Oral History*. Austin: University of Texas Press.

———. 2001. "O que podemos aprender do discurso kalapalo sobre a 'história kalapalo'?" In Franchetto and Heckenberger, *Os povos do Alto Xingu*, 293–307.

———. 2005. "Honorification and Avoidance." Keynote lecture, fourth meeting of the Society for the Anthropology of Lowland South America, Estes Park, Colorado.

Bourdicu, Pierre. 1977. *Outline of a Theory of Practice*. Translated by Richard Nice. Cambridge: Cambridge University Press.

Carneiro, Robert L. 1977. "Recent Observations on Shamanism and Witchcraft among the Kuikuru Indians of Central Brazil." *Annals of the New York Academy of Sciences* 293:215–228.

———. 1989. "To the Village of the Jaguars: The Master Myth of the Upper Xingú." *Antropologica* 72:3–40.

———. 1993. "Quarup: A festa dos mortos no Alto Xingu." In *Karl von den Steinen: Um século de antropologia no Xingu*, edited by Vera Penteado Coelho, 407–429. São Paulo: EdUSP.

Carsten, Janet, and Stephen Hugh-Jones. 1995. Introduction to *About the House: Lévi-Strauss and Beyond*, 1–46. Cambridge: Cambridge University Press.

Castro, Eduardo Viveiros de, and Manuela Carneiro da Cunha, eds. 1993. *Amazônia: Etnologia e história indígena*. São Paulo: NHII-USP/FAPESP.

Coelho de Souza, Marcela. 2001. "Virando gente: Notas a uma história aweti." In Franchetto and Heckenberger, *Os povos do Alto Xingu*, 358–400.

Cunha, Manuela Carneiro da, ed. 1992. *História dos índios no Brasil*. São Paulo: FAPESP, Companhia das Letras.

Fausto, Carlos, Bruna Franchetto, and Michael J. Heckenberger. Forthcoming. "Ritual Language and Historical Reconstruction: Towards a Linguistic, Ethnographical, and Archaeological Account of Upper Xingu Society." In *A World of Many Voices: Lessons from Documented Endangered Languages*, edited by Adrienne Dwyer, David Harrison, and David Rood. Amsterdam: John Benjamins.

Foster, Robert J. 1995. *Social Reproduction and History in Melanesia: Mortuary Ritual, Gift Exchange, and Custom in the Tanga Islands*. Cambridge: Cambridge University Press.

Franchetto, Bruna. 1986. "Falar kuikuro: Estudo etnolingüístico de um grupo caribe do Alto Xingu." Ph.D. diss., Universidade Federal do Rio de Janeiro.

———. 1992. "'O aparecimento dos caraíba': Para uma história kuikuro e alto-xinguana." In Cunha, *História dos índios no Brasil*, 339–356.

———. 1993. "A celebração da história nos discursos cerimoniais kuikúro (Alto Xingu)." In Castro and Cunha, *Amazônia*, 95–116.

———. 1996a. "A marca da palavra 'verdadeira' em kuikúro, língua karib do Alto Xingu." Manuscript.

———. 1996b. "Diálogos rituais no Alto Xingu: A rede de alteridades." Manuscript.

———. 2001. "La Parole du chef: Rencontres rituels dans le Haut Xingu." In *Les Rituels du dialogue: Promenades ethnolinguistiques en terres amérindiennes*, edited by Aurore Monod-Becquelin and Philippe Erikson, 481–510. Nanterre, France: Société d'Ethnologie.

———. 2003. "Céu, terra, homens: O calendário kuikuro." In *Idéias matemáticas de povos culturalmente distintos*, edited by Mariana Kawall Leal Ferreira, 101–118. São Paulo: Global.

Franchetto, Bruna, and Michael Heckenberger, eds. 2001. *Os povos do Alto Xingu: História e cultura*. Rio de Janeiro: EdUFRJ.

Gregor, Thomas. 1977. *Mehinaku: The Drama of Daily Life in a Brazilian Indian Village*. Chicago: University of Chicago Press.

Heckenberger, Michael J. 1996. *War and Peace in the Shadow of Empire: Sociopolitical Change in the Upper Xingu Region of Southeastern Amazonia, A.D. 1400–2000*. Ann Arbor, Michigan: University Microfilms.

———. 2005. *The Ecology of Power: Culture, Place, and Personhood in the Southern Amazon, A.D. 1000–2000*. New York: Routledge.

Hill, Jonathan D., ed. 1988. *Rethinking History and Myth: Indigenous South American Perspectives on the Past*. Urbana: University of Illinois Press.

Hill, Jonathan D., and Fernando Santos-Granero, eds. 2002. *Comparative Arawakan Histories: Rethinking Language Family and Culture Area in Amazonia*. Urbana: University of Illinois Press.

Ireland, Emilienne. 1988. "Cerebral Savage: The Whiteman as Symbol of Cleverness and Savagery in Waurá Myth." In Hill, *Rethinking History and Myth*, 157–173.

———. 1996. "Chefia e dinâmicas políticas entre os Waurá." Paper presented at the 20th annual meeting of the Associação Brasileira de Antropologia, Salvador, Brazil.

———. 2001. "Noções waurá de humanidade e identidade cultural." In Franchetto and Heckenberger, *Os povos do Alto Xingu*, 358–400.

Lévi-Strauss, Claude. 1987. *Anthropology and Myth*. Translated by Roy Willis. Oxford: Blackwell.

McIntosh, Susan Keech, ed. 1999. *Beyond Chiefdoms: Pathways to Complexity in Africa*. Cambridge: Cambridge University Press.

Nora, Pierre. 1989. "Between Memory and History: Les Lieux de Mémoire." Translated by Marc Roudebush. *Representations* 26:7–25.

Rumsey, Alan. 1999. "Agency, Personhood, and the 'I' of Discourse in the Pacific and Beyond." *Journal of the Royal Anthropological Institute* 6:101–115.

Sahlins, Marshall. 1985. *Islands of History*. Chicago: University of Chicago Press.

Santos-Granero, Fernando. 1998. "Writing History into the Landscape: Space, Myth, and Ritual in Contemporary Amazonia." *American Ethnologist* 25(2):128–148.

Scarre, Chris, ed. 2005. *The Human Past*. London: Thames and Hudson.

Seeger, Anthony. 1977. "Fixed Points on Arcs in Circles: The Temporal, Processual Aspect of Suya Space and Society." In *Social Time and Social Space in Lowland South American Societies*, edited by Joanna Overing Kaplan, 2:369–377. Paris: Peeters.

Steinen, Karl von den. 1886. *Durch Central-Brasilien*. Leipzig: Brockhaus.

———. 1894. *Unter den Naturvölkern Zentral-Brasiliens*. Berlin: Dietrich Reimer.

Turner, Terence. 1991. "Os Mebengokre Kayapó: História e mudança social de communidades autônomas para a coexistência interétnica." In Cunha, *História dos índios no Brasil*, 311–338.

———. 1993. "Da cosmologia à história: Resistência, adaptação e consciência social entre os Kayapó." In Castro and Cunha, *Amazônia*, 43–66.

Wagner, Roy. 1989. "Conclusion: The Exchange Context of the Kula." In *Death Rituals and Life in the Societies of the Kula Ring*, edited by Frederick H. Damon and Roy Wagner, 254–274. DeKalb: Northern Illinois University Press.

Weiner, Annette B. 1992. *Inalienable Possessions: The Paradox of Keeping-while-Giving*. Berkeley and Los Angeles: University of California Press.

Contributors

Jean-Pierre Chaumeil is senior research fellow at the Centre National de la Recherche Scientifique (CNRS).

Philippe Erikson is associate professor of anthropology at the University of Paris X–Nanterre.

Carlos Fausto is associate professor at the Programa de Pós-Graduação em Antropologia Social, Museu Nacional, Universidade Federal do Rio de Janeiro, and researcher at Brazil's Conselho Centro Nacional de Pesquisa e Desenvolvimento Tecnológico (CNPg).

Peter Gow is professor of anthropology at the University of Saint Andrews.

Michael Heckenberger is associate professor of anthropology at the University of Florida.

Eduardo Kohn is assistant professor of anthropology at Cornell University.

Fernando Santos-Granero is staff scientist at the Smithsonian Tropical Research Institute.

Anne-Christine Taylor is senior research fellow at the Centre National de la Recherche Scientifique (CNRS) and director of the research and educational division of Paris's new Musée du quai Branly.

Aparecida Vilaça is associate professor at the Programa de Pós-Graduação em Antropologia Social, Museu Nacional, Universidade Federal do Rio de Janeiro, and researcher at the Conselho Centro Nacional de Pesquisa e Desenvolvimento Tecnológico (CNPg).

General Index

Index of Indigenous Peoples